MERIT

A volume in the series
American Institutions and Society
Edited by Brian Balogh and Jonathan Zimmerman

MERIT

The History of a Founding Ideal
from the American Revolution
to the Twenty-First Century

Joseph F. Kett

CORNELL UNIVERSITY PRESS **ITHACA AND LONDON**

First published 2013 by Cornell University Press
Printed in the United States of America

Library of Congress Cataloging-in-Publication Data

Kett, Joseph F.
  Merit : the history of a founding ideal from the American Revolution to the twenty-first century / Joseph F. Kett.
      p. cm.
  Includes bibliographical references and index.
  ISBN 978-0-8014-5122-5 (cloth : alk. paper)
    1. Merit (Ethics)—Social aspects—United States.   2. Social values—United States—History.   3. National characteristics, American—History.   4. United States—History.   I. Title.

  BJ1500.M47K45   2013
  179'.9—dc23   2012027111

Cornell University Press strives to use environmentally responsible suppliers and materials to the fullest extent possible in the publishing of its books. Such materials include vegetable-based, low-VOC inks and acid-free papers that are recycled, totally chlorine-free, or partly composed of nonwood fibers. For further information, visit our website at www.cornellpress.cornell.edu.

Cloth printing   10 9 8 7 6 5 4 3 2 1

To the memory of Donald Harnish Fleming, 1923–2008

Contents

Acknowledgments

In conceptualizing and writing this study, I have received aid beyond my deserts from colleagues in the History Department at the University of Virginia. Several years ago, in response to my plea for help "getting pregnant again," Brian Balogh suggested the topic and assured me that it's "up your line, Kett." Having written books on the histories of medicine, youth, and self-improvement, I was uncertain about the location of "my line," but I have found the topic and its cousins (the histories of competition, rewards, rankings, and grades) boundlessly interesting. Balogh later critiqued drafts of the introduction and final chapter in ways that compelled me to investigate more deeply the tension among the Founding ideals of the American republic. In an act of supererogation, my colleague Elizabeth A. Meyer took time from her studies of Antiquity to browbeat me into paying more attention to historical contextualizations of merit, and in an act bordering on self-immolation, she read the first complete draft of the manuscript. I can assure readers that her criticisms are your gain. Mike Holt read an early version of Chapter 2 and suggested some good ideas for revisions; John C. A. Stagg read a later version of Chapter 2, along with Chapter 1, and saved me from some mistakes. Karen V. H. Parshall provided valuable criticism of an earlier draft of Chapter 6 and bibliographic leads for other chapters. Blake Hurt brought a useful non-academic perspective to his reading of the manuscript. Michael McGandy of Cornell University Press gifted me with an extremely helpful critique of the penultimate version of the manuscript. William R. Johnson of the Economics Department at Virginia, Paul Kingston of the Sociology Department, and Steve Railton of the English Department patiently responded to my requests for bibliographical references. I have also profited from discussing aspects of this book with Mark Thomas and Erik Midelfort. By nursing me through a serious illness, my wife, Eleanor, made the author, and thus indirectly the book, possible. To all of these individuals, I extend my warm gratitude while accepting full responsibility for flaws that remain.

MERIT

THE FACES OF MERIT

In early May of 1775 Benedict Arnold met up with Ethan Allen near Lake Champlain. Neither man was a professional soldier—Arnold a valorous druggist, Allen a frontier land speculator—but each looked smart in his new uniform: Arnold wore a scarlet coat, Allen a green coat with enormous gold epaulets. Arnold had been commissioned a colonel by the Massachusetts committee of safety; Allen had been elected colonel by the Green Mountain Boys, roughnecks from the disputed area between New York and New Hampshire. Sharing the same objective, to seize Fort Ticonderoga, a short distance across Lake Champlain, Arnold and Allen immediately engaged in a warm dispute, not about *how* to take the fortress that the British had spent a fortune rebuilding after capturing it from the French in 1759 (fortunately for the Americans, if also unknown to them, only a single sleeping sentry guarded its gate), but about *who* would first enter the fort. In the end, they settled this dispute by entering the fort side by side. Allen nevertheless received most of the publicity for the conquest, much to Arnold's dismay.

In the fall, Arnold, still eager for fame and now armed with a commission from George Washington to attack Canada, led an expedition through the largely uncharted wilderness between Boston and Quebec. The "merit of that officer is certainly great," Washington wrote on hearing that Arnold's force had survived the trip,[1] and although the attack on Quebec failed, Patriots compared Arnold to Hannibal crossing the Alps. Yet even now Arnold's merit was not to receive the degree of recognition that he expected. In February of 1777, when Congress appointed five new major generals, Arnold was left off the list; his native Connecticut already had two major generals. Pleading that the promotion "which was due to your seniority, was not overlooked for want of merit in you,"[2] Washington tried to console Arnold, but to no avail. Arnold, who persisted in interpreting Congress's action as an impeachment of his character and as a request for his resignation, demanded a court of inquiry into his conduct. His conduct, however, had never been at issue. He was simply the first victim of a congressional compromise to allocate promotions on the basis of seniority, quota, and merit.

Seniority was measured by the date of an officer's commission at his current rank; quota, by the number of troops raised and to be raised by each state. An officer who saw others promoted over him on the basis of these criteria had no reason to feel disgraced. In contrast, whenever invoked, merit, lacking any concrete measure, invited trouble. Having been promoted to brigadier general before any of the new major generals, Arnold could see their present advancement only as his own humiliation. Indeed, even in May 1777, when Congress belatedly promoted Arnold, it still declined to give him precedence over the others.

To argue over the dating of a commission was to argue about precedence— literally who went first in any procession. Protocol in our society usually settles issues relating to military and diplomatic etiquette without major eruptions. In the new republic that Arnold served until his sense of injured merit led him to defect to the British in 1780, however, such protocol was less established. Both Washington and John Adams believed that conflicts over precedence had no place in the republic, while Congress, frequently uninformed about the fine gradations of seniority and rank in the provincial militias that composed the Continental Army, often ended up kicking the hornet's nest when it promoted officers. To Arnold and the many officers like him, conflicts over the dating of commissions were, in fact, contests over comparative merit, and not just in the obvious sense that to promote a junior over a senior was to insult the latter. Arnold felt that Congress's delay in recognizing his merit, followed by its refusal to "restore" his rank (reestablish his precedence), left him so diminished in his own eyes that he would actually be useless to the cause. So to slight Arnold was not merely to disrespect his merit but also to drain the qualities that had *made* him meritorious.

I call this kind of merit *essential*. Essential merit, resting on an individual's visible and notable achievements and/or performances, is more than the sum of achievements/performances. Achievements/performances are seen as an accurate reflection of one's inner merit. The "Men of Merit," a favorite term of the Founders to describe themselves, viewed their merit as a quality that propelled their achievements/performances and that they carried through life. In sum, success constituted their merit made visible; failure was the child of Fortuna, events beyond human control.

Essential merit resembled honor, the public verdict on someone's qualities, but with the difference that an individual's honor consisted of his assessment of how others assessed his performance, while his merit lay in his imagining of the inner quality that accounted for his performance. Merit and honor were cousins of *character*, a word that today connotes inner rectitude but that in Arnold's day signified a visible mark and, in politics, the reputation acquired by a man for his acts on the public stage. In contrast to our more egalitarian society's familiarity with *personality* and ethnic or religious *identity*, expressions that connote difference rather than hierarchy, *Men of Merit* and *First Characters* were not only interchangeable terms in 1780 but expressions that implied one's rank in a hierarchy, earned in competition with fellow gentlemen.

To this Founding Generation, the American republic seemed notably conducive to the manifestation and reward of merit. Yet Americans did not invent the ideal of merit, which had its roots in antiquity and, more proximately, in Puritanism. During and after the English Civil War of the 1640s Puritans advanced the ideal of government by consent rather than by hereditary succession. Under Oliver Cromwell's Protectorate, they abolished both the English monarchy and the House of Lords. Republican theorists like James Harrington and Algernon Sydney tied the ideal of government by consent to a new conception of the qualifications of leaders. Instead of inheriting their positions, leaders were to earn the respect of the many. However grandly some English monarchs might have estimated their achievements, they almost always owed their place exclusively to hereditary succession, often while still young and entirely unproven. Ten kings of post-Anglo-Saxon England ascended to the throne during their minorities; one of these, Henry VI, ascended in 1422 at the ripe age of nine months, then was formally crowned king of England at seven and of France at ten. To be sure, there were exceptions to hereditary succession. William the Conqueror became king of England, as proclaimed by his sobriquet, by a kind of brute achievement. But this achievement little impressed Thomas Paine, who remarked in *Common Sense* (1776) that "a French bastard, landing with an armed banditti, and establishing himself king of England against the consent of the natives, is a very paltry rascally original" for Britain's monarchy. Anyone who traced dynasties to their first rise, Paine opined, would find nothing more than the "principal ruffian of some restless gang."[3]

Paine stood squarely in a tradition of English radicalism that first sprouted on the Puritan side during the English Civil War, gained momentum during the Protectorate, and then persisted in the less hospitable climates created by the later Stuarts and the Hanoverians. Historians call this line of thinkers "commonwealth men" or radical Whigs. They championed government by consent and the ideal of a "republic," a word with variable connotations that meant, minimally, rule by meritorious leaders whose virtuous policies earned popular consent. Radical Whigs admired America as a place where merit would rise unencumbered by the chains created in Europe by hereditary privilege. As inhabitants of a rude and provincial society, Americans impressed radical Whigs as free of the guile so often disguising the face of merit in Europe.

In this sense, America was "born meritorious," to adapt a phrase ("born liberal") coined by Louis Hartz.[4] At the heart of the American experience with merit lay a historical peculiarity. In major European nations merit became the rallying cry in the eighteenth century of groups that, while seeing themselves as meritorious—educated, virtuous, and fit to wield authority—attributed their exclusion from positions of power to arbitrary and factitious distinctions. The Dissenters in England (with few exceptions, radical Whigs were Dissenters), the *Bildungsbürgertum* in the German states, and the Frenchmen who marched under the Revolutionary slogan of "careers open to talents" fit this description. What distinguished the American experience was that the Whig gentlemen leading the Revolution based their claim to govern on their merit, which they grounded on their contributions to the Revolution. In America, then, merit became the property not of revolutionary outsiders but of revolutionary *insiders*, who styled themselves Men of Merit or First Characters. Not for a minute did these men doubt that the perpetuation of republican government would ensure the continuation of advancement by merit. Nor did they question that their own success was the product of that very same merit.

Although America was "born meritorious," it was born with many other values that, paradoxically, have boosted *and* obstructed the ideal of advancement by merit. For example, by affirming that no citizen had a birthright to rule over others, the ideal of equal rights substituted advancement by merit for bloodlines, but it also seeded jealousy (suspicion) of the motives of office seekers in the new republic. To a degree, jealousy was a legacy of the Imperial Crisis, when battered royal officials were forced to rely on imported "placemen" from the Mother Country to sustain their authority. In response, American Whigs identified *influence* and *connexion*—terms English Whigs already used to convey wire-pulling and back-scratching—as obstacles to advancement by merit. The vast compass of influence and connexion under the Hanoverians reinforced the burgeoning American belief that republics were far more receptive than monarchies to advancement by merit. By the late 1780s, however, the disruptive potential of equal rights was becoming evident in criticism of the Men of Merit themselves. Although few challenged the merit of the Men of Merit, many suspected that the First Characters, known to each other because of their prominent role in the Revolution, would form a power-hungry cabal. For decades after 1789, when Congress had assigned the president sole power to remove appointed federal officials, all discussions of appointment and advancement by merit were permeated by the underlying fear that a president would use his power of removal to establish despotism through the bestowal of patronage.

Similarly, the Founding ideal of popular consent had the potential both to nurture and to obstruct advancement by merit. In 1813 Thomas Jefferson put forward the ideal of republican governance by a "natural" aristocracy of talented and virtuous men, who would be chosen by an electorate enlightened by the progress of education and science. Yet as Benedict Arnold discovered to his mortification, republican legislators had found that to secure the consent of large masses of socially and geographically disconnected people, they had to apportion the appointment of major generals among the states by creating a quota system. Thus was born what later generations would call logrolling or distributive politics.

Finally, the notion of a meritorious birth of the republic, widely accepted by the Founding Generation, induced the complacent conviction that advancement by merit would persist as long as republican institutions endured. In reality, republics had no monopoly on merit. Absolute monarchs who owed their place to hereditary succession nevertheless had a clear interest in sponsoring merit by promoting talented and ambitious young men of modest social rank in order to curtail the power of barons. Thus, starting in the late eighteenth century, well before the American republic even contemplated the practice, absolute monarchies installed examinations for entry into the public service. Second, nothing in the nature of a republic excluded the exercise of influence—the manipulation, that is, by the politically potent of those less potent with offers of office as a reward for conforming to their will. By labeling influence and connexion diseases only of monarchy, Americans blinded themselves to the extent to which their own republic was permeated by the quest for status and its accompanying vices of unfettered ambition and trading on influence and family prestige. American Whigs of the Revolutionary era recognized that their fathers and grandfathers had ardently sought high social rank. But they assumed that, in the absence of hereditary succession, their ancestors had owed such rank as they had achieved to their meritorious qualities. Colonial hierarchies thus acquired a rather virtuous glow in the memories of Revolutionary Whigs, who often proceeded to conflate their own achievements with those of their immediate ancestors, considering *both* to be components of their own merit.

Essential merit has not disappeared in our own time. We glimpse the shade of Benedict Arnold in the sports pages when we read about star athletes who pout when offered four-year, $100 million contracts after a teammate has been offered $120 million over five years. Historians know nothing of such bounty; still, I recall a departmental meeting in which a senior colleague announced that we had to replace an aged colleague with someone of equal rank (full professor), not so much to fill a particular gap left by X's departure—X having been inactive for several years because of illness—but to avoid insulting X by intimating that he could be replaced by someone forty years his junior. Over the course of time, however, the scope of essential merit has been conscriped by a type of merit I call *institutional*.

Institutional merit differs from essential merit in several ways. The former attaches more importance to the acquisition of knowledge—especially "exact," specialized knowledge of the sort that may be assessed by written examinations—than to the act of extraordinary battlefield valor, the striking performance exhibited by the dazzling oration, or the marvelous cure. The evidence of institutional merit came to be represented by precedent-laden legal briefs, peer-reviewed scientific articles, command of the principles of military organization learned in war colleges, and diplomas from educational institutions whose high standards make it plausible to attach the "presumption of merit" to their graduates.

In advancing this distinction between two types of merit, I am not suggesting that those who thought of their merit as essential necessarily lacked ties to institutions. Essential merit permeated the professions of law, medicine, and arms for much of the nineteenth century. Indeed, it was incarnated in individuals who used the professions as platforms for self-promotion, kept themselves in the public eye, and were quick to take exception when their peers failed to acknowledge their claims to preference. It was the sort of merit valued by collegians between the Revolution and the Civil War. These young men competed with each other in exhibitions of rhetorical display, sought high academic rank that was measured by the distinction of the oration that they were nominated to deliver at commencement, and made trouble for the colleges whenever their pretensions were not suitably acknowledged. Collegians who insisted that their public display of their "genius" evidenced their merit resembled the politicians who volunteered for military service during the Civil War with the realistic expectation that their military rank would correspond to their political status. One of them said that he could write everything worth knowing about tactics on the back of his greeting card: what mattered was the innate ability *to lead*, whether the followers were voters or soldiers.

Institutional merit emerged in several spheres of endeavor in the mid-nineteenth century, in large part as a reaction against the disruptive, self-aggrandizing individualism that accompanied essential merit. For example, in the military the legacy of essential merit proved itself an incubus even before the Civil War. Essential merit made it nearly impossible to promote a junior officer over one more senior without triggering a confrontation, for the past services of the senior entered a kind of memory bank that entitled him to the perpetual deference of his juniors. Essential merit demanded rank as its reward, not only in the military but in the colleges, where commencements exhibited the digitally exact rank order, top to bottom, of the graduates. In contrast, within the sphere of higher education, institutional merit subordinated rank to categories of achievement, each expressed by such honorifics as *cum laude, magna cum laude*, and *summa cum laude* and each accessible by all students judged worthy of the category. By the early 1900s students were less likely to be subject to rank ordering than were the colleges and universities themselves; the first, second, and third scholars, in other words, were giving way to the first-, second-, and third-rate medical school, law school, or graduate school.

A persistent component of institutional merit has been its orientation toward identifying promise in the form of aptitudes and abilities likely to lead to superior performance at some future date. The vast mental-testing industry that sprang up after World War I typifies this quest. The United States has no peer when it comes to devising and administering mental tests, and although mental tests have occasionally sought to identify genius in the form of stratospheric IQs, the industry has primarily constructed tests to fit people whose scores place them near the middle of the curve of distribution into places in schools, corporations, and government bureaucracies.

Indeed, the American penchant for mental tests seems light-years distant from essential merit. Under the latter, individuals expected to be ranked by their public performance—easily judged—rather than by their promise, which more or less defied direct observation. Paradoxically, however, the republican ideal of equal rights connects essential merit and institutional merit, which resemble the faces of Janus. These faces look in opposite directions but are nevertheless joined.

The Founding Generation assumed that in a republic merit provided the only legitimate basis of distinctions. An individual who sought distinction had to rest his case, however implausibly, on his merit, and his merit had to be publicly demonstrated. In practice, however, merit proved to be a sandy foundation on which to base social distinctions, for the new republic rapidly became a society where all citizens, or at least those who really counted, claimed to be meritorious. Disruptions caused by rival claims to merit therefore became commonplace, and distinctions more difficult to establish. Viewed from this perspective, the American embrace of mental testing, a feature of institutional merit, can best be viewed as an inevitable development in a society where no hegemonic social class could claim the sanction of custom or blood to sustain fully its claim to essential merit.

In keeping with its republican traditions, the United States entered World War I without a real counterpart to a European officer class, and in 1917 the army's brass decided to allow psychologists to administer mental tests to recruits, mainly to identify likely officer candidates. The most widely publicized of these tests measured the intelligence of soldiers, but both the brass and the psychologists recognized that officers, while they certainly needed some intelligence, above all required character. The Founders viewed a man's *public character*, his reputation among his peers, as the outward measure of his essential merit. Many added that in a republic, with no fawning courtiers to disguise the face of merit, a man's public character faithfully represented his merit. Nothing would have astonished the Men of Merit more than to be told to take an examination to measure their character, let alone to be told that evaluations of the examinations indicated deficiencies in some component of character—that they had scored well on energy, say, while their initiative needed buffing. Inclined to think of their merit as an indivisible component of their personhood, they would have been equally astonished to hear that merit could be broken down into discrete units. In the Founding era there were no marks or grades in schools, no formal tests of merit, no examinations for entry into the public service—no written examinations, in fact, of any sort *anywhere* in the American republic.

Long before World War I and in reaction to the disruptions wrought by assertions of essential merit, colleges devised "merit systems" that established separate numerical scores for such activities as regularly attending class, paying attention, behaving courteously, and giving correct answers on examinations. These scores then became the bases for assessing underlying traits such as industriousness and persistence. But merit systems made no claim to measure character in adults. For grown-ups, psychologists recognized, assessments of character were often the result of random impressions based on brief encounters.

To remedy this acknowledged flaw in assessing character, Walter Dill Scott, a psychologist at Carnegie Tech, devised a "man-to-man rating scale" in 1915. Scott asked each member of the group being evaluated to think of "the best man you ever knew" and "the poorest man you ever knew," next an "average man" in his experience, a better-than-average man, and a poorer-than-average man. Collectively, these became the "scale men," and each was assigned a number (e.g., 15, 12, 9, 6, and 3). Next each member of the group asked himself whether, for example, Jones was better than the average man, worse than the poorer-than-average-man, and so on. All of this required the evaluators to know each other fairly well, of course. Army camps in which officers were confined together for long periods seemed to be ideal places to test Scott's scale, and in 1918 the army used this scale as the basis for its own Army Rating Scale, which was put through trials at two camps. The army brass and the psychologists agreed that a successful trial would strike a blow for advancement by merit rather than by prejudice (the personal impression), family influence, or political wire-pulling. And so, with nothing to gain from dishonesty, the evaluating officers were asked to rank their peers. Reflecting the times, however, they were not told to describe an officer's public character. Rather, each officer was to pick twenty-five fellow officers who shared his billet and whom he knew "intimately," and to rate each on nearly thirty qualities. Examples included endurance, energy, dependability, ease in learning, decision making, and tact.

Reflecting the ingrained American belief that nearly all citizens were likely to possess *some* comparative advantage in the competition of life, a striking feature of the Army Rating Scale, as indeed of most American attempts to measure merit, lay in the profusion of categories to be rated. (Americans did not invent intelligence testing, but they have outstripped other nations in their quest to identify different kinds of intelligence, just as they have built a case for an immense number of different vocational aptitudes.) After the war the army hired a young psychologist, Harold Rugg, to assess the validity of the Army Rating Scale—whether, that is, the scale measured real traits. Rugg and his team chose several measures of validity, including the degree of agreement among officers in rating each individual officer and the degree to which the officers' ratings of intelligence agreed with scores on intelligence tests. "Is the rating of human character practicable?" Rugg asked in 1922. "Most emphatically, NOT," he concluded.[5] The Army Rating Scale, in short, was a dud.

Rugg found that when the same person was independently rated by several officers, the difference in range of ratings was commonly as large as 30 points on an 80-point scale, that when the scores of officers picked to be scale men for intelligence were compared with their scores on intelligence tests, the "least intelligent man I ever knew" according to the rating scale varied according to intelligence tests anywhere from "most intelligent" to "least intelligent." Men listed as "the best captain I ever knew" by some officers were identified by other officers as "the poorest captain I ever knew." More fundamentally, Rugg discovered the same propensity that Edward L. Thorndike, a distinguished psychologist at Columbia University, was simultaneously naming the "halo effect": no matter how many traits of a subject were rated, ratings were governed by the evaluators' general reaction to the subject, which depended on how the evaluators interpreted the subject's actions toward them.

The halo effect is the bond that joins the faces of Janus, between essential and institutional merit. They face in opposite directions, yet in the American context they are inseparable. In retrospect, essential and institutional merit appear to be logical developments in a republic founded on the principles of equal rights and advancement by merit. Essential merit gripped Americans during the late eighteenth century and for much of the nineteenth century because, in the absence of hereditary succession, Americans imagined that advancement in their society could be based only on merit. But essential merit, deeply instinctive, turned out to be a formula for disruption. Eventually, Americans turned to institutional merit, and having exceeded the Western world in their embrace of essential merit, proceeded to do the same with institutional merit.

What Americans have come up against, however, is the realization that no matter how many categories they use to rate each other, in the final analysis they cannot avoid making a judgment: yes or no. And as is characteristic of Americans, no sooner do they make that judgment than they begin to question its fairness.

Strictly, merit is a "quality deserving reward." As with the concepts of equal rights and popular consent, the prevailing understanding of the elements of merit (the qualities deserving reward) has repeatedly changed. The same has been true of the practices deemed incompatible with advancement by merit, which have included advancement by bloodlines, nepotism, popularity, party loyalty, political pull, preferential legislation, regional quotas, racial prejudice, and racial quotas. In sum, as an ideal of the Founding, merit has been shaped by the values that have evolved since the Founding.

Following the American Revolution, the notion of merit resembled a lake created by a dam. The Revolution established something like a national directory of Notable Patriots whose achievements even their critics acknowledged and whose members controlled the discourse on merit for a brief period. After relating how the Imperial Crisis and Revolution transformed merit from a self-imagined attribute of the colonial gentry, closely allied with its conceptions of its honor, reputation, and public character, into a political concept, Chapter 1 relates how even the critics of these self-styled Men of Merit, while doubting whether they could be trusted with power, conceded their claim to meritorious distinction. The reliance of the Founders on an individual's public character as a signifier of merit created a problem when it came to transmitting their influence across generations, the subject of Chapter 2. In principle, a system of examinations modeled on those of Prussia and other European nations could have identified the most talented members of the next generation for advancement. Without either the experience of defeat or a revolution from below, Americans showed no interest in such a system. Their closest brush with one came when Alexander Hamilton decided to interview officer candidates for the Provisional Army in 1798. Hamilton's initiative triggered characteristically republican suspicion about his motives (would this army fight the French or the Jeffersonians?) and came to naught when John Adams made peace with France.

Ambitious members of the generation born during or just after the Revolution inherited the self-regard of the Founders without their conspicuous and validating achievements. Chapter 2 describes how, in the professions, the armed forces, and governments, members of this generation manipulated federalism to advance their ambitions. Frustrated in one venue, they shifted to another, proving adept at constructing the very ladders of merit they sought to climb. Where the Men of Merit both expected and received deference based on acknowledgment of their achievements, the combined effects of intensifying demands for equal rights and democratizing politics meant that members of the younger generation would find their claims to distinction disputed at every turn. Harvard graduate and Federalist Horace Binney expressed the thwarted expectations of his generation when he complained in 1815 that, in contrast to all other nations, public life in the United States was not a "profession" with its "peculiar and permanent rewards of wealth, reputation, and power."[6]

To refer back to an earlier metaphor, Chapter 1 describes the impounded lake; Chapter 2 depicts seepage from the dam. This seepage cut channels for several distinct discourses—all influenced by the Founding—that form the subjects of Chapters 3–7. Emphasizing parallels between the public life and the colleges, Chapter 3 describes the colleges in the post-Revolution era as training grounds for public men and as prone to disruption for many of the same reasons as public life. After 1820, colleges responded to student disruptions by introducing merit *systems*. In contrast to such terms as essential and institutional merit, which I have coined to draw a distinction clearer in retrospect than it was to contemporaries, these systems, and their obsession with precise, numerical calibration of small differences in merit, were familiar to contemporaries. In a society where a hegemonic class could no longer impose its rules for identifying merit, all rules had to be stipulated in exhaustive detail before the competition started.

The Founders did not expect that equal rights would lead to equality of condition. Their ideal, rather, was a hierarchical society in which American abundance would permit the multitude to achieve a "competency." Chapter 4 first takes up the challenges to this assumption that arose from an economy permeated by financial speculation, risk, and the alarming juxtaposition of wealth and ruin, and from the egalitarian thrust of mass politics. It then turns to the impact of these changes on public schools. After 1840, educators introduced numerical marks and report cards in order to turn public schools into microcosms of society. They expected *managed competition* in the schools that would promote moderate ambition in average children without encouraging the personal rivalries that were searing the social fabric. Under the regimen of managed competition, the child of average ability would gain promotion from grade to grade by keeping up with his or her average classmates. Competitions in which all industrious students gained a modest prize, promotion to the next grade, would habituate them to expect success, albeit bounded and achievable success, as a reward for the exercise of ability and effort within the reach of the average citizen.

Much of what I have just described changed between 1880 and 1930. The second half of Chapter 4 identifies a key component of this transition: the dawning recognition that divisions of rank and class in American society were increasingly based on the kind of work people did rather than on gradations in the merit of individuals. Economists began to describe society as a layer cake composed of *noncompeting* groups; sociologists introduced the concept of *social stratification*. Public educators responded to this recognition by abandoning the idea that all schoolchildren should be exposed to identical experiences that would forge character traits for life. In its place, they substituted tracking, vocational education, and vocational guidance—innovations that rested on the assumption that children, regardless of their merit, would have different "likely destinies" and required different treatment based on the scientific measurement of their aptitudes and abilities by so-called *mental* or *psychological tests*.

Chapter 5 carries the story of testing from its inception before World War I through the interwar years. Historians have devoted far more attention to mental testing than to any other part of the history of merit. The title of a prize-winning study of the testing movement by Stephen Jay Gould, *The Mismeasure of Man*, underscores the negative assessment of the movement in books on the subject published during the last three decades. Nevertheless, the historian's job is not to condemn (or praise) the movement but to understand why it aroused such high expectations and why it took the form that it did. By dismembering the individual into sundry traits and attributes—scholarship, industry, attentiveness, deportment—each one measurable and therefore improvable, the report cards favored by public educators after 1840 encouraged self-betterment but made no explicit attempt to forecast destinies. Forecasting destinies became important as the role of institutions and inherited social structures in shaping the lives of citizens came to be recognized. Dependence on institutional clients quickly became a feature of the American testing movement and shaped its trajectory. Most testers initially believed that intelligence was a fixed, heritable entity that was indispensable to progress, but their experience with institutional clients led them to doubt connections between high measured intelligence and such public benefits as superior productivity.

In contrast to most scholarly treatments of the testing movement, Chapter 5 describes testing as always a work in progress; critics found that they were shooting at a moving target. During the interwar years testers redirected their interests to the investigation of a wide range of aptitudes and abilities. Part of the appeal of mental tests lay in their promise to validate popular aspirations by identifying each citizen's comparative advantage in the race of life. I view this development as another of the many accommodations between merit and equal rights in the American past.

Chapter 6 examines the efforts of leading figures in higher education, allied with like-minded spirits in the professions, to vest the "presumption of merit" in institutions during the late nineteenth century. Chronologically, this chapter overlaps the second half of Chapter 4 and Chapter 5. Each looks at a different aspect of the same gradual shift from essential to institutional merit. It would not be far from the mark to say that the history of merit in the United States has witnessed a long-running battle between those who have argued for the self-sufficiency of the individual's ability and will to rise in the American republic and those who, fearing or merely questioning this self-sufficiency, have trusted more in the certification of individuals by institutions that have met the "presumption-of-merit" standard. The emergence of large, bureaucratically organized corporations and government bodies has slowly tilted the balance to those who have preferred the model of predictable and orderly advancement based on small and measurable increments of merit.

Chapter 7 turns to the installation, starting in the 1880s, of merit systems in the federal and state governments and uses these systems as a window on the continuing interaction of merit with equal rights and popular consent. Persuaded that republican institutions identified and rewarded merit, the Founders saw no need for examinations to identify it, and in contrast to their counterparts in Europe, the civil-service reformers of the 1880s did not envision examinations as a means to open the path to office for people like themselves. The "open, competitive examinations" required by the Pendleton Act (1883) aimed, rather, at killing the partisan distribution of public jobs—the spoils system—without ruffling equal rights. Examinations were acceptable only to the extent that they tested knowledge assumed to be possessed by all Americans who had graduated from the "common" (public) schools. The legacy of equal rights extended into the twentieth century, when it blunted attempts by a new generation of reformers to introduce a "higher," European-style civil service.

Chapter 8 ties together several earlier threads by describing the crisis that has enveloped the ideal of merit since the mid-1960s. It begins and ends with a paradox: Americans had spent two centuries devising ways to reconcile advancement by merit with equal rights and popular consent only to hear from critics, mainly academics, that merit could never be reconciled with these other ideals of the Founding. Entering the late 1960s, merit had one notably exposed flank: in seeking to reconcile merit with equal rights and popular consent, most Americans had never viewed the effects of class on life trajectories as indelible. In the prevailing American view, class posed a challenge to the ideal of universal advancement by merit, but a challenge that could be surmounted by some mixture of science, especially mental testing for aptitudes and abilities, and guidance. In this respect, critics of the New Left, who led the onslaught against merit during the 1970s, had a point: even the fairest application of merit-based selection could not overcome the legacies of birth. Since the 1970s, however, fears of America's declining international competitiveness, a culture of antagonism toward expert authority, and intensifying partisan divisions have deflected interest from merit-versus-equality to merit-versus-incompetence and to an obsessive concern with the evaluation of professionals.

Including books by Gould, Nicholas Lemann, and John Carson, the scientific measurement of merit, especially by tests for intelligence, has dominated the literature on the history of merit.[7] Carson's book has the advantage of both setting this history in a comparative context (France and the United States) and starting with the Enlightenment's philosophical and scientific discourse about "talents." Carson's wide net enables him to address what I also see as a fundamental issue: how to rationalize social distinctions in a republic. In contrast to Carson, I am less interested in the formal discourse about talents (which had negligible impact in late eighteenth-century America) than in selection procedures, in other words, in how examinations, tests, or any alternative procedures were actually deployed. Conceptually, my starting point is a paradox: on one hand, a Revolution led by a gentry whose claims to merit were conceded even by their fiercest critics; on the other, a Revolution fought for popular consent and equal rights (but not equality of condition) that would provoke challenges to assertions of authority by those nominally authorized to draw distinctions among citizens. Compared with the aforementioned historians, my book portrays selection procedures in the United States as more feckless than repressive.

1

REPUBLIC OF MERIT

Speaking on the second anniversary of American Independence, David Ramsay, the early historian of South Carolina, described the United States as a nation in which "all offices lie open to men of merit, of whatever rank or condition"; even "the reins of state may be held by the son of the poorest man, if possessed of abilities equal to the important station."[1] Ramsay recognized that Independence itself had boosted the cause of merit, but he traced the roots of merit to the colonial period. Even under British rule, he wrote in 1789, the colonists' distance from Britain had preserved them from "the contagion of ministerial influence." High colonial offices had been "confined to natives of Britain" and were "neither sufficiently numerous nor lucrative" to create an American class of idle dependents on government. With little prospect of breaking the grip of "placemen" (professional officeholders sent from the Mother Country) on high government posts, most colonists had learned that they could acquire only such rank as earned by their own efforts and those of the "immediate ancestors."[2] In a similar vein, in 1774 Alexander Hamilton distinguished natural inequalities based on talents and industry from artificial ones created by "ministerial tools and court sycophants."[3]

Social positions that were earned rather than inherited were evidence that merit—some combination of talents and efforts—accounted for an individual's rise. Yet the Imperial Crisis that led up to American Independence reminded the Anglo-American colonists that ways to advance that depended on neither merit nor inheritance abounded in the British Empire. For example, placemen acquired their jobs through the patronage of grandees; most parsons owed their positions to appointment by the king, or a local squire, or a great man. The beneficiaries of patronage were expected to supplicate, to remind patrons of their loyalty and past services, their shared acquaintances, and, where possible, their kinship relations. The frequent invocations of such terms as *interest* and *connexion* were reminders of the centrality of patronage to advancement.[4] Interest and connexion also figured prominently in Purchase, the British system for allocating military commissions. With the Restoration of the Stuart monarchy in 1660, England's ruling class gradually implemented the sale of commissions in the Royal Army. Until 1871, British officers, except for engineers and artillerists, gained commissions up through lieutenant colonel by buying them. As was true of church benefices and government jobs in Britain and the Empire, Purchase was mediated by interest, the persistent application to political patrons. Purchase fixed the rank, interest the place, whether in a prestigious unit like the Life Guards in London (an excellent locale for the further pursuit of interest) or in rude Scotland, barbarous Ireland, or some dismal outpost in the Empire.[5]

Patronage and Purchase were gray areas when it came to merit. In the colonies as in the Mother Country, the ambitious supplicated the influential for favor. Hamilton wanted no part of "ministerial tools" and "sycophants," but he basked in the aura of his patron, George Washington. At its inception after the Restoration, England's rulers saw Purchase as a conservative alternative to the New Model Army that Oliver Cromwell had led during the English Civil War. In Cromwell's army, educated soldiers rose in rank by displaying valor in combat; they were rewarded for their performance rather than social status.[6] After the chaotic collapse of Cromwell's Protectorate, conservatives remembered the New Model Army as a rabble and they saw Purchase as a buttress of social order. During the eighteenth century Purchase underwent several reforms, notably the abolition of "infant commissions" like the one that awarded a captaincy to the fifth Lord Ellibank in 1706, when he was only three. Infant commissions rested on the principle of hereditary privilege, which had been fiercely attacked by Puritans during the English Civil War and which American Patriots of the 1770s would target. Yet even after the British eliminated infant commissions during the 1760s, they continued to permit "purchasing over," which allowed the family of a young man without military experience—"fresh from the nursery," critics complained—to purchase commissions at a higher rank than battle-hardened officers.

The British never thought of Purchase as a merit system in the sense of a configuration of examinations to test or predict military competence. The Duke of Wellington, who had become a lieutenant colonel by Purchase, believed that military schools like those established in the early nineteenth century at Woolwich and Sandhurst just produced coxcombs and dandies, and is said to have exclaimed that he wanted to hear no more rubbish about merit. Over time, however, the British concluded that Purchase produced good officers by ensuring that most commissions were awarded to younger sons of the rural gentry, young men barred from inheriting the family estate by primogeniture, accustomed to the outdoor life, and likely to have learned the right mixture of authority and "condescension" by observing their fathers' conduct toward tenants. The eventual abolition of Purchase reflected the growing recognition that bankers and merchants were outbidding the rural gentry for commissions for their sons.[7]

Similarly, patronage lacked any features of a merit system. Sir Robert Walpole, Britain's prime minister from 1721 to 1742 who became notorious for using his control of royal patronage to win support for Crown policies in parliament, routinely exiled talented men to the wilderness for failing to bow to his will and allotted to his three sons offices in the Exchequer that collectively were worth an astonishing £13,400 a year.[8] Radicals in Britain equated "Robinocracy"—one of several plays on Walpole's given name—with corruption. As was true of Purchase, however, the British were slow to reform patronage. Britain did not initiate a merit system of competitive examinations for public jobs until the 1850s, decades after Prussia started examinations for its public service in the immediate wake of its defeat by Napoleon in 1806. Pressures for reform were milder in Britain, in part because Britain avoided both catastrophic defeat and, unlike France, revolution. Reflecting on their history from the vantage point of the post-Napoleonic era, Britons reminded themselves how much they owed to the products of a seemingly corrupt system of patronage, interest, influence, and connexion. Britain's greatest naval hero, Horatio Nelson, was a beneficiary of patronage. His mother was a grandniece of Sir Robert Walpole; her brother, a captain in the Royal Navy, secured young Horatio's initial appointment as a midshipman after her death and guided his early career.

American Contexts

An image of America as innocent of corruption and its train of abuses permeated the thinking of those eighteenth-century British writers who were quickest to find corruption at home. Americans were familiar with the writings of James Harrington and Algernon Sydney (seventeenth-century "commonwealth men" who championed government by consent), with their eighteenth-century successors (including John Trenchard and Thomas Gordon, the authors of newspaper articles collectively known as *Cato's Letters*, in the 1720s), and with the later self-styled "real" or "true" Whigs (usually called radical Whigs by historians), such as James Burgh, Richard Price, Thomas Paine, and Joseph Priestley. Cato and the radical Whigs especially were attuned to corruption, which they equated less with pilfering from the public purse than with executive manipulation of the House of Commons by the trade of office for votes. Walpole's Robinocracy undermined the principle of consent dear to radical Whigs by seducing the otherwise independent Country (landed gentry) with the blandishments of Court (ministerial) favors. Radical Whigs, most of whom were Dissenters, attacked the required oaths of allegiance to the Church of England which, into the nineteenth century, effectively barred Dissenters from public office and university fellowships; they did so on the dual grounds that such tests violated consent and barred talented and loyal Englishmen from public life. Whigs also assailed the underrepresentation in parliament of the talented and aspiring middle class of merchants and manufacturers.[9] In combination, corruption and religious tests nurtured arbitrary government and suffocated merit.[10]

Unflinchingly preferring merit, radical Whigs were uneasy about identifying it, mainly for the reason cited by Cato: "great abilities have for the most part, if not always, been employed to mislead the honest but unwary multitude, and to draw them out of the open and plain paths of public virtue and public good." "Popularity," Cato wrote, was "no proof of merit."[11] Burgh claimed in 1775 that "nations have often been deceived into slavery by men of shining merit."[12] As Dissenters, radical Whigs were prone to find corrupt motives behind appearances, especially that of virtue.

Cato often paraphrased Chapter 10 ("Of Power, Worth, Dignity, Honour, and Worthinesse") of Thomas Hobbes's *Leviathan* (1651), a work notable for its corrosive reduction of seemingly high-minded motives to self-interest. For Hobbes, no motives required more urgent deflation than the quest for fame and glory, impulses that had been much admired by Renaissance humanists. Seekers after glory cherished their reputations as visible signifiers of their merit and they protected their honor, the quest for distinction in the eyes of one's peers and posterity that had been so admired by the ancient Romans.[13] But Hobbes described the quest for distinction in a detached and satirical tone alien to the ancients: society valued men who coveted great riches and honors because it construed the act of aiming high as evidence of great inherent powers, while it counted evidence of ambition for "little gains, or preferments" as a mark of low self-worth. Paraphrasing Hobbes, Cato wrote that "little crimes and small criminals have been detested and punished; while great malefactors have been generally reverenced and obeyed." Cato viewed men as differing little in natural endowments but, "mischief frequently being introduced by merit," found claims of superior merit to be self-serving. All of mankind's "pomp, titles, and wealth are means and devices to make the world think that they who possess them are superior in merit to those who want them."[14]

Except in America. In the eyes of radical Whigs, Americans were strangers to the show and artifice that disguised merit in Europe. Paine, who famously conflated nobility with "No-ability," never wavered in his belief that merit alone governed America.[15] In *Observations on the Importance of the American Revolution* (1785), Price contended that nearly all evils would disappear were social distinctions based only on "personal merit," and he took great comfort from the Articles of Confederation's ban on hereditary titles. To Price, Americans appeared to live in a happy middle state of manners, between savagery and luxury.[16]

Americans were well aware of this image of themselves. Price and Burgh were personal friends of Benjamin Franklin, who conveyed this impression of all America whenever he traveled abroad. The promotional literature of the early colonies, especially Pennsylvania, had described America as a place where anyone could achieve a competence by dint of industry, a point extended by J. Hector St. John de Crèvecoeur's *Letters from an American Farmer* (1782). A Frenchman who had farmed in Orange County, New York, Crèvecoeur famously described America as a land with no parasites to suck the rewards from honest labor, "no aristocratic families, no courts, no kings, no bishops, no ecclesiastical dominion, no invisible power giving to the few a very visible one, no great manufactories employing thousands, no great refinement of luxury."[17] Three years later John Dunlap, who had been responsible for printing the Declaration of Independence, wrote to his brother-in-law in Ireland to urge "the young men of Ireland who wish to be happy and free [to] leave it and come here as quick as possible. There is no place in the world where a man meets so rich a reward for good conduct and industry as in America."[18] This idea proved resilient. A half-century later the Jacksonian Democrat economist Theodore Sedgwick Jr. printed England's *Table of Precedence*, from the royal family down through dukes, marquises, archbishops, barons, and knights to lowly tradesmen, to prove that "in this unnatural, perverted order, the first, the original, the greatest producers of wealth are placed beneath many who do nothing for the good of mankind."[19]

Several features of the colonial experience gave plausibility to this image of America and to the inclination of American Whigs to think that radical Whigs like Burgh and Price were expressing warnings more applicable to Britain than to their own situation. First, in striking contrast to Britain, where more than one-third of the members of the House of Commons in the mid-eighteenth century held "places" within the gift of the Crown, either as employees of the ministries or as holders of sinecures, pensions, or military or naval posts, in America, with neither a national church nor a regular army or navy, no royal governor had at his disposal more than a shadow of the patronage available to Walpole and his successors. Massachusetts governor Francis Bernard complained in 1768 that if punishments and rewards were the hinges of government, then in Massachusetts the door was "off its hinges."[20] Second, although most colonists accepted the state's responsibility for religion, the religious establishments in Massachusetts and Connecticut were Reformed, hence nonconformist under English law and by definition tenuous within the Imperial order. The multiplicity of denominations in the middle colonies prevented any exclusive establishment. The story was different in Virginia, where the established Anglican Church harassed Baptists before the Revolution. But once fighting broke out, Anglicans had to abandon discrimination against Baptists to secure Baptist allegiance to the Whig cause.[21] Third, like the House of Commons in Britain, American legislatures were malapportioned, but not, as in Britain, against the interests of the highly literate class of urban merchants, professionals, and publicists. Rather, relatively inarticulate western farmers were the ones to experience underrepresentation, and given the expenses of colonial officeholding, they rarely complained about it.

Finally, the American colonies lacked an "embodied" aristocracy. Eighteenth-century Anglo-American parlance distinguished a nation's embodied aristocracy, which rested on hereditary succession—a nobility—from its "conventional" or "natural" aristocracy, which consisted of its substantial property holders, with or without life titles. On one level, this difference was trivial. Compared with the Bourbon, Hapsburg, and Hohenzollern nobilities on the European continent, Britain's nobility was small, less tied to military service, much freer to enter trades, and much less endowed with tax exemptions and similar privileges.[22] Colonial political elites were so tightly bound by kinship that they scarcely needed titles to perpetuate their influence. On another level, the difference was important. Long before David Ramsay interpreted American Independence as a victory for merit, colonists had voiced the argument that in a "new country," prominent families rarely owed their rank to more than a few generations of ancestors. These colonists concluded that they, and their immediate forebears, had earned their rank. When in 1693 New York's governor called upon the assembly to give the province's council (in effect its upper chamber) a larger role in governance, Cadwallader Colden responded that since "the most opulent families" had risen "from the lowest ranks of the people," the council, in principle an elite within an elite, did not "embody a distinct rank of the people."[23] Hence it could not act as a check on the prerogative (executive authority) and should continue as a merely advisory body. In 1711 the New York assembly reminded the council that without hereditary status or life tenure, it was not "another distinct state or rank of people."[24]

Rank and Office

Ramsay's image of the colonial past as based on earned achievement had some foundation, but he nevertheless overlooked a great deal. Perhaps his most misleading assertion lay in his historical claim that creoles, their path blocked by placemen, restrained their ambition for office. True, both Hamilton's New York and Ramsay's South Carolina contained a lot of placemen. Most colonies, however, had few placemen, even during the Imperial Crisis. Placemen were rare in New England; there were few in Virginia; and even in South Carolina they were resented because they took offices sought by creoles. In 1774 the prominent South Carolinian William Drayton complained that the problem with placemen was that they were "Strangers from England" rather than "Men of Rank in the Colony," who certainly craved office. Drayton's complaint was evoked by his own displacement (by a placeman) from the province's highest court, a position Drayton owed mainly to the intervention of his uncle, the lieutenant governor.[25]

In a colonial society lacking a nobility but permeated by status seeking, office appealed to creoles as a signifier of status.[26] "The Influence which Preferments and Comissions have upon little Men is inexpressible," Cotton Mather wrote in 1709. Everyone, it seemed to Mather, sought to strut among his neighbors "with the Illustrious Titles of, *Our Major*, and *the Captain*, or *His Worship*."[27] Public offices themselves were graded, like military ranks. Even when individuals occupied the same office, they squabbled over precedence. In contrast to social hierarchy, which existed apart from its observation, precedence required spectators and evidenced itself on public occasions. Edmund Morgan has written of the late seventeenth-century "big men" of Virginia that a councilor or a judge "would sometimes refuse to sit at all if not placed higher than another on the list of councilors or judges, though the placement had no apparent function."[28] John Adams said on the eve of the Revolution that "the office of a Justice of the Peace is a great Acquisition, . . . enough to purchase and corrupt any Man,"[29] and right after the Revolution he observed that while in the absence of hereditary titles the United States had no orders of men, it had "different orders of *offices*."[30]

The importance that colonists attached to the link between office and status impressed no one more than Adams. Born in 1735, Adams belonged to the generation of "old revolutionaries," men who were more deeply impressed by the inevitability of social hierarchy and by the tenacity with which men clung to their social rank than men such as Thomas Jefferson and James Madison, born respectively in 1743 and 1751.[31] On entering Harvard in 1751, Adams received a quick reminder of his social position when he was "placed" fourteenth out of twenty-five students under Harvard's established system of "seniority." Since a student's age did not directly affect his rank, "social precedence" is a more accurate tag for this puzzling system. Until Harvard's class of 1772, students were ranked by Harvard's "immediate government" (president, professors, and tutors) toward the end of their freshmen year in a digitally exact order on the basis of "the supposed Dignity of the Families whereto they severall belong."[32] Rank had its privileges. It determined the order of seating in commons, the assignment of rooms, the order in which students processed and orated at commencement, and the order in which graduates were listed in triennial catalogues.[33] Yale had a similar system until late in 1767. Rank lists were conspicuously posted on the college's walls; no student could fail to know his rank.

Paine Wingate of Harvard's class of 1759, much later a U.S. senator, recollected that the students "were often enraged beyond bounds" at their placement and it took time to reconcile them to their "allotment."[34] Parents complained even more vociferously, hardly surprising since they were the ones being placed. Angry fathers did not argue that young Jonathan was a bright lad deserving of a higher place. Rather, they spoke the language of John Winslow, who reminded Harvard's president in 1749 that "Rank in our Way is looked upon as a Sacred Thing [and] it is generally allowed that the Sons of the New England Cambridge are placed according to the Degrees of their ancestors I have therefore put in my Pretensions for my son."[35] Winslow can be forgiven for failing to identify the main basis for the rankings, which was not a father's wealth or the luster of his ancestors but the prestige of the father's civil office, for Harvard's government never published the basis and voiced the "supposed Dignity" criterion only on the eve of abolishing the system. The son of a governor would have precedence over the son of a lieutenant governor, followed in order by the sons of councilors, justices of the peace (with precedence determined by the date of a father's first commission as a justice), college graduates in rough order of their fathers' graduations (this effectively squeezed in clergymen's sons), and then all others. Once placed, a student could do nothing to elevate his rank (nor could a father elevate his son's rank by gaining a higher civil office after the ranking), but the son could raise his rank by marching in place while those placed higher were "degraded" (demoted) for infractions.[36]

Degradation for disciplinary infractions was unrivaled as a form of humiliation, a type of discipline favored by Reformed Protestants. Samuel Melyen of Harvard's class of 1696 knew this when he pleaded with Cotton Mather, a supposed wire-puller as the son of Harvard's president, to intervene to restore Melyen's rank after his degradation to the foot of the class for an infraction. "Had I been at first Inferior to the rest," Melyen implored, "I should have been contented and thought it my place." What galled him was the distance he had fallen from his "Antient [original] standing."[37] The "Terrors of Degradation" help to explain the persistence of the system,[38] but its origin reflected the college's desire to publicize the putative social worth of its students in an age when an individual's likely value to a community was an accepted foundation of social distinctions. Town proprietors in seventeenth-century Massachusetts allotted land in new towns on just this basis.[39] In eighteenth-century Connecticut, church committees allotted seats for worship on the basis of members' social standing and perceived worth to the community.

John Winthrop, the first governor of Massachusetts, had explained in "A Model of Christian Charity" that "no man is made more honourable than another or more wealthy etc., out of any particular and singular respect for himselfe."[40] The precedence system punished those who failed to live up to their station or talents. Society's hierarchy of stations, possessions, and talents had been freely gifted by God for His glory and the welfare of His creatures, not to exalt individuals. Any Englishman, Catholic or Protestant, could have said the same. What distinguished Protestantism, especially in its Reformed incarnations, lay in the value it attached to reasoned consent. Children were not born into churches but joined them after professions of faith. Similarly, authority was not an indelible attribute of kingship; it could be forfeited by misconduct. As a Reformed bastion, Harvard treated rank as an attribute subject to degradation for misbehavior. In contrast, although an eighteenth-century visitor to England's ancient universities, Oxford and Cambridge, would have found students arranged in a hierarchy—noblemen, "gentlemen commoners," "foundationers," "commoners," "battelors," "bible clerks," and "servants"—each visibly distinguished by the sort of cap and gown he wore, he would discover that rank could not be lost by misconduct.

Rank at Harvard and Yale was not fixed, but neither did it depend on a student's meritorious performance, at least not primarily. A number of anomalous placements at Harvard before 1700, notably that of future poet Michael Wigglesworth ahead of a Cotton and a Dudley in the class of 1651, suggests that academic performance, most likely on Harvard's oral entrance examination, played some role in the initial placement of students, especially in the seventeenth century.[41] But in the eighteenth century scholarly promise appears to have affected rankings only after the college authorities had run out of sons of dignitaries to place. Although Harvard and Yale encouraged students to excel in their studies by granting awards like Harvard's Hopkins prizes and Yale's Berkeley prizes, winning awards did not affect a student's rank. Harvard's faculty singled out Samuel Chandler for a Hopkins prize after he had been degraded to the foot of his class of 1753 for serious infractions.[42]

When it decided to abandon the social-precedence system, Harvard's government did not reject the system's underlying principle; rather, it cited the system's "inconveniences," which included irritating influential fathers. It was not accidental that Harvard abandoned the system after the Massachusetts House passed a bill (subsequently blocked by the governor and council) to charter a rival college in Hampshire County. The leader of the western interests, Col. Israel Williams of the class of 1727, was known to have "great" rage against Harvard ever since one of his sons had been assigned a relatively low place (barely in the top half) in the class of 1751, while another son had been placed in the top quarter of his Yale class.[43] The immediate occasion of Harvard's decision was a tangled case involving the rankings of two students in the class of 1771, which boiled down to whose father held the more prestigious justiceship of the peace.[44]

After abandoning their social-precedence systems, each institution began to list students alphabetically in its catalog. Starting in 1777, Harvard began to distinguish its top scholar by an arabic 1 next to his name, but it did not begin to rank its top ten scholars until 1826. Yet we should not underestimate the significance of the change. A Yale charity student, predictably ranked low on the precedence scale, wrote in 1767 that with the impending abolition of the precedence system, "it is not he that has got the finest coat or largest ruffles that is esteemed here at present." Rather, as the class "henceforward are to be ranked alphabetically, the students may expect marks of distinction put upon their best scholars and speakers."[45] In sum, merit would count, and it is little wonder that in 1831 Harvard librarian Benjamin Peirce, who dredged up information about the social-precedence system (mainly by tapping Paine Wingate's nonagenarian recollections), pronounced the system at odds "with the genius of Republicanism."[46]

Merit in the American Revolution

The republicanism to which Peirce alluded had been a work in progress since the English Civil War. In *The Commonwealth of Oceana* (1656) James Harrington had imagined a commonwealth, a government lacking a king or hereditary aristocracy and devoted to the interests of the people, in which, among a body of twenty men, fourteen would recognize the superiority of six "natural aristocrats," who would be elected by ballot on the basis of their qualities of birth, wealth, education, and liberality.[47] Harrington and other republican (or "commonwealth") writers assumed that consent would occur among equals, but equals did not mean everyone. The seventeenth- and eighteenth-century Anglo-American political world rang with inconclusive debates over the extent to which the possession of reason, property, and religious orthodoxy were preconditions of civil equality. Whatever position defenders of government by consent took on the issue of who qualified for equal rights, few doubted that when equals gave their consent, they would choose superior governors.

In eighteenth-century Britain writers who occupied the ideological spectrum from Cato to the radical Whigs warned about the threat posed by the Court and its manipulation of patronage. Although creole officeholders benefited from influence and "connexion" and complained about the "avarice" of Crown officials, before the Imperial Crisis of the 1760s they did not see Crown corruption of colonial legislatures as a problem.[48] The conflict over taxing the colonies, however, turned local influentials into enemies of the prerogative and led many American

Whigs to complain that governors were passing over qualified candidates for office to appoint less fit ones.

In the 1760s John Adams had been on the periphery of a case that would sear itself into American political consciousness. When the death of Massachusetts' chief justice in 1760 created a vacancy on the province's highest court, James Otis Jr. sought the position for his father, a former speaker of the province's House and a Barnstable lawyer, who had been promised the position by a former governor. But the responsibility for filling the vacancy fell to Governor Francis Bernard, who appointed Thomas Hutchinson. Hutchinson was not a placeman but an American, a descendant, in fact, of the seventeenth-century sectary Anne Hutchinson, and a Harvard graduate. Adams, who had been laboriously preparing for the full-time practice of law since his graduation from Harvard, judged the appointment of Hutchinson by a standard more relevant to himself by expressing dismay because Hutchinson had been "bred" a merchant, not a lawyer. No less enraged, the younger Otis, according to Bernard, threatened to set the whole province ablaze, "even if he perished in the attempt," if the appointment went to Hutchinson, who, aside from the fact that he was not the elder Otis, already held several important offices (lieutenant governor, councilor, judge of probate for Suffolk County, and commander of the fort on Castle Island). To the younger Otis, Hutchinson was a self-seeking "engrosser" of offices and the holder of "incompatible" offices, such as legislator and judge.[49]

In reality, Hutchinson had not sought the chief justiceship, but he did sprinkle appointments among his friends and relatives, including his brother-in-law Andrew Oliver and Andrew's brother Peter. To favor kin was hardly a new practice in colonial politics, but the emerging Imperial Crisis gave it a new valence. Shortly after Hutchinson's appointment as chief justice, Adams watched as the younger Otis attacked the writs of assistance before the superior court, where Hutchinson upheld their legality. With passage of the Stamp Act in 1765, privately opposed by Hutchinson, Andrew Oliver secured appointment as the Stamp Act agent in Massachusetts, and protesters against imperial taxation for revenue quickly discovered a target in the so-called Hutchinson-Oliver Junto. After Hutchinson's appointment as royal governor of Massachusetts in 1771, the mounting fury of attacks on the Mother Country would force him into even greater reliance on family and friends, all seen by Adams as an abuse of executive patronage.

As a delegate to both the first and second Continental Congresses, Adams emphasized that an individual's fitness rather than his *connexion*, his merit rather than his family's friends, had to become the prerequisite for appointments. He declaimed that revolution would make "Capacity, Spirit, and Zeal in the Cause, supply the Place of Fortune, Family, and every other consideration which used to have weight with Mankind."[50] The Imperial Crisis left American Whigs with the view that the abuse of patronage was inseparable from executive power and a dis-ease of monarchy, and they wrote state constitutions in the 1770s that restricted the appointment power of governors and, as in New York, required rotation in office. In their search for the "most meritorious" leaders, however, American Whigs underestimated the weight of their colonial past. Leading a revolution that was not intended to overthrow the gentry, American Whigs did not stray far from the social bases of colonial officeholding.

The war itself provided fresh incentives to look for leaders within the gentry, the social rank most obsessed with status and precedence. Officers would have to raise troops, which meant they had to be recognized for their local weight and in-fluence. What could be said of colonial society—that the offices were more finely graded than their holders—was doubly true in the army, where ranks were very finely calibrated. The results often were chaotic. As Robert Morris complained, Congress was ever disputing over "Liberties, Priviledges, Posts, and places."[51] During the war the intensity of "their Colonial Jealousies and Distinctions" be-came virtually a hallmark of the Americans. The French were amazed by it and the British eager to exploit it.[52]

Predictably, regional conflicts occurred over military appointments. Wash-ington's appointment as commander of the Continental Army in 1775 was un-controversial: his military experience was valuable; his wealth gave the lie to the British charge that the rebels were unprincipled adventurers with nothing to lose; and as a Virginian he gave a national cast to the army at a time when most of the troops were New Englanders. Although New Englanders were miffed when two of the next three major-generalships went to Virginians, regional tensions would prove easier to control than conflicts over rank and precedence within regions. Congress's move to pour balm on regional wounds by appointing two northerners as major generals, New York's Philip Schuyler and Connecticut's Is-rael Putnam, soothed interregional envy, but Putnam's appointment infuriated two Continental brigadier generals, who had outranked him in the Connecticut militia, and each resigned his commission in the Continental Army. Still poorly informed about local hierarchies, Congress soon created new problems by ap-pointing eight brigadier generals, one of whom, John Thomas, recently pro-moted to lieutenant general in the Massachusetts militia, was left junior to two officers who had been his subordinates in the Massachusetts militia.[53]

Adams could scarcely believe the tenacity of adherence to rank and prece-dence in a supposedly republican army, and he lashed out at those who insisted on "the honor of maintaining a rank superior to able men." He angrily described small obsessions with the "delicate point of honor" as "one of the most putrid conceptions of absolute monarchy" and as "incompatible with republican prin-ciples."[54] Pleading with an angered Thomas not to quit the army, Washington also dismissed concern for precedence as an excrescence of monarchy. As a principled war, the Revolution required soldiers to subordinate their pride to the national interest, in contrast to "the usual Contests of Empire and Ambition," in which "the Conscience of a Soldier has so little Share that he may properly insist upon his Claims to Rank, and extend his Pretensions ever to Punctilio."[55]

In retrospect, the sensitivity of Continental officers to rank and precedence seems rather extraordinary, since only a handful of them, men such as Horatio Gates and Charles Lee, half-pay British officers who sided with the colonists, were professional soldiers. The vast majority of Continental officers knew nothing of the values of European professional soldiers. French officers serving in America after the alliance with France found themselves crowded with naive questions from Continental Army officers about their civilian trades. In reality, the war intensified the gentry's long-standing sensitivity to its dignity by awakening a new desire for fame and glory, a feature of monarchies and aristocracies that the colonists had gleaned more from literature than from their experience.[56] Combined with the stimulus of war, the tradition of colonial status seeking made it difficult for gentlemen to distinguish their honor and reputation from their sense of self-worth.[57] When in 1780 Congress tried to reorganize the quartermaster general's department, headed by Nathanael Greene, by appointing subordinates without gaining his approval in advance, Greene, in civilian life a Rhode Island ironmonger, did more than resign as quartermaster general. He wrote an extraordinary letter to Congress, which he provocatively referred to as the "administration," a term that conjured up images of corrupt British ministries, and then announced that it was unnecessary for him to list his objections to the reorganization plan; "it is sufficient to say that my feelings are injured."[58] Four years earlier Greene had complained that were he not promoted, his self-esteem would collapse and render him useless to the nation. More was at work here than Greene's touchy ego. The prevailing view among officers was that they were all equally courageous and differed only in opportunities to display their bravery; merit was the given, rank the distinction.[59]

Officers in the army and, later, the navy embraced this understanding of their merit as a fixed element of their public characters more explicitly than did civilians of the gentry class. Yet the officer corps of the army was composed of civilians of gentry rank who had put on uniforms. The terms (*rank, station*) used in eighteenth-century America conveyed fixity rather than fluidity in a society where many argued that rank had been earned by the individual or his immediate ancestors. Like the system of ranking collegians by social precedence, military ranks were more finely graded than civilian ranks. Similar assumptions permeated civilian life, however, where the effectiveness of officeholders was thought to depend on their public characters rather than their technical competence. Congress complained about the burning obsession with rank and precedence in the military but did more to fan than to douse it. If a general failed, the root lay in his character and not his tactics, or, more accurately, defective tactics evidenced vicious character.

One way to have avoided conflicts over precedence would have been to rely on seniority, as based on time in rank. Inasmuch as no clear regulations existed for translating seniority in state lines to the Continental line, seniority was far from foolproof, but support for it ran strong among Continental army officers, who recognized their own tendencies and who liked seniority's automatic quality. Were an officer passed over for promotion, he could attribute his treatment to circumstances rather than to an assessment of his merit. Greene staunchly defended seniority as the principle for promotion. Too often, he complained, cases for promotion based on merit merely amounted to "a single instance of bravery."[60] He may have been referring to Congress's controversial promotion of Israel Putnam to major general in 1775 after his victory in an insignificant skirmish on Noodle's Island in Boston harbor, where Putnam had used a 50:1 numerical advantage to overpower a detachment of British marines.

Reflecting the prevailing view in Congress, however, Adams and Washington saw seniority as the handmaiden of monarchy. Monarchs amassed power, they theorized, by creating comfortable dependents; the wise despot provided opportunities for his inferiors but only to bind them more effectively to his will. Officers who knew that they would be promoted in time, as long as they did their sovereign's bidding, made ideal subjects but not necessarily good fighters. When officers of a Connecticut regiment remonstrated against the appointment to a lieutenancy of recent Yale graduate and future Patriot martyr Nathan Hale, Washington retorted that "commissions should ever be the reward of Merit and not of Age."[61] As Adams developed his arguments for merit during the war, he also described it as a check on the concentration of power. Retaining the power to promote meritorious officers would diffuse power by giving Congress, and not just the military, a say in promotions.

Most army officers nevertheless viewed the invocation of merit as a guise for favoritism. Adams himself conceded that all members of Congress had "sons, brothers, and cousins, acquaintances, friends, and connexions of one sort or another," and that all assemblies were prone to favoritism. Early in the war he used his position in Congress to urge Washington to appoint one of his law clerks, Jonathan Williams Austin, as his secretary, despite Austin's past and present "Follies." Adams lived in a society where this sort of trading on influence was expected; for a patron not to do so would be to insult his dependent.[62]

Adams, then, appears to have been a hypocrite, the more so because he complained that leaving promotions based on merit to "the General and the army" would invite favoritism. Yet Adams's thinking about merit had some consistent elements. He defended merit as a basis of selection not because it promised the best possible outcome by identifying and elevating talent from a vast pool but because it checked arbitrary power. The big lesson he had learned from the Imperial Crisis was not that favoritism could be excluded from republican government but that favoritism became really dangerous when linked to the enhancement of concentrated power, the very sort of enhancement that he saw as the work of the Hutchinson-Oliver Junto in colonial Massachusetts. He believed that Congress contained more "guards and checks upon the infirmities of leading members" than did the military. As his relations with Washington frayed—Washington's low opinion of New England troops became a poorly kept secret—Adams even insisted that Washington should not be allowed to appoint his own staff, since the staff was supposed to act, according to Adams, as a check on the commander (a doubtful proposition, since a general's staff was colloquially called his "family").

The most visible evidence of Congress's desire to maintain control over army appointments was the Baltimore Resolution of February 1777, which urged "due regard" for "the line of succession," the merit of the persons proposed for promotion, and the quota of troops raised and to be raised by each state.[63] Gouverneur Morris dubbed this the "mysterious trinity of *Seniority, Merit,* and *Quota.*"[64] Within this trinity, merit was the Paraclete, the least embodied component. Applying it was difficult, but just asserting it gave Congress, which *was* the national government, a basis for overriding state rules and customs and preventing the devolution of all military power to the army's command. In reality, the first application of the Baltimore Resolution, briefly described in the introduction to this book, contributed to Benedict Arnold's treason in 1780. In appointing five new major generals in February 1777, Congress omitted Arnold, whose demonstrated bravery everyone conceded. None of the five new major generals had served as long as Arnold as a brigadier general; one, Benjamin Lincoln, held brigadier rank only in the Massachusetts line. Arnold fell victim to quota, for Congress judged that his native Connecticut had enough major generals for its share of troops. Writing to Arnold in April 1777, Washington, whom Congress had not consulted, described quota as a "strange mode of reasoning" and then reassured Arnold that his promotion, "which was due [owed] to your seniority, was not overlooked for want of merit in you."[65]

This assurance did not console Arnold, who took no comfort from any private thought that he was superior to other generals in courage and daring. Sounding much like Nathanael Greene, Arnold wrote to Washington that any officer who retained his commission "at the expense of reputation, I hold as a disgrace to the army, and unworthy of the glorious cause in which we are engaged."[66] Arnold could have taken Washington's advice and ignored the slight, since it clearly was based on an arbitrary quota system. But as a principle for distributing commissions, quota had only recently been institutionalized in the Baltimore Resolution; to Arnold it could not hold a candle to rank and reputation as a signifier of an officer's worth. Instead, he demanded a court of inquiry into his record, an awkward request since he had not been charged with anything, and he then set off in April 1777 to plead his case to Congress, pausing on the way to join a force of Connecticut militia that was attacking a British column retreating from a raid on Danbury. Impressed by this latest example of Arnold's bravery, Congress promoted him to major general on May 2 but then refused to backdate his promotion to February. Arnold always described this as a refusal to "restore" his "rank," seemingly an odd choice of words for one who had just been promoted. What Arnold meant was that Congress, by declining to restore the precedence he held over the other five new major generals when all had been brigadier generals, had dishonored him. James Lovell, a Massachusetts delegate to Congress, described the issue between Arnold and Congress as "really a question between Monarchical and Republican Principles, put at a most critical time." From Lovell's perspective, to insist like Arnold on precedence was to behave monarchically and to forsake "patriotic exertion." Arnold's "self-love" had led him to assert "a fanciful right incompatible with the general interest of the Union."[67]

As time passed, however, Washington, tired of finding a stack of resignations on his desk every time an officer was promoted out of the "common course" (seniority), called on Congress to restrict promotions "for merit" to "the most eminent and distinguished services"[68] and to establish a "*fixed*" principle of promotion.[69] While never relinquishing its power to reward merit, Congress gradually came around to this position. For example, in 1781 Congress divided the nation into eight districts, each with a specified allotment of general officers; promotions to brigadier general were governed by seniority within each district and to major general by seniority within the Continental Army.

The invocation of merit during the Revolution was a loose cannon on the deck, a principle that on the one hand seemed unarguable and on the other had profoundly disruptive potential. By the end of the fighting, Congress had developed procedures that promised to preserve merit as a principle while enveloping it with hedges, mainly quota and seniority, to restrain its disruptive potential. At the same time, Congress never abandoned merit as a basis of appointment or promotion because the invocation of merit gave Congress a basis for interfering with the military when it saw fit.

Merit and "Jealousy" in the Ratification Debate

The Revolution thus left an ambiguous legacy to the framers of the Constitution. As a gentry-led revolution, the war enhanced the status of the Patriot gentry, individuals who soon would style themselves "Men of Merit" and "First Characters" on the basis of their contributions to victory. Ironically, however, victory removed the Mother Country's placemen, "ministerial tools," and "sycophants" who had been the target of Whig suspiciousness during the Imperial Crisis, with the effect that the strain of suspiciousness embedded in republican thought increasingly searched for homegrown targets. In the late 1780s, suspiciousness found a roost in the thought of leading opponents of ratification of the Constitution, the antifederalists, who criticized the Men of Merit and First Characters on grounds laid out earlier by John Adams.

Adams came away from the Revolution with diminishing confidence in the self-enacting power of merit as an ideal. He spent much of the 1780s in Europe, where he had opportunities to expand his knowledge of history, witness court life, follow news from America about the sharpening conflicts of interest groups in state legislatures, and refine his ideas about government. Reflecting on his experiences during the 1770s, Adams, the innocent abroad, now recognized that even republican officials were prone to the courtly vice of deploying talents to secure influence and power. In his major work during the 1780s, his *Defence of the Constitutions of the United States of America*, published in two volumes in 1786 and 1787, he wrote that, faced with a need to raise an army and appoint generals, a popular assembly would always choose the man with "the most ample fortune, the most honorable descent, the greatest abilities." Once chosen, the general would fall in with other leading men to promote "men of family, property, and abilities." Since no assembly on its own could assess the "merits and pretensions of applicants," the man with friends "of aristocratic complexion" in the assembly would always gain preference.[70]

The *Defence* was a rambling response to a succinct letter written in 1778 by Anne-Robert-Jacques Turgot, the French financial reformer, to Richard Price, complaining that the American state constitutions, with their provisions for bicameral legislatures, betrayed an "unreasonable imitation" of Britain's Commons and Lords. Adams, who had defended senates as necessary to embody the aristocratic social rank, now set the conflict between hereditary and natural aristocracy within a broad historical framework. Hereditary aristocracies were prone to collapse from their own excesses, while natural aristocracies were dangerous because their proclivity to feed on the vices of human nature, especially blind reverence for the "great," made them potent. In both the *Defence* and his *Discourses on Davila* (1790) Adams drew heavily on Adam Smith's *Theory of Moral Sentiments* (1759), especially its rooting of the "passion for distinction" in human nature. What we admire in the great, Smith contended, is their greatness—their social rank—which controls how much merit we detect in them; "in equal degrees of merit who does not respect more the rich and the great than the poor and the

humble." The talents of Louis XIV, Smith wrote, were "not much above mediocrity," but all Europe fawned on his step, his "affecting" voice, and his "frivolous
accomplishments."[71] As Adams saw it, in any contest with this bent of human
nature, "humble, modest, obscure, and poor merit" stood little chance of being
noticed.[72]

In contrast to Thomas Jefferson, who would later link natural aristocracy to
merit, Adams insisted that natural aristocracy depended on appearances, with
which merit, an inner quality, could never compete. During the 1790s Adams's
prolonged ruminations on aristocracy contributed to his rift with Jefferson and,
more generally, Jeffersonian Republicans, who labeled him a defender of aristocratic rule. Ironically, however, during the 1780s Adams's notion that natural
aristocracy was inevitable was embraced by antifederalists, all of whom would
become Jeffersonian Republicans in the 1790s.

At New York's ratification convention, Alexander Hamilton clashed with Melancton Smith, a political ally of New York's antifederalist governor George Clinton and a future Republican, in a memorable debate over Article I, Section 2, of
the Constitution. This clause set the size of the House of Representatives until the
first census at sixty-five, smaller than all but two state legislatures and only one-
tenth the size of the House of Commons in Britain,[73] and thereafter permitted
no more than one representative for every 30,000 inhabitants. Smith, a Dutchess
County farmer, cited the small size of the proposed House as an invitation to
aristocracy, since "none but the great," those with "conspicuous military, popular,
civil, or legal talents," were likely to gain election where electoral districts were
so large.[74] (Smith would have been more alarmed had he known that only Washington's last-minute intervention at the Philadelphia convention—it was the
only time he spoke—lowered the ratio from 1:40,000 to 1:30,000.) It was Smith's
firm view that representatives in a republic should be drawn from the "middling
classes"; they should be "sensible, substantial men, who have been used to walk
in the plain and frugal paths of life."[75] Hamilton professed to be dumbstruck by
Smith's complaint that the Constitution threatened to establish an aristocracy ("I
hardly know the meaning of the word, as it is used").[76] But Smith, who had just
read Adams's *Defence*, had a ready response. Aristocracy in no way depended on
"titles, stars, and garters." "Natural aristocrats" with "conspicuous" achievements
would turn the public's head away from the leaders of the sober middle classes.
A similarly acrimonious dispute had arisen at the Philadelphia convention over
a different clause of the Constitution, Article I, Section 6, which prohibited the
appointment of senators and representatives during their terms to any civil office under the United States "which shall have been created, or the emoluments
whereof shall have been encreased during such time." This wording resulted from

interminable wrangling among the delegates, who remembered that awarding concurrent (or "plural") offices to legislators had been one of the means by which British ministries and royal governors had manipulated elected assemblies. To check the abuses of plural officeholding, several of the state constitutions had established the principle of rotation in office, often amounting in practice to term limits. But the framers of the Constitution, which did not provide for rotation in office, took a different tack by substituting institutional checks and balances, designed to restrain the *exercise* of power, for sharp restrictions on the tenure of officeholders.

At Philadelphia a number of supporters of the Constitution, including Rufus King of Massachusetts, Gouverneur Morris of New York (who wrote the final draft of the Constitution), Hamilton, and James Wilson of Pennsylvania, consistently advocated minimal restrictions on concurrent officeholding. These same individuals styled themselves "men of merit" or such equally republican-sounding alternatives as men of "conspicuous" talents and achievements and "first characters." The social backgrounds of these Men of Merit varied. King and Morris were well born. The "bastard brat of a Scotch peddler," in John Adams's words, Hamilton, the illegitimate son of a failed West Indian merchant, accurately described his social position before his emigration to North America from St. Croix as that of a "grovelling" store clerk.[77] Wilson, a Scottish immigrant who became one of just six men to sign both the Declaration of Independence and the Constitution and one of the original justices of the Supreme Court, devoted himself to law, drafting constitutions, and making money. That his penchant for land speculation eventually left him in penury, "hunted like a wild beast" by his creditors, should not obscure his passionate belief that America offered unrivaled opportunities.[78]

All of these men had gained fame during the Revolution and its aftermath, and all of them thought that the effectiveness of the national government would depend significantly on its ability to attract nationally famous notables into its service. Any restrictions on concurrent officeholding, King argued, "would discourage merit."[79] Most critics of restrictions on concurrent officeholding shared the view that republics, lacking the despot's resort to force, could be effectively governed only if they adopted features of the British system, with its reliance on ministerial influence as a way to secure legislative support for measures put forward by the executive. Gouverneur Morris cynically referred to public offices as "loaves and fishes," the "noble bait" that would attract the prominent into public service. He added, "No government will be good without Influence, that is unless Men of Merit or the Pillars of Govt. are rewarded with Offices of Honor and Profit."[80] Wilson, who at one point opposed even a minimum age for members of the House of Representatives as likely to dampen "the efforts of genius, and of laudable ambition," asked whether the "talents, which entitle a man to public reward, operate as a punishment."[81] Hamilton contended that restrictions on collateral officeholding blocked the "dispensation of those regular honors & emoluments, which produce an attachment to the Govt."[82] In the New York state ratifying convention Chancellor Robert R. Livingston would echo this language when he pronounced any restriction on pluralism "an absurd species of ostracism."

For the Men of Merit, nothing better signified their merit than their reputations. In America as nowhere else, they argued, reputation measured merit. James Wilson saw to it that a legally enforceable right to reputation was written into Pennsylvania's 1790 Bill of Rights, and in his *Lectures on Law* (1791) he argued that each person had a natural right to his reputation because reputation was a form of property. Yet Wilson preferred to call reputation "character," which he equated with the "just result" of the opinions that ought to be formed of a person's talent and conduct.[83] In other words, character was reputation in the American republic, where titles and legal distinctions did not inflate one's reputation. In a nation lacking "showy" courtiers and mobs to applaud them and marked by a prevailing "mediocrity of fortune" and equal rights, the self-inflation of any individual would meet with no adulation beyond his just deserts.[84]

Advocates of sharp restraints on plural officeholding, including George Mason of Virginia and Elbridge Gerry of Massachusetts (each would refuse to sign the Constitution), warned of corruption and creeping aristocracy in the absence of checks on it. At one point Mason sarcastically proposed to eliminate all restraints on plural officeholding in order to invite into government those "generous and benevolent characters who will do justice to each other's merit, by carving out offices and rewards for it."[85] The final version of Article I, Section 6, which owed a lot to James Madison, was a compromise. In addition to restricting the appointment of senators and representatives to offices under the executive's authority, it barred officeholders under the United States from simultaneously sitting in Congress.[86]

As a safeguard against a Walpole-style corruption of Congress, this language satisfied most delegates, who believed that, by restraining the *exercise* of power, the system of checks and balances embodied in the Constitution rendered unnecessary extraordinary restraints on the *agents* of power. In 1789, while debating the establishment of the department of foreign affairs, the first Congress under the new constitution dealt another blow to the idea that the reputation of a First Character could act as a trump card. To the amazement of its participants, this debate dragged on for weeks over whether the head of the department could be removed solely by the president, by some combination of the president and

Congress, or solely by impeachment. Early in the debate Representative William Loughton Smith of South Carolina, soon to become an ardent adherent of the Federalist Party, argued that a cabinet officer had so much of his reputation, and hence his property, invested in the office that removal by any other means than impeachment was unthinkable.[87] But only one other member of the House agreed with him, and the debate quickly turned into a conflict between advocates of sole presidential removal power and those who wanted to condition presidential removal with Senate consent. In these debates Madison was among the leading advocates of investing sole removal power in the president.[88]

As George Mason sensed, the Revolution and its aftermath nevertheless had created a kind of national directory of famous men whose merit even their opponents conceded. In 1783 Aedanus Burke, future antifederalist and Jeffersonian Republican, blasted the recently founded Society of the Cincinnati not only as a "deeply planned and closely executed conspiracy" against the republic but also as a "self-created" hereditary order whose members would soon be "grasping for every thing and rising from one usurpation to another."[89] What most troubled Burke was that the Cincinnati were chosen from "the first rate men," the Revolutionary officers who had so much "merit and claim to the applause of their countrymen at home and to fame abroad." Their "merit, services, and lustre of character" rendered the Cincinnati especially threatening.[90] Five years later Melancton Smith made the same point in the New York convention when he contrasted his "men in the middling class" not with the rich as such but with those in the "first" class, who were distinguished by their superior "birth, education, talents, and wealth." These were John Adams's natural aristocrats, who owed nothing to hereditary titles, legal distinctions, or titles, stars, and garters.[91]

Melancton Smith stood firmly in the antifederalist mainstream.[92] For these men, identifying the natural aristocracy was easy. It consisted of men who possessed abundant wealth, great abilities, a keen sense of honor, "general knowledge" and an expansive outlook on public affairs, exceptional ambition, and prominence (its members, that is, were "conspicuous"). Being conspicuous, they readily identified and allied with each other, and they would use this alliance to gain high office, not by rigged elections but by fair votes. Although Smith estimated the number of natural aristocrats throughout the nation as only four to five thousand men, the "natural democracy" consisting of small and middling farmers, artisans, traders, and professionals would be no match for it where electoral districts were large. The problem with rule by this natural aristocracy arose from its overall superiority. So elevated were these men that they could not represent the diverse interests of society. Much more than federalists, antifederalists like Smith adhered to an interest-group theory of politics. Farmers, artisans, and traders all had distinct and conflicting interests—for example, one group would favor taxing land, another taxing trade—and these diverse interests could be best represented by men engaged in each.

One can readily construct a list of principles that mainstream antifederalists did not assert. They did not assert that merit was blocked from rising in the republic. Unlike revolutionaries in France, they did not claim that careers needed to be opened to talent. The apathy of the "natural democracy" worried Melancton Smith more than its oppression. In fact, he did not think that the natural democracy was oppressed at all. In the American republic ordinary people could expect their abilities and exertions to receive their just deserts. Only in a limited sense did antifederalists champion the cause of groups underrepresented in government. They proposed increasing the size of the House to accommodate the plural interests of society, while accepting that the natural aristocrats would hold the high offices of state and acknowledging that natural democrats were so lacking in ambition that they needed goading to seek office at all. In contrast to Jefferson's later ruminations about natural aristocracy, antifederalists did not call for a more intellectually nimble and virtuous class of leaders. They did not propose that governmental and educational institutions be bound more tightly, for example, by a system of examinations for office of the sort being instituted in the late eighteenth century by Prussian monarchs.[93] Rather, they accepted John Adams's proposition that some individuals would make it to the top and they would do so by a combination of birth, wealth, education, talent, and virtuous acts, all of which would lead to accomplishments that would gain the awe of the natural democracy.

Conceding that the natural aristocracy was bursting with merit, antifederalists nevertheless distrusted it. They were heirs to a long tradition of colonial-era attacks on "cabals" dominated by self-anointed leaders, the sort of men Edmund Morgan dubbed "go-getters," who used their proximity to royal authority to enrich themselves. The Imperial Crisis redirected the fear of corruption to British placemen and "sycophants," and in seceding from the British Empire, American Whigs thought that they had also seceded from corruption. With Independence, however, this fear of corruption experienced a kind of repatriation. Now republican suspiciousness focused on homegrown agents of corruption.[94] Corruption itself was usually defined as the illicit quest for power rather than robbing the public purse. In the absence of customary and established rules for defining the scope of the licit quest for power, distrust resembled a bomb that could go off at any moment. It had exploded during the furor over the Society of the Cincinnati, and Washington worried sufficiently about it to consider rejecting Congress's proffer of the presidency of the new republic in 1789.

Republican suspiciousness notwithstanding, support for government by meritorious luminaries was backed at the end of the 1780s by a wide range of federalists, not all of whom followed the Men of Merit by viewing office as a reward for the eminent. James Madison did not conceive of high office as a reward for the First Characters, but he preferred rule by the eminently meritorious to that of the local notables likely to prevail in a system of small electoral districts. The First Characters' path to office need not be strewn with lilies, in his view, but it had to be made sufficiently inviting to ensure that they would be competing for votes only with their peers, and not with the sort of middling farmers and merchants favored by Melancton Smith. Fearing the mediocrity of the majority, Madison chided the antifederalist George Mason for failing to recognize that in Virginia "the backwardness of the best citizens to engage in the legislative service gave but too great success to unfit characters."[95]

After ratification Madison proposed to remedy this problem by establishing at-large elections (statewide) to the House of Representatives. The debates over drawing the first congressional districts revived the arguments used earlier in conflicts over concurrent officeholding and the small size of the House.[96] Writing to Jefferson in 1788, Madison contended that statewide elections would "confine the choice [of representatives] to characters of general notoriety, and so far be favorable to merit."[97] Other federalists echoed this view, usually linking it to an attack on small electoral districts for encouraging votes based on personal familiarity with candidates rather than on reputations that transcended local boundaries.[98] These federalists feared that small electoral districts would invite the "treating" of voters with rum that had scarred elections in the colonial period. In contrast to Melancton Smith, they also thought that the systems of checks and balances written into the Constitution provided an adequate safeguard against mischief by the First Characters.

Merit in Perspective

The Imperial Crisis and the Revolution turned merit, a self-imagined attribute of the colonial gentry that was tightly bound to their conception of their reputation and honor, into a political concept, an ideal on which public policy was to be based. Ironically, the Revolution both stimulated and stigmatized the quest for fame and glory among members of the gentry. In a society in which the gentry already had reason to think that it had earned its rank, conspicuous achievements on behalf of the Revolution were plausibly viewed as evidence of merit. Once the colonial order had given way to the republic, nothing seemed better to exemplify republican principles than rule by the meritorious. Merit as a personal attribute and as a basis of government seemingly merged. But not in the eyes of all citizens. Republican experience made it difficult to argue with the achievements of the First Characters, but republican principles cast a shadow over office seeking that would persist long after the ratification of the Constitution had apparently balanced the rival claims of rewarding merit and restricting the exercise of power and influence.

2

MERIT AND THE CULTURE OF PUBLIC LIFE

In his 1778 "Oration on the Advantages of American Independence" David Ramsay contrasted republics, "favorable to truth, sincerity, frugality, industry, and simplicity of manners," with monarchies, reservoirs of "insincerity, hypocrisy, dissimulation, pride, luxury, and extravagance." The "low arts of fawning and adulation" secured favor in royal governments, but Americans had been freed from "all pretensions to preferment, but those which arise from extraordinary merit."[1]

In fastening the tie between merit and republics, Ramsay set the bar for republican office seekers very high. Strictly speaking, they were not to seek office at all; rather, they were to await the bestowal of office as a reward for their conspicuous merit. The era of the Revolution had established a directory of notables in the form of gentry Whigs whose contributions to the Revolution awed even their critics. The conflict over ratification of the Constitution had brought to the surface antifederalist doubts about the disinterestedness of the Men of Merit and First Characters even while the checks and balances written into the Constitution restrained their exercise of power. During the 1790s, however, policy divisions between the rival coalitions of Federalists and Jeffersonian Republicans gave the Men of Merit a new lease on life. Each party recruited its leaders from the Revolutionary mainstream. Alexander Hamilton, the engine behind the Federalist Party, thought it important to attract eminent men to office in order to impress the people with the "splendor" and "energy" of their government; Republicans quickly got over the antifederalist suspicion of the First Characters and recruited their leaders from the Revolution's cast of notables.[2] Not until 1825 did a president who had not been conspicuous during the Revolutionary era take office, and that president, John Quincy Adams, was the son of a signer of the Declaration of Independence.

Yet the recruitment of leaders from the Revolution's notables did not exorcise the spirit of suspicion of the powerful or the would-be powerful in public life. This was true not only in politics but also in the military and the professions. It could scarcely have been otherwise at a time when army and navy officers owed their commissions to political wire-pulling, the legal profession was the main route to politics, and physicians often sought elective office. A combustible mixture of assertions of superior merit as a basis of advancement and suspicion of the motives of claimants to preferment also marked the early republic's colleges, which were incubators of public men, and led to frequent conflagrations.

The turmoil in the colleges was part of a larger tapestry of disruptive individualism, which this chapter and the next describe. This disruptive individualism took different forms in different spheres of activity. In politics, for example, the gradual acceptance of party loyalty as a legitimate basis for making public appointments, which became known as the spoils system, decompressed the high anxiety that surrounded civil-service appointments under the Federalists and Jeffersonians. Once it became clear that political parties would alternate in power, a president's appointments could favor his party without drawing charges of executive despotism. This normalizing of procedures for distributing routine public offices was at least partly intended to remove occasions for conflict inspired by the rival and irreconcilable claims of individuals to prestigious posts—high public office, elevated military rank, professorships in medical schools, and college honors—at a time when few accepted procedures for distributing such posts existed. In the absence of such procedures, all public competitions became collisions between the self-imagined self-worth of public men, which is to say between their self-imagined merit, character, reputation, and honor.

The Political Culture of Character and Merit

At a time when so many public offices that would later become elective were still appointive and when caucuses of elite public men made most nominations for elective office, the distribution of office almost invariably involved the exercise of "favoritism," supplication, an "unmanly" loss of independence, and the "fawning and adulation" so dreaded by Ramsay. Whether one gained public office by appointment or election, to win office required ambition and self-seeking, traits uncomfortably harnessed with the republican definition of virtue as the subordination of personal self-interest to the public good. Inevitably, the early political parties quickly became enveloped by this political culture's profound suspicion of personal motives. Neither the Federalists nor the Republicans were modern parties; neither saw itself as a permanent organization nor recognized the legitimacy of the other. They were nevertheless organizations in which individuals combined to gain power, the same grounds that had elicited antifederalist attacks on the Men of Merit during the debates over ratification.

Rather than publicly acknowledge their ambition, public men spoke of their *character*, *reputation*, *merit*, and *honor*, words whose connotations often overlapped but which nevertheless contained subtle differences. Strictly, a character was a visible mark, but in political parlance a man's public character amounted to the reputation he had acquired for his acts on the public stage. A public man also had a private character, and leading public characters were not above trading gossip about the private characters of their adversaries. The idea that public men wore masks was an eighteenth-century literary trope in Europe, and Americans were not unfamiliar with the idea. There is always a first time, exclaimed Hamilton, writing pseudonymously (as Catullus) in 1792 to build an inferential case that Jefferson had secretly been an antifederalist, "when characters studious of artful design are unveiled; when the vizor of stoicism is plucked from the brow of the Epicurean; when the plain garb of Quaker simplicity is stripped from the concealed voluptuary; when *coyly refusing* the proferred diadem is seen to be Caesar *rejecting* the trappings, but tenaciously grasping the sustenance of imperial domination."[3] For the most part, however, public men assumed that a public man's public acts revealed his private character or inner self, and they avoided public attacks on the private character of their rivals unless they suspected that an adversary's private character could be shown to have affected his public acts. When in 1797 the Republican hack journalist James Callender exposed the details of Hamilton's long affair with Maria Reynolds, Jefferson took no public notice; to have done so would have elevated the Callenders of the world. But Hamilton worried enough to publish the sordid details of the affair, not to defend his private character from charges of adultery, which he admitted, but to establish that that he had never betrayed the public trust by feeding Maria's blackmailing husband tips on government securities.[4]

In this culture of public life, honor walked a fine line between character and reputation. Honor can be defined as the public verdict on someone's qualities, but in practice honor was a possession of an individual, *his* imagining of how *his* reputation was assessed by his peers.[5] Public men in the early republic were no strangers to the code of honor, which committed them to a sequence of steps to defend their reputations. But Jefferson, Madison, and John Adams alike criticized the code of honor; John Quincy Adams detested it, and there were alternatives.[6] A public man might well value his reputation without resort to challenges and duels. For example, he could write a pamphlet defending his behavior, he could bring a civil suit for libelous damage to this reputation, or he could ignore the slight by attributing it to the shrill viciousness of the rival political coalition.

Merit was bound with character and reputation but also distinguishable. Men of Merit and First Characters were interchangeable terms. Merit could also signify an individual's private sense of his real but undervalued worth, especially when an individual thought himself underappreciated by his society. Here the prickly John Adams's ruminations on how easily the public was misled by impersonators of merit spring to mind. Yet Adams's cynicism about others' pretensions to merit—a product of his personality, his exposure to European courts during the 1780s, and his immersion in Adam Smith's *Theory of Moral Sentiments*—made him unrepresentative of American thinking about merit. James Wilson was closer to the mainstream when he averred that in America someone's reputation accurately reflected his public character because the path to distinction in the republic had been pruned of courtiers and hereditary titles. As noted in Chapter 1, even the antifederalists, who liberally quoted Adams's *Defence of the Constitutions*, conceded that the First Characters possessed genuine merit in the form of accomplishments in the Patriot cause.

An ability to evaluate the public character of others in ways that reinforced one's own authority was an indispensable component of the art of governance in this culture. Hamilton sprinkled his correspondence during the 1780s with cadenced analyses of men on the New York political stage, writing, for example, of John Morin Scott, "Nature has given him genius, but *habit* has impaired it. He never had judgment; he now has scarcely plausibility . . . ; His views as a statesman are warped; his principles as a man are said to be not the purest."[7] Collegians did much the same in what amounted to a preparatory exercise for public life. As a Harvard student in 1786 and 1787, John Quincy Adams recorded his assessments of each of his classmates, not to express his personal likes and dislikes but to explore the relationship between the inner and outer man. Of one classmate he wrote that "without possessing a superior genius," he "was literally mad with ambition," and though "determined to be distinguished from the rest of the world," he would always find "that the world will not respect the notions of a man, who pays no respect to theirs." Adams described another as blessed with popularity among both his classmates and the college's government, but "he is sometimes censured, and such is the instability of all populaces, that a small trifle might induce two thirds of the Class to deny the improvements and abilities of even this person."[8]

Enveloped by the culture of public life, the parties nevertheless also influenced it. In the context of the political divisions of the 1790s, one's public character came to include his measures or policies. Even before the ratification of the Constitution, supporters of ratification were contending that only "friends" of the

Constitution deserved to hold office under the new government. Failure to support ratification indicated a defective public character. When Jefferson's opposition to Hamilton's financial program became clear, Hamilton attacked Jefferson, who had been in France during the ratification debate, for having been a closet antifederalist. On the occasion of recommending a successful applicant for a high federal post in New Jersey in 1791, William Paterson, author of the New Jersey Plan at the Philadelphia constitutional convention and a future justice of the U.S. Supreme Court, wrote that his candidate "is a Federalist [i.e., one who had supported ratification]; this Fact in his Character ought not in my opinion to be overlooked."[9] Paterson's description of support for ratification as a fact in someone's public character, and not just an opinion about an issue, underscores the intimate bond that he and his contemporaries saw between men and measures. Linking a public man's policies to his public character made it difficult to resolve policy disputes as mere differences of opinion. A public man arrived as a total package. One effect of this association of men with measures was to turn conflicts over policies into conflicts between the rival claims of public men to possessing superior public character.

The intrusion of party differences into the culture of character and reputation intensified fears for the survival of the republic. At a time when republicans defined virtue as a willingness to put the public good over one's self-interest, it was tempting to think of any political or social organization in which individuals combined to enhance their influence as a "self-created" cabal. In 1783 Aedanus Burke had described the Society of the Cincinnati in these terms, and at the New York ratifying convention a few years later Melancton Smith had voiced distrust for the "great" on the grounds that they all knew each other and could easily league against the public interest. When the Democratic-Republican societies sprang up in 1793–94 in protest against Hamilton's financial program and the Jay Treaty, the Federalist lexicographer Noah Webster immediately attacked them, not primarily because of their stand on emerging party divisions or even because they were "running mad with the abhorrence of aristocratic influence," but because, paradoxically, these "self-created" societies were themselves aristocracies and had no place in the republic. They allowed little men to deploy their "private attachments" to each other to attain the power given European nobilities by birth and wealth.[10] Webster could find no threat to the republic from the eminent as long as they awaited the public's recognition of their superiority; the acquisition of public influence by private men would be benign in a republic so long as no special effort was made to attain it.

As noted, neither the Federalists nor the Republicans accepted the legitimacy of their rivals during the 1790s, nor did either party see itself as a permanent organization. Yet during the 1790s the "public character" of a public man included his political views, of which his adherence to a party organization, however rudimentary, was a signifier. Partisanship was incompatible with republican ideals, but party could serve as a uniform, distinguishing one combatant from another. Party allegiance could also serve as a signifier of merit at a time when no one thought of politics as a game in which winners and losers would regularly change places. A public man's measures provided insight into his character. Identifying the party allegiances of members of the rising generation also afforded the Men of Merit an opportunity to solve an otherwise intractable problem: perpetuating the influence of a class of leaders whose achievements were not likely to be replicated anytime soon.

Political Correctness

Hamilton, who had guided Washington through the maze of early appointments, seized the opportunity offered by the quasi-war with France in 1798 to perpetuate Federalist influence. Assured that in the event of war he would be Washington's second-in-command, Hamilton quickly compiled a list of "meritorious Officers" to recommend to Secretary of War James McHenry for the proposed new regiments.[11] Although Hamilton had to rely on letters of recommendation for most of the five hundred officer candidates, he supplemented these by personally interviewing many candidates and attaching grades, A, B, C, or X—in effect, must, should, can, or don't—and recommendations for specific ranks: ensign, lieutenant, captain, or major. Hamilton's marginal comments afford insight into what he was looking for. Letters of recommendation were indispensable to Hamilton; like the legendary Chicago ward heeler, he wanted nobody nobody sent. The surest way to earn an X was not to present letters. When he had letters, he looked for evidence of family and education and routinely recorded such comments as "good family[,] education and character" and "respectable parentage." He invariably attached high grades to candidates after whose names he wrote "classical education," "college education," "liberal education," or just "Columbia."[12] Manners and similar evidence of breeding were also important, negatively in the case of one young man who "remained *two hours in silence*" and positively for those who had written applications in clear prose and a good hand ("very handsome letter," "very good letter").[13]

Military experience in the Revolution, even when distinguished, appears to have made no impression on Hamilton, however. His disregard of military experience may have reflected his preference for *young* officers from families of rank. But family and education were inadequate qualifications unless accompanied by what can only be called *political correctness*. All of his recommenders were Federalists, but not all of the candidates, and Hamilton sprinkled his comments with such phrases as "violent Jacobin, ineligible" and "politics not correct," and, more favorably, "foederal principles," "politics correct," "friend to Government," and "foederal and Gentlemanlike."[14] In a letter to Jefferson in 1797 James Madison expressed amazement that young Republicans asked him to recommend them for public positions without realizing that any letter from an opponent of the Adams administration "was more likely to be of injury than service to the suitors for office."[15]

To the modern ear nothing sounds less consistent with identifying merit than Hamilton's careful recording of parentage and politics. He routinely graded sons of mechanics low, and he rated the sons of Federalist influentials high, even when recommended by their fathers or when he had independently ascertained that they were related to Federalist higher-ups.[16] Hierarchs elsewhere already had or were making use of formal procedures to control entrance into military and civil positions. Bourbons in France and Hohenzollerns in Prussia, especially Frederick William I and Frederick II (Frederick the Great), bent on centralizing royal authority, searched for talented commoners to appoint to high office, often capping the appointment with ennoblement, not from some abstract commitment to opening careers to talent but because it was easier to bind talented commoners than independent nobles to their wills. Prussia created a school-leaving certificate (the *Abitur*) and requirements for university degrees and examinations for some public positions, a system extended by reformers after Prussia's defeat by Napoleon in 1806.[17] In Revolutionary France, Bonaparte swept aside the universities and established the *grandes écoles*, national and highly competitive schools of administration, education, military science, and engineering. But these models held little attraction for America, where there was no nobility to break and no crushing defeat to spur reform, and where careers were thought already open to talents. Hamilton certainly exaggerated the extent to which careers in America were open, but he had only to look in the mirror or to examine the ranks of his fellow Federalists for compelling evidence in the form of men like Henry Knox (an obscure Boston bookseller who became a major general, secretary of war, and, through marriage, one of the great landlords of Maine) or the aforementioned William Paterson (the Irish-born son of a Princeton, New Jersey, storekeeper, whose education at the College of New Jersey led to a distinguished career in law and politics).[18]

Hamilton thought he was constructing an order of merit. Just as political correctness was a marker of character, eminent parentage signified a regard for reputation. Hamilton never called attention to his "obscene" origin, and in 1787 he voted against a law that, had it been in force in his native West Indies, would have legitimized his own birth in 1755.[19] In the deadlocked election of 1800 he would endorse Jefferson over Aaron Burr on the grounds that Jefferson's regard for his reputation would hold him on a steady course.[20]

Hamilton's procedures remind us that merit could acquire different meanings in different national contexts. Hamilton knew about the British system of purchasing officer ranks, described in Chapter 1, and by 1798 he probably knew of Bonaparte's revitalization of the principle of promotion from the ranks on the basis of demonstrated valor. The problems surrounding Purchase were obvious in a nation where the principle of equal rights argued against a birthright to command (the Republican poet and journalist Joel Barlow wrote that only nations with orders of nobility taught that some men were born to command and others to be commanded),[21] and, perhaps more telling, where the closest approximation to Britain's rural gentry were southern slaveholders, whose mastery of the habit of command was scarcely a recommendation for the ordering of soldiers in a republic. Further, American society was less finely calibrated and less wealthy than British society, especially at the higher ranks. In this context, Hamilton's emphasis on political correctness as a guide to merit can be viewed as an American substitute for the qualities that in Britain were embedded in the social system itself.

So much for Purchase; what about valor? Various factors help to account for the low weight Hamilton, himself a military man of insignificant origins and demonstrated valor during the Revolution, assigned to even distinguished military experience as a basis for appointment. Obviously, the practice of French revolutionaries and especially Bonaparte would never be a model for Hamilton. Further, restored to roughly regimental size in the 1790s after its near disbandment in the immediate wake of the Revolution and infrequently in action, the American army in the 1790s possessed few officerships to fill before proposals were made for the Provisional Army. Hamilton, Washington's former aide-de-camp, could never forget that the Continental Army's experience with promotions based on valor during the Revolution was unpopular among officers, who thought themselves equally valorous and who interpreted promotions out of the "due course" as personal insults.

Hamilton's plans for the Provisional Army collapsed after John Adams initiated peace overtures to France in 1799. The Federalists were left in the awkward position of having imposed a tax to finance a war that never took place. Wounded by an attack by Hamilton in the middle of the campaign of 1800, Adams lost the presidency to Jefferson and achieved the distinction of having been the last Federalist president. His son, John Quincy Adams, went over to the Republicans. Aaron Burr killed Hamilton in a duel. Federalist ascendancy ended.

Yet Republicans perpetuated many Federalist ideals about the characters suited to public life. Finding that to compete against the Federalists they had to recruit influentials to their standard, most Republicans abandoned the antifederalist suspicion of the First Characters. Distinguished service in the Revolution continued to weigh in an office seeker's favor. Political correctness persisted as a criterion for appointments. After coming to office in 1801, Jefferson initiated removals of Federalist officeholders, removals that he described as "moderate" but that were, in reality, far-reaching.[22] As the Republican ascendancy in national politics became more secure, his successors did not have to purge the few remaining Federalists, but neither did they show much inclination to appoint Federalists. James Monroe, for example, promised to conduct a nonpartisan administration but then appointed only Republicans.

Merit and Popular Sovereignty

Even as they recruited their own First Characters, Republicans devised new rationales for leadership. They scrapped the argument of the Rufus Kings that office was owed to Men of Merit by virtue of their talents and accomplishments. They then substituted an argument famously articulated by Jefferson in an 1813 letter exchange with Adams over natural aristocracy. In this debate Jefferson distinguished the "tinsel" or "artificial" aristocracy based on wealth and birth, which he expected to crumble before the "natural" aristocracy, based on talent and virtue. (Hidden in the text and usually ignored is Jefferson's classification of individuals who were talented, virtuous, *and* wealthy as natural aristocrats.)[23]

Jefferson had foreshadowed his position in 1779, when, as governor of Virginia, he had successfully engineered the abolition of primogeniture and entail in order to free property from hereditary descent and thereby complete the Revolution. As Jefferson saw it, the problem in Virginia was less the resistance of the Loyalists than the conservatism of the rebels, who thought their work finished with the separation from Britain. At the same time, he sent the legislature a Bill for the More General Diffusion of Knowledge, which proposed a pyramid of public education founded on a base of elementary schools in which all free children were to receive three years of free instruction in the elements of learning. A winnowing process marked the next layer, in which Jefferson proposed the establishment of twenty boarding schools for boys, each containing a mixture of tuition-paying scholars and "public foundationers." He spoke of the public foundationers as "twenty geniuses raked annually from the rubbish" and as destined to be reduced to one, who might eventually qualify for a scholarship to the College of William and Mary after subsequent rounds of scything.

The legislature never passed Jefferson's bill, but by the time of his 1813 exchange with Adams, Jefferson could plausibly assume that the triumph of his ideal of natural aristocracy was inevitable. The political ascendancy of Republicans led him to conclude that the progressive advance of knowledge and legislation had equipped or shortly would equip voters to recognize the natural aristocracy of talent and virtue. None of this persuaded Adams, who maintained that Jefferson had been beguiled by his party's and his own "popularity," in Adams's lexicon a noun joined at the hip with demagoguery and attributable to Jefferson's "invariable favorable opinion of the French Revolution." Adams's main point was that Jefferson was deluding himself in thinking that talent and virtue could be distinguished from other "Talents" ("Wealth, Strength, Beauty, Stature, Birth, Marriage, graceful Attributes and Motions, Gait, Air, Complexion, [and] Physiognomy") that led to influence and gave their possessors "the Character of an Aristocrat, in my sense of the word."[24] Adams compared the Americans' penchant for public funerals, escorts, dinners, and balls in honor of the great to the European practice of conferring titles, and he concluded that the two practices were identical, except that the American one was "more expensive, more troublesome, and infinitely less ingenious."[25]

What Adams labeled *popularity*, Jefferson called *public opinion*, a concept that gained momentum in the wake of the Sedition Act of 1798, when Republicans like New York's Tunis Wortman contended that the conduct of "public characters" should be open to public scrutiny and not be constrained by libel suits.[26] Public opinion was not always right, Wortman maintained, but it would never be wrong for long.[27] More than a decade later Jefferson's friend and fellow Virginian John Taylor amplified the Republican concept of public opinion in *An Inquiry into the Principles and Policy of the Government of the United States* (1814), a ponderous political treatise that Adams had read in manuscript in time for his 1813 debate with Jefferson over aristocracy.

In contrast to Adams's view that aristocracy was natural even in republics, an outgrowth of a gullible public's susceptibility to glitter, Taylor traced republican aristocracies exclusively to the "concubinage" between government and financial privilege.[28] A former antifederalist, Taylor had been voicing this opinion since 1794, when he had attacked Hamilton's financial program as a source of a new moneyed aristocracy. Paper money and financial speculation were parasites that subtracted from real wealth and thrived only because corrupt legislatures granted legal privileges to the "Paper Aristocracy." In making this point, Taylor also described knowledge and virtue as traits that reflected the impact of changing social and political conditions. The invention of the printing press had initiated the extension of knowledge to the multitude, a process largely completed in the American republic, which contained a "vast peerage" of abilities among average people. This peerage, in turn, was the source of public opinion, "the declaration of the mass of national virtue, talents, and wealth." Taylor's use of the singular "declaration" underscored his belief in the essential unity of public opinion. Temporarily, it might be misled and become the dupe of the Paper Aristocracy, but in a moral and "natural" society where landownership, information, and free inquiry were diffused, it could be trusted.[29]

In sum, Jefferson and Taylor constructed a coherent portrait of a natural aristocracy based on merit and identified and elected by the unclouded vision of an informed public. Yet the Republican ascendancy did not dispel the cloud of jealousy that enveloped public life and that continued to target hypothetical threats from combinations of men.[30] Even organizations without political aims were suspect. In the 1790s many Americans had looked on Masonry, which lacked the hereditary and caste features that had led to attacks on the Cincinnati, as a model for the virtuous and talented society they were building.[31] In 1793 De Witt Clinton had proclaimed that Masonry admitted "of no rank except the priority of merit."[32] During the uproar over Masonic lodges in the 1820s, however, Thaddeus Stevens would blast Masonry because it secured "an unmerited advantage" to its members over "the honest and industrious and uninitiated farmer, mechanic, and laborer, in all the ordinary transactions of life."[33] Just as Stevens and other anti-Masons assailed Masonry rather than individual Masons, John Taylor, a rich slaveholder, had no argument against wealthy men as such. Stevens and Taylor alike feared combinations more than individuals. Taylor truly reverenced farmers, not because they produced a tangible product—he also admired merchants, who produced nothing—but because farmers were too scattered ever to combine against the public good. What he could not abide was the deployment by the favored of their advantages of wealth and ability to secure personal benefits from public bodies.

Yet opportunities to secure illicit, or seemingly illicit, advantages were multiplying in the early republic. Boundaries between private and public were indefinite at a time when America was becoming a sprawling, decentralized republic with multiple ports of entry into public life and constructing a lavish profusion of new ladders of advancement. Each passing year brought the burning fuse of equal rights closer to detonation as the younger generation experienced the empowering effects of this founding principle. Jefferson's victory in 1800 opened the gates to Republican office seekers whose aspirations had been blocked by the Federalist ascendancy. The federal government was expanding at a much faster rate than the population; the number of federal civil offices rose from around three thousand in 1800 to six thousand by 1816 and to nearly twenty thousand by 1831. Eight new states entered the Union between 1803 and 1821, each with its own parcel of offices, civil and military. Periodic threats of war with Britain led to convulsive expansions of the army in 1808 and again in 1812, and whether old or new, states had their own militias and militia officerships.

Inventing Careers in the Early Republic

The generation that fought the Revolution had been accustomed to winning quick distinction. Benedict Arnold jumped from captain in the Connecticut militia in 1774 to brigadier general in the Continental Army two years later; Hamilton became Washington's aide-de-camp when barely out of his minority. Ambitious members of the generation born around the time of the Revolution were no less eager for fame,[34] and they conflated honor and merit just as their elders had. As had been true during the Revolutionary War, congressional efforts to reward exceptional merit continued to run afoul of the view of officers that they were all equally meritorious, that opportunities to display their merit depended on chance, and that any promotion out of the "due course" impugned the merit of those passed over. This configuration of values characterized essential merit. Adherents of this type of merit never forgot anything. When the gallantry of Lt. Charles Morris during the 1812 engagement between the USS *Constitution* and HMS *Guerrière* led Congress to promote him to captain, several officers protested, in part on the grounds that they all would have shown the same valor but also by invoking an incident in 1805, when Lt. Stephen Decatur had led a daring raid into Tripoli harbor to destroy the frigate *Philadelphia*, which had fallen into enemy hands. After Decatur was wounded, his subordinate, Lt. Charles Lawrence, took command, but Lawrence had not been promoted for his valor, and so, it was argued, to promote Morris, who had also taken over for a wounded commander, was to insult Lawrence.[35]

The conception of merit that officers embraced included more than just sensitivity to later and even hypothetical affronts. It also encompassed the idea that acknowledged success had to be a signifier of merit. A year after a fellow officer killed Decatur in a duel in 1820, over an incident that dated to the *Chesapeake-Leopard* Affair in 1807, Decatur's first biographer, S. Putnam Waldo, effectively captured this component of merit, whose roots extended as far back as Renaissance humanism. Decatur, Waldo argued, "left nothing to be decided by fortune, and submitted not the least event to its decision." Since only God controlled Providence, Decatur, "like other men," was "liable to have his most judicious calculations and active exertions *defeated* by misfortune." But his success owed nothing to luck; rather, it always resulted from his "skill, energy, and perseverance," his "active worth" and "positive merit." His reputation reflected his merit. If something happened to set back his reputation, the cause had to be misfortune, since his merit was fixed. Because dueling violated naval regulations, Waldo had to ask why Decatur had not declined the challenge to a duel and found consolation in his private sense of self-worth. Waldo answered with an argument that reminds one of Nathanael Greene's defense of his testy resignation as quarter-master general in 1780 (see Chapter 1). Had Decatur not accepted the challenge, Waldo argued, his feeling of self-worth would have experienced free fall, since he would know that others might not attribute his failure to misfortune.[36]

No less ambitious or infected with a sense of self-worth than those of the Revolution, officers of Decatur's generation faced ever widening opportunities for displaying their merit, often before total strangers. Continuing a precedent set by Washington, army officers were expected to be gentlemen, and Federalists established the same expectation for naval officers. The gap between noncom-missioned and commissioned officers in the American army was vast; the social distance between the highest NCO rank, sergeant major, and the lowest com-missioned rank, second lieutenant, was far greater than between any two com-missioned ranks. Commissioned officers just assumed that their commissions sealed their gentry status and legitimated their aggressive behavior toward their peers and superiors in the chain of command. For example, Winfield Scott was no sooner in the army and posted to the Mississippi Territory than he was court-martialed in 1810 for calling his commanding officer, General James Wilkinson, a traitor for his role in the Burr Conspiracy. Scott escaped punishment on a tech-nicality, but before long he and General Edmund P. Gaines began a decades-long conflict, ended only by Gaines's death in 1849, over whose promotion to major general in 1814 had occurred first.[37]

One historian has described "cantankerous individualism" as a feature of the American officer corps in the early republic.[38] Even officers less self-obsessed than Scott learned to become military entrepreneurs, advancing their careers by taking advantage of the permeable boundaries between private associations like the volunteer companies that proliferated between the Revolution and the Civil War and such public organizations as state militias, the regular army, and politi-cal office. Born into a wealthy and well-connected family (his father had signed the Declaration of Independence), William Henry Harrison entered the army in 1791 as an ensign and rose to captain before securing appointments as secretary of the Northwest Territory in 1798 and as governor of the Indiana Territory in 1801, the position he held in 1811 when he defeated the Shawnee Prophet Ten-skwatawa at Tippecanoe. As war with Britain loomed, the ambitious Harrison sought to return to the regular army, but he was left off the first list of brigadier generals. Capitalizing on his own popularity and his friendship with Henry Clay, he then secured an appointment as a major general in the Kentucky militia and next as a brigadier general in the regular army, in which he found himself sub-ordinate to another brigadier general. Rather than accept a subordinate role, he resolved to raise an army of Kentucky and Indiana militia (he commanded the latter as governor of Indiana) and then make a run at Detroit to retake it from the British. Harrison relented only when the secretary of war gave him command of the regular army in the Northwest.[39]

Such agile moves between private and public spheres also characterized the emerging professions of law and medicine. As a young man, John Adams had brushed up his Latin and read learned law treatises to bring himself to the "Consideration and perhaps favour" of the patriarchs of the Suffolk County bar and to ready himself to enter a stratified profession, like Britain's, where barristers, who did not deal directly with clients, stood higher than attorneys, who did.[40]

Similarly, in 1765 Philadelphian John Morgan, fresh from his medical studies at Leyden, had called for the establishment of a European-style medical profession in which physicians, who were educated in the classical languages and medical theory and who confined themselves to giving advice, would be distinguished from "Empiricks," surgeons, and druggists.[41] American social conditions worked against the specialization required to establish internal professional hierarchies, but the Revolution enlivened the legal and medical professions. As a legal and constitutional struggle against Britain, it added luster to the law, if not to each lawyer, and the proportion of full-time legal practitioners grew exponentially during and after the Revolution.[42] Law increasingly overshadowed the ministry as the profession of choice for college graduates.[43] The Revolution also opened new opportunities for doctors in the military's medical service and enhanced their contacts with public officials.[44] In the immediate wake of the Revolution, some bar associations successfully enforced standards for admission to practice, while several states incorporated medical societies with at least nominal power to control entry to the profession.

Ultimately, however, the Revolution's legacy of equal rights worked against ceding control of professional entry to bar and medical associations. Followers of the uneducated herbalist Samuel Thomson assailed doctors for their Latinate mumbo-jumbo and successfully argued that medical practice should be open to anyone. The resentment of Thomson's followers often boiled over into attacks on educated ministers who assumed that they alone were qualified to preach the word of God. Similarly, lawyers were charged with creating incomprehensible jargon to mystify the law. The trouble with lawyers, wrote the Jacksonian Democrat Frederick Robinson in 1832, was that they acted as if they were officers of the government (which, of course, they often were in Europe) when in reality they just followed a trade.[45] In 1835 Massachusetts, which had devised a system enabling college graduates to gain admission to practice after briefer apprenticeships than nongraduates, stripped bar associations of their control over entry into legal practice; other states moved in the same direction, not only eliminating the public functions of bar associations but repealing statutes that required specified preparatory study for the profession.

The disestablishment of the professions did not dim their attractiveness to ambitious young men, but it changed the rules of the game. The path to distinction for a lawyer or doctor depended less on presenting credentials to a circle of superiors and then mounting ladders constructed by those superiors than on horizontal thrusts in which the young man brought himself to attention in activities only tangentially related to his profession. Some of these activities, like delivering public addresses, required mastery of rhetoric more than technical competence; their attractiveness as routes to public distinction helps to explain the extraordinary proliferation of literary and debating societies. As Abraham Lincoln's Lyceum Address in 1838 suggests, public addresses constituted an uncontroversial way for young professionals to bring themselves to attention.[46] But as the case of medical schools indicates, there were alternative and more controversial routes to distinction.

In 1965 historian Daniel Calhoun concluded that the turbulence of medical politics in the early republic reflected the absence of a "set of legitimate opportunities for the individual physician to advance himself and claim special distinction."[47] The key words here are "legitimate opportunities" and "special distinction." Respecting special distinction, the combativeness of physicians—mostly aimed at each other—was a byword among contemporaries. In contrast to the medical profession in the half-century after 1880, when reformers focused on elevating standards for entry into the profession and for medical practice, the most prominent doctors of the early republic sought to enhance their reputations in the public's eyes, whether by advertising remarkable cures, writing pamphlets defending their conduct, manipulating politics to advance their personal ambitions, or starting medical schools.

In 1850 the United States contained forty-two degree-granting medical schools (up from two in 1780 and four in 1800), more than any other nation.[48] Medical schools proliferated even as legal requirements for medical practice were collapsing. Although no state required the M.D. for the practice of medicine, the degree had sufficient cachet with patients to spur a flourishing trade in the sale of degrees. But the primary impetus behind the dizzying spread of medical schools was to satisfy the ambition of doctors to become medical professors. Securing a professorship boosted a doctor's reputation among patients and local influentials, and since nearly all American medical schools were proprietary ventures, owned by their professors and run for a profit, professorships could be lucrative supplements to income from patients. The one foolproof way for doctors to become professors was to start medical schools and then appoint themselves to their faculties. In this respect, medical schools resembled those state-chartered banks that Secretary of the Treasury William Crawford attacked in 1820 on the grounds that they were founded primarily to lend money to their directors for land speculation.

Few doctors in the early republic could match Daniel Drake when it came to entrepreneurial flair. Born in New Jersey in 1785 and raised in Kentucky, Drake arrived in Cincinnati in 1808 to serve a medical apprenticeship to a family friend. Taking a year to study medicine at the University of Pennsylvania, Drake returned to Cincinnati, where in short order he established a circulating library, a debating society, a monitorial school (the older pupils taught the younger ones), and a lyceum. He also wrote two books about the geography, topology, and botany of the city and its environs, all while building a medical practice and running a drugstore.[49] After returning to Philadelphia to earn his medical degree in 1817, Drake secured a medical professorship at Transylvania University in Lexington, Kentucky. No sooner had he joined this faculty than he ran into a dispute sparked by the dislike of two professors, Benjamin Dudley and John Overton, for a third, William Richardson. Alleging that Richardson lacked a medical degree, Dudley and Overton tried to force him out. Drake sided with Richardson, and before returning to Cincinnati in 1818, he arranged for Richardson to receive an honorary medical degree from the College of Physicians and Surgeons in New York City.

Dudley then accused Drake of breaking his promise to spend two years in Lexington, to which Drake responded with a pamphlet, *An Appeal to the Justice of the Intelligent People of Lexington*, in which he described Dudley as "one of the vermin that infest our modern Attica" (Lexington billed itself as the Athens of the West).[50]

Back in Cincinnati, Drake initiated what contemporaries called the "Thirty Years War" when he procured charters for the Medical College of Ohio and Cincinnati College, the latter a largely paper institution that served the former as a degree-granting authority. Drake's plans to reserve half of the professorships at the Medical College of Ohio for nonresidents of Cincinnati angered local doctors, who forced Drake out in 1822. A few years later he was back, this time with doctors from Jefferson Medical College in Philadelphia in tow, and he induced the trustees of Miami University in Oxford, Ohio, to start a medical school, headed by him, staffed by his Philadelphia recruits, and intended to suck students from the Medical College of Ohio. But the latter institution staged a preemptive strike, hiring Drake's allies from the Miami school by offering them more distinguished chairs (there was a pecking order, based on subject taught, among medical professorships), forcing Drake into the humiliating position of accepting a minor chair, and then in 1832 ousting him a second time. Not to be outdone, Drake then resuscitated Cincinnati College, which had folded in 1826, and announced the formation of a new medical department under its nominal aegis (one of its professors was Samuel Gross, later immortalized by Thomas Eakins's painting *The Gross Clinic*). Three years later Cincinnati College's medical school collapsed, mainly because the Medical College of Ohio, Drake's original creation and continuing nemesis, blocked the access of its students to clinical facilities in Cincinnati.[51]

The Ohio medical "war" would go on for another decade and justify the observation of a contemporary that the medical profession was notorious "for the belligerent propensities of its professors." Beyond question, Drake was belligerent; at one point he was convicted of breaking into the house of a medical rival and clubbing him. But he was not a cannonball fired into a placid lake. The disruptive individualism typified by Drake also characterized medical politics in established cities like Boston and New York.[52] Whether in Cincinnati, Boston, or New York, the conflagrations that swept the medical profession also reflected what Calhoun described as the absence of "legitimate opportunities" for distinction in the medical profession. In contrast to Europe, where professions had established ladders to climb, in America professional ladders resembled the political parties; they were "self-created," established by the very people who were trying to climb them.

The Ambiguities of Patronage

Historians long debated (without reaching a consensus) whether the democratization of politics between 1820 and 1840 lowered the competence of appointed officials by substituting the partisan "spoils" system for merit. But contemporaries subordinated issues relating to competence to what struck them as a far more important question: the fear that the exercise of power, including the power of appointment and removal, would crush liberty by turning public officials into vassals of higher-ups empowered to hire and fire. To avoid the appearance of impropriety, appointing officials necessarily emphasized that they were making appointments based on merit or such synonyms as *fitness* or *qualifications*. The self-interest of appointing officials dictated that they not appoint those known to be unfit, but public figures had to take much on report. No formal measures of merit such as examinations or requirements for academic credentials screened prospective officeholders, nor was there any pressure to introduce such measures. George Washington, who vowed to make merit the basis of his appointments, defined merit negatively; he would not appoint his relatives to office. Yet this criterion, seemingly straightforward and sanctioned by long-standing American complaints about Walpolean corruption, proved difficult to implement. As in

the colonial era, when intermarriage among gentry families led to strong kinship ties among officeholders, officeholding continued to run in families after
the Revolution, including families made by the Revolution. Tall, handsome, and
well educated, a veritable Magnus Apollo, De Witt Clinton cut a striking figure
in New York politics, but neither his political allies nor his enemies forgot that he
was the nephew of the state's first governor. In view of the importance attached
by American Whigs of the Revolutionary era to British-instigated corruption—
illicit influence and connexion were legacies of British imperialism—it is unsur-
prising that after the Revolution, Americans found it easy to equate their own
characters with those of their fathers.[53]

Removals were even trickier than appointments in this political culture.[54]
Congress's decision in 1789 to give the president sole removal power left executive officeholders serving at the president's pleasure and seemingly deprived them
of the manly independence thought necessary for republican government. Policy
divisions between Federalists and Republicans provided presidents with some
cover. After taking office in 1801, Jefferson justified his "moderate" removals of
Federalist officeholders partly on the grounds that the elected administration had
a responsibility to appoint men who supported its policies and who would lend
dignity and weight to its measures.[55] Reasonable on its face, this principle nevertheless proved difficult to administer. Jefferson also announced that, in principle,
he would not remove "good" men who differed with him merely in opinion (except for federal marshals and attorneys, the legacy of John Adams's "midnight
appointments"), but in a letter to his attorney general he distinguished good men
from "industrious" opponents, the sort of people Martin Van Buren would later
call party "brawlers."[56] The difference between a principled noncombatant and
a party brawler was easier to draw than to substantiate. Much depended on the
social rank of the seeker. The idea that the office should seek the man and not the
other way around legitimated the expectations of the First Characters for high
office, but it did not come equipped with any mechanism to adjust it downward
for the claims to minor offices put forward by those lacking public characters.
In context, Jefferson was asking just how "industrious" a surveyor in Gloucester,
Massachusetts, had been on behalf of Adams. Surveyors were functionaries more
than public characters, and the number of federal offices suited to functionaries
was ever growing.

Writing in 1854, former senator Thomas Hart Benton criticized the "sweeping" removals "now practised by both parties" as a "great political evil," in large
part because each change of administration deprived the public of experienced
public servants.[57] Benton's argument would permeate the thinking of the reformers who introduced competitive examinations into the federal civil service in
1883 and who contended that the distribution of public jobs on the basis of

partisan loyalty impaired the efficiency of the public service. But the genuine terror and fury that swirled around patronage in the early republic had a different source. From 1800 well into the 1830s, the main argument, dispersed across the political spectrum, was that executive removals undermined the separation of powers and thereby invited despotism. In 1825–26 a Senate select committee, chaired by Benton and including Martin Van Buren, unanimously proposed several bills. One would have required the president to communicate to Congress his reason for dismissing any civil officeholder for whom he nominated a replacement. Another, adopted in practice and regularized by statute in 1843, gave members of Congress a direct role in nominating cadets to West Point. Still another, an attempt to stop the executive branch from advertising vacancies only in sympathetic newspapers, would have required the postmaster general to provide Congress with a list of papers delivered by the postal service that contained advertisements of civil-service vacancies. The shared purpose of these proposals was to restrain executive patronage to the point where it could not invite despotism or the sort of corruption of legislatures that the Revolutionary-era Whigs associated with British ministries.[58] For example, Benton thought that the framers of the Constitution had erred when they failed to ban members of Congress from holding any executive offices. When Andrew Jackson took office in 1829, executive removals were still evaluated through a window tinted by the old-fashioned republican principle of the separation of powers.

One notable effect of the link between executive patronage and threats to the separation of powers was to turn every controversy about the distribution of offices into a debate about the survival of the republic. In 1820 Jefferson complained to Madison that the Tenure of Office Act of that year, which established a four-year term for the principal federal officers responsible for the collection and disbursement of money, would excite "all the hungry cormorants for office," render existing officeholders "sycophants to their Senators," multiply "cabals," and turn the government into a sink of "corruption and faction."[59] This was strong language for a law whose likely purpose was to increase congressional rather than executive patronage (witness Jefferson's reference to turning officers into "sycophants to their Senators").[60] Under the law, officers whose terms expired would lose their jobs unless reappointed. As president, Quincy Adams routinely reappointed financial officers at the expiration of their terms, so the issue of executive patronage did not surge to the fore until Andrew Jackson instituted mass removals in 1829. But Jefferson's feverish reaction, shared by Madison and Quincy Adams, reminds us that any measure that opened public offices to new occupants triggered terror that it would reduce manly republicans to sycophants cringing before elected despots, whether in Congress or the White House, not that it might lower the competence or efficiency of public servants.

Patronage also sat uneasily with the Republican principle of popular sover-eignty. In theory, the two could be reconciled: the popular will was the remote enabler of government appointments, patronage the immediate instrument. In practice, however, the two often conflicted, since patronage involved not merely bestowal from above but also application and pressure from below. The remark-able career of Andrew Jackson illustrates all of these elements. In some respects, Jackson was a creature of patronage. Making his way through western North Carolina to Tennessee in the 1780s, Jackson lacked family, education, and wealth. His main possessions were his pretensions to gentry status and his regard for his reputation, which burned in his breast even before he had any reputation of which to speak. He issued his first challenge to a duel, at the age of twenty-one, to an opposing lawyer, in fact his former law teacher, for ridiculing his arguments in an obscure Tennessee court case in 1788. "My charector you have injured," he wrote in his challenge, "and further you have Insulted me in the presence of a court and a larg audiance."[61] Needing a patron, Jackson found one in William Blount, the governor of the Southwest Territory and then of the state of Tennes-see. Before the Panic of 1819 there were no issues in Tennessee politics, just rival squads of land speculators led by chieftains like Blount and his archrival John Sevier. A Tennessee legislature packed with Blount loyalists elected Jackson to the U.S. Senate in 1797, and in 1802 Jackson won an election over Sevier as major general of the state militia when the current governor, a Blount loyalist, inter-vened to break a tied vote among the militia's field officers in Jackson's favor.[62]

Jackson thrived by patronage, but he never interpreted his success as any-thing other than the unsolicited popular verdict on his merit. In his own eyes, he never sought popularity, a defect he was quick to detect in others. In 1797 he accused Tennessee's senator William Cocke, whom he would shortly challenge to a duel, of showing Sevier a letter that Jackson had written to him and thereby "stepping forward to raise your own popularity by sacrificing your private con-fidence."[63] The trouble with popularity was that it involved the manipulation of public opinion by some artifice and hence was necessarily transient, in contrast to the fixity of merit. Jackson attributed his election to the U.S. Senate and to the militia rank to the "unsolicited suffrage" of the people. In 1825 he congratulated himself for not having solicited the presidency by midnight cabals, and he de-clared his conscience free of any insinuation that he had ever sought "an office not sanctioned by [my] merit."[64]

Responding to one of Jackson's innumerable taunts, Sevier once proclaimed, "My reputation, Mr. Jackson[,] is to me my only treasure."[65] Jackson could have said the same and so could have Hamilton. By some measures, Hamilton and Jackson had much in common. Each had a high regard for his reputation, served as second in duels, issued challenges to duels, and fought them. (Two years after

Hamilton was killed in a duel, Jackson was nearly killed in one.) Neither man started with wealth or family name. Hamilton's mother's adultery barred him from an inheritance; Jackson inherited some money and then squandered it in gambling. Each owed his rise to patrons, respectively Washington and Blount. Yet a crucial difference separated the two. Hamilton took his world of patronage and sponsored mobility for granted.[66] He expected his qualifications to be judged by his peers, not by the public; the public's role was merely to approve or disapprove of the administrative performance of its superiors. In contrast, Jackson readily accepted the public as a judge of the qualifications of its leaders.

The idea that the public was a legitimate judge of candidates' qualifications, rather than just of their policies, proved an especially volatile mixture in the 1820s, before the bloated Republican coalition had split into the issue-defined rivalries of the second party system. Albert Gallatin astutely recognized that the Republican Party was falling victim to factionalism because of its preoccupation, inevitable in the wake of the Federalist collapse, with men more than measures and, more particularly, with men who viewed their reputations as calibrations of their merit.[67] In what amounted to a justification of enduring two-party competition, in 1824 the *Albany Argus*, the organ of Van Buren's Bucktail faction of the New York Republicans, contended that a party was always weakest when opposition to it was weak.[68] Partisanship nevertheless remained under a cloudy if not entirely overcast sky. In 1823 Madison, who three decades earlier had called for statewide voting to elect congressmen as a way to ensure the continuing dominance of the First Characters, responded to the increasingly common practice, called the "general ticket," of assigning all of a state's electoral votes to the candidate who won the popular vote, by calling for small electoral districts in each state to "break the force of those geographical and other noxious parties."

Deflating Merit

No one declared the idea of basing appointments on merit to be rubbish, but a serious debate about merit's scope in politics developed at the end of the 1820s in response to the presidential campaign of Andrew Jackson. In August 1828, when Jackson's supporters were booming him for the presidency, Postmaster General John McLean engaged in a remarkable exchange of letters with Edward Everett, then a rising congressman from Massachusetts. The two men formed a study in contrasts. Everett owed much to his virtual anointment by his liberal Congregationalist-Unitarian sponsors: entering Harvard at thirteen, he graduated at the top of his class of 1811, became the minister of the prestigious Brattle Street Church at nineteen, left the pulpit at twenty for a Harvard professorship of Greek, which provided for two years of study in Europe (he took four), and at twenty-six accepted the editorship of the *North American Review*.[69] "The low game of politics, I disdain," he informed McLean. In contrast, McLean was adept at the "low game."[70] With little formal education, he climbed through the rough-and-tumble of Ohio politics to Congress and to important positions under presidents James Monroe and Quincy Adams.

From this, one would expect that Everett would take the high ground, denounce party, and defend merit. Yet it was Everett who attacked Quincy Adams "for making an exclusive regard to merit" his guiding principle in appointments. "For an administration to bestow its patronage without distinction of party," insisted Everett, "is to court its own destruction."[71] When Everett spoke of party, he meant a candidate's "friends." Party divisions were ignited and fanned by the zeal of camp followers for the rewards of victory, especially appointments to office. Everett approvingly cited the comment of British foreign secretary George Canning that Americans sought public office more avidly than the British. As Everett saw it, the walks of private life were open in each nation, but "office here is family, rank, hereditary fortune, in short everything out of range of private life," and Americans would endure "incredible humiliations" to gain it.[72] Pro-Jackson editors were already assuring "Jackson men" (the Democratic Party was still an embryo) that once in office Jackson would "REWARD HIS FRIENDS AND PUNISH HIS ENEMIES."[73]

There were two subtexts to this exchange. First, unbeknown to Everett, McLean was hedging his bets in the upcoming election by secretly making overtures to Jackson. In 1830 Jackson appointed McLean to the Supreme Court, where he spent the next thirty years casting bait to hook the presidency, so much so that he became known as the "Politician on the Supreme Court." Second, Jackson kicked McLean upstairs because McLean had become a strenuous critic of Jackson's removal policy. Although McLean played the "low game" of politics, he had tried to write some rules for it by distinguishing offices belonging to the administration, legitimately open to partisan distribution, from posts belonging to the nation, like the postal service, where he thought that merit should prevail. He had worked hard to inculcate postal workers with the belief that they held a sacred trust, and he was sure that should the appointment of officeholders come to depend on party, public confidence in the government would dissolve.[74] In 1835 Daniel Webster added the army, navy, land offices, and customhouses to the list of "institutions of the country" rather than of the party in power. Politicize the institutions of the country, Webster argued, and the resulting "scramble for office" would undermine public confidence in the government and, in McLean's words, turn the Union into "a great electioneering arena."[75]

Jackson paid no attention to the McLean/Webster distinction between offices open to party and offices open to merit. He based his removals, which were among his first acts on taking office, on his twist on the eighteenth-century principle that rotation in office would prevent despotism. In Jackson's version, all public offices belonged to the people, and the president, as the direct representative of the people (and not, as Jackson's predecessors had thought, merely the chief administrator of the executive branch), could dispose of them as he saw fit. Jackson was not the first president to engage in removals, but he was the first to make removals a policy. In Jackson's eyes, executive removals were as indispensable to republican principles as they were incompatible in the eyes of McLean and Webster.

National Republicans like Webster, Quincy Adams, and Henry Clay derided rotation as a "stale sophistry" that merely rationalized Jackson's penchant for rewarding his friends and punishing his enemies.[76] Although Jackson left most of the dirty work of removals to lieutenants like Isaac Hill, Duff Green, and Amos Kendall, he contributed to controversy by refusing to give any reason for the removal of individual public servants. Webster drew his distinction between offices of the country and those of the administration in an 1835 speech in which he supported a bill to require the president to state the grounds for each removal. But as Webster conceded, Jackson stood on substantial constitutional ground. Although Webster thought that Congress had erred in 1789 when it had given the president sole removal power, in so doing it had explicitly rejected the alternative of impeachment. No one was owed office; no one had property in office; and a president who removed a public official was not obliged to allege misconduct by that official. Webster nevertheless insisted that forcing the president to state a reason for removing public officials would compel "more entire regard for their real merits and demerits."[77]

By 1835 many Americans were familiar with the juxtaposition of *merit* with *demerit*, which formed the basis of a widely publicized system introduced by Superintendent Sylvanus Thayer for ranking cadets at the U.S. Military Academy at West Point. Good conduct was merit; misconduct, demerit. Although merit and demerit at West Point were each written in the singular, each was expressed as a numerical sum. Widely employed by other colleges between 1820 and 1860, Thayer's system deflated merit by grinding it down into little piles of numbers that could be compared. In the colleges, merit systems were imposed from the top by college "governments." College governments had many autocratic features, but no one argued that the sometimes despotic behavior of college presidents threatened the survival of the American republic. In contrast, although politicians could allude to the merits and demerits of public officials, these were subordinated to the overriding fear of executive patronage as the highway to executive despotism. Webster wrote in 1835 that as long as the president possessed unrestrained removal power, "manly independence" would disappear from public life, for public servants would be evaluated only by their subservience to the will of an autocrat.[78]

After winning the presidency in 1840, Whigs adopted the same practice of removals and partisan replacements for which they had attacked Democrats during the 1830s. In his brief presidency (1849–1850) Zachary Taylor, the last elected Whig president, would try to revive the nonpartisan heritage of Whiggery, only to meet stiff resistance from established Whigs, including Webster. In view of Whig partisanship after 1840, it is tempting to dismiss Webster's forebodings about the impact of Jackson's removals on the safety of the republic as partisan blather, but it is more likely that Webster meant what he said in the mid-1830s. In the mid-1830s leading Whigs were still ambivalent about whether they formed a permanent political organization rather than a league of the best men against the dictatorial "King Andrew I." Jackson himself valued personal more than partisan loyalty as a basis for appointments. When Jackson took office in 1829, the issue of removals was still bound tightly to the view that executive patronage threatened to eviscerate the separation of powers and thereby establish despotism. In the mid-1820s Thomas Hart Benton, already a staunch Jackson supporter, had voiced a concern similar to Webster's a decade later.[79] The key change was the onset of the Panic of 1837 and the ensuing severe depression, which sharpened the ideological differences between the Whigs and Democrats over issues relating to banking and reform and contributed to the Whigs' embrace of partisanship as a legitimate basis for filling offices. Partisan differences rooted in clear division over issues took the edge off the complaint, often made by National Republicans and Whigs before 1837, that widespread executive removals contained the seeds of despotism because they pushed officeholders into supine subjection to those in power. Recommending a Whig editor for a federal job, a Louisiana Whig wrote to Henry Clay in 1841 to assure him that the editor was not a "mendicant for office" but a willing adherent to "the Cause."[80]

Downsizing Leaders

The intensifying ideological divisions between the parties facilitated the outright acceptance of the legitimacy of partisanship in appointments. At the same time, the long-standing fear that executive patronage provided a route to despotism eroded. None of Jackson's successors before the Civil War gained reelection, and none matched his autocratic and uncompromising temper. On a parallel track, the rise of mass parties reduced the fear of executive patronage. In 1824 as in 1800 a president who sought to succeed himself had to gain the support of the leading members of his party in Congress, but after 1832 he needed the support of his party's national convention, which meant that he required backing from the state party conventions and from the factions within state parties that ultimately controlled the selection of delegates to national conventions. One of the many features of the spoils system that angered President James K. Polk was that he was besieged daily by factions of his own party seeking the dismissal of officeholders appointed by rival factions.[81] Increasingly, presidents, historically the chief focus of fears of executive patronage, were reduced to disposing of patronage appointments proposed by much lower ranks within their parties. In sum, executive patronage was becoming an incubus—the president took the blame when appointees proposed by others proved incompetent or crooked—more than an engine of despotism.

Although Whigs eventually embraced the partisan character of their cause, Democrats had moved much more swiftly in that direction, and in their train they had carried a new conception of relationship between men and measures, between individual talents and the needs of the party. In 1835 Tennessee Whig John Bell pronounced high office an honor to be gained by "high-souled emulation" in a kind of Tournament of Champions.[82] Bell expected the losers to generously acknowledge that the better man had won, and he condemned the "excess of party" because it forced a man to choose between party loyalty and the public interest, or at least where his conscience told him the public interest resided. Bell's view of high office as a public trust, to be held by the best men, would decline in the estimation of both parties after 1840. The individual who benefited most from the decline of this ideal was Martin Van Buren, who had been well in advance of his contemporaries in envisioning interparty competition as necessary to implement majority rule. As a presidential candidate, Van Buren presented a challenge to the idea of presidential politics as a "War of the Giants," a phrase coined by a Virginia editor in 1820, for he was no giant. Van Buren, the Whig *American Review* opined in 1845, had "no commanding traits in his character" and no reputation in philosophy or letters; next to De Witt Clinton, his archrival in New York politics and a man of "noble and elevated intellect," Van Buren was a cipher and his followers devoid of "all meritorious ideals."[83]

Democrats conceded as much. An 1835 campaign biography of Van Buren by William Holland acknowledged that the brains, the "men of splendid talents," those who had achieved reputation by their exhibition of "striking parts," were all on the Whig side. But none of this mattered, for the "individual [candidate] is nothing; his individual merits or demerits are nothing."[84] What mattered was Van Buren's adhesion to the Democratic Party as the agent for implementing the popular will. It was no accident that the Democratic Party was the first to nominate and elect "dark horse" presidents, James K. Polk and Franklin Pierce, men selected for their "availability."[85]

Spoils and Merit

In the mid-twentieth century Leonard D. White, a distinguished political scientist at the University of Chicago, ardent supporter of the Progressive Era's Good Government movement, and a leading student and historian of civil services—federal, state, local, and foreign—associated merit with the establishment of civil-service careers. He defined such careers as marked by an ascending series of steps on a bureaucratic ladder, to be mounted on the basis of political neutrality and some combination of academic qualifications and demonstrations of competence at each rung. This conception became the guiding ideal of White's academic specialty, public administration, among the most prestigious fields in political science during the second quarter of the twentieth century. When White looked at the history of the federal civil service, he discovered few figures who fit his ideal of a career service, "with its opportunity to rise to higher, more responsible, and better paid positions reaching into what in a later age would be called middle management, except for the very few who became chief clerks."[86] Partisanship, which White associated mainly with the Jacksonians, snipped whatever buds of a career service had appeared under the Federalists and Jeffersonians.

From White's perspective, partisanship and merit systems based on examinations and ladders for promotion were antagonists. That the relationship between partisanship and merit was more subtle, however, was grasped by one of White's forerunners, Carl R. Fish. Fish, who had the advantage of writing the history of the civil service before professors of public administration had cast their shadow on the field, observed in 1904 that before the Pendleton Act of 1883 established "open, competitive examinations" for civil-service positions, government service often was a species of entrepreneurship, which attracted "clever, sometimes brilliant men" because it had no rules. Any position "might lead anywhere, and that quickly."[87] Although White was uncertain what to make of such men, he provided examples of the sort of people Fish had in mind. These examples included Connecticut's Elisha Whittlesey, who, after serving five terms in the House, held a succession of auditorships and comptrollerships under several administrations; Albion K. Parris, a former Maine Supreme Court justice who held the office of second comptroller in Treasury from 1836 to 1850, when he was succeeded by Hiland Hall, a former Vermont Supreme Court justice and governor; and John Appleton, a Maine lawyer who edited a Democratic newspaper before being appointed by George Bancroft to the chief clerkship of the Navy Department in 1845. Subsequently, Appleton became chief clerk of the State Department and chargé d'affaires in Bolivia before being elected to Congress in 1850 and rising to assistant secretary of state in 1857.[88] None of these men fit White's conception of career civil servants as proto–middle managers. In fact, they were not career civil servants at all. Their career was public life. Jobs in the civil service were ports in a storm or springboards to something better.

The spoils system, in sum, did not bar the rise of the talented. The system nevertheless cast a cloud of suspicion over all proposals for formal procedures to reward merit. The ideal of merit sometimes pushed its way onto the national agenda between 1840 and 1860, only to be treated as a gate crasher. When Navy Secretary George Bancroft proposed in 1845 to break the grip of seniority on naval promotions by establishing a board of officers to make selections on the basis of merit, he was immediately accused of trying to create a wedge for Democratic spoils. Although Bancroft was a Democrat serving the highly partisan Polk administration, the charge was unfair. As Bancroft observed, seniority "demands promotion as its right." The effect was to overload the navy with aged officers; in 1845 the average age of captains, then the highest naval rank, was nearly sixty. Further, Bancroft devised a criterion for promotion by merit, a considerable accomplishment in a navy that had not fought a battle for three decades: the length of an officer's service at sea. His assumption that the most excellent and ambitious officers would seek perilous and "wasting" duty at sea rather than desk jobs was plausible. No matter. Congress declined to implement the proposal, and the navy would not develop a system of selective promotion until the early twentieth century.[89]

There was a flip side to this story. Partisanship eased fears of presidential autocracy, of oppression initiated at the top and then spreading downward tentacles. Consider, for example, the decision to allow each member of the House of Representatives to nominate one young man from his district to the military academy at West Point. This was a matter of no small importance since, by 1830, West Pointers held 63.8 percent of army commissions, up from 14.8 percent in 1817. Presidents also had parcels of nominations to distribute. Nominees had to pass West Point's entrance examination, but only nominees could take the examination, and those who failed it could retake it after receiving free tutoring. No hard-and-fast rule dictated that politicians base their nominations to West Point on partisan loyalty; instead, they might follow the example of President Polk, who nominated his nephews. But party-based appointments guaranteed that the political composition of the officer corps would more or less reflect the diverse political composition of Congress. The effect was to quiet fears, rife in the early 1800s, that Federalists would use their domination of the officer corps, a holdover from the 1790s, to check the policies of elected Republican administrations.

The triumph of party politics also undermined the extreme political individualism of the early republic. An elective or appointed officeholder who professed to stand above and apart from parties was in for trouble as the nineteenth century wore on. Zachary Taylor discovered this when veteran Whigs like Webster and Clay subverted his plan for admitting the whole of the Mexican Cession as states. The legitimization of partisanship and the entrenchment of the spoils system gave to the distribution of public office a measure of predictability and routine that earlier had been lacking. Now an individual who pulled political wires to advance himself was not violating the public trust or turning government into a sink of corruption. When Quincy Adams appointed Henry Clay secretary of state after the election in 1825, the air was filled with charges of a "corrupt bargain," but no one complained when Abraham Lincoln gave cabinet appointments to several wire-pullers who had helped him win the Republican nomination over William Seward in 1860.[90]

Parallel to the deflation of political individualism, a deflation of individualistic behavior was occurring in the professions. After reviewing medical politics in the early republic, Daniel Calhoun identified a clear trend toward "a kind of moratorium on attention to individual achievement" by midcentury.[91] Increasingly, physicians exerted pressure against "the man who sought repute for himself as an individual rather than as a member of the profession." The effect was a "dampening" of both "intellectual arrogance and intellectual individualism." Ironically, the ease of chartering medical schools, which initially contributed to the turmoil within the profession, eventually had a pacific effect. The proliferation of medical schools by 1850 made it practical to fill vacant professorships with medical graduates, without the brazen and disruptive self-promotion and self-fashioning that had characterized the profession a decade or two earlier. Initiating a practice that would continue into the twentieth century, even the "irregular" practitioners of herbalist, homeopathic, and osteopathic medicine started their own medical schools, so that rival armies of doctors marched on parallel avenues.[92] The fractious relations between army officers, which had been so notable a feature into the 1820s, also experienced a cooling down. Historian William Skelton has put forward a persuasive reason for this. As the military academy at West Point became the main source of commissioned officers, the rigorous West Point experience rubbed off the rough edges of young men.[93]

By the 1820s one major component of the experience at West Point had become submission to its merit system, which substituted seemingly unarguable numbers for the self-inflated pretensions of officer candidates. Thayer's system and the many college systems modeled on it were known as *merit systems*. In contrast, no one called the political spoils system a merit system. Later advocates of merit in government dedicated themselves to killing the spoils system as the first step to introducing a merit system based on competitive examinations. In view of the Founding commitment to merit, the ascendancy of the spoils system can plausibly be viewed as a retreat from Founding ideals. The problem did not lie in patronage as such. The Founders saw no inherent incompatibility between a patron's sponsorship of a young man into a career in public life and selection by merit; they understood that sponsoring dullards, debt defaulters, or rakes could threaten their own reputations. But in a republic that was both new and federal, one where the bases of power were mainly local or regional, and where the Revolution's legacy of suspicion still glowed, appointments to federal office were long enveloped by fears that the appointment power opened the door to congressional or executive despotism. The gradual acceptance of political parties as legitimate vehicles for identifying and channeling the popular will dissolved these fears; intensifying two-party competition came to be seen as a guarantor of the republic's security. However much they might disagree on banking, tariffs, internal improvements, and slavery extension, Americans continued to view the republic itself as the ultimate guarantor that, in all really important ways, advancement in America would be based on merit.

Viewed as a system for the mass dispensing of public jobs, the political spoils system resembled the merit systems that the colleges were initiating. Neither sought to open careers to talents—the republic itself accomplished that objective—nor did either aim at finding buried talent in the form of promising young men whose value to society lay undiscovered. Both sought to calm disputes over precedence that arose from the regime of essential merit by establishing procedures for the distribution of rewards.

3

SMALL WORLDS

Competition in the Colleges

The contours of competition for honors in colleges paralleled competition in public life. In each case the American Revolution stimulated more intense competition, more striving for fame, more prizes and rewards. Students in the early republic who insisted on recognition of their genius resembled the Men of Merit and First Characters who rested their claims to high office on their possession of preeminent and conspicuous merit, which was comprehended as a unitary superiority.

The Early Colleges

That striking similarities existed between the conception of merit in public life and in the colleges is hardly surprising, for the colleges were virtual training grounds for public life.[1] Most college graduates entered the professions of divinity, law, or medicine, each of which was public in several senses. Ministers performed in public, not only from the pulpit but as orators on public occasions. Law was universally acknowledged as the main route into politics, and doctors served in legislatures to a much greater extent than now. Daniel Drake was typical of prominent and ambitious physicians in writing pamphlets aimed at the public, to justify either their medical theories or, more frequently after 1800, their conduct in the public controversies that tore at their profession. Similarly, the college was a stage on which students performed. Before 1830 all examinations were oral and most were public. The principal form of instruction in all of the colleges was the recitation, a public exercise in which tutors, recent graduates who acted as the drill sergeants of the colleges, called on students to rise and answer questions, based on the assignment, in front of their classmates. Graduating seniors were required to pass public oral examinations in which a college's trustees, themselves leading public men, often participated. In 1790 Harvard's governing boards required all students to undergo annual oral examinations to test their mastery of the year's material. The student literary societies, the mainstays of the extracurriculum in colleges, engaged in debates and other rhetorical exercises in which students performed before audiences of their peers.

In the colleges as in public life, merit proved to be an extremely disruptive force: before the 1820s all claims by students to academic distinction rested on their self-assessed reputations among their peers. The merit system installed by Sylvanus Thayer at West Point, widely copied elsewhere, represented the first such *system* for allocating academic rank. College governments judged Thayer's plan and its many imitators to be successful because, by using numerical assessments of the legion of activities in which students engaged instead of self-promotion as the basis of students' self-imagined reputations, merit systems cooled the tempers of hotly competitive students.

To understand the competitiveness of students in the early republic we have to recognize that virtually none of the features we associate with academic competition today were present in colleges. With the exception of Thomas Jefferson, who successfully recruited distinguished European professors to the fledgling University of Virginia, colleges rarely sought to attract scholarly notables.[2] Jefferson had no real successor until the 1870s, when Daniel Coit Gilman lured eminent professors to the new Johns Hopkins University. Tutors, who carried the instructional workload of the colleges, usually were drawn from their college's alumni and appointed in exact order of seniority (years since graduation). After assuming Yale's presidency in 1778, Ezra Stiles created controversy when he occasionally considered "literary Merit" in appointing tutors.[3] Meritocratic pressures on students hovered between nonexistent and modest. Entrance examinations, always oral, sought to establish whether the student was prepared for the curriculum, not to choose the best applicants from a pool. Highly qualified students were often admitted to higher classes; in 1786 John Quincy Adams, well traveled in Europe as his father's secretary and fluent in French, was admitted to Harvard as a junior. Barely qualified students were admitted on condition that they make up deficiencies (this remained the case at most colleges throughout the nineteenth century).

There were no numerical marks or letter equivalents before the 1810s. Written examinations, introduced in the late 1820s, did not become the main form of examination until after 1870. A half-century elapsed between the abolition of the system of ranking students at Harvard and Yale by social precedence and the establishment of ranking systems based on examinations and marks. Throughout the period from 1780 to 1850 the baccalaureate degree remained more a certificate of attendance than a prize for academic accomplishment. In 1785 Stiles devised a grading system, probably the first in an American college, which classified seniors as *optimi*, second *optimi*, *inferiores*, or *pejores*. Stiles primarily targeted the *pejores*, the seniors whose minds he characterized as "poverty itself." His one known application of the system was to bar some students from graduating and to demote others. This was sufficient to provoke "disturbances," "with the express purpose of offering insult, indignity, and violence to the Persons of the Tutors," and the departure of several seniors, who left the college "for fear of having the degree depend on Merit."[4] In 1791 the junior and senior classes petitioned for exemption from the annual examinations decreed in 1790 by Harvard's governing boards, and when their petition was denied, "disturbances occurred in consequence."[5]

The moves by Stiles and Harvard's governing boards to assess the "literary merit" of students were part of a trend, affecting most colleges after 1760, to tighten the academic screws on students.[6] Adhering to their traditional minimalism, however, students clashed with their superiors at every turn. For example, a new rule requiring students to provide excuses for their absences from class triggered a rebellion at Harvard in 1768.[7] Accepting academic requirements in principle, students ingeniously dodged them when applied. As a student at Harvard, John Quincy Adams observed that his classmates evaded attending recitations by holding class meetings. "I am told," he primly recorded in his diary, that "there have been fellows so lazy and stupid as to call a class meeting for that purpose."[8] His classmates also cut classes on the flimsiest excuses (to return home for warmer clothing), and they routinely extended their winter vacations by weeks. Two weeks into the spring term of 1787, Adams wrote, "about one-half the class is here."[9] As a student at Union College in the late 1810s, future statesman William H. Seward became enraged when tutor Francis Wayland, future president of Brown University, called on him out of alphabetical order in a daily recitation. Wayland then ordered Seward to leave the room when he refused to answer any questions. That Seward could not answer questions is hardly surprising; he had not even brought his Homer to class. But his muteness was intended to insult Wayland for violating unwritten protocol (calling on students in alphabetical order), and it created enough of a row to elicit an apology to Seward by the college's president, Eliphalet Nott, on behalf of Wayland, and a corresponding apology from Seward for having been unprepared.[10]

Students not only resisted basing the baccalaureate degree on measured merit; they also showed little interest in competing with each other for prizes.

Although Harvard, Yale, and the colleges founded during and after the Great Awakening offered a variety of prizes in the form of books, cash, or medals for student "dissertations," collegians were becoming selective when it came to prizes worth seeking. For example, as governor of Delaware, John Dickinson established medals in 1782 for the best student dissertations at the College of New Jersey (Princeton). But competition for the Dickinson medals ceased within a few years because of lack of student interest.[11] There was little change during the next six decades. The same fate befell the system of premiums for academic excellence that Francis Wayland established at Brown University during the 1840s.[12]

Yet the foregoing requires one major qualification, for students in reality were becoming extremely competitive. Undergraduates showed little interest in competing for cash or medals because these distracted from the only competition that really mattered to them: winning "parts," also called "appointments," at so-called exhibitions and at commencement. As a graduating Harvard student observed in 1798, parts were the "golden coin" of the student body.[13]

It had not always been so. College commencements had become public extravaganzas long before 1750, but graduating seniors had not been the center of attention. True, graduating seniors spoke Latin set pieces, called disputations, at commencement. As Samuel Sewall described it in his diary, disputations would start the ceremony at Harvard's early eighteenth-century commencements, but these would cease as soon as the governor and his entourage entered. Then the main event took place, a carefully crafted Latin oration by Harvard's president. This was followed by orations by masters of arts, graduates who for a fee could acquire the M.A. on the third commencement after their graduations. Sewall's diary indicates that one graduating senior delivered an oration, but the masters of arts played a much more prominent role than graduating seniors at commencement. Further, the graduating senior orator was selected on the basis of his rank under the social-precedence system, which was also the basis of assigning parts in disputations.[14]

Commencements changed in several ways after 1750. Princeton, which quickly became the largest of the colleges founded during the Great Awakening, never had as many candidates for the master's as for the bachelor's degree, and the same was true of colleges founded during and after the Revolution. This change partly reflected the shifting goals of students, who increasingly aimed for the legal or medical professions rather than the ministry, the objective of most masters of arts. Harvard and Yale continued to graduate nearly as many masters as bachelors, but even at these colleges the masters' ceremony was pushed from the morning to the afternoon, where it was crowded by a continuation of the morning bachelors' ceremony.[15]

Prizes to Die For

As seniors became the focus of commencements, the components of commencements became more varied in response to the new academic culture embodied in
belles lettres, which entered the English language with the translation in 1734 of
Charles Rollin's *De la manière d'enseigner et d'étudier les belles lettres*. Belles lettres
included rhetoric, poetry, languages, history, and moral philosophy, but these
were less subjects to be studied in the modern sense of learning about them than
boosts to performance and behavior in public. For example, history was valued
as a treasure trove of models on which to base conduct. In the 1760s the colleges
were coming to be described as "literary" institutions and as ideal places to educate the men of letters who, according to Princeton's first historian in 1764, were
urgently needed to fill "the bench, the bar, the seats of legislation." The image
of the man of letters, James McLachlan has written, was based on the revival of
the Greek and Roman classics, particularly Cicero, and especially Cicero's model
of the orator who combined civic leadership, learning, and eloquence.[16] Belles
lettres persisted as a curriculum for public life long after the Revolution.[17]

In 1761 Harvard's Overseers introduced periodic "exhibitions," public oratorical performances by students, to coincide with the Overseers' semiannual visita-
tions.[18] President John Witherspoon of Princeton, who would become the only
clergyman to sign the Declaration of Independence, and Yale's Stiles supported
the new emphasis on orations in English. But the main impetus behind the ascendancy of belles lettres came from the student literary societies that became
features of all of the colleges after 1760. Examples of these were the Brothers in
Unity and Linonian societies at Yale and the American Whig and Cliosophic societies at Princeton.[19] In contrast to the secret fraternities that emerged in the colleges toward the mid-nineteenth century, the literary societies usually included
most if not all students. At Yale and Princeton, college officials assigned students
to one or another society; Princeton students derided those who chose not to
join either society as "neuters." At many colleges the societies competed to enlist
new members. Regardless of the method of selection, the literary societies in each
college—there were usually two of them—rivaled each other. As an American
Whig at Princeton, James Madison scrolled Hudibrastic ridicule of the rival Cliosophics. When not deriding their adversaries, society members conducted their
own debates and exhibitions in English, which ran parallel to officially sponsored
exhibitions; in some instances the societies printed their own diplomas and conducted parallel commencements. They also compiled their own libraries, always
more accessible and sometimes larger than the college's library.[20]

In combination, pressure from trustees, the efforts of progressive presidents
like Witherspoon and Stiles, and the literary societies transformed the content

of commencement parts. Syllogistic disputations, whether in Latin or English, became less frequent and plummeted in prestige. "Syllogistics," Harvard student John Quincy Adams related, were "very much despised by the scholars." To be assigned one, he wrote, was like having "DUNCE" written on one's forehead.[21] As exercises in logic rather than belles lettres, syllogistics constrained students from parading historical and literary allusions. In contrast, orations in Latin and especially in English became more common. Harvard students called these the "good parts," and Adams happily related that Harvard's government assigned more such parts in 1786 than formerly.[22] So-called conferences, or "dialogues," which resembled discussions but with the speaking parts crafted in advance, also became features of commencements after 1760. Although less prestigious than the assignment of a solo part (Adams rated "ignominious" the assignment of a part in a dialogue), these were nevertheless sought because the topics of dialogues closely resembled the topics students debated in their literary societies.

Exhibitions and commencement parts licensed personal display and resembled dramatic performances. When Harvard's Overseers decreed that periodic exhibitions of student oratory be held in advance of commencement, they also voted that college laws against theatrical entertainments should not be construed as preventing the exhibitions.[23] The dramatic features of exhibitions and commencements brought collegians to public notice; indeed, commencements were virtual coming-out parties for young men who aspired to public life, "the first young budding of fame to a collegian."[24] Not only did the high and mighty attend commencements, but newspapers closely followed commencement events. For example, newspapers in New Jersey and Pennsylvania reported Princeton's commencements in detail, one noting that the valedictorian of the class of 1769 gave an address "eloquently composed and pathetically delivered."[25] In what was likely an indirect stab at John Adams, whose talk about the inevitability of aristocracy in his recently published *Defence of the Constitutions of the United States of America* had inspired controversy, two Massachusetts newspapers unfavorably compared John Quincy Adams's address at Harvard's 1787 commencement ("the public expectations from this gentleman, being the son of an Ambassador, the favorite of the officers of the College, and having enjoyed the advantages of European instruction, were greatly inflated") with that of another student.[26]

By the 1780s the gentlemen's clubs springing up in Boston, New York, and Philadelphia, which brought recent graduates into contact with well-placed elders, were becoming virtual alumni clubs of the collegiate literary societies.[27] But students could parade their literary attainments before influentials, especially a college's trustees, without leaving campus. The University of North Carolina's first board of trustees included the governor, three signers of the U.S. Constitution, two justices of the U.S. Supreme Court, several U.S. senators and representatives, five future governors, and two Revolutionary War generals. The University of Virginia's first board of visitors included three former presidents of the United States. As fledgling institutions, North Carolina and Virginia benefited from the support of such luminaries, but even in 1844, when the survival of the University of North Carolina was no longer in doubt, its board of trustees numbered sixty-four, compared with a faculty of eight. Rival literary societies offered honorary memberships to leading public figures, hung portraits of them in their rooms, and displayed their rhetorical skills in public exhibitions.[28]

The literary societies also competed for commencement parts for their champions. In principle, membership in a society served to prevent competition for parts from turning into individualistic rivalry. A student's success, Princeton sophomore Joseph Cabell Breckenridge wrote to his father (Jefferson's attorney general) in 1806, "must confer honour on the body of which he is a member."[29] Students acquired the habit of ranking each other on the basis of their performances in the "exercises" of literary societies, and they expected their rankings to be taken seriously by the college's government. In most colleges most of the time, the college government made the final selection of commencement orators, but students had an acknowledged voice in the selection. Students always chose their orator for Class Day, the day when the seniors left college before returning for commencement. At Princeton, John Witherspoon experimented before the Revolution with allowing students to choose their commencement orators. He abandoned the idea when it produced "confusion and ill blood," and while serving in the Continental Congress he cited this experience as the reason for not allowing army generals to choose new ones.[30] Versions of this practice nevertheless were introduced at Princeton in 1809 and again in 1812, when the assignment of parts was delegated to the literary societies.[31] Dickinson College had a similar system in the 1790s; future chief justice Roger B. Taney counted his election as valedictorian as his first entry into public life.[32] In 1807 the government of South Carolina College allowed juniors to elect their twelve "most respectable scholars," who were then awarded parts at commencement.[33] University of Virginia students and faculty battled furiously over the choice of commencement orators in the 1830s, a scrimmage ended only by the adoption of an electoral college in which each had a voice.[34] At the University of North Carolina in the early 1840s the faculty grouped graduating seniors deemed eligible for honors into three classes and then allowed the top class to elect commencement speakers.[35]

Such deference to student opinion conflicts with the conventional image of the early colleges as tiny despotisms. But a college's government had every reason to put its best foot forward at commencement. A disrupted commencement was certain to anger notables. According to John Quincy Adams, Harvard's government rebuffed a request by his class to be allowed a private commencement in view of the state's financial distress in the wake of Shays' Rebellion, on the grounds that it would offend public officials and deprive the governor of an opportunity to show himself in "splendor and magnificence."[36] Inasmuch as students composed as well as spoke their parts, dazzling rhetorical performances showed the college at its best. Whether governments allowed their students to choose their commencement speakers or merely consulted them, it was to their advantage to encourage a consensus about the allotment of parts both to ensure a trouble-free commencement and to ennoble competition (or "emulation"). As far back as 1669, when the citizens of Portsmouth, New Hampshire, having heard "the loud groanes of the sinking colledg," raised money for Harvard, they announced the hope that their example would "provoke the rest of the country to jealousy [envy]," but quickly added that "we meane an holy emulation to appear in so goode a worke."[37] Emulation became holy when it was collective and benevolent, and it could be noble if it encouraged one person to model his behavior on that of a superior. But rivalry, connoting competition in which one person's success depended on another's failure, could breed un-Christian envy, vanity, and anger.

Reflecting on the old-time colleges, Henry D. Sheldon wrote in 1901 that students spent an extraordinary amount of time assessing each other and viewed "the applause won by the leading members as belonging to the common fund of class credit."[38] Future Supreme Court justice Joseph Story of Harvard's class of 1798 recalled, decades later, that students' performances in recitations made it possible for all members of the class to assign "generally correct, impartial, and satisfactory" rankings to each scholar. Story wrote these words to assure the son of William Ellery Channing that his father, who had edged Story for the top honor, had fairly won his rank because his class, marked by a "generous spirit of emulation" and "proud of its best scholars," agreed with the decision of Harvard's government to assign the top honor to Channing.[39]

Story was right at least on one count. Students took pains to acquire distinction without seeming to seek it. For example, John Quincy Adams was eager to win the first honor, valedictorian, at Harvard's 1787 commencement, but he had to settle for the second honor, salutatorian. As secretary of state thirty-five years later, he was still sore at the slight, and the fact that his closest rival for the valedictory "sunk at the age of 35, to be forgotten," just rubbed his open wound.[40] But when Adams was approached shortly after his graduation to have his commencement address published in the *Columbian Magazine*, he demurred, or appeared to demur, on the grounds that since another student had already turned down an offer to have his commencement poem published, "it might with reason be considered a mark of presumption in me, to assume a distinction, which others, much more meritorious, had declined through modesty." Adams relented only when offered a patriotic motive: publication would enable the "Friends of Liberty" to see "the features of the Parent in the Son."[41]

Story's sexagenarian recollection of "generous emulation" nevertheless was oblivious to the commotion that surrounded Harvard's 1798 commencement. After Harvard's government censored Channing's address for its extreme Federalist partisanship, bound to offend Republicans in the state legislature, Channing threatened to refuse to deliver it unless the government backed down. Story's recollection also obscured the rage of disappointed students that threatened commencements. Daniel Webster was so demoralized by his failure to be assigned the English valedictory at Dartmouth's 1801 commencement that he refused to present himself for his degree.[42] The decision of Dickinson College officials to refuse a commencement part to future president James Buchanan for routinely having cut recitations nearly provoked a student rebellion in 1809. At Dartmouth in 1811 a student who thought his part too low appeared on the commencement stage in slovenly dress, his stockings down at the heels; did not bow to the president and trustees; read his part in a monotone inaudible ten feet away; and was denied his degree.[43] A dispute over assignment of a commencement part contributed to Harvard's Great Rebellion of 1823 and to Amherst College's 1830s "Gorham Rebellion," which seriously threatened the college's survival.[44]

These upheavals had sundry roots, including the students' accusation that college governments practiced favoritism in assigning parts. Inasmuch as the colleges usually recruited their tutors from their alumni, it was not unusual for faculty members who had belonged to one or another of the rival literary societies and who continued to attend its meetings to favor students from their own society.[45] Charges of favoritism arose even in the absence of literary societies, however. For example, although possessing a variety of speaking clubs, Harvard lacked an equivalent to the usual two-society rivalry. But in 1798 William Austin, a graduating senior, blasted its government for equating merit with obedience to the college's mountain of petty rules—he wondered whether Harvard was really a "house of correction" rather than an institution receptive to "superior genius." Austin gave examples of such genius: Isaac Newton, Edward Gibbon, and, rapidly descending the steps, recent graduate and future Federalist intellectual Joseph Dennie. In Austin's eyes, the assignment of parts had become the "political engine" by which the college kept the students in line. It would confer an English oration on a "blockhead" as long as he did its will. Dennie, Austin's paragon, who had been degraded for "insolence" as an undergraduate (class of 1790), described Harvard's tutors as "invariably low-born despicable rustics, lately emerged from the dung-hill, who, conscious of their own want of genius, were determined to discountenance all who possessed it."[46]

The predominantly Federalist students of the northern colleges equated their "merit" less with specific skills than with a total package they often labeled *genius*, which connoted the public manifestation of inner quality.[47] As a Harvard student in 1824, Charles Francis Adams, John Quincy Adams's son, recorded the lectures of Edward Tyrell Channing, the Boylston Professor of Rhetoric, in which Channing equated genius with "style," the "picture of a man's mind and character."[48] Just as the Federalist Men of Merit expected spontaneous recognition of their unitary superiority, students expected their superiors to acknowledge their genius. To tell a Joseph Dennie that his genius fell short of his pretensions was to make a harsh statement and to invite a petulant response.

In theory and at times in practice, the collegiate literary societies subordinated self-inflated members to group norms. Customarily, each society elected a *censor morum* charged with reporting to the society any breaches of decorum on the part of members that were likely to bring the society into disgrace. But self-policing was merely a component of the intense competition between the societies; members of one society rarely associated with those of the rival society and sometimes trashed its rooms. John Witherspoon observed that his ill-fated plan to allow the American Whigs and Cliosophics at Princeton to choose commencement orators failed because neither society would put forward even a single member of its rival. Roger Taney recalled that at Dickinson the larger literary society voted itself all of the commencement parts. Daniel Webster came to grief at his Dartmouth commencement because the college's two literary societies deadlocked on choosing commencement speakers, forcing the college's government to intervene with an assignment of parts that short-changed Webster. At times, rivalry between societies reflected political and regional divisions. By 1806 Brown University's two literary societies had divided along Federalist/ Republican lines.[49] William Seward wrote that Union College's two societies split between northern and southern students during the Missouri crisis.[50] At the University of North Carolina the division, political and cultural, between the state's east and west was reflected in the composition of the literary societies.[51] But often there were no identifiable political or regional differences between the rival societies, and they still collided like enemy armies.

College governments nevertheless sought to perpetuate the societies. For example, Yale's government awarded students a half-holiday the day after the literary societies' bimonthly debates. What governments did not encourage was the proliferation of societies; more than two was always a crowd. Yet disaffected members of a society were prone to secede to start a new society. At North Carolina in 1838 a faction within one of the college's two societies, the Dialectic, seceded to form a third society after the majority of Dialectics had failed to name its champion the Dialectic's commencement orator.

Even in the absence of such secessions, the colleges were bursting with student factions. At the conclusion of his Dartmouth career Amos Kendall, future postmaster general and patronage dispenser under Andrew Jackson, wrote an account of his student days that provides remarkable insight into the extent and functions of campus factionalism. The Dartmouth that Kendall attended from 1807 to 1811 was still a small college, with classes numbering forty to fifty students. Nearly all students belonged to one or another of the college's two literary societies, the Social Friends (Kendall's society) and the United Fraternity. Kendall also joined a secret mutual improvement club composed of a dozen of his classmates and devoted to "composition, declamation, and forensic discussion," and he would be selected for the Philoi Euphradias, an honor society unique to Dartmouth, and for Phi Beta Kappa, an honor society with chapters on many campuses.[52] Kendall's mutual improvement society and the two honor societies shared two features: they encouraged rhetoric, thereby preparing their members for parts in exhibitions and commencement; and they were self-selecting. The Philoi Euphradias was composed of members who had anointed themselves the "flower" of the student body. Phi Beta Kappa, although not a secret society, drew a veil over its proceedings and chose its members by methods sufficiently mysterious to invite controversy. (One Harvard Phi Beta Kappan devised a cryptogram to record the society's proceedings in his diary.)[53] In contrast, Kendall's mutual improvement society was truly secret; its members pledged never to mention its existence to other students. It seems odd that a dozen students would try to conceal their activities from the remaining two or three dozen in the class, but Kendall provided a clue when he recorded that the society's members always participated in its exercises "not by appointment but in alphabetical order." In effect, they had insulated themselves from the rivalry that pervaded all other aspects of the student culture, not from rejection of rivalry—all would soon enter the lists—but to prepare themselves in seclusion for competition.

Kendall's main allegiance was to the Social Friends, who competed fiercely with the rival United Fraternity. By custom, each society's members voted to assign parts at its senior exhibition, which was held two days before commencement. To be assigned an oration at this exhibition was thought to be "the most honorable appointment," but Kendall preferred an appointment as poet at the Social Friends' exhibition. Receiving it, he composed a long tragedy, "Palafox, or the Siege [by Napoleon] of Saragossa." The Social Friends then wrangled with the United Fraternity over whose poet would recite on the day before commencement, when the campus would be filled with visitors, or two days before, when the audience was likely to be sparse. The faculty intervened, after a fashion, to appoint a committee composed in equal measure of students from both societies, but the committee predictably deadlocked along society lines. Only when the Social Friends, at Kendall's bidding, voted to boycott the exhibition did the United Fraternity back down. Shortly thereafter the college's government appointed Kendall to deliver the Latin salutatory at commencement, the most prestigious appointment at Dartmouth.

Kendall's triumph was clear but its basis was cloudy. Like other colleges, Dartmouth administered annual oral examinations to students, but as usually was the case elsewhere, they were not graded, served the sole purpose of governing promotion to the next class, and were passed by nearly everyone. Kendall also attended recitations, but these were not graded and he missed more than his share. A serious student, he also was impoverished, and he often left college to work. He learned of his appointment as salutatorian after an interlude during which he was away from November 28, 1810, to April 13, 1811. He had taken comparably long leaves in the preceding two years to "replenish" his funds by teaching school. All of the colleges had long winter vacations for just this purpose, but Kendall's leaves were so long that he had to be reexamined and formally readmitted to his class on each return.[54]

Ultimately, Kendall's rank depended on his reputation. He attributed his success to being thought the best scholar, "by the class first, and afterwards the government." In part, his reputation rested on his rhetorical skills, demonstrated in frequent exhibitions. But his political skills may have been equally important, for Kendall was an outsider. He stood out in a predominantly wet Federalist student body as a dry Republican Baptist. He had fallen out of favor in his sophomore year when he and a handful of students signed a petition against "treating," the practice that dictated that students who had received appointments in exhibitions buy alcoholic beverages for the entire class.[55] His selection for the Philoi Euphradias also alienated him from many of his classmates, who razzed the Philoi when they marched into the meeting hall for Kendall's reading of "Palafox."

Kendall attributed his eventual success to his "decision of character," which meant what Emerson would later call "self-reliance," a determination to stand on one's own convictions rather than bow to the crowd. Yet Kendall's description of his decisiveness makes it clear that what he really aimed at was to *appear* independent. In addition to his lively imagination, he wrote, "my reserve in not connecting myself with any of the officers of government has carried an appearance of independence, and these causes . . . have enabled me to bear the palm from those more studious and knowing than myself."[56]

As an outsider, Kendall could stand back from his Dartmouth experience and see collegiate competition for honors as a game, just as Martin Van Buren, another outsider, would later see politics as a game. A game tested skills and wits, but the prize went to the one who was proclaimed the winner, not necessarily to the superior person. Kendall wrote that "at a university of this kind, a few glowing pieces of composition, with one or two public declamations, written and spoken with spirit, have more effect in raising the reputation of a student, than the reasoning of a Locke, the application of a Newton, or the wisdom of a Solomon." He added that "upon this tinsel foundation was my reputation in great degree established."[57] Most students thought that their reputations measured their merit, but Kendall conceded that his reputation exceeded his merit. His reputation boiled down to his popularity, and "college popularity is as variable as the wind." In later years, as one of Andrew Jackson's hatchet men on removals, Kendall would often hear the anguished protest of victims of the spoils system that their removal from office scarred their reputation, but he had already become a cynic about reputation.

Marks and Marking Systems

Kendall won the first honor at Dartmouth without ever having received a numerical or letter grade. Marks and marking systems did not enter the colleges until the 1810s and spread only after 1820. Once established, marking systems had an effect that resembled the spoils system in politics. The spoils system did not pretend to reward merit, but it did establish a routine and largely depersonalized method for the distribution of offices; marking systems, although promoted as an unarguable measure of merit, established an automatic basis for distributing commencement parts. Just as the explicitly partisan basis for distributing public jobs undermined the culture of honor and reputation that had made men more important than measures, marking systems deflated collegians' preoccupations with their cherished honor and sacred reputations. Commencement parts now would depend on class rank, and rank on numbers.

Marking systems came into the colleges on the heels of a wave of student rebellions. Rebellions had started in the 1760s, but those occurring between 1800 and 1830 were much more disruptive.[58] In 1805 nearly the entire senior class at the University of North Carolina seceded in protest against a new regulation that students inform on one another. Harvard and Princeton experienced major rebellions in 1807. After becoming Princeton's president in 1812, Ashbel Green, who had vowed to treat "every pupil as a child," was driven to despair when the "children" barred tutors from their rooms, rang the college bell at night, set fire to outbuildings, and exploded bombs in the chapel, even on the Sabbath.[59] In the 1820s Harvard students stole gunpowder and used it to set off an explosion in a residence hall. Harvard's Great Rebellion of 1823 led to the expulsion of forty-three of seventy seniors, including a son of John Quincy Adams, almost on the eve of commencement. Yale's Conic Sections rebellion in 1832 led to the expulsion of one-third of the sophomore class.

College rebellions had no relation to extramural political or social causes. Rather, rebellions always commenced over intramural issues like bad food, the refusal of the faculty to grant a holiday, a new requirement about attendance at recitation, or disappointment over the allotment of parts. For example, an attempt in 1805 by the trustees of the University of North Carolina to force the *censor morum* of each literary society to report infractions to the college's government spurred the "Great Secession" of 1805. Harvard's Great Rebellion of 1823 was triggered by student outrage when a member of the class of 1823, George Trask Woodberry, was accused by his classmates of attempting to influence the assignment of parts at an exhibition by informing "some gentlemen in Boston" that his rival for a part was "an immoral character." In response, the class chose the rival as its orator and mercilessly hissed Woodberry's efforts to speak at the exhibition.[60] Rebellions typically began with petty vandalism. Student protest developed into full insurrections when the college government demanded that malefactors confess and inform on other students. Invoking their collective honor, students then formed combinations to resist these demands, so that, regardless of the occasion of trouble, college discipline itself became the real issue. Wealthier and more secular than their colonial forerunners, students actively pushed back against the college governments' attempts to humiliate them.

Reacting to rebellions, college governments gradually changed the colleges' disciplinary systems after 1820 by substituting the bureaucratic administration of rules for personal confrontations.[61] Trustees, who had played prominent roles during the founding era of individual colleges, gradually delegated discipline to the faculty and began to fade from the picture. Marking systems were components of the new bureaucratic approach to discipline, and several of them were modeled on the merit system introduced by Thayer as superintendent of West Point in 1818. To each course, Thayer assigned a numerical weight—mathematics weighed more than French—and to each student a numerical grade, which was the product of the course's weight and the student's performance in it. The system included numerical "demerit" for infractions of rules. In the end, each student would have a composite score, and this score formed the basis of his class rank. Thayer installed the merit system at West Point with a specific objective: to counter the influence of Acting Superintendent Alden Partridge, who was forced out after a court-martial in 1817. Deciding the future assignments of cadets, taking over classes when in the mood, selecting capable students for private instruction, and erratically administering discipline, Partridge had run the academy like a charismatic dictator. In contrast, Thayer had the mind of a bureaucrat: he would administer and the faculty would teach. Thayer's system infuriated some cadets, but most seem to have accepted it and even liked it. It gave students something to strive for, since a student with high rank was more likely to be assigned to the branch—infantry, cavalry, artillery—of his choice. Class rank also established a graduate's initial place on the army's seniority list (the higher his rank, the earlier his commission's dating), at a time when army promotions were governed exclusively by seniority. Thayer's mechanical system had at least the appearance of eliminating favoritism, which had become a problem under Partridge. Favor and merit had long been viewed as incompatible, but the only way to eliminate the appearance of favor in an honor culture was to impose the kind of obsessively detailed merit system that Thayer initiated.[62]

Thayer's system found an influential supporter in Harvard's George Ticknor, who publicized it during the 1820s.[63] The grandson of a poor farmer and the son of a sometime grocer and schoolteacher, Ticknor had risen to a professorship at Harvard. Ticknor sought to use academic merit as the basis for an intellectual aristocracy, which would then diffuse knowledge among the multitude (Ticknor would become the moving spirit behind the founding of the Boston Public Library in 1852). Ticknor's support for Thayer's marking system was well timed. Harvard's Great Rebellion of 1823 led to intervention by the Overseers and the initiation of reports to parents on each student's conduct and scholarship. By the late 1820s Harvard was scoring students on a 1–20 scale in each subject. After becoming president of Harvard in 1829, Josiah Quincy, former congressman and mayor of Boston, established his Scale of Comparative Merit, which awarded or subtracted points, up to a pinball-machine maximum of 29,980, for nearly every activity in which a student could engage over four years. Quincy's system, which lasted into the 1870s with only minor modifications, reflected the same bureaucratic mentality as Thayer's.[64]

Marking systems were direct responses to the rebellions that were threatening the survival of some colleges; by conflating scholarship and conduct as elements of merit, they provided college governments with a numerical rationale for suspending or expelling students. Such systems were components of the new bureaucratic administration of discipline, which deemphasized personal confrontation. No longer was the malefactor called on to confess; he was just told the score. Instances of violence between students and faculty persisted, especially in the South; a professor at the University of Virginia was murdered by a student, in front of a crowd of students, in 1840. But mutinies by entire classes had become a memory by 1860.[65]

Marking systems also aimed at eliminating favoritism in a hotly competitive student culture. Distributing college honors by some combination of faculty and student opinion invited at least the appearance of favoritism. Dreading any appearance of favoritism, Quincy assigned himself the laborious task of gathering weekly reports from professors and tutors on each student before he did the addition and subtraction. Each of the marking systems devised by individual colleges in the 1820s and 1830s had its own peculiar features, but all of them relied on keeping daily records of scholarship and conduct, and they made misconduct a negative component of class standing. One immediate effect of their implementation was to elevate the importance of recitations, the most humdrum of all student activities, in determining rank. Calling for correctness rather than brilliance, recitations offered few opportunities for display. An excellent record in recitation was just the sum of many correct answers. In contrast to Thayer, who based marks primarily on periodic oral examinations and who used recitation marks to break ties, Quincy made performance in daily recitation the centerpiece of his marking system. In Quincy's eyes, rank would no longer depend "on occasional brilliant success, but on the steady, uniform, satisfactory performance of each exercise."[66]

Coming from opposite directions, Kendall, a Republican who became a Jacksonian Democrat, and Quincy, truly a diehard Federalist (his biographer called him the "last Federalist"), reached negative conclusions about the collegiate culture of reputation. Kendall discovered that reputation was really just transient popularity. Quincy, who belonged to the family that lorded over young John Adams in Braintree, was haunted by the thought that anything so sacred as rank could be subject to a vote. He attacked the "wickedly aspiring," and he was determined to make Harvard the one place in America where "worth and merit shall be measured by something other than the polls."[67]

The features of American marking systems come into sharper focus when they are contrasted with Cambridge University's Tripos. By 1830, after nearly a century of evolution, the Tripos consisted of two written examinations, the Mathematical Tripos and, after 1824, the Classical Tripos. Reflecting the legacy of Isaac Newton, the former, which included natural philosophy, was the more prestigious. Until 1850 a candidate for honors in the classics had first to secure a place in at least the lowest honors classification on the Mathematical Tripos, the so-called junior *optimes*, but his rank on the Classical Tripos did not otherwise reflect his performance on the Mathematical Tripos, while a candidate for mathematical honors could skip the Classical Tripos. Cambridge's emphasis on mathematics helps to explain its early use of written examinations, which dated to 1740, for it was difficult to test mathematics orally.[68]

The Tripos was probably the most ferociously competitive examination in the history of the English-speaking world. Each examination lasted a week. Examiners moved among the tables in the university's unheated Senate House—ink regularly froze overnight in its wells—distributing questions, sometimes printed but usually dictated. As soon as a "questionist" (candidate) had finished one question, he would be given another while his answer to the first question was being marked. Marks were awarded not just for correctness but for brilliance. As a way of stimulating more intense competition, questionists were grouped into brackets at the start of the examination on the basis of their previous performances in examinations and disputations. The higher one's bracket, the tougher the questions, so a student was always competing against opponents who had a chance to beat him. The practice of continuous marking made it possible to arrange the candidates into new brackets after the first few days of the examination, and a questionist unhappy with his bracket could challenge one higher to a kind of playoff. At the conclusion of each examination (mathematical and classical) the marks of each candidate were summed. The sums often ran into thousands of points. Candidates then were arranged in an order of merit. First came the "wranglers"; the highest scorer was listed as the senior wrangler. Next in the descending order of merit came the senior *optimes* and finally the junior *optimes*. A few candidates, such as future prime minister William Gladstone in 1831, won the coveted "double-first" as senior wrangler on both examinations.[69]

The quest for Tripos honors resembled a horse race. As interim results were posted, students placed bets on the final outcome. "The senior wrangler," Leslie Stephens wrote in 1865, "is the winner of the Derby."[70] Glory and money were the rewards for high wranglers on either examination.[71] Their names were "published in all the London papers," wrote an American who sat for the Tripos in the 1840s, "as regularly as the Queen's last drive, or the Spanish Queen's last revolution."[72] As long as a high wrangler subscribed to the doctrines of the Church of England, a requirement becoming controversial by the 1830s but persisting until the 1870s, he was assured of a fellowship, a share of his college's endowment which might be worth as much as £2500 a year for life, with no stipulated duties.[73] The stakes were high, but charges of favoritism rarely clouded the outcomes of the Tripos. Cambridge's colleges engaged in fierce rivalry; an examiner from, say Trinity College, might favor Trinity questionists. But the presence of so many examiners from rival colleges checked favoritism.[74]

The differences between the Cambridge Tripos and the practice of American colleges were profound. American colleges started to introduce written examinations only in the 1830s. No American college installed an examination and marking system even remotely comparable to the Tripos. In *Hereditary Genius* (1869) Francis Galton, Charles Darwin's cousin and the founder of eugenics, used the enormous difference between the highest and lowest number of marks gained by Cantabridgians on the honors list, as much as a factor of thirty-two, to prove that the differences among men in natural ability were vast.[75] But the American marking systems did not aim to distinguish differences in ability. All of the American systems conflated scholarship and conduct to determine rank; none of them awarded points for brilliance. The total number of points attainable under Quincy's Scale of Comparative Merit was high, but only because so many student activities unrelated to academic ability, such as attending recitation or chapel, were allotted points. Quincy opposed ranking students solely by academic distinction. During the 1820s Ticknor had proposed sectioning Harvard classes (for recitation) by academic proficiency; indeed, Ticknor would have been happy to see academic classes (freshmen, sophomores, etc.) abolished. But Quincy's predecessor, Joseph Kirkland, and the faculty blocked sectioning by proficiency, and Quincy did not revive the idea.[76] So, contrary to Ticknor's ideal, sharp and dull students continued to recite together.

These differences between Cambridge and American colleges can be explained in various ways. Examinations at both Cambridge and Oxford became much more daunting after the French Revolution, which impressed Englishmen with the need to sharpen the wits and boost the energy of their own ruling class. Fearing the godlessness of the French Revolution more than its egalitarianism, American educators responded by promoting religious revivals among collegians, and the low-church Protestant clergymen who headed most colleges targeted the wayward more than the brilliant students. In addition, the financial resources of England's ancient universities greatly exceeded those of American colleges, which lacked the endowments to fund the fellowships that attended academic success in England. For example, Yale's Berkeley prize yielded an income of less than $50 a year for up to three years, conditioned on residence in New Haven. The American system of using commencement parts as rewards for merit cost essentially nothing.

The number and extent of rewards also distinguished England's ancient universities from the American colleges. The majority of Cantabridgians, roughly two-thirds of each graduating class, made no effort to win honors. Rather, they were content to belong to the Poll (from *polloi*, the many) and graduate only with a degree. By all accounts the academic demands made on the Poll were negligible; Anthony Trollope was among the commentators who thought that the academic requirements for Oxford and Cambridge students who sought an "ordinary" degree were less than those imposed on average American collegians. To seek honors was, in effect, to volunteer for a hazardous mission, and any number of Cantabridgians who went on to luminous intellectual careers, including William Wordsworth and Charles Darwin, elected to watch the game rather than to play it. When it came to honors, American colleges also had their bystanders, but the proportion of graduating seniors to win a part at commencement was higher than in England. At new colleges it was the custom to give all seniors parts at commencement in order to build public support for the college. Established colleges were more selective but far from restrictive; the proportion of graduating seniors to be awarded commencement parts ranged from one-third to two-thirds. At Quincy's Harvard those whose cumulative score put them in the top half of their graduating class received parts.[77]

Marks led to orders of merit, but in contrast to the Tripos, during which questionists learned their standing on an almost hourly basis, the American custom was to keep students in the dark about their class rank. This had been the case even before the rise of marking systems. In 1787 John Quincy Adams observed that Harvard students eagerly awaited the government's announcement of parts in periodic exhibitions and at commencement because only then could they surmise their class rank. "My appointment, they tell me, is considered the fourth in the class," a surprised Henry Wadsworth Longfellow wrote of the part assigned him in Bowdoin's 1825 commencement. "How I came to be so high, is rather a mystery to me, in as much as I have never been a remarkably hard student, touching College studies."[78] The rise of marking systems changed nothing on this count. William Gardiner Hammond, an Amherst student who sought highest honors in the 1840s, related that a Latin tutor marked each recitation with a number, "denoting its degree of merit, and the general average of these settles the student's standing. But this is kept secret from them."[79] As late as the 1860s instructors at Yale used ciphers to compile recitation marks in their "score-book," so that a student who got hold of the book could make no sense of it.[80]

The mystery surrounding rank, the strangeness of this horse race in which neither jockeys nor spectators knew the position of the contenders until the finish line, is puzzling. One of the main functions of marking systems was to establish an unarguable standard for awarding graduation honors. The Thayer and Quincy marking scales were obsessively detailed, but other systems were far from vague. When Yale started to mark recitations in 1813, it employed a 1–20 scale, calculated to two decimal places, so really a 400-point scale. Under Quincy's system a student would learn his class standing at the end of each academic year. At other colleges students sailing close to suspension or expulsion were told their standing. Yet the usual practice was minimalist; a student would learn his relative rank only if some reason required informing him.

Keeping students in the dark may have been a way to stop them from resting on previous laurels, but this is unlikely since students scarcely knew which laurels they were already wearing. More likely, it reflected the ambivalence of college governments about "emulation."[81] Suspicion of emulation, that Janus-faced coin that could so easily be flipped to the side that read bitter envy, was deeply ingrained in the values of the low-church Protestant clergymen who ran the colleges. College governments encouraged rivalry between student literary societies, at least as long as there were only two of them, as a way to defang individualistic competition and its concomitants like envy and ambition. Governments also continued to promote the solidarity of each academic class, even after the decline of colonial customs like "trimming" (hazing) and fagging, which had been enforced by college authorities. Fearing anything that exalted an individual student, college governments encouraged the bonding of each academic class. In 1804 Yale president Timothy Dwight secured the abolition of fagging, but the Yale faculty, persuaded that trimming was necessary to ensure the subordination of freshmen "from rude towns and families," blocked his plan to eliminate hazing. Oxford and Cambridge were congeries of colleges whose champions competed for university honors. The college taught; the university examined. In contrast, the American college, even if it called itself a university (as Harvard did after 1824), was a free-standing institution with no division between teaching and examining. Whereas a Cambridge student's loyalty was to his college, an American collegian's "patriotism" was to his class.

College governments were reluctant to take any action likely to undermine class unity, which the continuous publicizing of rank threatened. For example, students' charges that Phi Beta Kappa encouraged a "discrimination" among the students had long clouded the status of its chapter at Harvard. In 1789 a committee of the Overseers, chaired by John Hancock, concluded that Phi Beta Kappa's overall effect was salutary because, as Quincy later wrote, "literary merit was assumed as the principle on which its members were selected."[82] The goal of maintaining class solidarity led Harvard to inter Ticknor's plan to section the class by proficiency. There is no evidence that students opposed this and much to indicate they approved it. In the early 1820s students in the Greek class of Ticknor's friend George Bancroft, future secretary of the navy, had rebelled when Bancroft tried to initiate sectioning by proficiency rather than alphabetically.[83] Among the objections students launched against Quincy's Scale of Comparative Merit was that it eroded class unity.

Ambivalence is the mot juste when it comes to describing the authorities' view of emulation. At Harvard, Bancroft championed sectioning by proficiency, but in 1821, a year before he accepted a position at Harvard, he wrote that "emulation must be most carefully avoided, excepting the general and mutual desire of excelling in virtue." No one "ought to be rewarded at the expense of another," for those who fail to win prizes "may have been impeded by the nature of their talents, and not by their own want of exertion."[84] This widely held view—it united Transcendentalists like Bancroft with low-church Protestants—maintained that talents came from God and deserved no reward; success resulting from individual exertion was meritorious. There was nothing new in this idea, but it is impossible to measure its acceptance throughout the society. A general who won a battle or a politician who won an election could always attribute his success to his virtuous concern for the public good. Schools and colleges were microcosms of society in some respects, but factors like ability and effort were easier to disaggregate in educational institutions, and the tendency of marking systems to elevate the importance of recitations in determining class rank has to be scored as a victory for effort rather than ability. In short, effort was the ground of "proficiency."

Honors are valued to the extent that the activity honored is valued, and in this respect England's ancient universities and the American colleges presented a striking contrast. Charles Astor Bristed, a wealthy New Yorker (related to John Jacob Astor) who attended Yale from 1835 to 1839 and Trinity College, Cambridge, from 1841 to 1844, immediately recognized that at Cambridge the system of university examinations, crowned by the Tripos, formed "the staple and life of the whole system," the only standard of merit.[85] Success depended on knowledge, and "reading men" were valued. At Cambridge there were no rewards for "disconnected and single exhibitions of brilliancy," in contrast to Yale and other colleges, where the "dazzling" performance, composing and speaking a part in an exhibition, was treasured.[86] Bristed would have been happy to see Yale abolish its Junior Exhibition, but he added that for the government to have done so would have provoked a student insurrection because of the political character of the student culture. American collegians were apt to compare winning an election to the presidency of a college literary society with winning a seat in the state legislature. Just getting a door closed in a college residence hall required a quasi-legislative procedure ("I move that Mr. Smith be a committee of one to close the door"). Compared with English students, whose diffidence Bristed traced to their awareness of what they did not know, American collegians were "precocious" in the ease they displayed around adults. Bristed attributed this to "our national over-encouragement of oratory" and to the predilection of American collegians to take their cues from public men, especially the latter's "habit of talking and writing about things of which they have but small knowledge."[87]

To state Bristed's point more abstractly, there were differences between the British and American reward structures. In 1842 Brown University president Francis Wayland asserted that in no other country "is the whole plan for the instruction of the young so entirely dissevered from the business of subsequent life." Scholarly distinction as such was little valued, in contrast to the European continent, where gaining offices "of honor and emolument" required high university standing. Wayland recognized that Britain formed a special case, since a Cambridge fellowship did not lead directly to political preferment. Fellowships were useful principally for those who contemplated careers in the national church or a university professorship or the headmastership of an endowed school and who were willing to remain celibate for the duration of their fellowship. Still, a high wrangler became famous within the circles that mattered in Britain, a nation whose elite, in Wayland's estimation, "form one great family." The American situation, where there was no national church and where securing a college professorship scarcely required a national reputation (the very thing awarded a high wrangler), was profoundly different. Wayland concluded that the American college "forms no integral and necessary part of the social system."[88]

Wayland proposed various remedies, including publishing the rank of each student at the close of each term and establishing a system of cash premiums for scholarly distinction, to spur scholarly competition. But where the sources of authority were mainly regional or local, the boundaries of civil society at once expansive and amorphous, and the attraction of public life keen—in other words, in the United States—collegians did not require the prospect of national fame or direct access to positions of preferment or a chance for contemplative study to induce them to compete.

The introduction of marks changed the character of college competition. The immediate effect of marks was to strip students of any say in the award of parts, which now was based on a student's class standing. Commenting on Harvard's 1843 commencement, Rev. John Pierce, who attended nearly every Harvard commencement from 1784 to 1848 and who commented in his diary on the performance of each part ("eloquent," "mediocre," "Coleridgian" and hence "dreamy," or just "too long"), observed that one of the graduates, Thomas Hill (a future president of Harvard), delivered an English oration that was "so eloquent I thought he would have the first assignment in the class," but Hill had been "exceeded in recitation exercises by [Horace Binney] Sargent, whose attention had been perseveringly and uninterruptedly devoted to the attainment of the first honor."[89] Marking systems aroused student protests during the 1830s. In 1834 most Harvard students in each class signed a protest against Quincy's Scale of Comparative Merit. The freshman protest, signed by David Henry Thoreau among others (Thoreau later reversed his given names), blasted the system for arousing "envy and jealousy" among the students at a time when "literary standing must depend on something more than mere college rank."[90] Similarly, Amherst's Gorham Rebellion erupted in 1838 when nearly all members of the three upper classes signed a petition, five feet long, calling for either the distribution of parts to all students or the abolition of the whole system of "distinctive and honorary appointments."[91]

These protests are open to interpretation. They can be read as affirmations of egalitarianism—everyone should have a part—or as rejections of basing parts on marks because by ignoring the display of genius, marks failed to calibrate true merit. Recitations continued to form the main basis of marks, but by the 1830s performance on the newly introduced written examinations also counted. Their advocates praised written examinations for their fairness, since each student now had to answer the same question, rather than, as in a recitation, a different one, and for testing the range and depth of a student's knowledge. Students disliked them, probably for the same reasons. In 1831 Yale students smashed their inkstands against the side of the examination hall on exiting a written examination.

We should also allow for the ambivalence of student opinion. William S. Tyler, an Amherst graduate and a faculty member before, during, and after the Gorham Rebellion, wrote that some of the petitioners were unhappy with the parts assigned them while others objected to the whole system of appointments.[92] Ambivalence fairly describes Harvard's Richard Henry Dana Jr., who would achieve instant fame in 1840 with the publication of *Two Years before the Mast.* In his journal, written five years after his graduation in 1837, Dana recollected that he so loathed Quincy's system that he cherished the memory of his rustication to Andover in 1832 for his participation in a chapel disturbance. He could "hardly describe the relief I felt at getting rid of the exciting emulation for college rank, and at being able to study for the good of my own mind, not the sixes, sevens, and eights, which, at Cambridge, were set against every word that came out of a student's mouth," and he compared his return to Harvard to "a slave whipped to his dungeon."[93] Yet his journal also recorded his delight at rising from fifteenth to seventh in his class by the end of his sophomore year and his disappointment in not securing a commencement part commensurate with his class rank (he was the victim of a technicality).[94]

If Dana is any indication, students who disliked marking systems learned to work within them and to compete for appointments. But by severing the relationship between a student's reputation among his peers and his academic rank, marking systems removed a key motive for competing for rank, whether one defines this motive as seeking public flattery or seeking the self-validation about one's "genius" that attended peer acknowledgment. As long as a student's merit depended on his reputation among his peers, and as long as college governments took reputations into account when allotting parts, any determination of merit was bound to involve favoritism, for what could reputation be but the sum of qualities attributed to an individual by others? Those qualities had to be displayed in public and assessed by the witnessing public. Although targeting favoritism above all else, marking systems undercut reputation as the basis of rewards.

Students still accepted parts when offered them, but the traditional forums of student competition were gradually losing their resonance. By the late antebellum years the student literary societies were widely acknowledged to be in decline, and neither exhibitions nor commencements were faring well. In 1871 Lyman Hotchkiss Bagg of Yale's class of 1869 described Yale's Junior Exhibition and commencement, long public galas, as shadows of their former selves. Consisting mainly of students, their relatives, and girlfriends, the public that now attended these events was narrower than in 1800 and 1820, and many students who were assigned parts no longer performed them. Similar developments occurred at Harvard, where the custom of assigning nonperformed parts dated to the 1840s and where students increasingly treated commencement with detached amusement. In the 1840s Harvard students who were ranked in the bottom half of their class began to stage a burlesque commencement at the Navy Club in Boston. In charivari fashion, the lowest became the highest: the student most frequently disciplined was deemed the Lord High Admiral; the laziest, the Rear Admiral; the most profane, the chaplain; and so on.[95]

The New Age

Students continued to seek validation from their peers, but increasingly by election to the Greek-letter fraternities that spread like a prairie fire from campus to campus in the 1830s, the very time when marking systems were taking root. Several features of the early Greek societies distinguished them from their modern descendants. Far from having residence houses, the early fraternities were secret societies that shielded themselves from the hostile gaze of college governments by shrouding their membership and procedures in mystery. At times, they professed "literary" aims, but literature usually took a backseat to cards, singing, and terrifying initiation rites.

The early Greek societies nevertheless thought of themselves as honor societies because they competed to enlist the students highly reputed among their classmates, the college's "big men." To win a prestigious appointment or an essay contest remained a legitimate avenue to bigness. So did election to literary-society office. Typically, a Greek fraternity would form a voting bloc to win elections for members to literary-society offices. As Bagg recognized, no relation existed between faculty and students rankings of merit. Class standing (called "stand" at Yale) as such counted for nothing when Greek fraternities chose members. Rather, a Greek society valued the stand of its members only to the extent that it helped them secure prestigious exhibition parts, and even exhibition parts gradually became less significant to the fraternities than success in a campus essay contest, especially, according to Bagg, when won by a student thought to have low stand. As Bagg observed, in the absence of the Greek societies "these honors and prizes would lose a good share of their value, since their chief attractiveness consists of their supposed efficacy in securing [Greek] society elections for their winners."[96]

Bagg was describing the end of one era and the beginning of a new one. Just when the old era ended varied from college to college; as is often true of historical change, the old and the new ran on parallel tracks for a few decades before the old era's extinction. What can be said is that from the Revolution well into the antebellum era, competition for rewards in the colleges resembled competition in public life in several ways.

In 1829 Samuel Lorenzo Knapp recalled the era of the Revolution as a time when "all the ambitious were striving to be statesmen; and no other path to distinction was open." Born in 1783, Knapp had achieved minor distinction as a lawyer, newspaper editor, and orator on public occasions, just the sort of public activities that had expanded after the Revolution. In the wake of the Revolution, collegians primarily sought public distinctions, distinctions that were earned by performances in public at recitations and literary-society debates and orations, and bestowed at public events like exhibitions and commencements. Like public men, collegians were sensitive to their reputations and expected consensual recognition by their peers and elders of their meritorious qualities. Consensus was important because it gave the lie to the charge that a successful candidate for honors owed his success to his ambition and cunning. Like Andrew Jackson and many other public men, collegians believed that their triumphs resulted from unsolicited verdicts. To the extent that college governments allowed students a voice in awarding honors to each other, they encouraged consensus, and to the extent that students participated in one or another of a college's rival literary societies, they kept up the appearance, and at times also the substance, of seeking honors for the good (reputation) of their group.

4

MAKING THE GRADE

Managed Competition and Schooling

As long as merit was equated with significant public achievements and with talents capable of public display, it was difficult to imagine gradations of merit among ordinary people. Patriot writers of the Revolutionary era maintained that American conditions were uniquely conducive to the achievement of a "competency," an achievable medium between misery and abundance.[1] The ideal of securing a competency neither invited comparisons between one person and another nor encouraged a view of life as an endless competition among the common people.[2]

By the 1790s some Europeans were describing an excessive love of wealth as an American trait, but Joel Barlow, the Republican poet and cultural nationalist, brushed aside this criticism. If some Americans were greedy, he argued, the cause lay in the fading residue of British colonialism; purity was native, corruption foreign.[3] In so responding, Barlow was aligning himself with the ingrained view that no American should be criticized for seeking betterment since the attraction of America lay in its opportunities for gaining a "competency." In contrast, during the second quarter of the nineteenth century anxiety arose in many American quarters about the demoralizing effects of unrestrained competition for riches among ordinary citizens. In response, public educators, hostile to individualistic competition that created a loser for every winner, devised a system of graded, free schools that would come to be recognized by Europeans as a uniquely American system of mass education based on equal rights. In this system, "managed competition" aimed to instill aspirations to self-betterment in children without any experience of personal triumph over others. The ideal of these public schoolmen was not the merit of the First Characters of the Founding era, the package of total superiority. Rather, their ideal resembled Sylvanus Thayer's merit system at West Point and Josiah Quincy's Scale of Comparative Merit at Harvard, for they envisioned merit as the product of small, different, and measurable units. These units included school subjects like arithmetic and English and moral traits like industry and promptness. Decomposing merit into sundry parts put it within the reach of average children.

The Transformation

Starting in the 1820s writers in many fields began to complain about "emulation" as a national disease. These writers equated emulation with the nearly universal desire of Americans to surpass each other in the accumulation of wealth. To be sure, favorable assessments of emulation continued to appear in print. In 1836 Joseph Cogswell, cofounder (with George Bancroft) of the elite Round Hill Academy in Northampton, Massachusetts, linked emulation to the benefits that naturally accrue to superiority in knowledge, virtue, and ability, and he criticized the students at Amherst and Dartmouth who were attacking the system of commencement parts. Collegians valued their "literary reputations" as qualifications for public office, and any hint that they would allow envy to rule competition was a "libel" on them. Cogswell concluded that attacks on competition were the pedagogical equivalent of "radicalism and agrarianism," which would reduce everyone to a dead level of uniformity.[4] Cogswell, who drew all of his examples from the colleges, acknowledged that the tenor of opinion in school periodicals had turned against him, and on this count he was right.

When Horace Mann became the secretary of the newly founded Massachusetts Board of Education in 1837, the preponderance of opinion among writers on pedagogy had been shifting against emulation for about a decade. These writers equated emulation with the desire for "personal superiority" over a competitor, and they alleged it bred envy and discord.[5] No sudden change of the word's meaning accounts for this; dictionary definitions of emulation had long portrayed it as both a spur to excellence and an incubator of envy. But during the 1830–60 period nearly everyone writing for school journals fastened on the latter connotation. When in January 1848 an article defending emulation and school prizes as appropriate preparation for "the great drama of life" appeared in the *Massachusetts Teacher* (the organ of the Massachusetts Teachers Association), it drew such a cascade of criticism from readers that the editors apologized in the February issue for having published it and claimed that somehow the article made it into print because the editorial board had neglected to read it.[6]

Public educators who bashed emulation feared that children who competed for school prizes would succumb in adulthood to the epidemic of greed seemingly sweeping America. In 1840 Alexis de Tocqueville speculated that in democracies "most human passions either end in the love of riches or proceed from it."[7] Americans valued wealth as the only acceptable basis of distinction in a democracy, where reverence for the past, birth, and calling scarcely distinguished one person from another. William Gouge, the best-informed Jacksonian Democrat on currency issues and a foe of banks, wrote that in the United States "talent is estimated only as a means of acquiring wealth," and "wealth alone can give permanent distinction, for he who is at the top of the political ladder today, may be at the bottom tomorrow."[8] Freeman Hunt, editor of *Hunt's Merchants' Magazine* and a friend of many bankers, concluded that in America "there remains but one basis of social distinction, namely wealth." Aristocracies of talent, education, and refinement could flourish off the beaten path, "but in society at large, gradations of social position are measured by stock certificates, rent rolls, a bank account." In a nation where seeking public office was an uncertain venture, "wealth has gained an importance far beyond that which belongs to it where it is used only to keep up an estate and display rank, to enjoy life, to procure advantages of education and of travel." In America, wealth "creates rank; it gives social position, even without antecedent respectability or correct education; and hence pride and vanity, that in other countries have so many and varied outlets, here crowd into one channel."[9]

Hunt knew whereof he spoke. Biographical directories like Moses Yale Beach's *Wealth and Biography of the Citizens of New York City* were starting to rank their subjects by their net worth. The appearance of this and similar volumes in other major cities coincided with the rise of the first credit-rating agencies, themselves a testimonial to the increasingly depersonalized character of economic transactions. Many Americans celebrated competition as the way to spur economic development and to identify merit. The first edition of Beach's compilation in the 1840s functioned more as a guide to credit ratings than as an order of merit, but between this edition and the twelfth in 1855 Beach added biographical details and inspirational commentary to show that the talents once displayed in war and conquest now could be found in the countinghouse. Beach led a trend, persisting for decades, to construct orders of merit based on wealth, especially the wealth of "self-made" men.[10] Others worried that the economy was coming to resemble a gigantic lottery that spun off rewards by chance. Legislatures reacted in contradictory ways. Most states banned lotteries between 1815 and 1840 in an attempt to extinguish the gambling spirit.[11] At the same time, legislatures made it easier for insolvents to cancel their debts and they acknowledged that failure was an unavoidable product of risk taking. On visiting America in 1830, Tocqueville's traveling companion Gustave de Beaumont was advised never to bring up the subject of bankruptcy in polite society, since most present were likely to have declared bankruptcy at some point.[12] Edward Balleisen has estimated that at least one in three and perhaps one in two antebellum business proprietors eventually succumbed to an insupportable load of debt; during the thirteen months of operation of the federal Bankruptcy Act of 1841, roughly one in every one hundred white men in the United States came before the federal courts as a debtor.[13]

Just Deserts

Reflecting the influence of David Ricardo, the founder of what Karl Marx later called the British school of classical economics, American writers began the systematic analysis of economic issues during the 1820s. Like Ricardo, they looked into the relative contributions of the so-called factors of production—land, labor, and capital—and into the distribution of the national product into rent, wages, and profit. American economists nevertheless faced a distinctive challenge; they had to reconcile economic developments with the nation's founding ideals and especially with the principle of equal rights.[14] Applied to economic endeavors, equal rights meant that merit should be the only basis for rewards: economic rewards should match the economic contributions of individuals, and social inequalities should reflect individual differences in merit. One would expect this from upholders of the existing social order, but critics said much the same. As early as 1799 in *The Key of Liberty*, William Manning, a former antifederalist and self-taught and self-conscious advocate of the lowly, averred that because of the great range of capacities among men, "there will always be a very unequal distribution of property in the world."[15] Like the idea that Europeans were worse off than Americans because monarchies and courts siphoned off the fruits of honest labor, this idea had considerable staying power. The broad acceptance of this principle shaped American thinking for at least a century after 1820. Eventually, American economists would embrace marginal-productivity theory with unique enthusiasm and feminists would rally behind the banner "Equal Pay for Equal Work" because each promised to bring the nation closer to the ideal of just deserts.[16]

Compared with Americans, British writers were less inclined to construe wealth as a mark of merit, which is hardly surprising in a society where social rank, while dependent on wealth, relied on so much beyond wealth. Even in 1869, when Britain's preeminence in manufacturing had established it as the leading world power, Francis Galton's *Hereditary Genius*, which contended that "genius," superior talent and capacity for exertion, ran in families, rested its case on the lives of eminent statesmen, warriors, artists, poets, scientists, and jurists. But Galton said nothing about manufacturers or merchants. Although trade carried less of a taint in England than on the European continent, in no Western nation would it acquire the glow that surrounded it in nineteenth-century America. Neither Galton nor his cousin Charles Darwin came from nobility. Rather, their families had achieved eminence in the professions, manufacturing, and commerce, and both Galton and Darwin held Whig-Liberal views in politics. Along with like-minded Englishmen, they championed free trade, the rights of Dissenters, antislavery, and careers open to talents. But when they thought of talents, those relevant to business did not spring to their minds.

The distinctiveness of the American approach can be clarified by distinguishing *merit* from *desert*. Since merit implies rewards that are deserved, merit and desert appear to be inseparable. Yet British sociologist Keith Hope wrote in 1984 that "when Americans talk about merit, they really mean *desert*."[17] In the English context, Hope contended, the modern ideal of merit originated in the "swamp of frustration" felt by the leading members of the middle class toward the end of the eighteenth century. These people, mostly Dissenters, experienced the sting of exclusion. Barred from matriculating at Oxford and Cambridge, they gained a superior education at Dissenting academies. They made money in trade and the professions, but their exclusion from the highest offices of state left them without influence on public policy. Their "ideology of merit was the collective belief of a meritorious group that they were being excluded from public employment which, given the chance, they would carry out . . . with much greater address and efficiency than the hangers-on of the aristocracy who currently monopolized them."[18]

Late eighteenth-century America did not contain a counterpart to this class, that is, a group that was well-educated, self-conscious, eager for office, and excluded. To the extent that America gave rise to an ideology of merit during the Founding era, it was the property of the self-styled Men of Merit. Highly diverse in their religious, regional, and class origins, these men thought that they deserved office as a reward for their contributions to the Revolution. Their antifederalist opponents conceded their merit but, reflecting the pervasive republican suspicion of authority, distrusted them precisely because their merit was so conspicuous. The perceived task in the early republic was not removing barriers that blocked merit from rising. Rather, it was to restrain the exercise of power by any well-organized and ambitious body of men, whether the Cincinnati, the Federalists, the Republicans, or the Masons.

Although Americans have tended to use merit and desert interchangeably, desert carries somewhat different connotations. Merit implies some sort of selection of individuals by a superior body. Hope compares it with justification by grace and, completing the Calvinist analogy, substitutes "meritelection" for the modern "meritocracy." On the other hand, desert (and Hope even refers to "desertocracy") connotes a society where each person's rewards, primarily economic, correspond to his "inputs" (for want of a better term), his skill and effort. In Hope's analogy, desert resembles justification by works. In principle, works righteousness is universally accessible, at least in America; its connotations approximate those of the American Dream.

By the Jacksonian era, American ideas about rewards for economic efforts, desert, were becoming engulfed in controversy. But it was an odd sort of controversy. The occasional Henry David Thoreau might argue that Americans should learn to live with less, but the real controversy revolved around a different question: were ordinary Americans receiving economic rewards calibrated to their skills and efforts, or were these rewards being stolen by a conspiracy of the few, the financiers and speculators whom John Taylor, the Virginia Republican and soul mate of Jefferson, dubbed the "Paper Aristocracy"? Taylor contrasted the owners of "substantial, real, or honest property" arising from "fair and useful industry and talents" with those fraudulent property holders who had taken advantage of "privilege, hierarchy, paper, charter, and sinecure."[19] These were the new and homegrown equivalents of the royal placemen.

A planter who by 1798 owned an estate of over two thousand acres and more than sixty slaves, Taylor never advocated equalizing property. Any move in that direction, he warned, would throw farmers, who merited their rewards and who were too isolated from each other to combine against the public good, into a defensive alliance with the Paper Aristocracy and the demonic engine that supported it, Alexander Hamilton's Bank of the United States. While serving in the U.S. Senate from 1792 to 1794, Taylor foreshadowed the attacks on the Bank later mounted by Jacksonians. Pillaging the productive classes, the Bank illustrated how the wealthy were ever seeking to acquire something for nothing and effectively violated the republican principle that wealth be distributed "by merit and industry."[20]

Hostile to banks, monopoly, and paper money, Taylor's ideals eventually became orthodoxy among mainstream Jacksonian Democrats. Much like Taylor, Jacksonians envisioned a "natural" economy based on exchanges between small producers—farmers and artisans—and they extolled competition, whether in politics or business, as liberating. "Each man," wrote Theodore Sedgwick Jr. in 1836, "should have perfect freedom, unrestrained by monopoly and unjust privilege, to exert his talents and to rise to any height he can."[21] True, there would be winners and losers in all competitions, but most Democrats thought that differences among whites were modest and would diminish as competition spurred each citizen to discover and cultivate his abilities. Indeed, the rival Whigs often attacked Democrats for minimizing individual differences.[22]

Just as Democrats viewed their political leaders (after Jackson) as interchangeable servants of their party, they rejected the idea that one person's economic contribution deserved exponentially greater rewards than another's. The persistence of legislated privilege alone enabled the few to accumulate wealth far out of proportion to their talents and exertions. Jackson himself proclaimed in 1832, in his message vetoing recharter of the Bank of the United States, that the common people had no cause for complaint as long as governments did not add privileges to the natural differences in merit that would lead some to accumulate more than others.[23]

Most Democrats most of the time believed that mass literacy and universal white manhood suffrage were sufficient remedies for the evils of legislated privilege. Banish privilege, and natural competition would prevail. Yet an undercurrent of doubt leaked into Jacksonian thought.[24] Jeffersonians had warned of tendencies. For example, Taylor cautioned that five thousand Americans were *seeking* to enrich themselves at the expense of five million; in the tradition of classical republican thought, he drew his examples of predatory behavior from ancient Rome or Renaissance republics rather than from his own society. In contrast, confronted as much with realities as tendencies, during and after the Panic of 1837 mainstream Jacksonians turned to attacks on paper money. John L. O'Sullivan, a leading Democratic editor, wrote in 1840 that wealth acquired by the movements of paper money "controlled by a few gambling speculators" could never be "the test of merit." "Merit" became "a mere evanescent quality. The only standard of character is to be found in the quotations of a board of brokers."[25]

Along with other Jacksonians, O'Sullivan then added a psychological dimension by contending that paper money tempted ordinary Americans into an otherwise unnatural level of speculative enterprises. The problem, in other words, lay not only in the pillaging of the many by the few but also in the susceptibility of the many to the vices of the few. Echoing a point Jackson had made in his 1832 message vetoing recharter of the Bank, O'Sullivan still believed that, absent legislated privilege, rewards would follow merit and that economic ruin would be the natural "requital of ill-desert."[26] But he added that wherever rewards were based on merit, the bitterness spawned by "the deadly animosity of classes feeling themselves equal" would shrink.

Competition and Public School Reform

Defining the problem as illicit privilege, the remedy for which lay in the ballot box, the sacristy of the American republic, Democrats supported public schools less as agencies of social betterment than as institutions that guarded individual rights by diffusing literacy.[27] Targeting illicit privilege as the source of social conflict, Orestes A. Brownson and other leading Democrat intellectuals argued that, contrary to Whig expectations, free schools would not dissolve social tensions by teaching different social classes to cooperate.[28]

Admittedly, generalizations about such diverse coalitions as the antebellum political parties are risky. School reformers often complained about partisanship; their allegiance was to reform more than to a party. Some conservative Democrats like Robert Rantoul Jr. of Massachusetts embraced the agenda of the public-school reformers. But in state legislatures Whigs gave much more consistent backing to the reform agenda—including central state boards of education, state tax support for public schools, and graded schools—than did Democrats, who were more likely to back locally controlled, ungraded schools.[29] Rantoul, in fact, was the only Democrat on the Massachusetts Board of Education, established in 1837 and headed by Horace Mann. Mann's annual reports from 1837 to 1848 established his national reputation. Reforms that first sprouted in Massachusetts spread across the northern tier of settlement between 1840 and 1900. In place of ungraded schools that occasionally intersected the lives of children, reformers would develop systems of graded schools that would be as coextensive with the lives of children as conditions would permit.

There are striking parallels between the way in which reformers envisioned advancement in schools and the way in which Whigs envisioned economic development as the rising tide that would lift all ships. Where Democrats saw a self-sufficient economy of small producers, Whigs saw a backward nation in need of state action to improve the standard of living "as a sufficient form of compensation for the existence of social distinctions."[30] Compared with Jacksonians, Whigs were less impressed by America's natural resources, especially land, than by its dearth of capital.[31] Whigs viewed capital accumulation as the basis of progress. Northern Whigs, usually protectionists, contended that factory laborers learned new skills on the job, which gave them leverage—they could threaten to leave for self-employment—to pry higher wages from their employers. Horace Mann described factories as merit-based hierarchies in which workers were rewarded according to their skill and effort.[32]

Whenever their projects drew fire, school reformers renewed their association between schooling and economic development. In his 1841 annual report, written in the turbid wake of a narrowly unsuccessful attempt by rural Democrats and evangelicals to abolish the Massachusetts Board of Education, Mann reported the results of a rather loaded questionnaire that he had sent to the state's manufacturers, who had predictably responded that they preferred sober, educated, and industrious workers to intemperate illiterates.[33] The school reformers were sure that schooling would economically empower and morally renovate its beneficiaries, which in principle meant the entire free population. Universal free schooling led to progress; the absence of free schools explained backwardness. Why did England produce more food than Africa? Because the English possessed some free schools. Why were Americans paid higher wages than the English? Because the United States had more free schools.[34]

Although soldering the connection between schools and economic development, neither Mann nor other reformers proposed the direct teaching of trade skills. "Industrial" education was reserved for delinquents, defectives, and dependents rather than for the children of responsible citizens. Instead, schools imparted "character," habitual rectitude. Northern Whig economists and educators expected free schools to produce a more disciplined and industrious work force. A point less often appreciated, they also linked character to capital formation and saw a high ratio of capital to labor as the basis of progress.

The notion that diffused moral habits could boost production had roots in the writings of conservative British interpreters of Ricardo like John R. McCulloch. McCulloch equated capital with the fruit of prolonged abstinence by the capitalist, who chose to let his profits accrue to invest in tools. McCulloch contended in 1823 that capital was "accumulated labor," and since wages remunerated labor, all profit was a form of labor. In the following year James Mill incorporated this "abstinence theory" of profit into his *Elements of Political Economy*; his son, John Stuart Mill, would eventually incorporate it into his *Principles of Political Economy*.[35] In America northern Whigs embraced this line of thinking because it established the ultimate harmony of interests between capital and labor (an important point for Whigs since they knew that not all citizens would immediately share the benefits of banks and tariffs), and they then added an insistence on the superior quality of American labor. Capital was not Adam Smith's "stock" of tools and implements but a composite of material elements and immaterial qualities that created wealth.[36] Michael Hudson has described this tendency to treat skills and ingenuity as components of political economy as a "distinctly American trait" that separated American value theory from the European mainstream.[37] Rantoul, the trophy Democrat on the Massachusetts Board of Education, characterized the possessors of skill as forming a "great interest" in society. Rantoul even put a number on it. He calculated that in 1838 the products of Massachusetts's industries and farms totaled in excess of $100 million, of which $54 million was paid to labor as wages and $18 million to capital as profit; the residue, $28 million, he classified as the reward of "talent, skill, and ingenuity."[38]

If we ask how free schools nurtured these qualities, we are led to an argument advanced by Francis Wayland, whose *Elements of Political Economy* was probably the most widely used textbook on political economy during the 1840s and 1850s. Wayland's relentless moralism led him to conclude that skill was just an intense form of human industry and that the effort to acquire knowledge was as valuable as knowledge itself. The frequency of exchange would always be proportional to the "*intelligence, wealth*, and *moral character* of a people," which would be spurred by the "universal diffusion of common education."[39]

A Whig in politics and a Unitarian in religion, Mann linked schooling primarily to moral reform through character building, an ideal articulated by his pastor, William Ellery Channing. In Whig thought, Jackson's 1836 Specie Circular had unleashed all of the shortsighted, self-seeking passions of Americans. Whig economists envisioned capital formation, the key to prosperity and progress, as the product of prolonged abstinence and steady accretion.[40] Similarly, Unitarians believed that life was a process of gradual self-improvement, often called "self-culture."[41] Unitarians criticized religious revivals for encouraging conversion experiences likely to be followed by let-downs, and they were joined in this criticism by liberals in other denominations. The most notable antebellum defense of steady accretion as the basis of spirituality, Horace Bushnell's *Christian Nurture* (1847), was the work of a liberal Congregationalist. Not surprisingly, evangelical Protestants formed a major bloc of opposition to the school reformers. As noted above, evangelical Protestants in Massachusetts, with strong backing from Democrats who resented the reformers' allegiance to state control of schools, nearly succeeded in abolishing the state board of education in 1840 and again in 1841.[42]

Under Mann's leadership, the entire Massachusetts Board of Education, including even Rantoul, was composed of Unitarians. The attacks on emulation that permeated the early school journals expressed the fear, articulated by Unitarians and shared by other liberal Christians, of individualistic competition. Channing warned that the "mighty impulses" that swept the nation stirred up "restlessness, wild schemes, extravagant speculation, a grasping spirit, ambition, and fanaticism in a thousand infectious forms."[43] Mann agreed. Republican government gave men freedom but it also unleashed "uncontrollable impetuosity," the "love of gain and the love of place," and a scramble by the many for "posts of honor and emolument which but one only can fill."[44] Aside from their shared Unitarianism, Channing and Mann expressed the common anxieties created when men who accepted the principle of deferential hierarchy that had permeated Federalist America confronted the messy egalitarianism and aggressive materialism of the 1820s and 1830s. Where deference was perceived as the norm, one man's superiority did not threaten anyone; where equality was the expectation, the desire for betterment intrinsic to emulation looked like unrestrained ambition.[45]

Yet in many ways the school reformers left the public schools more competitive than they found them. To comprehend this paradox, we need to examine the kinds of competition that reformers favored and the kinds they opposed.

It was an article of faith among reformers and their allies in the teaching profession that motivating schoolchildren to seek prizes embodied a defective pedagogy, one that elevated the importance of the quickly regurgitated answer over understanding, the knowledge of words rather than things, and the eager resort to corporal punishment rather than to the child's natural eagerness to enjoy the good opinion of "the wise and the good." In part, these sentiments reflected the influence of the Swiss reformer J. F. Pestalozzi, who emphasized teaching by objects, linking words to things, and appealing to the understanding rather than feats of memorization. In rightly constituted schools, affectionate authority would replace terror, and "moral suasion" would supplant corporal punishment.[46] Mann himself became involved in a long tangle with the masters of Boston's grammar schools, whom he thought displayed an excessive reliance on spurring competition among schoolchildren, and in 1845 Mann's allies on the Boston school committee staged a surprise attack by arriving at each of the city's nineteen grammar schools at eight o'clock in the morning and distributing 154 printed questions to the most advanced class in each school, a total of 530 students out of 7,526. Traditionally, the city's school committee had staged year-end oral examinations in each grammar school, but as Boston's population quadrupled between 1820 and 1860, oral questioning became less feasible. Mann's preference for written examinations rested on more than practical considerations. Using a strikingly up-to-date metaphor in 1845, he praised written examinations for giving a "Daguerreotype likeness" of the contents of students' minds.[47]

The results of this surprise attack dismayed Mann without really surprising him. Students answered only around 60 percent of the questions and only around 30 percent of these correctly, and even their partially correct answers revealed their defective understanding: they could date an event such as the embargo but not describe its meaning.[48] Mann was sure that the root cause of the problem lay in the reliance of the usual school competitions on some form of public approbation as a reward for achievement. On a tour of European schools in 1841 Mann had taken copious notes on their systems of competition, and he devoted part of his 1843 report to summarizing his findings. His targets included the Scottish universities, where medals and prizes were awarded even for essays on religion, and French boarding schools, where pomp and ceremony accompanied the award of prizes. He conceded that the French system, in which the reputation of each school depended on the prize scholars it sent on to universities, identified "the latent talent of the country." But this was not an important goal for Mann or other American educators, who took it for granted that under free institutions talents would rise without extraordinary intervention. The baleful moral effects of the French system impressed him more than the benefits of discovering talent. Especially disquieting for Mann was his perception that the United States "is perhaps second only to France, in the love of approbation as a prompter and guide to action."[49]

Mass politics and the mass market afford a context for understanding educators' complaints about school prizes, the sort of rewards they routinely labeled "glittering." In reality, American schools, much like American colleges, had a rather meager range of prizes to award. For example, no public school or state or local school board offered scholarships to colleges, nor would any until the 1880s. But a brief survey of existing school prizes illuminates the fear of reformers. These prizes included the Franklin medals, awarded by Boston's city council since the late eighteenth century to superior male students in the city's grammar schools. One recipient recalled that on winning a Franklin medal in the late 1820s, he and all the other winners were invited to a celebration at Faneuil Hall. All of the city fathers, and no women, were present. The boys were seated at a separate table, each with his medal hung by an elegant blue ribbon around his neck, given a glass of wine for a toast, and then escorted out while the gentlemen prepared for a night of serious toasting.[50] With fewer resources, rural schoolmasters sometimes devised colored tickets as rewards, an idea also used in Sunday schools and recalled by Mark Twain in *The Adventures of Tom Sawyer*. In some versions of ticket rewards, students who recited correctly earned black tickets, which in sufficient number could be exchanged for red ones, which could eventually be exchanged for a book.

Another competitive technique favored by schoolmasters, the head-and-foot method, required arranging pupils in lines. Those who correctly answered a question moved higher; those who stumbled, lower.[51] The head-and-foot method became a favorite of teachers in monitorial (or Lancasterian) schools, which rested on the principle that one schoolmaster could oversee the education of hundreds of children in a single room by stirring competition. Student monitors, older and more advanced than the others, each taught a circle of ten to twelve pupils, who competed to become monitors or at least to move higher in the line or closer in the circle to the monitor. Such "moving up" was a reward that usually accompanied catching the monitor or another student in small errors during recitation. Even advocates of monitorial schools conceded that students were too eager to correct small mistakes in order to move up.[52]

Just as Jacksonians viewed life as a series of small competitions for betterment, with no big winners or losers as long as the playing field was level (free of legal privilege), no student in the head-and-foot system enjoyed any anterior privilege based on age or previous attainment. Each dawn brought a new competition, and each day might see several fast changes of place from high to low. As Jean Baker has observed, head-and-foot competitions resembled Jackson's ideal of rotation in office.[53]

Monitorial schoolmasters also devised crude rewards based on money or monetary facsimiles, presumably just the sort of spur that the poor required. William Bentley Fowle, who conducted a monitorial school for girls in Boston during the 1820s, described how each pupil would contribute twenty-five cents to a pool totaling some twenty dollars. Fowle then created a nominal currency, called "merits," with a specified number of merits fixed for each school exercise. At the end of each quarter a pupil's cumulative merits were summed and each was rewarded from the pool of real money in exact ratio to her merits.[54] Most monitorial schools devised rewards similar to Fowle's by distributing tickets that could be redeemed for prizes like tops, books, or pictures, each with a stated monetary value. In Detroit some monitorial pupils created a scandal when they passed facsimile coins as legal tender.[55]

Rural and town schools also had their year-end exhibitions, which combined features of the colleges' ritualistic senior examinations and commencements. School committeemen would briefly examine pupils in reading and arithmetic, and, like collegians, pupils would speak "parts." Warren Burton, who wrote an illuminating memoir of New Hampshire's rural schools in the early 1800s, recalled that pupils spent so much time rehearsing for the exhibition and "flourishing off" their speaking parts, usually extracted from readers like the *Columbian Orator* or *American Preceptor*, that they had little time left for study.[56] Academies, which offered a broader range of subjects than the rural common schools, also ended each year with an exhibition. William H. Seward recollected that the academy he attended in Florida, New York, as a sixteen-year-old staged a semiannual and annual "dramatic exhibition" for which students prepared "select pieces" and wrote "original compositions."[57] Charles Coon's exhaustive study of hundreds of North Carolina academies in the early 1800s reveals a similar picture of term-end exhibitions in which pupils were showered with praise by approving trustees and routinely judged "best," "very best," "perfect," and "most perfect."[58] Community festivals that affirmed the support of a town or rural neighborhood for its schools and teachers, exhibitions flourished where schools were perceived merely as extensions of their neighborhoods.

Reformers, who viewed the public schools through the lens of the putative needs of the nation rather than the desires of local communities, attacked all of these competitions on pedagogical and moral grounds. Exhibitions that encouraged ten-year-olds to flourish off their pieces distracted teachers and pupils from the serious business of education and amounted to a massive deception. They encouraged an unnatural manner, especially in girls. Bashful girls became "pert" and "impudent" when they acted out parts.[59] Teachers became part of the deception when they fed pupils questions in advance of the oral examination. Burton observed that children who effortlessly spelled long words posed by the teacher flubbed easy ones tossed by the clergyman.[60] Above all, reformers disapproved of competitions that encouraged rivalry, on which they blamed a train of national evils, from the squabbling of religious denominations to extreme partisanship in politics to the unbridled speculative spirit of the commercial economy.[61]

Yet Mann's generation of reformers favored some forms of competition. To this generation of reformers we owe written examinations and report cards based on numerical marks, instruments of what Michel Foucault called "the régime of disciplinary power."[62] All of the reward systems attacked by reformers featured visible, individual rewards such as medals, colored tickets, and movements from foot to head, and all of them encouraged students to seek public approval. In all objectionable forms of competition, children performed as individuals and their success or failure was instantly visible. Reformers rejected anything smacking of show or display, like school exhibitions in which the child affected an "unnatural manner," behaved "precociously," and sought applause for his "solitary performance."[63] In contrast to crowd-pleasing exhibitions, written examinations were never evaluated by the amount of happiness they spread. They afforded "no attraction whatever to beholders" and therefore left no room for "deception."[64]

Why the school reformers saw their innovations as improvements is a fair question. Mann's metaphor of the written examination as a "Daguerreotype likeness" offers one clue. In public oral examinations each child answered a different question (or the same question until someone got it right) whereas in written examinations each pupil had to answer the same question without the benefit of prompts from the questioner. Another clue lies in the reformers' preference for monthly report cards. Reformers favored report cards based on numerical marks because they tracked results over a month or a term rather than daily. In this respect, they resembled Thayer's merit system at West Point and Quincy's Scale of Comparative Merit at Harvard. In contrast, monitors in Lancasterian schools were familiar with the daily command, "Take Down Lists!" That is, they were to remove from the walls the rankings of pupils from the previous day, so that each day initiated a new competition. Reformers compared report cards, which they called the "credit" or "merit" system,[65] with merchants' ledgers. Like the ledger, which encouraged the merchant to think in terms of months rather than minutes and hours, report cards encouraged teachers to take the long view. Rather than reprove each infraction at once, when emotions were high, report cards kept "a *record of attainment*" and exhibited "the true desert of the pupils."[66] They rewarded persistence, not striking display.[67]

Written examinations, marks, and report cards were also valuable aids to the classification of pupils, a subject on which reformers placed an extraordinary amount of emphasis. Today we take it for granted that children will advance from grade to grade through a sequence of promotions, followed by graduation to a higher level of school—for example, middle school to high school. But before 1850 (and for long after in many areas) few public schools were organized like this. Rural schools gathered pupils of widely varying ages, anywhere from five or six years old to their mid-twenties, in a single room. The great variation in the age and attainments of students posed staggering problems for teachers. One teacher recalled that "it was by no means uncommon to see a dozen or more classes in the same room, studying the same book, but at a dozen or more stages of advancement in it."[68] Typically, a teacher could attend to only one group of pupils at a time, usually by gathering them around his or her desk and asking questions during a recitation. The other children quietly read or copied passages from books, often brought from home, or just made trouble. Under such conditions, teachers often classified pupils merely by their size—the same method used to classify books in libraries—with the "large" or "tall" boys and girls grouped separately.

More numerous and sophisticated classifications were possible in towns and cities, where sorting pupils by attainment was feasible. Until midcentury, however, town schools were organized by the subject taught rather than by an average of attainment in all subjects. Boston's grammar schools, which took pupils from the primary schools, were long divided into writing schools, where students learned penmanship and rudimentary arithmetic, and reading schools, often located in a different part of the city, which taught reading and spelling, along with some grammar, composition, and geography. In order to encourage students to master the components of both writing and reading, Boston's school committee initiated a reform in 1819 by which writing and reading schools became divisions within the same building, each on a different floor.[69] Each floor might contain several hundred students, but the floor's headmaster could divide his flock into smaller "classes," usually four, that were loosely graded by level of attainment, and within these classes he could create such subdivisions as he saw fit. Grammar schools usually contained a few rooms off the main one on each floor where the headmaster or his assistants, called "ushers" (usually men) or "assistant teachers" (usually women), could hear smaller recitation groups.

Under this system a student could stand high in one subject and low in another. This came to be seen as a problem as urban populations mushroomed. In the wake of the publication of Calvin Stowe's influential report on the Prussian schools, which attributed their success to their age-graded and stepped curriculum,[70] educators across the northern tier of states engaged in a relentless quest for a superior method of classifying students and grading schools. Grading schools involved consolidating many small schools into a few large ones, some-times called Union schools, and establishing "intermediate" schools between primary and grammar schools. By 1840 a graded school system meant a sequence of schools at different levels.[71] Within each grade of schools pupils continued to be classified by their level of attainment in a subject, "writing" or "reading," which made it difficult to establish any uniform method of advancing pupils from one grade of school to the next.

With Boston in the lead, educators hit on a different way to classify pupils that would become the norm in urban school systems by the Civil War. A turning point occurred in 1847 when John D. Philbrick became the headmaster of the Quincy grammar school. Philbrick, who would go on to become Boston's school superintendent for all but two years between 1858 and 1878, introduced a course of study, initially called simply "the experiment," in which the materials of all subjects were arranged in a sequence of ascending difficulty that was divisible into annual segments. He then placed an assistant teacher, usually a woman, in charge of one classroom in which she would teach a particular segment of the materials in all subjects. Under this system, pupils would advance from level to level based on their numerical average of attainments in all subjects.[72]

Contemporaries, who complained of the "WANT OF SYSTEM" in unclas-sified schools,[73] saw this approach as an effective application of the division of labor, comparable to that in railroad corporations, factories, and large mercan-tile establishments, where one "master-mind" directed many assistants. At a time when Boston's grammar schools, designed to accommodate three hundred to four hundred students, were ballooning toward one thousand each, the division of the course of study into annual segments made it possible to assign a large but manageable number of students, sixty to seventy, to each teacher. The system was efficient, but not cheap, for it required large school buildings. Boston constructed eleven of these between 1847 and 1858. The Dwight school, built in 1856, was representative. It had four floors above the basement, the first three with four rooms each, and the fourth with two rooms. Each room contained sixty-three desks (a desk for each pupil was a Philbrick innovation), making exactly 882 for the whole school. The Dwight school could accommodate roughly twice the number of pupils as the typical grammar school two decades earlier, but by sub-dividing pupils into manageable units of sixty-three per class and by establish-ing a single graded course of study, Philbrick was able to reduce the number of headmasters from two to one while employing more female teachers, who were paid little more than half the salary of a man. Before Philbrick, a "graded" school system signified a sequence of independent schools at different levels: pri-mary, grammar, and high school. In the wake of Philbrick's innovations, a graded school also signified a sequence of ascending internal grades.[74]

As had been true in the old grammar schools, race and gender remained acceptable bases of classification. African American students were segregated into black primary and grammar schools, and with some exceptions, girls attended female grammar schools. But public high schools, which reformers envisioned as the capstones of the system, were coeducational in most cities, and where they were not—Boston and Philadelphia maintained separate female high schools—the required entrance examinations were of identical difficulty. The system resembled a pyramid with a thick pedestal composed of primary, intermediate, and grammar schools, narrowing at the apex of the high school. In contrast to contemporary European schools, which sorted children by social class, American educators were constructing a system that sorted them by their average level of attainment in all subjects. "In giving credit for a good recitation," a Massachusetts educator wrote, "we do not take as a standard what would in all cases be called a perfect lesson, but such as is within the reach of the average of the class, by proper application and study."[75] Arranged into classes based on "the average capacity of the pupils"[76]—numerical marks and report cards made it easy to ascertain "average attainments"—children would learn that if they were sufficiently industrious to keep up with their class, they would rise to the next grade level within their school, and so would all of their industrious classmates. Promotion itself was a reward, and retardation a punishment.[77]

The prospect of promotion through the grades offered what Massachusetts's George Boutwell called "logical, symmetrical, perfect education."[78] Implicit in the language was an image of a ladder of schools, each linked to its predecessor. Pupils would always have before them the prospect of advancement on the basis of their industry or retardation for laziness. Reformers were quick to recognize the potential of this type of classification of students to encourage ambition without personal and visible rivalry. If all of the students in a school were sorted into large classes based on "equality of attainment," Connecticut's Henry Barnard wrote in his 1851 treatise on school architecture, "there would be a spirit, a glow, a struggle."[79] Although Barnard's reference to struggle suggests that he welcomed rivalry, in fact he deplored it. James Pyle Wickersham, a prominent Pennsylvania school official, observed that the division of public schools into ascending grades, each based on an average level of attainment in all subjects, absorbed personal rivalry into the group. As long as the child focused on staying abreast with his group rather than surpassing anyone in it, schooling would come to resemble games of ball or cricket, which, as Wickersham observed, produced friendship among rivals.[80]

This sort of classification was not feasible outside the cities and larger towns, but reformers devised ways to classify schools that lacked classrooms. First in a series of articles in Mann's *Common School Journal* and then in a coauthored book on school management, George B. Emerson, an ally of Mann, proposed that rural schoolmasters sort their pupils into numerous contiguous "divisions" according to their "general progress and deportment." Emerson applied this principle to the one-room schoolhouses still prevalent in many parts of Massachusetts and Connecticut and in which a single teacher would instruct one group in arithmetic and then turn his or her attention to another group in reading or geography.[81] Emerson's divisions were not these small study groups but rungs on a hypothetical ladder of achievement within the school. He acknowledged that his divisions might exist "only on paper, in the [teacher's] record of the school." They were nevertheless indispensable. A child who stood high in reading or deportment for three months would learn from the teacher that he, along with several of his classmates, had been boosted into a higher division in reading, but within this group of achievers, no divisions would be drawn, nor would the seating arrangement of the school be affected. Thus, fifteen or so pupils might "have the satisfaction of having raised themselves, from grade to grade, to the first division, without having any emulation, as no one of the number shall know which is the highest or lowest of the fifteen."[82]

Emerson saw several advantages to this approach. First, in contrast to the head-and-foot competition in which advancements were frequent and visible, under Emerson's proposal advancement would occur slowly and only after prolonged efforts. Second, each child would be ignorant of his or her standing relative to others in his or her division, and hence personal competition, the "worst passion" of the heart, could be avoided. Third, because the distance between contiguous divisions was small, the child could readily envision moving up. "The desire for advancement and progress is a commendable motive," Emerson wrote. "The only difficulty is, so to direct and control it, as to prevent competition from becoming personal."[83]

Finding the most appropriate method of advancing pupils was a key component of the organization of schools, a subject about which reformers wrote far more extensively than about what schools were to teach. When they talked about organization, they displayed a high degree of sensitivity to the relation between school and social organization, but it would be misleading to think that they wanted schools to mime society. In fact, they criticized competition between individuals in the larger society, and, not unlike contemporary political economists, they imagined a larger society in which merit would receive its just deserts without spurring bitterness and chaotic rivalry.

The reformers took universal education very seriously, more seriously than any other group of educators in the Western world at the time. In their ideal, all students would attend school and experience predictable, but not automatic, advances as part of their group. It was on just this basis that reformers attacked private schools. If the reformers had had their way, there would have been no private schools. They criticized private schools because these schools charged fees and thereby divided the rich from the poor. But some private schools did not charge anything. A notable example was the endowed Norwich Free Academy, founded in Connecticut in 1857. The Free Academy posed a challenge to reformers since it evaded their usual criticism of private schools, but they attacked it anyway, and on grounds worth comment. Rather than assail the quality of education it offered, they condemned it because it lacked any connection to the ladder of public schools, or to any ladder of schools. Like other independent academies, it was not part of a system in which those occupying the higher rungs would provide energy and ambition to those on the lower rungs.[84]

The school reformers' ideal of promotion through the grades was intended to make the public school a place that instilled in children the possibilities of orderly advancement in a developing society. Orderly advancement meant moving up as part of a group rather than as an individual leaving rivals in his wake. Partly to respond to the familiar Democrat refrain that the artisans and farmers formed the only productive classes, northern Whigs preached the interdependence of the finance capitalists, managers, foremen, and "operatives," who occupied distinct niches in the hierarchy that made the factory system hum.[85] Individuals rose as members of interdependent groups and in a process by which each group prospered while keeping its position relative to other groups. Far more than Democrats, whose ideal society—a harmonious republic of artisans and farmers—lay in the Jeffersonian past, Whig economists and educators alike projected a harmonious future based on economic and moral development.[86]

Two Nations Divided by a Shared Language

British investigators of American education were immediately struck by how the same terms had different meanings in each nation. In Britain *secondary education* signified a more complete education than an *elementary* education. The youngest students in a secondary school were to be found in its primary department, not in an elementary school. Similarly, a *grade* referred both to the quality of a school and the likely occupations of its graduates. Established in 1869, the Endowed Schools Commission proposed dividing schools into three grades: the first would take boys at eighteen to prepare them for universities and the higher professions; the second would take boys at sixteen and prepare them for business; the third would take boys up to fourteen. In America, as Francis Adams, an English school inspector who visited the United States in the early 1870s, grasped, a grade referred to a level within a school, not to its quality. Adams acquired the habit of referring to the class within the grade, and what he saw impressed him. The American system spurred each student to stay abreast of the group to gain promotion to the next grade. "The class is everything; the individual scholar is merged," with the "very healthy effect" that "the emulation of the pupils is excited, and effort is created. The higher grades draw up the lower ones."[87] Similarly, in America elementary and secondary education referred to levels rather than to species of education. An American secondary school was one that provided a more advanced education in what were known as the "common branches" than did an elementary school, and public secondary schools were outgrowths of and appendages to elementary schools. To use the language of contemporaries, secondary schools were common schools even though only a small fraction of young people attended them; indeed, it was on just this basis that public educators turned back legal challenges to tax support for public high schools.[88]

Grade also had different connotations in each nation. In England *grade* referred to the quality of the school. A first-grade school provided a more complete secondary education than did a second-grade school. In American public education a grade referred to a level within a school and each grade contained several classes, meaning groups of students studying the same subjects at the same level under different teachers.

From the 1840s into the 1890s public educators puffed the ideal of graded schools in which, in principle, most children would advance more or less in lockstep from level to level as long as they kept up with the average of their class. Although variations were common, elementary education was usually divided into primary schools or departments, encompassing grades one through three or four, and grammar schools or departments, covering grades four or five through seven or eight. Since promotion was not automatic and would not become so until the 1940s, completing the grades resembled running an obstacle course, but one that an average child with average effort was expected to finish. Teachers saw their task as bringing all their pupils "up to grade." Marks and report cards would measure pupils' progress toward promotion with their peers to the next grade.

Applied to workplaces rather than schools, the ideal of predictable promotions within the reach of most employees captured the interest of Edward Bellamy, author of the best-selling utopian novel *Looking Backward, 2000–1887* (1888). Dr. Leete guides the time traveler Julian West around the Boston of 2000. In the new Boston the government owns all industry, competition has given way to cooperation, and scarcity to abundance, and all workers in the "industrial army" are paid the same. Thanks to the planned coordination between manufacturing and consumer needs, there is no unfulfilled desire, no restless striving for personal ascendancy, no disagreement, and hence no political parties. Bellamy's pen could erase competition, but not merit. Informed by Dr. Leete that all workers are paid the same, Julian asks, "How can you do that, I should like to know, when no two men's powers are the same?" "Nothing could be simpler," Leete replies, since all that is required of each is the same effort. There is no unfairness because "desert is a moral question." A man's endowments, "however godlike," merely fix the measure of his duty, not of his reward.[89]

Leete's reply rolls so smoothly from his mouth that it sounds rehearsed; critics of "emulation" had made the same point in the pages of school journals. But it does not satisfy Julian, who wonders how workers can be stimulated to effort. Leete, who now seems a tad defensive, explains that there are grades within each industry, and "according to his stand as an apprentice, a young man is assigned his place as a first, second, or third grade worker." Workers are not paid by their ability and industry, but they are nevertheless graded by these traits, and periodically regraded on the basis of their performance. Those with highest ratings can jump from apprenticeship to the highest (first) grade, "so that merit never need wait for long to rise, nor can any rest on past achievements unless they would drop into a lower rank."[90] The exceptionally meritorious can gain further promotions, for the industrial army contains officers, such as captains, who are the equivalent of industrial foremen, and colonels, the superintendents. In sum, the new Boston is simultaneously egalitarian and meritocratic, and all merit-based distinctions arise from performance in the workplace.

Even in the new Boston, rank has its privileges. The preferences of high-grade workers for a particular line of work carry more weight than those of low-grade workers. Unwilling to motivate workers by appeals to their greed, Bellamy substituted appeals to their pride. The results of each regrading, Leete tells Julian, are "gazetted in the public prints," and those promoted are publicly invested with a badge. Each industry has its own "emblematic device," in iron, silver, or gilt, depending on the rank achieved. Further, so that indifferent or poor workers "shall be able to cherish the ambition of rising" and "that no form of merit shall wholly fail of recognition," each grade of industry is divided into classes, with honorable mention and other prizes for work "less than sufficient for promotion." As a result, only a "trifling fraction" of workers are apt to remain in the lowest class of the lowest grade," and these are "likely to be as deficient in sensibility as to their position as in ability to better it."[91]

Bellamy had a knack for giving practices familiar to his nineteenth-century audience a futuristic spin. The reward for high standing in Sylvanus Thayer's West Point merit system had been preference in assignment to a branch of the army, the same reward Leete proposes for excellent workers. Leete's reference to keeping detailed records of performance to evaluate workers foreshadowed the rating cards of the personnel management movement of the 1920s, but it also resembled the report cards that became fixtures in public schools after 1840.

The Boy Scouts of America, established in 1910, made extensive use of merit badges of the sort Leete proposed for grades of workmanship, but Bellamy could have derived the idea from the long-standing use of colored ribbons or medals as school prizes, and he must have known about the growing use of medals as rewards for valor in the military during and after the Civil War.

Bellamy's conception of promotion from grade to grade within each industrial branch corresponded to the growing practice of large corporations, especially the railroads, of rewarding salaried employees with promotions. It was also congruent with the ideal of graded and steady advances for everyone, which public educators had been implementing in urban schools since the late 1840s and which promised to reconcile egalitarianism with rewards for merit that encouraged social cohesion rather than individualistic competition.

Ultimately, even Bellamy had to make room for merit in his egalitarian utopia. Merit resembled one of those oblong party balloons that, squeezed in the middle, bulges at the ends, and squeezed at the ends, bulges in the middle.

The Death of the Average Child

Many of the assumptions that had guided the public-school reformers of Mann's generation were in shreds by 1910. Written examinations to govern annual promotion from grade to grade left a trail of controversy. Mann had compared written examinations to daguerreotypes for their promise to reveal the contents of children's minds. By the 1870s and 1880s they were more often described by their critics as lotteries in which the winners were the lucky ones who remembered trivial chips of information on judgment day. Examinations resembled Gatling guns in action: in geography name the six highest mountains, the five largest indentations of the coastline, the seven longest rivers, and the six largest lakes in North America; in literature three works by Shakespeare, Scott, Chaucer, Byron, and Milton and one by Hume, Goldsmith, and Pope, and also the authors of *Evangeline*, *The Marble Faun*, and *The Last of the Mohicans*. Realizing that they themselves were assessed by their pupils' performance on written examinations, teachers vied with each other to increase the percentage of correct answers by their pupils. Newspapers published the performance of different schools, the classes taught by different teachers, and the proportion of correct answers by different students on promotion examinations. What had started as an effort to substitute invisible rewards for prizes and other visible measures of success became highly visible.[92]

None of this passed without challenge. Written examinations for promotion made a lot of enemies among teachers and principals, whose classes and schools were assessed by the performance of their pupils on examinations. In the early 1870s Emerson E. White, who in the course of a long career served as principal of Cleveland's Central High School, Ohio's commissioner of education, president of Purdue University, and superintendent of Cincinnati's public schools, attacked the "examination fiend" and spurred a debate over examinations and marks that resembled a long-running play in which the actors spoke the same lines every night. To their defenders, examinations for promotion were necessary to impose standards on schools, to guarantee uniform attainments at each grade level, and to introduce children to the harsh struggle of life. One educator compared annual examinations for promotion to the ledger balancing of merchants at the end of each year; another lauded their "bracing" effect on pupils. In response, critics argued that examinations for promotion encouraged teaching to the test and "overpressure" (thought to be especially a problem for girls), and were more likely to assess a pupil's luck in remembering a trivial fact than his or her "power" of understanding. Better, argued the critics, to depend more (or wholly) on class standing ("teachers' estimates"). Defenders of examinations for promotion countered that teachers' estimates invited favoritism and that there was no substitute for an examination drawn up in the office of a school superintendent or by a committee of principals to measure results objectively. Some argued, predictably, for governing promotion by a combination of examinations and teachers' estimates, a position that invited the response that, recognizing that they were assessed by the performance of their students on examinations, teachers found ways to hold back their best scholars in order to make themselves look better.[93]

This debate raged among schoolmen from 1870 to around 1900, after which its terms began to change in response to two issues, "elimination" (attrition from grade to grade) and "retardation" (the presence of pupils thought to be overage for their grade level). Both issues were by-products of the spread of graded schools. Ungraded rural schools continued to be filled with older boys and girls who attended them a few weeks a year, during slack times in the farming cycle, into their late teens and even early twenties. Far from encouraging the persistence of these older youths, especially the troublesome "large boys," Mann had cheered their exit. As the expectation of promotion from grade to grade solidified, the raw numbers pointing to attrition aroused alarm among educators.[94] Teachers had always known that some of their pupils had duller wits than others, but before the rise of compulsory school laws (mainly a development of the period from 1870 to 1915) it was plausible for them to think that the vast majority of their pupils could complete the course. Although sporadically enforced and rarely requiring more than a designated number of weeks in attendance each year (typically between four and twenty, not necessarily consecutive), these laws increasingly scooped into the public schools the sort of incorrigible, truant, and foreign-born youngsters who earlier had been mostly out of sight and out of educators' minds. In 1887 the superintendent of schools in Erie, Pennsylvania, told the State Teachers' Association that it was the duty of the common schools to "hold as long as possible children differing in race, heredity, surroundings, strength, health, and faculty of learning."[95]

Retardation was another consequence of graded schools. Once elementary schools had been sliced into grades, superintendents started to calculate the average age of the pupils within the classes in each grade. The individual ages from which averages were derived varied widely, but, numbers having a certain motive power in themselves, published averages formed the expectation that pupils would enter the first grade at ages five, six, or seven and finish the eighth between thirteen and fifteen. Compulsory school laws, which more often than not set fourteen as the school-leaving age, tended to reinforce this expectation.

Before 1910, however, no consensus united educators against either attrition or retardation. To assure taxpayers that public schools were fully utilized, superintendents reported high rates of promotion, usually in the 80–90 percent range, from grade to grade. While accurate, such figures were misleading, in part because many of the pupils "eliminated" had not failed promotion (they had dropped out to work, or moved, or died), because promotion rates were based on the number of students finishing each year (although many had left schools during the year), and because the cumulative effect over eight grades of even 90 percent promotion rates was huge. In contrast to superintendents, many teachers and principals construed attrition as a sign that they were doing their jobs by maintaining standards. Similarly, in line with Philbrick's division of the curriculum into annual segments, many teachers saw their job as ensuring that each pupil mastered each subject regardless of how long it took.

Most children, especially in the lower grades, were likely to gain promotion to the next grade, but there appears to have been an intensifying expectation in graded schools during the second half of the nineteenth century that pupils perform all classroom tasks at a kind of double quickstep. Most likely, this expectation was nurtured by the departure of children for jobs in commerce and manufacturing, which, unlike agricultural jobs, were incompatible with part-time schooling. Over-age students were bound to attract attention, but before 1900 public educators focused more on accelerating fast learners through the grades than on special treatment for slow learners.

The groundwork for acceleration was laid by the one clear effect of the debate over written examinations for promotion in the 1870s and 1880s: increasingly, city school systems replaced annual promotions with semiannual and, in some instances, quarterly promotions (without abandoning written examinations, they also gave more scope to class standing). More frequent promotions meant that pupils who failed promotion would not have to repeat the entire year and that fast learners could move ahead more quickly, for it was easier to skip a semester or quarter than an entire year. It was revealing of the times that the individual who did the most to bring retardation to the attention of public educators, Harvard president Charles W. Eliot, had negligible interest in slow learners.

Schools According to Charles W. Eliot

In a series of addresses and articles between 1888 and 1892 Eliot raised awareness of retardation in grammar schools. His examination of Boston's grammar-school data from the 1870s and 1880s revealed that anywhere from 20 to 24 percent of pupils in the grammar schools were over the age of thirteen, the age at which they should have entered high school or taken a job.[96] Eliot blamed the expectation of many public-school officials that all pupils in a given grade would be promoted in "lockstep," without regard to differences in "capacity or merit."[97] Because teachers, as we have seen, contrived to hold back their brightest students, the ranks of the retarded pupils were filled with bright boys and girls who should have been accelerating through the grades.

Eliot's ideas about the public schools have to be set within his embrace of the old-fashioned ideal of natural aristocracy. Because America lacked "caste" in the form of institutional or hereditary barriers to mobility, he argued, it was uniquely receptive to the ideal of careers open to talent. Like Thomas Jefferson, Eliot revered rule by a natural aristocracy recruited from the smart children of the common people, who first would be identified by their performance in schools. The sons of the poor deserved the same educational opportunities as those of the rich. The wealthy sent their children to private schools, where they received "a suitably varied course of instruction, with much individual teaching."[98] The logic of democracy, which Eliot boiled down to equality of educational opportunity, demanded that public schools match private schools in the range and depth of their offerings. On this ground he urged the introduction of algebra, foreign languages, and natural sciences at the grammar-school level.

Like Jefferson, Eliot lived comfortably in a hierarchical world as long as hierarchy was based on talent, virtue, and opportunity for all boys. (Neither man made room for females in the ranks of nature's *aristoi*.) Like Jefferson's natural aristocracy, Eliot's required infusions of fresh blood, which Eliot thought coursed in the veins of upwardly mobile public-school graduates. Yet Eliot had far less confidence than Jefferson that voters would elect and empower the natural aristocracy. Jefferson forged his ideal of a natural aristocracy selected by the schools and voted into office at a time of his political party's ascendancy. In contrast, Eliot, a blueblood with extensive family ties to Boston's intellectual aristocracy, was tortured by his realization of how ineffectual his own social class and its values had become. Politically a Mugwump who served as vice-president of the Cambridge chapter of the National Civil Service Reform League, Eliot called civil-service reform the "reform of reforms." His nightmare was the prospect of a democracy run by loutish businessmen, half-educated professionals, and corrupt politicians. Rather than trust the voters, Eliot was persuaded by his reading of Francis Galton's *Hereditary Genius* (1869) of the power of heredity to produce new and energetic "family stocks."

Unlike Galton, Eliot believed that acquired characteristics were heritable and, hence, that education would nurture more good stocks. The success of American democracy depended on its ability to recruit new families into the circle of excellence. He was pleased to discover that most Harvard alumni were the sons of fathers who had not been "college-bred." The United States would "undoubtedly" see a great increase in the number of "permanent families" in which honor, education, and property would be transmitted with "reasonable certainty."[99]

All of this would make higher education the parade ground of the natural aristocracy, but as Eliot reluctantly recognized, it would also drag out the period of formal education. "The man of action cannot forever be in the schools," Cornell's Ernest Huffcut declaimed during an exchange with Eliot at a 1902 conference of the Association of American Universities.[100] Eliot was already at work devising answers to the lengthening of education. These included taking advantage of electivism to make it possible for students to acquire the baccalaureate in three years and providing for the acceleration of bright pupils through grade school. Eliot dissented from the increasingly prevalent idea that semiannual and quarterly promotions formed the best way to break the "lockstep" by facilitating the promotion of pupils to the next grade when they were ready. In his view, the effect of more frequent promotions would be to increase the range of intellectual ability in each class; the hares in 2B would jump into the company of the tortoises in 3A, where their new teacher would force them to slow down. Rather, although he did not use the term, Eliot could plausibly claim paternity of *tracking*. Contemporaries credited an 1892 address by Eliot to the National Education Association (NEA) on "desirable and undesirable uniformity" in schools with spurring interest in "parallel" courses. Our understanding of tracking is shaped by a form it gradually took after 1900: separate tracks for slow, average, and gifted pupils, each running through the eight grades of elementary school, but each with greater or lesser degrees of within-grade enrichment on the basis of pupils' tested ability and achievement.[101] What Eliot proposed was very different: that pupils of different ability move through the grades not only on different tracks but at different speeds, so that fast learners could complete their elementary and secondary educations in as few as nine grades.

By 1910 the preponderance of opinion among public educators had shifted away from Eliot's plea for acceleration, largely in response to two highly influential studies of attrition: Edward L. Thorndike's "The Elimination of Pupils from School" (1908) and Leonard P. Ayres's *Laggards in Our Schools* (1909).[102] Thorndike, who had assumed that nearly all children who did not go to high schools finished elementary schools, was shocked to discover that only one-third of the pupils who began the first grade finished the eighth. Ayres remarked that Thorndike's study had initiated a storm of editorial criticism of the wastefulness of public schools.

Thorndike (a psychologist and pioneer of the science of educational measurements) and Ayres (a former superintendent of schools in Puerto Rico) brought a high level of sophistication to the interpretation of data that led the two to tangle over whose simplifying assumptions were more realistic. Each study nevertheless marked a huge advance over the primitive methodology of earlier studies, which had failed to control for child mortality, spatial mobility, or population growth (each cohort entering the first grade was all but certain to be larger than its predecessor, with the effect that, without any elimination, the number of pupils in each grade after the first would show a decline) or to establish whether over-age students were spread evenly over the grades or concentrated somewhere along the spectrum.

On these counts, Ayres's findings were sufficiently striking to transform the entire debate: the vast majority of children in city schools persisted through the fifth grade, but only one-half reached the eighth grade and one-tenth completed high school. The key to understanding attrition lay in age-grade ratios, which revealed that a very substantial proportion of thirteen- and fourteen-year-olds in elementary school were still below the sixth grade. For example, data from Cincinnati in 1907 indicated that nearly one-third of fourteen-year-olds in elementary school were in grades 1–5.[103] Ayres established that most retardation did not occur because pupils entered school late and that it was not offset by late entrants who accelerated through the grades (for every child making swifter than normal progress, eight to ten were moving at a slower than normal speed). Neither decisions made by parents (when to send their children to first grade) nor the class or ethnicity of the pupils had much effect on levels of retardation. Rather, retardation was primarily created by two realities: "our schools' courses are too difficult to be completed in eight years by the average child who starts at the age of five, six, or seven, and our systems of grading are too inflexible to permit the more mature child to make up the handicap he is under through a late start."[104]

Eliot's bright child who became bored by the lack of an enriched curriculum disappeared under Ayres's mountain of data, which evidenced that the real problem arose from retardation in the first five grades. The retarded pupils were not being "held back" but "left back," forced to repeat grades, often several times, until they were too big for their seats, grew dispirited, and quit, all in the name of maintaining high standards. As Ayres observed, "There is a feeling among school workers, not always or even often expressed, but generally more or less forcibly present, that retardation is a symptom of good schools."[105] For Ayres, retardation signified bad schools, not merely because it wasted resources but, more fundamentally, because "the average city school system trains its pupils well in the habit of failure."[106]

Unequal Starts

By 1910 Eliot had become a member of an endangered species—officials of elite colleges and universities and private-school headmasters who sought to legislate for public schools. After 1910 American public education came to be dominated by a different breed of educators, typified by Clarence Kingsley, who chaired the NEA's Commission on the Reorganization of Secondary Education (CRSE, 1913). Born in 1834, Eliot was forty years older than Kingsley, and aside from a brief detour to teach at MIT, he spent his entire career at Harvard. Kingsley, a Colgate graduate, spent most of his career as a public high school teacher and state supervisor of high schools in Massachusetts.

This new generation was far more engaged than Eliot in the problem of the slow pupils and in the retention of pupils in junior high schools, high schools, and junior colleges. It cried for experts rather than natural aristocrats, and it called for "adjusting" the curriculum of the public schools by introducing vocational courses for those unable to succeed in academic courses. The nightmare of the new generation was not Eliot's dread of ineffectual and/or corrupt national leadership but its image of the school "dropout" (a word apparently coined in the early 1900s), who drifted first into a "dead-end" job and then into the ranks of malcontents and agitators.

Eliot assumed that completion of grammar school would terminate formal schooling for most children. But even as Eliot was speaking, the number of public high-school students was rising. It doubled in the 1890s, a decade in which the proportion of fifteen-through eighteen-year-olds in high school rose from around 5 percent to just over 10 percent. In 1890 only 3 in every thousand Americans were enrolled in high schools, a number that rose to 7 in 1900, 10 in 1910, 21 in 1920, and 32 in 1930. These enrollment leaps reflected many factors: the decline in the farm population; greater wealth, which made it possible for families to prolong their children's education; and compulsory-school and child-labor laws, which sufficiently harassed employers to lead them to prefer adult immigrant to juvenile labor.

This trend toward a rise in average educational attainment (the number of years spent in school) also contributed to a change in the way that school officials thought about the relationship between schooling and occupations. For much of the nineteenth century, public educators had portrayed schools as places to acquire the right sort of competitive values—ambition, self-control, and fair play— rather than job-specific skills. Despite a noisy minority's agitation for educating children in the "mechanic arts," so-called industrial education retained its pejorative associations. In 1885 the Illinois Industrial University changed its name to the University of Illinois so that its graduates would no longer be badgered with questions about why they had been "sent up." Although public schools taught far more subjects in the 1870s than in the 1830s, public educators continued to think of the curriculum as an obstacle course to build character rather than as preparation for a specific occupation, just as they continued to think of the life trajectories of students as likely to be shaped by their character and ability more than by the structure of economic opportunity itself.

Toward the end of the nineteenth century, however, economists, soon followed by educators, began to present a different image of the labor market. In England, J. E. Cairnes had advanced the idea in the late 1870s that society resembled a layer cake composed of "noncompeting groups." A lot of frenetic movement occurred within each layer, but custom and limited opportunity usually restricted children to the layer occupied by their parents.[107] This theory would gradually gain traction among American economists and social thinkers, who would name it the *theory of social stratification* and who admired it as a realistic alternative to success ideology. But it flew in the face of belief in the accessibility of opportunity in the United States. While not dismissing the idea that society was stratified, public educators of the Progressive Era concluded that prolonging schooling would enable young people to start their working lives at higher strata. Boys and girls who dropped out of school before age sixteen faced bleak job prospects, either hanging around waiting for "something to come up" or restricted to "dead-end" jobs as casual, unskilled laborers. The effects were as much moral as economic. In the words of Paul Douglas, University of Chicago economist and later U.S. senator, the dropout "is not at work nor in school; he is industrially adrift," likely prey for the "gang spirit."[108]

By 1920 the most influential voices among public educators were committed to the principle of keeping students in school well into their teens. Even with exponential increases in high-school enrollments, this was still an ideal rather than a reality. But it was the spur behind any number of schemes to "reorganize" American public education. These included the establishment of "junior high schools," the preferred term for institutions that split the seventh and eighth grades from elementary schools and linked them to the first two years of high school as a form of "post-primary" education. Educators rationalized junior high schools in the au courant language of encouraging early adolescents to sample different subjects, including vocational subjects, as a prelude to deciding their future choice. But their primary goal was to encourage students to persist longer in school. Instead of having to wait until age fourteen or fifteen to enter high schools, elementary school students could now enter a type of high school at twelve. A similar goal motivated the establishment of "junior colleges." Their many advocates hailed these institutions, which added grades thirteen and fourteen to existing high schools, as forms of "post-secondary" rather than higher education. Junior colleges offered something for everyone: an academic track for general education that would substitute for the first two years of college (an idea embraced by a number of elite university presidents, most notably William Rainey Harper of the University of Chicago) and a vocational track. Regardless of the junior college's prescribed purposes, its fundamental appeal was its promise to prolong public education.

The New American Way

In 1936 Isaac L. Kandel of Columbia University's Teachers College described the American educational system as built up on the "vertical system, each stage of education being articulated with the next following, so that pupils pass normally on the completion of their elementary education into the public high schools and thence into the college under certain conditions, or on completion of the primary schools into the junior high school, thence into the senior high school and from there into the college."[109]

The feature of this system of vertical organization that contrasted most sharply with European education lay in the Americans' negligible use of examinations as sieves. In Europe, examinations sorted students at the thresholds of each level of education; in America, sorting occurred within each level.[110] That is, American educators were preoccupied with identifying individual differences among pupils in order to guide them into institutions in which they were most likely to persist. This was known as articulation, which aimed at a noiseless transition from rung to rung. Noiseless transitions did not exactly mean automatic promotions, but the tendency was in that direction. Progressive Era educators increasingly embraced the idea that a student not ready for promotion to the next grade or level be promoted anyway, subject to "conditions," specifically the requirement that students who had failed one or more subjects had to make them up in the next grade. This was a plausible solution at a time when even elite colleges like Yale admitted a significant proportion of their students "on condition" that after admission they make up subjects failed on the entrance examination. But large school systems faced nightmarish administrative difficulties in keeping track of students in different grades who were working off conditions. In the wake of the Depression, which shrank the job market for dropouts, automatic promotion became the norm.[111]

Like Sherlock Holmes's dog that did not bark, what is missing from this listing of elements of *reorganization* and *articulation* is competition, or, to use the old-fashioned word, *emulation*. In 1927 the aptly named William S. Learned, a staffer for the Carnegie Foundation for the Advancement of Teaching, published a scathing report, *The Quality of the Educational Process in America and in Europe*, in which he tore into American educators for having denuded the educational process of competitive striving. True, compared with England, a much higher proportion of the American population was in school full-time: in 1921, 43.8 percent of males and 46.9 percent of females aged fifteen to eighteen in the United States versus 6.9 percent of males and 7.5 percent of females in England. According to Learned, however, mass education extinguished excellence. The United States was under the "bane of the average." To retain students, schools lowered standards to the point where all but the notably defective persisted. Students in high schools and colleges were allowed to take a nondescript crop of electives, from botany to band and journalism. Most universities admitted students on certification from their high schools, without examinations, and once enrolled, even the students who took serious academic subjects found that courses had been minced into those ubiquitous measures called credits, which basically rewarded them for being present. The competitive spirit lived on in interscholastic and intercollegiate sports rather than in "head-work," but Learned averred that if Americans governed their sports the way they did their classrooms, they would be obliged to minimize achievement, reward contestants for their effort rather than for success, invite an athlete to compete chiefly with himself, make up teams alphabetically rather than by selection, and keep failures on the squad.[112]

As with any broad indictment, one can think of exceptions, but Learned was not far off the mark. In *The Adolescent Society* (1961), which quickly became a classic study of American high-school youth, sociologist James S. Coleman described the trend of American public education since Learned's day in identical terms: a move away from scholastic competition and toward minimizing differences in academic achievement.[113] As Learned observed, Americans made little use of competitive examinations. In England the Education Act of 1902 established a system of free places in grammar schools, which corresponded more to American secondary schools than to American grammar schools, on the basis of performance on competitive examinations, but by then American public high schools had ceased to require entrance examinations. With the notable exception of the Regents' Examinations in New York State, American high schools did not have school-leaving examinations, like the French *baccalauréat* or the German *Abitur*. Except for the small number of prestigious colleges that accepted the results of the examinations set by the College Entrance Examination Board, established in 1899 to ease the burden on private-school headmasters who had to prepare their students for the different examinations at each of the small number of colleges that required entrance examination, most American high-school graduates gained admission to college without examination. The main innovation in college admissions in the United States after 1870 was the initiation of the "certificate" system by which university educators visited high schools and encouraged them to expand and deepen their courses, especially in the sciences and modern languages, by guaranteeing admission for their graduates to state universities without examination.[114] (In contrast, English reformers with the same agenda secured control of examinations for university entrance as their first step.) Even the colleges that set examinations for entry admitted a high proportion of their students on condition that they make up deficits once enrolled. As late as 1920 few higher educators viewed examinations as competitive and selective mechanisms. The purpose of an entrance examination was to establish whether a student was qualified for college, not to select him from a large pool of applicants for a limited number of places.[115]

A few colleges experimented in the 1920s with the newfangled intelligence tests as part of their admissions procedure, but none relied on these tests of "mental ability," and the main purpose of the few colleges that used them was not to exclude applicants but to encourage the persistence of those already admitted beyond the first year or two of college.[116] At all levels, American educators showed little awareness that education was a device for rationing scarce rewards in adulthood. Not until the 1920s did a handful of public educators describe the role of public schooling as sorting children with different "social destinies," and even then educators described the "selective" role of schooling in a tone of amazement as "hitherto unnoticed."[117]

The Contrast

A considerable temporal and intellectual distance, then, separated the Progressive Era educators and economists from the public-school reformers of the 1840s and

1850s. Fearing the effects of mass democracy and economic individualism, the school reformers envisioned public schools as institutions in which individual children would strive to excel but without rivalry and without triumph over others. The child would learn to advance with his group on the basis of ability and effort within reach of most pupils. Having learned in childhood to excel without desiring to exceed others, the adult would be primed for success and inoculated against the demoralizing effect of failure.

In contrast to Mann's generation of reformers, who saw a society gripped by predatory individualism, analysts of the Progressive Era saw society as moving of its own momentum toward a harmonious and cooperative future. The world of business now looked more predictable; big corporations offered careers based on small but steady steps upward. (They were becoming more like schools.) Simon N. Patten announced in 1909 that efficient production was leading America into a new age of abundance in which the ruinous rivalries of the past age of individualistic and predatory competition were giving way to social cooperation.[118] Also in 1909 the pioneer social psychologist Charles Horton Cooley, who had started his career as an economist and written his doctoral dissertation on the railroad industry, proclaimed that the present epoch was marked by the "wider application of intelligence" and that "the general and popular phase of larger consciousness is what we call Democracy."[119] In the same year, the journalist Herbert Croly contended that the essential condition of democracy was a rising standard of living; only by offering material abundance could the American state retain the allegiance of the losers as well as the winners in economic competition.[120] Competition would persist, but it would primarily engage collectivities—corporations (Cooley) or cities (Patten). The midwives of abundance through social efficiency would be "bodies of experts," not captains of industry, wrote Stanford University sociologist H. H. Powers.[121] In the emerging "non-competitive" society, the ordinary man could look forward to a life of small but predictable rewards rather than a chance to gain exceptional advantages over his peers, the economist and editor Albert Shaw argued.[122]

Shaw's reference to small but predictable rewards resembled the ideal voiced by the antebellum school reformers, but with one notable difference. Mann's generation of reformers assumed that, for better or worse, citizens of the republic controlled their destinies. Graded schools and predictable promotions would inculcate traits of mind and character that would enable the young to navigate their way through the larger society, seen by reformers as a sphere of unrestrained ambition and reckless individualism, without losing their moral compass. What most alarmed the antebellum school reformers was that moral defectives, like Andrew Jackson, could rise to the top. By Shaw's day, educators were coming to see society as less malleable by exertion of the individual's will; more complex social structures had created a denser atmosphere. It was not enough merely to equip youth with character. Increasingly, finding ways to identify specific aptitudes and abilities in the young and guiding youths to their appropriate "destinies" became a preoccupation of social thinkers. In this context, the mental testing movement galloped across the landscapes of both education and business in the two decades after 1910.

5

THE SCIENTIFIC MEASUREMENT OF MERIT

Written examinations, numerical marks, and report cards measured achievements, but not the sort of public achievements that I have associated with essential merit. Rather, by subordinating impressions of single and visible achievements to silent measures of unremarkable behaviors over a lengthy time period (a month or a semester) and by slicing merit into measurable units, these instruments that first appeared during the antebellum era more closely resemble institutional merit. Yet none of these measures of merit explicitly aimed at forecasting the futures of students. This is a point worth mentioning because tests to identify promise in the form of IQ and special intellectual and/or occupational aptitudes became a major component of the way in which institutions of every sort identified merit during the twentieth century. Putting it this way makes it sound like the enterprise to identify abilities and aptitudes is best viewed as a later addition to institutional merit: first the report card and much later the IQ test or the Scholastic Aptitude Test (or the Strong Vocational Blank, the Coudert Preference Test, the Minnesota Multiphasic Personality Inventory, etc.). Numerical measures of achievement unarguably preceded scientific forecasts of destinies. At this point, however, we need to push our inquiries a little farther. Neither the word nor the concept of *promise* (or *talent*) was an invention of the early mental testers. Jefferson, who developed his idea of a natural aristocracy, selected by public schools, between 1779 and 1813, assumed that his "geniuses raked from the rubbish" would rise as far as their merit would carry them. Although they wrote about average pupils rather than geniuses, nineteenth-century public educators made a similar assumption. The more merit one acquired before exiting school, the farther one would advance in life, and for a simple reason: hierarchies in the American republic were based on merit. It was just this assumption that new theories about noncompeting groups and social stratification, described in the previous chapter, challenged.

Forecasting destinies became important in the context of a growing recognition that institutions and inherited social structures fundamentally shaped the lives of individuals. The fictional characters in Edward Bellamy's utopian novel *Looking Backward, 2000–1887* (1888) are all but swallowed by the institutions that manage and direct their lives; two years later the psychologist James McKeen Cattell, who believed that institutions were playing an ever larger role in the lives of real Americans, coined the term "mental tests" to describe newfangled tests of abilities and aptitudes that he expected to fit people better to institutions.[1]

American Adaptations

The history of the scientific measurement of merit is replete with irony. It began as an enterprise to identify extraordinary merit in the form of *genius*; it turned into an enterprise to identify trivial (but putatively consequential) differences between ordinary people. Americans adopted tests for intelligence and aptitudes with more gusto than any other nation, but they contributed few of the seminal ideas that would shape the movement. Their inspiration for the experimental study of psychology sprang from Wilhelm Wundt at the University of Leipzig. They borrowed hereditarianism and coefficient correlations from two Englishmen, Francis Galton and Karl Pearson. An Englishman, Charles Spearman, taught them that consistently positive correlations between the performance of large numbers of people on different tests pointed to the existence of an underlying "general factor," which Spearman labeled g and equated with the brain's stock of energy. Another Englishman, Godfrey Thomson, instructed them that there were other ways to interpret these positive correlations and that intelligence might consist of several discrete factors.[2]

For age-normed tests for higher mental abilities, Americans were indebted to two Frenchmen, Alfred Binet and Théodore Simon, who, having been asked by the French government to study subnormal children, published in 1905 the first series of tests of the higher mental processes of children. Three years later Binet and Simon published a revised version of their first test series. The revised series assigned to each child an age level, which signified the earliest age at which a child with normal intelligence could be expected to complete the test. This became the child's "mental age." Soon translated with adaptations for American children by Henry H. Goddard, a research psychologist on the staff of the School for the Feeble-Minded in Vineland, New Jersey, the Binet-Simon Scale aroused the interest of Lewis M. Terman, whose 1906 dissertation at Clark University in Worcester, Massachusetts, investigated the intelligence of very bright and very dull children. Terman's 1916 revision of the Binet-Simon tests, known as the Stanford-Binet (Terman by then was teaching at Stanford University), quickly became the accepted American version. Terman also popularized the concept of "intelligence quotient" (IQ), invented by a German and obtained by multiplying the ratio between mental and chronological age by 100.[3]

American contributions to the movement for precise measurement of human differences, however derivative, were ingeniously adaptive. For all of their borrowing, Americans gave mental testing a distinctive spin, or more accurately several such spins, all of which reflected American culture. Interest in testing for intelligence and aptitudes developed at a moderate pace in the United States until World War I, when Terman, Robert M. Yerkes, and other psychologists attached to the U.S. Army's Committee on the Classification of Personnel (CCP) administered a battery of intelligence tests, known as army alpha (for literates in English) and beta (for illiterates and non-English-speaking foreigners) to more than 1.7 million soldiers. In the wake of World War I, testing became a fad in the United States. In 1919 the army released the alpha test for general use, and leading CCP psychologists devised the National Intelligence Test.[4] More than 500,000 copies of this test were sold in its first year and 800,000 in 1922–23. Each passing year saw new tests enter the market. In 1922–23 a single firm that specialized in publishing tests sold more than 2.5 million copies of various types of intelligence tests. By the mid-1920s more than forty different group intelligence tests were on the market. A contemporary concluded that the language for describing mental abilities had become incorporated into popular language; "the possibility of measuring an individual's intelligence by a short and simple test has captured the imagination of school people and the general public."[5] Terman's former student Florence Goodenough wrote in 1949 that the multiplication of testing devices "has hardly any parallel in the history of scientific method."[6]

The extraordinary growth of mental testing in America owed a great deal to the client orientation of the testers themselves. The movement's leaders saw themselves as applying psychology to solve problems, and this objective led them to market their services to public schools, the military, and corporations.[7] The implications of this orientation were profound. The testers tended to accept their clients' definitions of problems, whether retaining pupils longer in school, selecting suitable officer candidates for the military, or identifying productive workers, and they adapted their technology for measuring differences in IQ and vocational aptitudes to their clients' expectations.

This client orientation reflected the life experiences of the leading testers. Goddard was born into a downwardly mobile Quaker farm family in central Maine (losing his farm, his father became a farm laborer) and educated first in rural schools, which he later called "a travesty upon education," and next as a scholarship student at Haverford College. After his graduation from Haverford, Goddard secured a one-year appointment at the University of Southern California, where he did double duty as the football coach. He returned to Haverford to earn his M.A. in mathematics and then went back to his hometown to teach at an academy before enrolling at Clark University, which, under its president G. Stanley Hall, had become a Mecca for advanced study in pedagogy and psychology. Goddard's next stop was a teaching post at the State Normal School in West Chester, Pennsylvania, an institution that Yerkes, also a farm boy and a decade younger than Goddard, briefly attended to acquire a high-school education before enrolling at Ursinus Academy and Ursinus College.[8] Terman also was educated in one-room rural schools and then, because high schools were rare in his native Indiana, enrolled at the age of fifteen in the Central Normal College in Danville, Indiana, not far from the farm where he grew up, the twelfth of fourteen children. With frequent interludes teaching in one-room country schools to earn money, Terman spent the equivalent of four and a half school years from 1892 to 1898 acquiring three different degrees. But the unaccredited "C.N.C." did not offer well-regarded degrees, and in 1901, after another interlude as a rural teacher, Terman, now married and twenty-four, enrolled as a junior at Indiana University, received another bachelor's degree, and went on to graduate study under Hall at Clark University.[9]

Provincials without noteworthy family connections, these men uncomplainingly accepted their role as servants of powerful interests. Edward L. Thorndike of Columbia University, who fashioned both intelligence tests and standardized achievement tests, would later write that his career had been marked by "its responsiveness to outer pressure or opportunities rather than inner needs"; Terman thought that "chance" had governed his career; and Goddard titled his unfinished autobiography "As Luck Would Have It."[10] Having pursued any number of blind alleys only to emerge as successful—famous and in some cases even wealthy—it was natural for them to conclude that talent was not blocked in America so much as wasted by the lack of standards in the content and measurement of education. Lacking easy access to sophisticated circles and influential people, the testers became entrepreneurs as well as professionals, ever seeking to find new and imaginative uses for mental tests and measurements.

On the whole, this enterprise failed: by the end of the 1920s the movement was in disarray and the testers were folding their tents. The testing movement nevertheless had a huge impact, much of it unintended by the testers themselves, on how merit was understood. It publicized the distinction between knowledge and information on one side and ability on the other.[11] Although the immediate effect of mass testing was to reinforce stereotypes about Americans of African or southern European descent, the quantitative bullets fired by the testers often flew in unanticipated directions. Whatever the content of intelligence, test results indicated that women had roughly as much of the stuff as did men.[12] The same results indicated that it was much more difficult than initially thought to correlate intelligence with socially valuable behaviors, like the work ethic. Still more results left the dismaying conclusion that character, traditionally believed to be a key element of merit, was not the sturdy moral ballast of lore but prone to vary from one situation to another. Finally, although it was not any tester's original intent, the testing movement subtly established the principle that the way to find out about someone was not to look at him (or her) to gain a total impression but to administer a paper-and-pencil test that sliced and diced the subject into tiny morsels.

The Shadow of Galton

The mental-testing movement, which was part of a larger movement for the scientific measurement of human differences, had several fathers, of whom Binet was probably the most important, and one grandfather, Francis Galton, Charles Darwin's second cousin, scion of an eminent Whig-Liberal family, African explorer, student of heredity, pioneer of statistics, and a founder of *eugenics*, a word he coined (he also coined *nature/nurture controversy*). After having been smothered with praise from an older sister, who had constantly told him how smart he was, Galton entered Trinity College, Cambridge, with the expectation of becoming a high wrangler in the mathematical Tripos, only to suffer a nervous breakdown, abandon any plans for honors, and settle for an ordinary "poll" degree. This shattering experience had the odd effect of inducing Galton to study examinations, not to condemn them but to establish that the high wranglers indeed were much smarter than even the low honors men. Drawing on his researches into the scoring, over several years, of the mathematical Tripos, in which marks were added for brilliance, he concluded that the examinations revealed "prodigious differences" in ability among honors candidates. In one documented case the senior wrangler received thirty-two times as many marks as the lowest honors man.[13]

Darwin's *Origin of Species* (1859) suggested to Galton that natural selection might be speeded up, at least for humans, through the mating of superior men and women. Eugenics drove nearly all of Galton's speculations and experiments between 1865 and his death in 1911.[14] (In 1865 he proposed that in a "perfect" England, examinations would select the ten most talented men and women, who would be wed in a festive ceremony in Westminster Abbey in the presence of the Sovereign, with each couple receiving a prize of £5,000.)

The germ of eugenics can be found in two articles called "Hereditary Talent and Character" that Galton published in 1865 and in *Hereditary Genius* (1869).[15] Persuaded that all the really important advances of civilization depended on geniuses, Galton equated genius with a person's merit, a term he used interchangeably with "civic worth," which was a composite of his mental ability, zeal, and capacity for work. Galton's investigations of collective biographies of eminent Britons and foreigners over several centuries and in some instances back to antiquity convinced him that genius was rare; regardless of his source, genius occurred roughly in the ratio of 1:4,000.[16] Next, to show that genius was hereditary, and not (as widely supposed) a random gift of God, Galton emphasized the frequency of kinship in a biographical directory of English judges since 1660; about 10 percent of the eminences had eminent kinsmen, usually proximate (father, son, brother) rather than remote.[17]

Galton wrote mainly about England's intellectual aristocracy, whose members belonged to a small world and knew much about each other. Consider his treatment of his own family in *Hereditary Genius*. His mother was the daughter of the second wife of Erasmus Darwin, early evolutionist, poet, and physician. It was said of Erasmus Darwin, Galton wrote, that he "sprang from an intellectual and lettered race, as his father was amongst the earliest members of the Spalding Club." Further evidence of genius: his son Charles, though he died young, "obtained the gold medal of Edinburgh University for a medical essay." Another son, Robert, was a physician with a large practice in Shrewsbury and the father of Galton's second cousin, *the* Charles Darwin. One of the sons of this Charles Darwin became "second wrangler at Cambridge in 1868, and another was second in the [Royal Military College] Woolwich examination in the same year." This indeed was a small world and it was Galton's. The key figure in Britain's Eugenics Education Society was Charles Darwin's son Leonard Darwin.

The task that absorbed Galton after 1870 was to explain how genius ran in families. He was skeptical of the prevailing view, advanced by Jean Baptiste Lamarck and shared by Darwin, that characteristics or traits acquired by an organism's interaction with the environment were heritable.[18] No evidence indicated that the sons of generals learned military drill faster than the sons of poets. Galton possessed a strong will to believe that the elements of genius were passed from generation to generation in the "stirp" or root, an idea that foreshadowed the notion that only components of the fertilized egg, which the Freiburg cytologist August Wiesmann baptized the "germ plasm" in 1883, could be passed from generation to generation.[19] Neither Galton nor other investigators knew anything about Gregor Mendel's experiments on plant breeding until their "rediscovery" in 1900. In the interim, Galton conducted his own experiments, weighing the seeds of sweet-pea plants and comparing the weights of mother and daughter seeds. These experiments came close to puncturing his hopes for eugenics, for Galton discovered that, regardless of the weight of the parent seeds, the daughter seeds fell closer to the mean weight of the total population than to that of the parent seeds.[20]

Eventually, Galton's disciple Karl Pearson came to his rescue by developing the mathematical tools of correlation and multivariate analysis. Pearson's new tools of analysis led him to conclude that while unusual and isolated traits might well regress to the mean, the offspring of exceptional parents would experience little reversion.[21] Pearson assured Galton that it would take only a few generations of proper mating to breed better stock.[22] Better stock meant not only more mental ability. Galton was sure that geniuses were superior to ordinary people in nearly every manner. They were smarter and more robust and possessed keener senses. In 1884 Galton opened the Anthropometric Laboratory in London, in which paying customers could undergo tests for cranium size, reaction time, and sensory discrimination. Reflecting Galton's influence, Pearson also assumed that a relationship existed between the distribution of physical and mental traits. To measure this relationship, he devised "biometrics," or Saint Biometrika, as he reverently called the application of statistics to biological variations.

In 1903 Pearson announced conclusions from information he had gathered on some four thousand pairs of siblings from nearly two hundred British schools. Since no tests for intelligence as such were available, teachers were asked to rate their pupils' mental abilities as bright, average, or dull. Obviously, comparable assessments for their parents were unobtainable. So Pearson compared such physical characters as height, hair color, and eye color and discovered a consistent correlation of around .5 for each pair, and a similar correlation for the mental ability attributed by teachers to each pair. Equal correlations for physical traits and mental abilities, he concluded, meant that mental ability, like physical traits, was heritable. Nurture could not improve mental ability any more than it could change eye color.[23]

Galton's ideas were deeply rooted in British culture. During the 1880s English periodicals were bursting with attacks on and defenses of competitive examinations, and for good reason: the British used competitive examinations to a degree that startled even Europeans. British audiences heard Sir Joseph Porter recall wearing clean collars and a brand-new suit for the pass examination at the institute (*H.M.S. Pinafore*, 1878) and the fairy queen in *Iolanthe* (1882) sing of the duke's exalted station gained by competitive examination. Aside from competition for university fellowships (e.g., the Tripos), the British devised examinations of different degrees of difficulty for different tiers of their civil service, with examinations set for the highest tier, the so-called Administrative Class, that essentially called for the kind of knowledge possessed only by Oxbridge honors graduates.[24]

Galton's influence nevertheless crossed the Atlantic. President Eliot of Harvard took his inspiration from Galton's *Hereditary Genius* and forged ideas about a new natural aristocracy that would be rooted in hereditary talent but would be saved from becoming an ossified caste by injections of fresh blood from the public schools. This was ironic, for Galton argued that the *absence* of free schools in England proved that heredity counted far more than environment. England was awash in men of "genius," but the United States, for all of its free schools, contained nothing better than "the newspaper-article-writer or member-of-congress stamp of ability."[25] Another American devotee of Galton was James McKeen Cattell, who coined the term "mental tests" in 1890.[26] After studying the new experimental psychology in Leipzig, Cattell submitted to tests at Galton's Anthropometric Laboratory. Accepting Galton's view that mental ability was somehow related to the physiological and nervous systems, Cattell devised tests for strength of squeeze and short-term memory. But when in 1901 Clark Wissler, one of Cattell's graduate students at Columbia University, correlated the performance of Columbia and Barnard students on Cattell's tests and their college grades, the results were sufficiently discouraging—the highest correlation was a dismal .16 (between short-term memory and grades) and several were negative—to drive Wissler from psychology to anthropology. Losing interest in testing, Cattell turned to editing scientific journals, notably *Science*, and a career as an academic statesman.

The void created by the failure of Cattell's tests was soon filled, first by Binet and Simon and then by Goddard. The establishment of scientifically precise distinctions among people, an objective of the larger, Galton-inspired movement that spawned mental testing, continued to arouse scholarly interest. One aspect of this quest lay in the explosion of criticism of the marking of written examinations. A key figure was the British economist, mathematician, and great admirer of Galton, F.Y. Edgeworth, who in 1888 and 1890 published influential articles in which he deployed Karl Friedrich Gauss's "law of error" to examine the likely disagreement between different examiners marking the same paper.[27] A few years earlier J. Rendell Harris, a British philologist and paleographer who had moved from the University of Cambridge to Johns Hopkins University in 1882 and to Haverford College in 1886, started to call on American colleges to mark their students on the curve of distribution in order to establish their rank order rather than just their comprehension of the subject tested.[28]

The storm over subjectivity in marking examinations blew up later in the United States than in Britain (it had not been present in the debates over the "examination fiend" in the 1880s). American educators were more likely to argue about whether marks should include character. On this issue, faculty opinion bounced like a tennis ball, with some contending that conflating scholarship and conduct measured merit, for character was a component of merit, and others responding that conflating the two gave a clear picture of neither. Columbia tried four different marking systems between 1869 and 1870.[29] The founding in 1899 of the College Entrance Examination Board, which produced the first entrance examinations for applicants to different colleges, finally led American academics, mostly psychologists and mathematicians, to investigate the scoring of examinations. These scholars quickly came upon a chamber of horrors: different professors who rated the same paper differently, even in mathematics (in one instance, a math paper was rated 92 by one examiner and 28 by another); the same instructor who scored the same examination differently at different times; and huge differences between different university departments in the distribution of grades.[30]

Despite this evidence, the American embrace of mental testing quickly soothed anxiety about subjective marking. The results of IQ tests were plotted on a bell (deviations from 100 in both directions). From this perspective, it seemed likely that mental testers measured the distribution of abilities far better than did fussy teachers who graded papers on a scale of perfection (e.g., 0–100).

The Uses of Testing

Urban public schools afforded the most numerous opportunities for applying the principles of scientific measurement and testing. Thorndike sought to make teaching more efficient by providing teachers with new technologies to discover exactly what their pupils had learned. By 1900 compulsory school laws combined with an exploding immigrant population were placing enormous pressures on city schools to keep their students moving up the ladder of grades in orderly fashion. In this context Thorndike and his student Leonard P. Ayres pioneered new methods of educational bookkeeping to puncture the myth that public schools were forging equality out of diversity. Fourteen-year-olds sitting alongside seven-year-olds in the second grade were not equal inputs and were unlikely to emerge as equal outputs. Thorndike had no problem with schools running like machines, if only they did or would. Although he was sure that a strong correlation existed between a child's intelligence and education performance, his first interest lay in measuring the latter by devising performance tests for handwriting (1910), English composition (1911), and drawing (1913).[31]

Thorndike intended his standardized achievement tests to combat waste in public education. He had no quarrel with universal free public education, but the intrinsic wastefulness of such education was his starting point. Scientific measurement documented variation more than uniformity. By underscoring the wide differences among pupils in the same schools, the testers' involvement with public education intensified their hereditarian convictions. Terman wrote his doctoral dissertation, "Genius and Stupidity," on the mental processes of "bright" and "stupid" boys in the Worcester, Massachusetts, schools. Thorndike's investigations into the performance of schoolchildren buttressed his belief that "men differ by original nature."[32] Of a thousand children selected at random, he wrote in 1911 in language reminiscent of Galton, "some will be four times as energetic, quick, courageous, or honest as others, or will possess four times as much refinement, knowledge of arithmetic, power of self-control, sympathy, or the like."[33] Reviewing Lester Frank Ward's *Applied Sociology* in 1906, Thorndike complained that profligate expenditures to provide everyone with equal education would deplete the public purse to no useful end, since education had to be adjusted to "the differing capacities of children."[34]

Mental testing's potential to prolong education made it nearly irresistible to educators. The results of the first Binet-Simon tests administered to U.S. schoolchildren, by Goddard in 1910, indicated that the mental ages of most children did not correspond to their grade levels and thus reinforced Ayres's major argument in *Laggards in Our Schools* and the arguments of educators who thought that sorting children within each grade by ability levels would encourage their retention.

The contours of the American approach to tracking come into sharper focus when compared with tracking, or "streaming," in England. The English had a history of finely calibrated language to describe their social structure and the type of schooling appropriate to each tier. Observing in 1868 that "the different classes of society, the different occupations of life, require different teaching," the Schools Inquiry Commission called for schools for the higher-middle, middle-middle, and lower-middle classes, nomenclature that did not come into fashion in the United States as a description of social class, let alone schools, until the 1950s. In the late nineteenth century most English working-class children who received any formal education did so in elementary schools that lacked any link to secondary education, while upper- and middle-class children received their elementary schooling in the preparatory departments of what were usually called grammar schools and would eventually be called secondary schools. At the top of the secondary ladder stood the endowed "public" schools, most of which were boarding schools for the children of parents who occupied or aimed at gentry status. Below these a variety of nonresidential fee schools served parents who were content to have their children achieve "respectability." No state-supported secondary schools existed.[35]

A turn came in England with the Education Act of 1902 and subsequent regulations, which laid the foundation for a system of tax-supported ("maintained") grammar schools. Despite tax support, these schools charged fees to most parents, but regulations following the 1902 Act made it a condition of receiving the full state subsidy that at least 25 percent of these schools' places should be free and open on the basis of a qualifying examination only to children from state elementary schools, in effect working-class children. During the 1920s and 1930s regulations gradually fixed eleven as the age for transfer from elementary, or "primary," schools to grammar, increasingly called "secondary," schools, and with the fixing of a transfer age the so-called Eleven Plus examinations took shape. Administered by local education authorities, who had been empowered by the 1902 Act, these examinations varied in format from locale to locale, but whether they featured testing for IQ or for subject matter or some combination of the two, they were selective.[36] Performance on the Eleven Plus determined whether one entered a grammar school or one of the fast-proliferating trade schools, a distinction of no small importance since grammar schools commanded access to the universities and to the more respectable forms of white-collar work.

Streaming developed primarily in state elementary schools, which by the 1920s served middle- and working-class children. It did so in the context of the looming Eleven Plus examination. The aim of streaming was not, as in the United States, to raise the overall level of educational attainment; the English assumed that most children would fail to gain a free place in a grammar school. What mattered was that those who did gain such places possessed merit, defined as intellectual ability. This assumption reflected values that could be traced distantly to England's aristocratic tradition of precise distinctions between superiority and inferiority, with distinctions based on property and manners slowly and partly yielding to those based on ability. More proximately, it reflected the views of Fabian Socialists, who, accepting the class-divided system of education, sought access to grammar schools for talented working-class children.

Profound differences between English and American values imparted different valences in each country to the idea of schools as sorters. Americans persisted in thinking that the function of schooling was merely to add a good thing, education, to original nature. Even when Americans took note of the selective role of schooling, as more did during the 1920s, they made little of it. Instead, they argued that different ability groups were to proceed at different paces and that grades were to be normed by ability group so that everyone would graduate. A committee of the National Association of Secondary School Principals recommended in 1922 that a passing grade in all prescribed subjects was to be within the reach of all normal students, and it urged that "to foredoom to failure any earnest boy or girl admitted to the high school, is thoroughly unjustifiable, undemocratic, and indeed vicious in all its effects."[37] The National Education Association proclaimed in 1924 that failure was to be considered "abnormal," and four years later a California educational bulletin advised that "the word 'failure' should have no place in a proper school system."[38]

Intelligence versus Character

As late as 1917 applied psychology aroused only fitful interest among businessmen, and applied psychologists themselves divided over whether intelligence, beyond a bare minimum, was necessary for achievement. These skeptics included Walter Bingham, who in 1915 established the nation's first department of applied psychology at Carnegie Tech and who a year later lured Walter Dill Scott there as director of its Bureau of Salesmanship Research. Bingham and Scott doubted the practical value of intelligence testing and put more faith and energy in devising tests for character traits that were useful in business.

American entry into World War I gave both the intelligence testers and the character testers unprecedented opportunities to demonstrate the applications of psychology. Initially, the army was more receptive to the ideas of Bingham and Scott, who were sure that character tests held forth unprecedented promise to select officers on the basis of merit.[39] Their dealings with businessmen appeared to give them more real-world experience than the intelligence testers could claim. In 1917 the main evidence that any intelligence test met the criterion of "validity," meaning that it correlated with some real trait, lay in the correlation between its results and those of other intelligence tests. The constituents of character—such as energy, leadership, resourcefulness, and zeal—sounded more like the stuff that soldiers were made of than did intelligence. Scott and Bingham also proposed to classify every man entering the army for specific duties, since each army division required a specified number of radio operators, electricians, mechanics, blacksmiths, teamsters, surveyors, and topographers, not to mention, as Scott added in passing, men armed "with the skills of destruction and defense that can be acquired only in the Army."[40]

The character testers also had superior connections to the army's chain of command. In August 1917 the army established the Committee on the Classification of Personnel (CCP), with Scott as director and Bingham as executive secretary, under the Office of the Adjutant General of the Army.[41] On a parallel track, Yerkes, who was a self-professed "psychobiologist" with an interest in animal intelligence (shared by Thorndike), president of the American Psychological Association, and chairman of the National Research Council's Psychology Committee—the National Research Council had been established in 1916 to advise the government on science—had to settle for the headship of the new Psychological Division, which was placed under the office of the Surgeon General in the Army Sanitary Corps. Although Yerkes doubted the validity of testing for character, he was forced to seek Scott's support for an appointment to the CCP and for the army's approval for intelligence testing.[42] In contrast to the character testers, the intelligence testers had little experience with administering group tests. They mainly had administered individual tests, which Terman called "Binet's *mode de luxe*." Individual intelligence tests required careful evaluation by a professional, and they had been administered to either very inferior or very superior subjects. Initially, the army's interest was confined to testing for "feeblemindedness," a likely bar to soldiering.

The wartime experience nevertheless boosted intelligence testing far more than testing for character. The big winners were Yerkes, Terman, and Goddard. Their success reflected the publicized failure, described in the Introduction, of the Army Rating Scale, adapted from Scott's "man-to-man" rating scale, to meet scientific standards of validity and reliability. Harold Rugg, hired by the CCP to evaluate the trials of character rating at two camps, averred that the trial conditions were "difficult if not totally impossible to duplicate in peacetimes" and then concluded that it was "most emphatically, NOT" possible to apply science to the rating of human character.[43] Merely increasing the number of persons who evaluated each individual's character and decomposing character into numerous traits did not produce an objective result.[44] More fundamentally, Rugg discovered the same propensity that Thorndike simultaneously was naming the *halo effect*.[45] Regardless of the number of traits rated, all ratings were governed by each rater's general reaction to the officer being evaluated. In turn, Rugg speculated, each evaluator's reaction depended on how the evaluator interpreted the subject's actions toward him.[46]

Yerkes, Terman, and the other psychologists interested in testing intelligence made no strong impression on the army but at least managed to avoid the fiasco of character testing. Their first step, initiated by Terman, was to develop a group test, called "Army *a*," which consisted of multiple choice questions and which, with the aid of stencils, could be quickly scored. Their second was to depart from Yerkes's original plan, which called for testing only soldiers whose mental behavior suggested mental deficiency. Between May and early July 1917 Yerkes and his co-workers reached two key decisions: to persuade the army to test all recruits and to try to correlate test results with the evaluations of recruits by their officers instead of merely with other intelligence tests. Rather than just screen out defectives, Yerkes's group planned to test for the likelihood of military success.

Mass intelligence testing started in April 1918. Heartened by trial evidence that the results of Army *a* correlated at a moderate level (roughly .5) with officers' evaluations of recruits, the testers modified Army *a* so that by the time it became what was called "alpha," it was more discriminating at the high end of the scale, a valuable alteration from the army's standpoint because it wanted to use the tests to select officer candidates and NCOs. Alpha was also tougher to fail, a useful refinement because the army wanted to discourage deliberate flunking in order to secure a discharge.[47]

The intelligence testing program had little effect on the army. The military continued to test recruits for a year after the war and adopted a policy of excluding those whose scores labeled them *morons*, a term coined by Goddard to describe "high-grade defectives," but in this respect the tests just accomplished what the army long had effected by its medical exam, the exclusion of those deemed mentally deficient. Many officers viewed the psychologists as pests who were mainly interested in using the military as a laboratory. At no point did the army rely on intelligence tests to select officer candidates.

Wartime intelligence testing nevertheless accomplished several enduring results. It created a community of mental testers, some of whom, like Terman, had worked in isolation before the war. Analysis of the results of alpha persuaded psychologists that they were actually testing intelligence, partly because the plotting of scores on (most) of the individual tests that composed alpha resembled a bell and partly because alpha scores correlated with scores on some other intelligence tests, notably the Stanford-Binet. But none of this addressed the issue of whether intelligence correlated with success in the actual world. An apparent answer to this question lay buried in army's data on testing.

Testing and Success

In his massive *Psychological Examining in the United States Army* (1921) Yerkes observed that alpha scores correlated positively with army rank and with the prestige of civilian occupations, but published as a Memoir of the National Academy of Sciences, filled with Pearsonian coefficients and many qualifications, and nearly nine hundred pages long, this volume had limited public impact.[48] More important were handy distillations, of which two stood out. In 1920 *Army Mental Tests* by Yerkes and Clarence Yoakum conveniently translated the numerical scores on alpha and beta into letter grades, which they then expressed in a series of bar graphs. These were widely reprinted and showed that 83 percent of officers made alpha grades of A and B ("very superior" and "superior" intelligence) compared with 73.2 percent of candidates in Officer Training School, 53.4 percent of sergeants, 39.7 percent of corporals, and 18.8 percent of privates.[49] On this basis, Yerkes and Yoakum asserted that while the tests did not "infallibly" predict soldierly qualities and did not measure bravery or power to command, in the long run these qualities "are far more likely to be found in men of superior intelligence." Yerkes and Yoakum felt sufficiently confident to urge their letter grades as a basis for the army's future selection policies: the A men were the officers of the future, the B men would make good officers or NCOs, the C+ men (high average intelligence) had the makings of NCOs, the C men (average intelligence) would usually remain privates but a few could rise to NCO, on down to the D men—"many of them are illiterate or foreign"—who would never rise above private, and the E men, unfit for service.[50]

The other important distillation of the results of wartime testing was Carl Brigham's 1922 *A Study of American Intelligence*, which carried a glowing introduction by Yerkes. A former army tester who would devise the Scholastic Aptitude Test (SAT) in 1926, Brigham did much to publicize the evidence from the military tests that supported the movement for immigration restriction by showing that the lordly "Nordics" outperformed the "Mediterranean race."[51] Brigham also reprinted the bar graphs from *Army Mental Tests* showing the relationship between intelligence testing and military rank, and, more important for the direction of testing in the 1920s, bar graphs indicating a relationship between alpha scores and soldiers' civilian occupations. Brigham drew his material on occupational correlations from Yerkes's *Psychological Testing*, but he presented it in a popular format that omitted all of Yerkes's qualifications.[52]

The discovery of a relationship between intelligence and occupations was an accidental by-product of the army testing program. This story began in 1918 when the personnel officer at Camp Wadsworth detailed twenty clerical workers to the testing unit. The psychologists quickly concluded that one-third of these clerks were incompetent and that the same third had below-average alpha scores. Although the CCP was already compiling information on the occupations of recruits in order to assign them to military tasks, the Wadsworth incident prompted it to secure support for a tabulation of occupational data from sixteen camps. Converted to letter grades, alpha scores indicated that unskilled laborers scored from mid-D to mid-C, plumbers from low to high C, file clerks from mid-C to low B, accountants from high C to mid-B, and doctors and engineers from high C to A.[53]

If intelligence correlated with the prestige of occupations, then it seemed likely that those with higher IQs would earn higher wages. On this count, classical economic theory was not much help, since it merely explained general wages (or the wage "level") as a return to labor. In an 1889 textbook the economist Richard T. Ely complained about the barrenness of economics when it came to explaining wage differentials, and then, as if to prove his point, offered no better explanation than the whimsies voiced by Adam Smith in 1776: the need to handsomely remunerate public executioners for their disagreeable work and men of "high account" to maintain their "splendid manner."[54] This vacuum was filled by marginal-productivity theory, which originated in Europe and received its principal American formulation in John Bates Clark's *The Distribution of Wealth* (1899). As Clark expressed it, the margin was the final increment or last unit of labor added in response to the estimated value of a product. The marginal wage was the last wage worth paying—the wage paid, for example, to the last farm laborer added to ensure the harvest of a crop before the storm. In 1904 Harvard's Thomas Nixon Carver rolled the new doctrine into a simple formula: find out what the group could produce with the extra laborer, then what it could produce without his help, "and the difference between the two amounts is the measure of his worth to the group—as a man's worth is calculated in the industrial world."[55]

Although originating in Europe, marginal-productivity theory took American economics by storm, chiefly because it maintained that, at least in theory, each producer would receive a return proportionate to his economic contribution.[56] In other words, it reinforced the ideal of just deserts, long a key element in the American conception of merit. Clark updated John L. O'Sullivan's assertion in 1840 that as long as rewards were merit-based, the "deadly animosity of classes feeling themselves equal" would shrink, by stressing that while the welfare of the working class depended on whether it received much or little, social harmony depended on each worker's receiving a return proportionate to his economic contribution.

Although marginal-productivity theory explained returns to individual workers, it was compatible with the Progressive Era theory of noncompeting groups. Princeton economist Frank A. Fetter, a leading marginalist, cited the working class's limited natural ability, its ignorance of alternative opportunities, and its lack of training as factors that routinely prevented young workers from entering higher grades of labor than their fathers. He then classified occupations into a four-tier pyramid based on *ability* and *skill* (words he used interchangeably): those requiring "rare" ability, those requiring "specialists," skilled labor, and unskilled labor. He assumed that marginal-productivity theory would regulate wages within each of these grades. Adam Smith was wrong, Fetter maintained, when he said that men differed little in natural ability (Smith believed that differences in ability arose from the division of labor). Rather, Fetter argued, differences in "talents" were rooted in nature. Just as no two pigeons have the same wingspan, no two people have the same abilities. "Nature by numberless devices is experimenting with variations on either side of the established mean."[57]

Given the limits of the science available to him, Fetter could mount sugges-
tive arguments, but before the discovery of a correlation between alpha scores
and civilian occupations, there was little reason to believe that either trades or
professions were mainly stratified by mental ability.[58] In a widely cited typology
advanced in the first edition of his *Principles of Economics* (1912), Harvard
economist Frank Taussig, a leading advocate of the theory of noncompeting
groups, devised a five-tier hierarchy of occupations: (1) the professions and
"managers of industry"; (2) the lower middle class of bookkeepers, teachers in
the lower grades, railway conductors, and foremen, all of whom looked down on
manual labor and aspired to better things for their children; (3) skilled workers;
(4) semiskilled workers like factory operatives and miners, whose jobs required
some attentiveness and responsibility; and (5) day laborers. Although Taussig believed that intelligence was hereditary and that an exceptionally talented person
could rise from one tier to the next, he initially based workplace hierarchy on the
distribution of pay, not ability.[59] "Any one of intellectual capacity who consorts
with the average person of the 'superior' classes and observes their narrowness,
their dullness, their fatuous self-contentment," he wrote, "must hesitate before
believing that they or their descendants achieve success solely because of their unusual gifts." The only certainty about the rich was that they had inherited capital
and connections.[60]

Stimulated by evidence of a relation between an individual's score on an intelligence test and his occupation, Taussig would change his mind about the relationship between ability and pay.[61] Correlations between alpha scores and
occupations had an electric effect on mental testers, educators, and social scientists in the 1920s. As a mark of the validity of intelligence testing, these correlations easily surpassed the principal existing method of establishing validity,
which merely involved correlating an individual's scores on one test with his
scores on another.[62] Evidence of a correlation between IQ and occupation made
it easier to detach IQ tests from their military context and to deploy them as a
basis for general conclusions about brains and jobs.[63] This was true even when
no data existed about the relationship between intelligence and specific occupations. In the mid-1920s Terman and another psychologist, Douglas Freyer,
publicized the so-called Barr Scale of occupations, which ranked one hundred
occupations, from hobo to "inventive genius (Edison type)" by the amount of
intelligence required by each, as estimated by a board of "judges" who did not
actually test anyone.[64] In 1927 Harvard's Pitirim Sorokin concluded from the
Barr Scale that occupational hierarchy "is based on the principle of a decreasing
intellectuality and controlling power of the occupations, which is at the same
time parallel to a decreasing payment and hierarchical place in the occupational
stratification."[65]

A leading theorist of social stratification, Sorokin postulated that in all societies some jobs were more important for group survival than others and demanded that their incumbents be more skilled and intelligent. Yet Sorokin's personal experience told him that societies would not necessarily fill their key positions with their best people. A refugee from Lenin's Russia—he had served as Alexander Kerensky's personal secretary and narrowly escaped execution by the Bolsheviks—Sorokin knew that aristocracies could become sufficiently decadent to collapse.[66] Evidence that the scores of individuals on intelligence tests correlated with their occupations nevertheless made a big impression on Sorokin, as it did on Taussig. In 1927 Sorokin concluded that "the higher social classes, on the whole, are more intelligent than the lower ones," and that "as a general rule, the social and mental distribution of individuals within a given society are positively correlated."[67] Citing studies, many spun off from the eugenics movement, from most corners of the world and in a host of languages, Sorokin assigned a near total superiority to the upper classes. They were taller, weighed more, had larger cranial capacity and larger brains, and were even better looking than their inferiors. American presidents of universities were taller and heavier than presidents of small colleges; bishops were bigger than small-town preachers; sales managers towered over salesmen; presidents of state bars were taller and heavier than county attorneys; station agents were shrimps next to railroad presidents.[68]

Taussig was an early American admirer of Sorokin, to whom he sent complimentary letters before Harvard snatched Sorokin from the University of Minnesota to fill its first chair in sociology. In 1932 Taussig authored *American Business Leaders: A Study in Social Origins and Social Stratification*, which had the distinction of being the first and for a long time the only serious study of economic mobility in the United States.[69] Drawing heavily on Sorokin's spirit, *American Business Leaders* based its evidence on responses to a questionnaire sent to a sample of around fifteen thousand business leaders, mostly corporate directors and partners in investment houses rather than founders of industrial or financial enterprises, drawn from the 1928 edition of *Poor's Register of Directors*. The responses spoke to an issue that long had interested Taussig: whether success in business resulted mainly from the environment, which Taussig equated with access to capital, personal connections, and higher education, or from heredity, which he based on the innate superiority of intelligence and merit. In earlier writings Taussig had dismissed the idea that the rich necessarily owed their position to merit; on the other hand, he had argued, intuitively, that success in business depended more on innate superiority than in other spheres of endeavor like the professions, where access to training and academic credentials largely accounted for hierarchies. Taussig's interpretation of the responses to his questionnaire confirmed his intuition. If top executives were paid ten times more than bookkeepers, there was "no question" of the reason. Differences in compensation arose "from the comparative supply of the several grades of ability required in these occupations."[70]

In Taussig's hands, merit trumped privilege on every page. Yet much of his evidence pointed to privilege. True, top executives were far more likely to have attended or graduated from college than the average American, but this only proved they were smarter. (On this count, Taussig could have taken a cue from Sorokin, who thought that college degrees were too easily acquired in the United States.) Taussig's data indicated that top managers clearly had benefited from their family connections. For example, 11.6 percent reported receiving more than $10,000 in aid from relatives and friends in the early stages of their careers, and 39.2 percent reported receiving a mixture of financial aid and door-opening interventions from influential relatives and friends. Over half of the top executives were sons of businessmen, 30 percent were sons of big businessmen, and 45 percent worked in the same firm as their fathers. Among this last group, over 70 percent held positions as chief executive, partner, or owner of their fathers' businesses.

To the untutored eye, top executives might resemble a "caste-like" group, but Taussig hammered away at the incorrigible metal shards that jutted out from his taut ship. For example, the proportion of leaders reporting benefit from influential connections was greater in the smaller firms (those with gross receipts under $5 million annually) and higher among subordinate than chief executives, so "the degree of success in business is not conditioned to any great extent by the factor of influential connections." Taussig acknowledged instances of upward mobility by sons of farming and laboring parents but immediately added that these sons were concentrated in comparatively small firms, proof that their parents had less talent to pass on to them than did the parents of corporate titans.

Despite its blinkers, *American Business Leaders* acquired a high reputation by default. No comparable studies existed until the 1950s, when a new generation of researchers, less wedded to hereditarianism and more focused on shoring up America's ideological foundations in the context of the Cold War, turned to the study of social mobility to establish the continued vitality of the American Dream. Social mobility was not high on Taussig's list of characteristics of a healthy society. The ability that carried a man to the top of the corporate ladder was both heritable and, in principle, distributed among all social classes, but it was also rare. From this perspective, one would not expect to find many sons of laborers or farmers at the top. It would never have occurred to Taussig, just as it had never occurred to Galton, to inquire into the proportion of children of ordinary parents who rose above their parents' station.

Taussig's hereditarian bias was fully shared by the mental testers of the early 1920s who examined the correlations between intelligence and occupation spun off from the army mental tests. Nothing would have pleased Terman and God-dard more than to advance the scaling of occupations by intelligence through the use of mental tests that sorted gifted young people into schools leading directly to the class of professionals and managers. But public educators were uninterested in using mental tests in this way; rather, they saw testing as a device for facilitating tracking and the prolongation of education. Lack of support from educators was not the only problem confronting psychologists who wanted to promote the scaling of jobs by intelligence. A much greater problem arose when it became clear that someone's score on an intelligence test, while a good predictor of his occupation (according to available evidence), was not a very good predictor of his productivity on the job. Identifying the mixture of skills and abilities that predicted productivity became a preoccupation of the personnel management movement. Illustrating the ironic consequences of the client orientation of the American testing movement, the founders of personnel management carried rigid hereditarian convictions, similar to Taussig's, into their work, only to find that their experiences within the movement led them in unexpected directions.

Testing and Personnel Management

Personnel management grew out of the convergence of several trends. Before 1918 Bingham and Scott had pioneered the field of industrial psychology, and Harvard's Hugo Munsterberg, who spurred Yerkes's interest in animal psychology, devised tests for selecting trolley conductors and marine officers.[71] After the death in 1915 of Frederick Winslow Taylor, who founded scientific management and who assumed that workers would produce more only if spurred by pay incentives, Henry L. Gantt led a new generation of scientific managers who stressed procedures for selecting workers and binding them to their firms, such as instituting promotion ladders, in order to reduce labor turnover and unrest.[72]

After 1918 the personnel management movement became a port of call for many of the former army testers, including Terman, Thorndike, Scott, Bingham, Yerkes, Yoakum, and L. L. Thurstone. In 1919 Scott founded the Scott Company to advise business on personnel policies and devised a "graphic rating scale" to simplify the evaluation of employees.[73] Bingham edited the *Journal of Personnel Research*, organ of the Personnel Research Foundation (est. 1922).[74] Yoakum acted as its managing editor, while Terman served on its editorial board and Yerkes was a contributor.

Primarily a response to the wave of strikes between 1916 and 1922, the personnel management movement drew support from business executives who sought a stable and contented work force, engineers interested in scientific management,

and social workers and educators who embraced the ideal of vocational guidance and were attracted by the idea that, properly structured, even routine jobs
could be turned into careers with ladders of advancement. The fortunes of this
movement would wax and wane over the next four decades, depending mainly
on changes in the economy. The movement nevertheless embodied a cohesive
set of ideals that promised social harmony and social differentiation through
testing, ideals that had a significant impact on American social thought until the
early 1960s.[75]

In the eyes of its progenitors, the personnel management movement required
a full package of reforms: reducing the number of jobs in a plant to a manageable number of classifications, each encompassing similar tasks; establishing
wage rates for each classification; introducing clearly articulated and published
promotion ladders; and administering performance-predicting tests to select
workers.[76] For example, Goddard, who believed that workers were productive in
direct proportion to their intelligence, thought that workers should be paid by
their IQs.[77] But firms wanted quick results, "not a booklet of psychological tests,"
as a business representative told the 1919 meeting of the APA. "The advertised
success of the latter has not sold the idea to manufacturers."[78] Part of the problem
faced by industrial psychologists arose from the long-standing control over hiring and promotion exercised by foremen on the shop floor. Under the reign of
foremen, prejudice ruled hiring decisions (Italians were womanizers, Romanians
dishonest, Slovaks stupid). Vague criteria for promotion ensured discontent in
the ranks.[79] In their efforts to wrest control over hiring and promotion from
foremen, personnel managers had some success in the immediate postwar era,
when labor markets were slack and firms had more scope for choice. Even then,
however, mental testers had to compete against firm managers who hired on the
basis of an applicant's facial or skull characteristics, height (the company officer
who only hired six-footers as salesmen), hair color, and, of course, race. In the
1910s Katherine Blackford, M.D., popularized the notion that blonds were "invariably" quick, active, and dominating compared with the plodding, painstak-
ing, and submissive brunets.[80] Blackford's *Analyzing Character: The New Science
of Judging Men, Misfits in Business, and Home and Social Life* (1914) and *The Job,
the Man, the Boss* (1914) went through numerous editions before and after her
early death in 1916, and are still in print.

Blackford combined Darwinian evolution with older ways of judging individuals which could be traced through phrenology back to the eighteenth-century
interest in physiognomy and which by 1915 usually passed under the name "characterology." Her approach rested on the assumption that all mental and psychical
states have evolved, with the fittest surviving, and leave physical marks, not only on
hair color but on the shape of one's nose, one's hands, size, and race.[81] Providing

instant results, characterology was a hard act to follow for the mental testers, with their paper-and-pencil tests, the more so because the mental testers quickly found that "general intelligence" did not correlate strongly or consistently with the performance of employees. IQ proved a poor predictor of performance in highly routinized workplaces and an inconsistent one elsewhere.[82] Why, for instance, did captains and lieutenants in Cleveland's police department score much higher on an intelligence test than did their counterparts in Detroit, who scored lower than patrolmen?[83] Why was there a strong correlation between supervisors' ratings of stenographers and the stenographers' scores on the Scott Company Mental Alertness Test in two departments of a firm but no correlation at all in a third department? Psychologists responded to these questions in various ways. They blamed employers for failing to provide enough opportunities for promotion. They kept searching for the perfect employee rating form, the one that recorded fundamental rather than composite traits and that eliminated the halo effect, for example by forcing raters to shift from one side of the page to another to locate "excellent." They also developed tests to measure traits that were more directly related to highly standardized jobs. In his widely cited *Employment Psychology* (1919) Henry C. Link described his experiments with testing female inspectors of artillery shells in a munitions plant. Deciding that the job required good eyesight, keen visual discrimination, quick reactions, and steady attention, Link assessed each worker's "general intelligence" and then administered various tests for each specific quality, including a card-sorting test, an accuracy test (inserting a brass-tipped pencil into progressively smaller holes on a board), and a "tapping" test that required the subject to push down a telegraph key as rapidly as possible. After working out the correlations between the scores and each worker's monthly production (measured by the number of shells inspected), Link applied the same tests to workers whose job was to test the heads of shells by fitting each onto a gauge.[84]

Link failed to discover a significant correlation between general intelligence and productivity for either the inspectors or the gaugers. But he did find strong correlations between the inspectors' productivity and their performance on the card-sorting and accuracy tests and very weak correlations for the gaugers on all but the tapping test. He explained the latter result as evidence that gaugers required speed of movement and endurance, which the tapping test aimed to measure, and he concluded that industry would save money if it applied similar tests to all prospective employees. Neither Link nor Thorndike, who wrote a glowing introduction to *Employment Psychology*, considered an alternative explanation. None of these workers had been selected on the basis of psychological tests. If the productivity of shell gaugers correlated with their performance on the tapping test (.52) better than that of shell inspectors on the same test (.14), it may have been that the sort of work the gaugers did ten hours a day resembled the tapping test far more than the number-checking test.[85] Jobs, as Adam Smith knew, developed aptitudes.

The wider the range of workplaces studied by psychologists and the more traits they tested, the more bewildering became the results. By the early 1920s vocational psychologists were mired in a swamp of empirical studies whose results ("good salesmen are not more frequently large than poor salesmen") pointed in no direction.[86] Beardsley Ruml of the Carnegie Corporation complained in 1921 that vocational psychology's obsession with practical applications and its buckshot discharge of correlation coefficients was contributing nothing to psychology.[87]

The number of studies of personal traits that might have some occupational utility nevertheless kept increasing, partly because the spread of psychology departments on college campuses gave the testers a bottomless pool of undergraduates to use as test subjects. For example, one investigator culled the eighty most commonly used descriptive words in five hundred letters of recommendation written by Oberlin College professors for seniors and then told each male student in a psychology class to select five men and each female five women from among their peers to rate on each term. The conclusion was not without interest: the men agreed most strongly on untypical male traits, like neatness, and the women on untypical female traits, like forcefulness.[88] Such studies lacked applications to business, but they sustained vocational psychology as an academic industry. This was an accomplishment of some significance. Once a subject and an approach to it—testing for vocational aptitudes—had been grafted to a university department, it was likely to persist, if only in the form of calls for more research. The persistence of vocational psychology in university departments and journals for specialists helps to explain why it eventually prevailed over the sort of character profiles, which relied heavily on visual evidence, popularized by Katherine Blackford. Although Blackford could draw on established traditions for reading character by visual signs, her approach smacked too much of phrenology, thoroughly discredited among scholars by 1900, to dent the academy. We should also bear in mind that books like Link's *Employment Psychology*, published during the postwar recession when employers could do more selecting than in the tight wartime labor market and filled with promises to enhance productivity through scientific selection at the gate, gave at least a veneer of plausibility to vocational psychology.

Unintended Effects

The practical orientation of American psychology pushed its practitioners in unexpected directions. One such direction involved the relative influences of heredity and environment. All of the important progenitors of mental testing were ardent hereditarians, but the nature/nurture issue became irrelevant to vocational psychologists, to whom it scarcely mattered whether an individual's aptitudes for a job were inherited or shaped by environment. The "distinction between innate and acquired abilities may be disregarded entirely in constructing tests," the vocational psychologist Max Freyd wrote in 1923, for vocational psychology is concerned "only with the abilities possessed by the [job] applicant."[89] Similarly, the more they examined jobs, the more psychologists talked about multiple abilities rather than a single general intelligence, which Spearman had called *g*. Terman never wavered in his belief that intelligence was a unitary trait, specifically the ability to think abstractly, and in 1921 he asserted that "the races which excel in conceptual thinking could, if they wished, quickly exterminate all the races notably their inferior in this respect."[90] But research had shown that intelligence was a disappointing predictor of workplace performance, and in the same year Terman called for more tests for "success in particular kinds of vocational employments" and for tests for "leadership ability," "scientific ability," and "manipulative-mechanical ability."[91]

As psychologists became more receptive to multiple factors in ability, they also began to explore the relationship between job performance and *character*, a term often used interchangeably with *personality* at the start of the 1920s. Thorndike wrote reassuringly in 1920 that "the abler persons in the world in the long run are the more clean, decent, just, and kind,"[92] but businessmen wanted direct tests for honesty, responsibility, and initiative rather than just ability. Harold Rugg's widely cited tabulations of data from the Army Rating Scale had underscored the extent of disagreement when humans rated each other's character traits. But it was still possible to devise tests for specific character traits; several contributors to a major symposium in 1921 on the nature of intelligence concluded that assessing character would become testing's next frontier.[93]

Character testing also gained momentum from numerous studies indicating only modest correlations between IQ and academic grades, which prompted the conclusion that "the discrepancy is due to some characteristic of the individual other than intellectual capacity."[94] Without abandoning their belief in the validity of intelligence tests, psychologists concluded that when bright students failed in school, the culprit was character. The moral perils associated with the emerging teen culture and the widespread apprehensions about moral decline that accompanied rising divorce rates enlisted the energies of the churches in moral regeneration. Character education became a mass movement after World War I. Schools installed so many character-education programs that the National Education Association established a Committee on Character Education to evaluate them. Between 1924 and 1926 John D. Rockefeller Jr.'s Institute on Social and

Religious Research funded the Character Education Inquiry, conducted at Columbia University's Teachers College.[95]

By the mid-1920s psychologists and religious educators had produced a forest of paper-and-pencil tests that purported to assess a subject's sensitivity to moral issues or to elicit the presence and intensity of moral traits. A 1925 inventory of works on "objective methods of measuring character" listed twenty-three "tests now available."[96] Some of these were tests for ethical discrimination. For example, the subject would arrange a series of words, phrases, sentences, or pictures in "the order of their [ethical] merit," or cross out some words or phrases. Others aimed to test the subject's character by placing him in a contrived situation. For example, a test required a child to close his eyes and then attempt to place a pencil mark in each of five circles on a card. Since this was virtually impossible, a student who succeeded must have taken a dishonest peep at the card.[97]

These tests rested on assumptions similar to those that had led the army to experiment with man-to-man rating scales. In 1917–18 both the army brass and the CCP psychologists held the old-fashioned view that character could be judged and some individuals had more of it than others. This approach to character had roots in nineteenth-century self-help guides like William Makepeace Thayer's *Tact, Push, and Principle* (1885), dedicated "to the young men of the United States, facing difficulties, subject to reverses, unassisted by influence or capital, the brave and hopeful of success."[98] The components of Thayer's categories sound much like what the Army Rating Scale purported to measure. For example, *push* included decisiveness, energy, effort, punctuality, and perseverance. Garbed in the new language of social science, the army scale substituted multiple judgments and correlation coefficients for decisions once made on the basis of a stern look in the eye or an inquiry into a soldier's family or political connections. The army testers thought that they were substituting science and merit for prejudice and political intrigue, but they also viewed moral traits as both deeply seated and persistent elements of the individual. One person might be strong on honesty and weak on energy, but he was unlikely to be strong one day and weak the next on either. Otherwise, there would be no point in ranking individuals by the components of character.

The Subversion of Scales

These assumptions about the persistence of character traits began to erode after the war. Whether they called the entity they studied *character* or *personality*, prominent psychologists were shifting their interest away from Thayer's categories. As Gordon W. Allport, already starting to attract attention as a pioneer of personality theory, observed in 1921, the traits usually classified as components of character were not "psychologically basic." They represented "complexes of habits (neatness, tact, and the like) rather than truly fundamental aspects of personality."[99] In Allport's terminology, "personality" connoted the dynamic forces underlying behavior, while "character" signified how society judged the social expression of these traits from a legal or ethical viewpoint. For example, society might judge someone neat but the motive force behind neatness might stem from deeper traits, such as a passive attitude toward parental authority or a phobia toward dirt arising as a defense mechanism against infantile habits or an extreme sensitivity toward the attitudes of one's peers.[100] By invoking *attitude*, a word that had only recently been decoupled from its long-standing denotation of physical posture and applied to predisposing emotional orientations, Allport underscored the direction that personality theory was starting to take. Personalities were configurations of attitudes, and they were not comparable. Like faces, Allport averred, "they have no duplicates; each one is a unique mixture of various degrees of divers traits."[101]

Allport notwithstanding, a few psychologists had already devised personality "tests and scales." In particular, Allport cited the pioneering work of the University of Wyoming psychologist June E. Downey. Born in 1875 to a prominent Wyoming family—her father was among Wyoming's early territorial delegates to Congress and her younger brother would serve as a U.S. senator from California—Downey held a doctorate in psychology from the University of Chicago and in 1927 was given a star, denoting outstanding achievement, in Cattell's misnamed *American Men of Science*. Perhaps reflecting her status as a woman in a male-dominated field, she was the only American psychologist of note to take handwriting analysis (graphology) seriously. Her research indicated that differences in the handwriting of men and women reflected social rather than innate sex differences.[102] By the 1910s the employment of handwriting "experts" to testify in court about the character of the accused had been widely discredited, but Downey revived graphology by giving it a twist. As part of her self-described "experimental prospecting," an apt metaphor given her roots in a silver-mining territory, she concluded that a person's handwriting, while irrelevant to his or her moral worth, did yield insight into the "will-temperament." As Downey defined it, temperament was an innate tendency that revealed itself in various patterned forms of activity. These were determined by an individual's nervous energy and whether this energy was immediately discharged to the motor areas of the body, which activated the muscles and glands, or was discharged in a more "roundabout" way.[103]

Downey drew much of this theory from William James. Her innovation was to devise and in 1919 to market a series of twelve tests that aimed to produce a "will-profile" for each subject. Four of her tests purported to measure "mental speed," four to measure one's degree of impulsive versus inhibited action, and four to measure carefulness and persistence. Most of her tests relied in one way or another on handwriting. For example, to measure "mental speed," the subject was required to write "United States" as fast as possible; to assess levels of inhibition, her tests forced the subject to write in a hand completely different from his normal hand ("disguised handwriting") and to write a memorized verse while his attention was distracted by the reading aloud of a story.[104]

Downey wanted to understand how the traits that composed the temperament were integrated in the individual's personality, but she dug her own grave by marketing the tests. These brought her some fame, but they also exposed her theory to testing by vocational psychologists, whose interest never extended beyond correlating her results with those of IQ tests, academic grades, and vocational aptitude tests. When these correlations turned out to be weak, interest in her tests waned. As for her idea of studying how traits were integrated in individuals, one researcher wrote the predictable obituary: "that has presented great difficulty to the test-makers and statisticians."[105]

On the other hand, it was to Allport's advantage that he did not devise a test for sale to schools or businesses. He described his aim as "personality study and description rather than personality testing."[106] His primary goal was to identify personality types, not to rank-order traits. (For example, extroverts tended to have "narrow but strong emotions" while introverts had broad but superficial ones.) With his brother Floyd, Allport did devise paper-and-pencil tests for personality. One such test, which asked subjects to imagine that they were applying for a job as a detective, was designed to plot their position from expansiveness (the letter would be filled with self-revelation and assurances of suitability) to reclusiveness (the letter would merely announce the applicant's credentials and interest). But Allport had no interest in rank orders, in judging whether one personality was better in any sense than another. Personalities "of divers sorts succeed equally well in the general adaptations of practical life," he wrote.[107]

As Allport was distinguishing personality from character, the unexpected results of the Character Education Inquiry were delivering a devastating blow to the tradition of character rating. The Inquiry consisted of administering and evaluating a great variety of tests for intelligence, vocabulary, arithmetic, moral knowledge, and moral behavior to more than eleven thousand schoolchildren aged eight to sixteen and to a control group of graduate students at Teachers College. Some of the tests were borrowed from Thorndike's Institute of Educational Research at Columbia. Others were taken over from an influential 1921 dissertation at Teachers College by Paul Voelker. Voelker's research had been widely cited in popular magazines; Mark A. May and Hugh Hartshorne, who were hired to evaluate the Inquiry, stated that Voelker's research was "probably familiar to hundreds of thousands of readers."[108] One of Voelker's tests for honesty first asked children if they could name all the oceans and then in a retest asked them to name the oceans again. Another involved sending a subject out to buy an item and then arranging for the merchant to give him too much change. May and Hartshorne criticized these as forms of entrapment, since the examiner himself engaged in the deception, but in one way or another nearly all of the ethical-behavior tests were traps. For example, one test approved by May and Hartshorne involved collecting completed tests, taking them to an office where they were duplicated and then scored, then returning the original to the child along with an answer key for self-scoring, and finally comparing the results.

May and Hartshorne were liberal Protestants committed to both religious education and social science. With Allport, they believed that the best way to study character was in situations; with John Dewey, they viewed education as a process that expanded understanding of society by encouraging inquiry; with John Broadus Watson and the rising school of behaviorism, they thought that science wasted its time studying mental states and that its proper focus was activity. These predispositions shaped their interpretation of the Inquiry, a preliminary version of which was published in six articles in *Religious Education* in 1926–27 and in final form as the three-volume *Studies in the Nature of Character* (1928–30).[109] May and Hartshorne concluded that an individual's moral conduct varied so much from situation to situation that it was idle to talk of general character traits like honesty. The "low correlations between the scores of the same children in different situations indicate quite clearly that a child does not have a uniform general code of morals but varies his opinions to suit the situation in which he finds himself."[110] For example, children who cheated on tests did not cheat their classmates, and those who did cheat on tests were counterintuitively more prone to do so when the likelihood of exposure was greater. Traditionalists could have interpreted the same data to mean that most children needed more character, but May and Hartshorne saw everything through the lens of pragmatism and behaviorism. To talk of a quality such as honesty was as scientifically empty, they contended, as explaining an act of remembering by referring it to "some faculty of memory."[111]

Nearly two decades later Terman's former student Florence Goodenough observed that May and Hartshorne had virtually killed scientific interest in the subject of character education and in the idea of rating people on a scale of character traits. "Their results," she wrote, "ran so strongly counter to the generally accepted idea that conduct is merely the outward expression of generalized character traits such as honesty or dishonesty, generosity or selfishness, and the like that for some years but little further effort was made to develop tests by which such behavior may be predicted. Even up to the present day, most people have preferred to steer clear of these topics or have employed other methods for studying them."[112]

Something for Everyone

Goodenough's obituary for character testing was matched by the recognition by many psychologists that the vast expectations aroused by testing in the wake of World War I—Walter Dill Scott wrote that "tests became regarded as a new form of magic"—had not been met.[113] The onset of the Depression blasted the testers' assumptions about the future of the economy. As the psychologist Sidney Pressey wrote plaintively, the Depression "was making it ironic to facilitate the progress of young people into careers when there were no careers to be found or to save labor in teaching when there were many more teachers than jobs." For Pressey, the Depression's effects were also personal. "The manufacturer of the one crude teaching machine I had been able to get on the market withdrew it from sale. The publisher of my tests went out of business. And—my wife asked me for a divorce, having plans for a second marriage."[114]

Even as the Depression sucked the wind from its sails, the testing movement persisted. But as testimony to the continuing vitality of the principle of equal rights, it took a more egalitarian direction. All along, some influential American social analysts had distanced themselves from Galton, and with good reason. The American context differed significantly from Galton's. The fine calibrations of academic performance that Galton drew on lacked a real counterpart in America. The leading universities had no equivalent of the Tripos and, as the next chapter describes, were becoming reluctant to distinguish their best students by any visible mark. There was much less overlap between political, intellectual, and business elites than in Britain. Multimillionaires who lit their cigars with hundred-dollar bills boasted of their grade-school educations; politicians talked up to the people. American success ideology disparaged determinism. When the pioneer sociologist Lester Frank Ward submitted an essay criticizing Galton's theory of genius to *Forum*, the editors changed the title from "Heredity versus Opportunity—or Nature and Nurture" to "Broadening the Path to Success."[115] In the American view, typified by Thomas Jefferson's theory of natural aristocracy, genius was randomly distributed across social classes. Charles Horton Cooley stated in 1897 that the idea that ability correlated with social class would strike most Americans as "monstrous."[116]

A reconciliation between these values and the technology of mental measurement would become possible if science could identify traits, whether innate or

acquired, that were likely to be valuable somewhere along the spectrum of occupations. The mania for vocational aptitude testing during the 1920s reflected
this belief, but it failed to produce results that could withstand scientific scrutiny.
In 1937 Walter Van Dyke Bingham, who was said to have spent his life worrying
about cobblers who might have been generals, warned that 75 percent of the
more than three thousand existing tests for vocation-specific aptitudes would be
blown away by a single blast of criticism.[117]

A more promising line of inquiry was initiated during the 1930s when psychologists began to reexamine the nature of intelligence itself. A key figure was
L.L. Thurstone of the University of Chicago. Trained as an engineer, Thurstone
assisted Thomas A. Edison (Exhibit A for anyone who wanted to explore different kinds of intelligence) in Edison's New Jersey laboratories before becoming a psychologist. To Thurstone we owe the idea that intelligence, rather than
resembling a pyramid topped by the general mental ability that Charles Spearman had labeled *g*, consists of seven "primary mental abilities" (PMAs): word
fluency, verbal comprehension, spatial visualization, number facility, associative
memory, reasoning, and perceptual speed.[118] PMAs were not vocational aptitudes; rather, they were "multiple factors" that collectively had come to be called
intelligence.[119]

American psychologists embraced the multiple-factor approach with much
more gusto than their British counterparts. With their more explicitly hierarchical society and long history of examinations like the Cambridge Tripos that
aimed to establish a rank order among examinees, the British tended to explain
imperfect correlations among the scores on the different group questions that
composed an intelligence test by invoking *g* or something like it. Adherents of *g*
acknowledged the existence of different factors but within a hierarchy with general mental ability at the top. From this perspective, weak correlations among a
subject's scores on different parts, or groups, of a mental test (this was often the
case) could be explained by supposing that some groups tested more important
factors of intelligence, the ones more reflective of *g*. In contrast, with their history
of believing that nearly everyone had some comparative advantage in the race
of life, the Americans preferred to explain weak correlations among factors by
postulating that different abilities were nearly independent of each other.[120] In
the 1960s University of Southern California psychologist J. R. Guilford, who had
joined with Thurstone to found the journal *Psychometrika* in 1935, claimed to
have discovered a virtual periodic table of 120 distinct abilities.[121]

Popular, as distinct from academic, psychologists also claimed to have discovered a cornucopia of abilities. Books like Charles and Margaret Broadly's *Know
Your Real Abilities: Understanding and Developing Your Aptitudes* (1948) listed
"personality" (do you work better with others or by yourself?), the "ability to

discern pleasing proportions," "tweezer dexterity" (ease in handling small tools), and "grip" among seventeen basic job aptitudes.[122]

The American Council on Education (ACE) distributed the first set of tests for PMAs to schools in 1938, but these tests lacked any validation before World War II. The war marked a turning point for the multiple-factorists like Bingham, who served as chief psychologist for the War Department from 1940 to 1947. Analysis of the specialized tests developed by the armed forces during the war, the most publicized of which was the Army Air Force (AAF) Qualifying Examination and the Air Crew Classification Battery, disclosed a strong correlation between examinees' scores and their likelihood of completing the military's training programs for pilots, bombardiers, and navigators.[123] The AAF results exhilarated multiple-factorists. In 1946 the ACE's Commission on Implications of the Armed Forces Educational Programs concluded that "so-called intelligence tests or tests of general learning ability are not likely to provide as efficient or even as accurate a prediction of any stated criterion as a set of carefully selected specialized tests."[124] Three members of a notable presidential commission on education appointed by President Harry S Truman—ACE president George Zook, the noted black educator Horace Mann Bond of Lincoln University, and T. R. McConnell of the University of Minnesota—had served on the Commission on the Implications of the Armed Forces Educational Programs, which had endorsed the multiple-factor theory. Echoing McConnell and certain that the nation was failing to identify "the latent intellectual talent and potentialities of our citizens," Ordway Tead, another member of the Truman Commission, wrote in 1947 that verbal manipulations of abstractions were just one kind of ability useful in college; others included artistic ability and "social sensitivity."[125]

The search for multiple factors in intelligence preoccupied American psychology from the 1930s into the early 1960s, when it began to crumble under the weight of its own empiricism. In 1957 John Flanagan, a psychology professor and former AAF tester, began to secure funding for Project TALENT, which resulted in the administration in 1960 of a battery of tests to nearly half a million ninth-graders. Flanagan's battery included tests for learning foreign languages, electronic ability, creative potential, vocational interests, sociability, sensitivity, vigor, calmness, tidiness, self-confidence, dating habits, and reading habits.[126] Once all the data had been assembled and scored and follow-up studies conducted, schools would be able to tailor their curricula and guidance counseling to individual abilities. Or so Flanagan believed. In reality, educators could scarcely assimilate the sixty test scores for each student or the more than one billion pieces of information dredged up by Project TALENT. After 1970 Flanagan's mountain of information did arouse the interest of economists and sociologists, who mined it to answer a different question—not how to guide youth into suitable careers but to understand the relationship between social class and schooling in American society.

By the mid-1960s Spearman's g was rebounding.[127] Americans were starting to debate *meritocracy*, a term coined in 1957—by an Englishman, predictably enough—the same year in which Flanagan began to coax funding from federal agencies for his exercise in overkill.

6

THE "PRESUMPTION OF MERIT"

Institutionalizing Merit

The mental testers resembled a migrating gaggle of geese, alighting on one pond before flying to another. They acted as consultants to institutions rather than as architects or implementers of policy. As consultants, they aided institutions in identifying and rewarding promising employees. In their own eyes, they used science to identify merit. But the kind of merit they had in mind had nothing in common with the overall superiority of the Founding Generation's Men of Merit. Nor did they have much in common with those who had devised merit systems in the nineteenth century to settle disputes over rank orders in competitions. Mental testers had little interest in competition. There were no first and second places on aptitude tests, just positions (rarely revealed to the test taker) on the curve of distribution. What mattered to the mental testers was that their institutional clients functioned efficiently, an objective that depended on identifying promising employees and aligning them with suitable jobs.

This kind of merit bears much closer resemblance to what I call institutional merit than to essential merit. A group of educators, along with kindred spirits in the professions (including the profession of arms), added flesh and muscle to the concept of institutional merit after the Civil War. These individuals shared a deep dissatisfaction with the way in which existing hierarchies in higher education, government, and the professions were constituted, and in response to this dissatisfaction they sought to vest the presumption of merit in institutions rather than in individuals.

A Gathering of Luminaries

Future president Woodrow Wilson was among the dignitaries from more than eighty colleges and universities who assembled in Baltimore in 1902 to celebrate the twenty-fifth anniversary of the opening of The Johns Hopkins University. Neither Wilson nor anyone else dissented when Charles W. Eliot, president of Harvard since 1869, proclaimed that the organization of the nation's universities had changed on an unprecedented scale during the preceding quarter of a century.[1] Eliot recognized several key movers of this transformation in the audience, including the University of Chicago's William Rainey Harper, Stanford's David Starr Jordan, Johns Hopkins's Daniel Coit Gilman, and Columbia's recently inaugurated president, Nicholas Murray Butler. Other speakers readily acknowledged that the pioneers of the transformation were Eliot, Cornell's Andrew Dickson White, and Gilman. After becoming its president in 1869, Eliot guided the transformation of Harvard from a provincial college to a nationally renowned university. Gilman set Johns Hopkins University on a course that made it the locus of the nation's leading graduate school, medical school, and hospital by 1900. As president of Cornell University from 1868 to 1885, White had effectively reconciled two ideals, practical and "philosophical" (academic) education, that had been antagonistic in the late 1860s.

Eliot, White, and Gilman, the three pioneers, were far from presenting a united front on educational reform. White loathed Eliot for his Harvard snobbery, his opposition to federal aid to education and to a national university, and his hostility to coeducation, a feature of both Cornell and (more tentatively) Johns Hopkins.[2] (Eliot construed coeducation as a university's public confession of its inability to attract males.)[3] Gilman and White remained close friends, but the institutions headed by each profoundly differed. Cornell University owed its founding to an endowment from Ezra Cornell, a self-made telegraph magnate obsessed with practical education and with students working their way through college in campus factories; he was determined to found a university where "any person can find instruction in any study." Andrew Carnegie admired Ezra Cornell; he included Ezra's widow on his private pension list. As New York state senators, White and Cornell teamed up to secure New York's allotment under the Morrill (Land-Grant College) Act of 1862 for the new university. As president, White blunted Cornell's hard-core utilitarianism, but when asked for advice by the trustees planning the curriculum of Johns Hopkins University in 1874, White envisioned Johns Hopkins primarily as a school of applied science.[4] Eliot's advice to the same query was to establish Johns Hopkins as a college of arts and sciences with free electives.[5] Neither suggestion fit Gilman's idea of a university founded primarily on research-oriented graduate programs.

These educators nevertheless shared several values, including a commitment to nonsectarianism in higher education, which minimally meant opposition to control of universities by religious denominations and which at times went further. In an extremely controversial move, Gilman invited Thomas Henry Huxley, "Darwin's bulldog" and self-styled "agnostic," to give the inaugural address at the opening of Johns Hopkins in 1876. In varying degrees and with Eliot the most extreme, all three favored expanding student choice in electing courses (electivism).[6] Harvard and Yale had made some provision for elective courses before 1860, but less in principle than as a concession to human weakness. They continued to require the study of Latin and Greek and even stipulated the exact order in which classical authors had to be read, a practice, White recognized, that contributed to the colleges' failure, despite the classical curriculum, to produce classical scholars.[7]

Eliot, Gilman, and White were also committed to the identification and advancement of merit. On the surface, there was nothing new in this goal. With their commencement honors, rank orders, and scales of merit, colleges had long professed to establish orders of merit, which they expected would be translated into positions of prominence in the republic. These three pioneers knew all about this sort of merit. Born between 1831 and 1834, they attended college at a time when public life, the public professions, and public address were the apples of collegians' eyes and when prize compositions in rhetoric, composing and speaking, permeated collegiate culture. What the pioneers came to describe as "special," "exact," or "accurate" knowledge played very little role in this culture of merit.[8] As the astronomer Simon Newcomb observed in 1876, Americans preferred versatility and adaptability to special training and did so with "entire success."[9] The high opportunity costs of full-time schooling, weak traditions of apprenticeship, and popular individualism nurtured a type of education based on the principle of catch-as-catch-can. Ralph Waldo Emerson lauded the lad "who in turn tries all the professions, who *teams it, farms it, peddles*, keeps a school, preaches, edits a newspaper, goes to Congress, buys a township, . . . and always, like a cat, falls on his feet."[10] While James Burrill Angell, future president of the University of Michigan, was traveling in Europe during the 1850s, Francis Wayland, Brown University's president, wrote to him with an offer of either a professorship of civil engineering or a professorship of modern languages. Angell had graduated first in his class at Brown, but his knowledge of civil engineering came from his brief employment by a water company, and although he chose the modern-languages professorship, he did not know French, German, or Italian. (Wayland told him to stay a year and a half in Europe to learn the first two.)[11]

Martial Fitness

In 1888 James Bryce, the most astute foreign observer of American values since Alexis de Tocqueville, described "an undervaluing of special knowledge" accompanied by "an enthusiasm for anything that can be called genius, with an over readiness to discover it," as one of "the salient intellectual features" of Americans.[12] In his preface to *The American Commonwealth* Bryce thanked several Americans for having guided him through American institutions and values. Among them was Thomas Wentworth Higginson, a minister and abolitionist who had raised the first black regiment in the Union Army during the Civil War. Bryce had probably read Higginson's "Regular and Volunteer Officers," published in the *Atlantic Monthly* in 1864, in which Higginson stated his preference for "regulars."[13] In Europe there had long been tension between graduates of military academies and aristocratic officers, who viewed military leadership as an art to be grasped intuitively, a kind of "natural genius," by those born to command.[14] The rough American equivalent lay in the tension between regulars, a term that connoted attendance at a military school or extensive combat experience or both, and officers who owed their commissions to political wire-pulling.

At the start of the Civil War, as in previous American wars, political influentials raised units of volunteers (the United States had never drafted anyone into its army) and were often rewarded with military rank proportionate to the number of volunteers raised. In order to create opportunities for political patronage, the government chose, as it had in previous wars, to create new regiments rather than to bring old ones up to strength.[15] In both the Union and the Confederacy, volunteer officers owed their commissions to patronage or to election by their men. Volunteers deferred to their officers only to the extent that their officers' courage in battle merited deference. Orders issued by volunteer officers read more like supplications.[16] Volunteer officers were known to leave their units to lobby for promotions. Like politicians, they sought popularity. Higginson averred that a regular officer would be more likely to inspect a sentry's rifle for sand, just the sort of nit-picking apt to arouse recruits' anger. Ulysses S. Grant thought that regular officers were more likely to say no.[17]

With the nation's history of maintaining a small army in peace and engineering quick expansions in war, its reliance on volunteers during the Civil War was inevitable. But the decision to raise new regiments officered by volunteers rather than sprinkle regulars into new regiments reflected values that were deeply entrenched by 1861. In the eyes of critics of regular-army officers, understanding human nature and dealing with people in the mass rather than technical or special knowledge formed the stuff of a good officer. Union general Jacob D. Cox, formerly an Ohio state senator, said that the principles of war were so few that they could be written on the back of his greeting card.[18] (In contrast, volunteers for the navy could rise no higher than lieutenant; no one assumed that a politician knew anything about seamanship.) Critics of West Point portrayed the Academy's products as "paper pedants." The Prince de Joinville, an unofficial French military observer at General George McClellan's headquarters during the Peninsula campaign, thought that sixty thousand regular soldiers would outperform "double or triple the number of volunteers." But he cannily added that "in America they do not know this, and besides they do not wish to know it. It would involve a renunciation of the general and deeply rooted creed, that every American, when he wishes to do a thing, may find within himself without any apprenticeship, the power to do it; and, consequently, there is no volunteer who, when he puts on the uniform, does not at the same time put on the qualities of a soldier."[19]

The debate between volunteer and career soldiering had two sides. Inasmuch as some political generals performed well and some regulars poorly, the Civil War did not settle the issue. The Franco-Prussian War of 1870–71 did more than the Civil War to boost the stature of advocates of professionalism like West Pointer (class of 1861) Emory Upton, who rose during the Civil War from second lieutenant to brevet major general. In his short but remarkable life Upton provided abundant examples of two different conceptions of merit which were straddled by the Civil War and which I have called essential and institutional merit. Essential merit refers to merit as a personal possession, evidenced by an individual's performance, recognized on the spot, and rewarded. In military terms this meant bravery in combat followed by brevet promotions. Requiring personal assessment of visible performance, essential merit persists in American culture, but over the long course of time its sphere has been constrained by the demands of institutions. For example, lessons learned the hard way during the Civil War gradually led to greater respect for professional soldiers. The practice of electing officers declined, especially on the Union side. Although new regiments continued to elect their officers, and state governors often put forward their own candidates, by 1863 "balloting had largely given way to advancement by merit, as defined and located by commanders rather than the men."[20]

Although Upton repeatedly demonstrated bravery under fire, he had a military intellectual's zeal for tactics and strategy. At Spotsylvania he devised a new tactic for assaulting a Confederate redoubt. Although the attack failed, Upton's tactic would become widely influential. After the war Upton became a favorite of General William T. Sherman, who dispatched him to study armies in Europe and Asia, and emerged as the leading advocate of military professionalism. Upton equated professionalism with reliance on career soldiers rather than volunteers, separating the military from politics, and establishing both a general staff and a war college.[21] Those who shared his outlook spoke a similar language. "In any office of the military service, whether of the line or of the staff," students at the army's School of Application for Infantry or Cavalry (founded by Sherman) at Fort Leavenworth were told in 1907, "search should be made nowadays, not for the brilliant solider, not for the genius, but for one that knows thoroughly the duties of the office."[22]

At his death by suicide in 1881, Upton left an unrevised manuscript designed to expose the "folly and criminality" of American military policy since the start of the Revolution.[23] This manuscript, Elihu Root wrote, lay "filed and forgotten among the millions of documents in the archives of the War Department" until 1904, when it was published as *The Military Policy of the United States*.[24] As war secretary, Root implemented many of the reforms urged by Upton.[25]

Reformers had to navigate obstacles left by legacies of essential merit. The main obstacle to substituting selection for seniority (as measured by date of first commission) as the basis for promotion lay in the widely held view that to do so would be inequitable to older officers, whose past services would be dishonored by the promotion of younger officers with far less service. Historian Donald Chisholm has contrasted equity (fairness) with economy (saving money) and efficiency (the greater good of the navy). By the equity criterion, the combat performances of naval officers during the Civil War entered a kind of memory bank and became part of an officer's self-imagined self-worth. Throughout the 1870s and 1880s many officers and public officials, including congressmen, accepted equity as the ruling criterion for promotion. In effect, they accepted past services as evidence of merit. But equity had long posed problems for efficiency by overstocking the navy with aged officers; at the start of the Civil War every captain on the navy's active list had served at least forty-two years. The problem intensified with the establishment in the 1860s of the grade of rear admiral and mandatory retirement at sixty-two. Lieutenants, typically in their mid-fifties, would have only a handful of years of service at the higher grades of lieutenant commander, commander, captain, and rear admiral.[26]

Congress frequently addressed this problem. Building on some earlier precedents, it established a "Naval Efficiency Board" in 1855 with authority to pension (the first use of retirement pay by the federal government) or discharge officers deemed "incapable" of performing their duties. Prodded by Lincoln's energetic navy secretary Gideon Welles, Congress established mandatory retirement ages for both navy and army officers. It no longer was necessary to prove that an officer was incapable of performing his duties to separate him from the service. In 1866 Welles boldly proposed to fill vacancies by alternating seniority and selection. One senator called this a "new principle." In substance, it was. Since the time of Stephen Decatur, all but six officers had been promoted by seniority.[27] But nothing came of Welles's proposal, and by 1866 the U.S. Navy, briefly the world's largest, was shrinking. Authorizing promotions of officers for "meritorious conduct," as Congress did during the Civil War, scarcely dented seniority. Officers' meritorious conduct became their "past services," which, in turn, kept them on the active list in the modern steam-and-steel navy that Congress authorized in the 1880s. Reflecting deference to the reigning principle of equity, in 1899 Congress provided for the separation of Civil War officers below mandatory retirement age on expensive terms: retirement at current rank with three-fourths sea pay of the next higher rank.[28]

In contrast to essential merit, the evidence for which lies in action, institutional merit introduces two key elements. First, it demands knowledge as a prerequisite of intelligent action. Along with Sherman, Upton had studied at West Point under Dennis Hart Mahan, who argued that military professionalism was rooted in knowledge of the history of warfare. Mahan's son, Alfred Thayer Mahan, more famously made the same point about naval professionalism in *The Influence of Sea Power on History* (1890).[29] Mahan based this book on his lectures at the Naval War College, established in 1884. With Root's encouragement, the Army War College was established as a postgraduate military school in 1901. Second, institutional merit introduces the element of promise. The mental testers, recall, were concerned with identifying promise or potential, and in this respect they can reasonably be called modern. Advocates of institutional merit look for talent that has not been actualized and devise methods of identifying it.

Modern armies, navies, universities, and corporations have sought to identify institutional merit for several reasons. Obviously, it is less expensive to administer than essential merit and more compatible with mastering the technical requirements of modern jobs. Institutional merit suits the large-scale institutions of modern society, institutions that are no longer lengthened shadows of their founders: the corporation more than the partnership; the university more than the small college; the army division more than the company or regiment of volunteers recruited and captained by a person. Institutional merit is also more congruent with the reward structure of modern society, which is characterized by a much greater profusion of ranks than antebellum society, and with the value—inculcated in the public schools—of stepped and predictable promotions.

By today's measures the structure of ranks in pre–Civil War America was notably flat. The old-fashioned law firm had a few partners and several apprentices, but no equivalent of the modern associate; colleges had a handful of professors and many tutors but no assistant or associate professors. The U.S. Navy in 1860 contained no rank higher than captain. The U.S. Army possessed a finely calibrated structure of ranks, with promotion regulated by seniority, but during wars it had always relied on volunteers who gained both commissions and promotions by political influence. What Carl R. Fish wrote of the public service under the spoils system—any position "might lead anywhere, and that quickly"—could be applied to volunteer army officers and to the antebellum professions, where self-promotion and display earned rewards.

The U.S. Navy, whose officer corps was far less subject to political influence than that of the army, differed in this regard. Through the period from 1865 to 1912 a minority of naval officers and congressmen called for a new system that would allow promising officers to be promoted over their seniors. Their key objective, to establish the principle of "up or out" at a specified age, came to fruition in a 1916 act, later known as the Line Personnel Act and described by Chisholm as the "pivotal point in the navy's history." This act established boards to select officers for promotion at specified ages in specified grades in the expectation that officers who reached the higher ranks would do so before their dotage.[30]

In their sphere the university presidents Eliot, Gilman, and White attacked practices and values similar to those attacked by Emory Upton. Just as Upton aimed to wrest military affairs from politicians, nothing more outraged Eliot, a stalwart of the National Civil Service Reform League (NCSRL) who called civil-service reform the "reform of reforms,"[31] than the infiltration of political patronage into higher education. He thought it a national disgrace that whereas Britain required examinations for entry to its royal military colleges, political patronage continued to control admission to West Point.[32] Gideon Welles had the same view, but the idea of examining applicants for the service academies ran into a stone wall based on the objection that examinations would privilege young men from wealthy families. Inasmuch as applicants were rarely from poor families, one suspects that shrinkage of patronage was the real objection. Gilman, who served as president of the NCSRL, claimed that the spoils system had multiplied with "the fecundity of bacteria" during the presidencies from Jackson to Andrew Johnson (each infected by the "Bacillus Tennesseeensis"), drew up lists of civil service reformers since ancient times, and took comfort when a geologist, a man of facts and not party, was appointed to head the Civil Service Commission established by the Pendleton (Civil-Service Reform) Act of 1883.[33] White proposed in 1881 that the NCSRL offer prizes for the best college essays on the evils of the spoils system, which he saw as demoralizing the nation's youth by severing advancement in public life from merit. The United States, White believed, needed only two reforms: universal education and civil-service reform.[34]

Eliot, Gilman, and White believed that the education of most public men left them incompetent to deal with the complicated issues of their day. One of Eliot's early faculty appointments at Harvard, the political economist Charles Dunbar, observed in 1876 that while the Civil War had brought questions of currency and public finance to the fore, the nation lacked "leading men in public life who could speak upon them authoritatively or command general attention."[35] In the same year, Yale professor William Graham Sumner attributed the intensifying critique of public life to rising public expectations of competence in public men.[36] The three pioneers gradually devised new structures in higher education that effectively bound universities more closely to the professions, which they envisioned as a sphere in which "exact" knowledge would be valued as the professions became more closely tied to higher education. By 1910 Eliot was describing business enterprise—long imagined by Americans as a great theater for the display of genius—as a profession whose practice would be improved by university schools of business. Gilman looked to the day when law professors would arbitrate international disputes, when scientists would solve the world's problems, when philologists would interpret the texts on which theologians based their opinions, and when the press would publish the opinions of the learned.[37]

The pioneers were notably more inclined than previous generations of college presidents to identify untapped talent. Gilman listed the discovery and development of "unusual talent" as among the characteristics of a university. In the same breath, he dismissed the discovery of genius as an objective of universities. The problem with genius lay in its connotation of an irrepressible force that would rise regardless of education and training.[38] Maintaining that the proliferation of feeble and squabbling sectarian colleges interfered with the development of the nation's "stock of talent," White called for a national public university, and he inserted in Cornell's charter a provision for free tuition for merit scholars selected by examination from New York's state legislative districts (he preferred this to exempting all students from tuition). Gilman shopped for brains, men of the "first rank," for his faculty, including Basil Gildersleeve, the classicist plucked from Virginia's faculty; James Joseph Sylvester, the brilliant British mathematician whose Jewish origins and refusal to subscribe to Anglican tenets had sentenced him to scrounging for decades around the periphery of Britain's institutions of higher education; and Henry Rowland, the physicist who had little American reputation but whose brilliance had caught the attention of Clerk Maxwell in England.

By 1915 the efforts of the pioneers and their successors had fashioned a university structure characterized by its absorption of professional education and, increasingly, the mounting of professional schools on top of colleges of arts and sciences. Although historians routinely invoke the influence of German universities on American universities in the late nineteenth century, this was not the structure of any German university. The pioneers borrowed features of European universities when it suited their objectives, but their goals developed primarily from the personal experiences of each man.

Origins

The pioneers' quest for a "real" American university began with their dissatisfaction with the opportunities for advanced study in the United States, even in well-established institutions like Harvard and Yale that called themselves universities. Otherwise a conventional undergraduate, Eliot had conceived an unconventional interest in chemistry before his graduation from Harvard in 1853. Besieged with cui bono questions from his friends and relatives, he justified his decision to become a "student and teacher of science" in a lengthy apologia to his mother and then accepted an assistant professorship at Harvard's Lawrence Scientific School, established in 1847 as Harvard's concession to demands that it make greater provision for teaching the sciences.[39] But the Lawrence School disappointed Eliot. It admitted nearly all applicants and paid its professors directly out of student fees, a "money relation" that Eliot found "extremely repugnant to my feelings as a teacher and as a student of science."[40] Although several colleges started scientific schools, Eliot was close to the mark when in 1869 he called them collectively the "ugly duckling" of higher education.[41]

Gilman and White faced similarly meager options. After graduating from Yale, Gilman spent more than a year in a frustrating attempt to acquire advanced instruction as a private student, first in New Haven and then in Cambridge.[42] Gilman and White, both from wealthy families, then secured positions as unpaid secretaries to the new American minister to Russia. Disappointment greeted them on their return. Gilman held a succession of posts at Yale as a fund-raiser, librarian, and eventually professor of physical and political geography at Yale's scientific school (called, after 1860, the Sheffield Scientific School), where he was caught between the distrust of businessmen for higher education and the distrust of Yale educators for schools of applied science.[43] Tiring of being treated as a poor relation by Yale's administration, in 1872 Gilman accepted the presidency of the University of California, where the educational utilitarianism dictated by the state legislature plunged him into misery. White, who had detoured from Russia to study history at the University of Berlin and who hoped to become Yale's first professor of history, found his path blocked by the Yale Corporation's hostility to his religious liberalism. He then took an instructorship in history offered by the University of Michigan's visionary president Henry Tappan. Tappan had called in 1851 for the establishment of a true American university, preferably public and located in New York City, where college graduates would be free to pursue knowledge in what would be essentially a graduate school. White shared Tappan's dream of a "worthy" American university, but he abandoned academe for politics when sectarian pressure forced Tappan out in 1863.[44] At a time when the "true" university was still a gleam in the eyes of a handful of visionaries, White might never have returned to higher education had he not been elected to the New York State Senate, where he chaired the committee on education and met Ezra Cornell.

Despite their limitations, the scientific schools and land-grant colleges signified impending change. So did the American Association for the Advancement of Science (AAAS, 1846) and the American Social Science Association (ASSA, 1865), societies joined by the pioneers. These were organizations that sought to forge what Thomas Haskell has called "communities of the competent" in a society where exact knowledge was undervalued.[45] Opened in 1865, Cornell University quickly became one of the largest American universities. Eliot interpreted the scientific schools, which he called "polytechnics" and of which there were around thirty at the time of his inauguration as Harvard's president, as evidence that more people were demanding knowledge that was exact and specialized but not necessarily practical. Advising the trustees who were planning Johns Hopkins University in 1874, Eliot proclaimed that the national interest required training men who were "thoroughly instructed in something," a vision similar to Gilman's vision of a university promoting "the best of every sort of culture."[46] Reviewing the mounting number of treatises on higher education, Ralph Waldo Emerson recorded in his journal in 1867 that "the treatises that are written on University reforms may be acute or not, but their chief value to the observer is in showing that a cleavage is occurring in the hitherto firm granite of the past and a new era is nearly arrived."[47] A year later White became Cornell's president, and in 1869 the thirty-five-year-old Eliot was elected president of Harvard. When Yale elected the sixty-year-old Reverend Noah Porter its president in 1871, Porter's main rival had been the forty-year-old Gilman, who had already turned down the presidencies of the universities of Wisconsin and California (he then accepted a re-offer of the California post) because he wanted the Yale presidency.[48]

With its medical and legal faculties and the Sheffield School, Porter's Yale called itself a university, and by 1871 it had more graduate students than Harvard. But these were not the features of Yale that interested Porter. In *The American Colleges and the American Public* (1870) Porter criticized "the limited class of lecturers and writers known as educational reformers."[49] Triggered by White's 1866 Plan of Organization for Cornell, Porter's book reviewed plans, starting in the 1820s, at Amherst, Harvard, Brown, and Michigan, for widening the range of student choice, either by increasing the number of elective courses or by establishing parallel classical and scientific courses. The lesson of history was that such plans collapsed when their sponsors discovered that reform failed to attract more students. Porter was confident that the same fate would befall Cornell because students attended college to prepare for public life rather than for specific occupations and professions.[50] When it came to meeting the "just demands of public life," nothing could match traditional pedagogy, especially the face-to-face encounters in recitations that trained students to bring their powers to act "with their utmost energy."[51] Beyond the classroom, the collegiate experience itself prepared students for public life. Every day collegians observed a clearly etched "natural aristocracy of eminent scholars, distinguished writers, prize and honor men, boating men, and gymnasts."[52] In no community other than the college "is real merit more likely to be discerned, or when discerned is it more generously acknowledged."[53]

Porter's "real merit" resembled essential merit. He was sure that it was best assessed by the personal observation of students in public competitions. Having studied at the University of Berlin in 1853–54, Porter was by no means indifferent to learning.[54] But, born in 1811, he was a generation older than Eliot, Gilman, and White (he graduated from Yale in 1831, the year Gilman was born) and far more wedded to the traditional conception of the college's function, to train public men who would lead by example. Porter's ideal was the whole man—pious, ethical, informed if not necessarily learned, and above all ambitious for public distinctions fairly won and hence "generously" acknowledged. Public competitions among collegians for rank were indispensable to this conception. There were lectures, written examinations, and even some electives at Yale, but Porter showed far more interest in the daily recitation, which required public performance, and in students running the "common course" of the fixed curriculum.

Eliot would later describe Yale under Porter as a porcupine on the defensive. But Porter's defense of tradition nonetheless still had the ring of plausibility in 1870. In his view, the curriculum and the student culture that valued wide-ranging competitions for prizes were complementary ways to identify merit, which was measured by public performance. Rhetorical exercises were still the staple of the collegiate extracurriculum. Five days after the opening of the University of Illinois in 1868, students formed two rival literary societies, and by the 1880s intercollegiate debates and oratorical contests kept the rhetorical tradition alive at colleges where the literary societies themselves were in decline.[55] At Yale the traditional competition for "parts" at commencements was weakening even before the Civil War, but into the 1890s academic attainment was still a valued asset when it came to selection for elite student societies. Students with high academic marks ("stand") were selected by the junior fraternities and elite senior societies out of proportion to their numbers. By the 1890s Tap Day at Yale—the day when the college's senior societies chose their members from the ranks of juniors—had become a public event, thronged by students eager for the tap and by faculty and college officials whose "intense interest" in the proceedings reflected their view that the societies chose men "most conspicuous in the college world, for athletic triumph or scholarly achievement or executive management of college affairs, or any other proofs of leadership."[56]

In defending recitations, competition, and the quest for rank in 1870, Porter added some practical considerations. He warned that infiltrating features of European universities—"freedom of election, the gratification of special preferences or tastes, real or supposed, and a direct preparation for the student's contemplated profession or business in life"—ignored the realities of American colleges, whose students were younger and less well prepared than German university students and more in need of the drill of recitation, and further risked stripping the American college of its traditional role without substituting a plausible alternative. American colleges had little to offer undergraduates beyond the honor attending the attainment of high rank. No American college, Porter noted, could approach Oxford University's annual distribution of some £120,000 in scholarships and fellowships to spur its "reading men." What was true of the colleges was true of the nation, he continued, for the United States did not offer any rewards for the acquisition of knowledge as such. It lacked any equivalent of the German system of "prizes in the civil and professional appointments, which are determined by the result of every examination from the beginning of the gymnasial to the end of the university life, and which are most powerfully reinforced by the intense and prevailing intellectual activity of the cultivated classes."[57]

All of this was true in 1870, and much of it was still true in 1900. (The Pendleton Act would never have been passed had it privileged university graduates in any way and thereby nurtured the dreaded "office-holding aristocracy.")[58] The absence in the larger society of direct rewards for academic distinction formed a major part of the context within which Eliot, Gilman, and White developed their ideas. As late as 1870, the pioneers were stumbling in the dark, largely bereft of allies either inside or outside universities. In what amounted to an acknowledgment of the ineffectual public support for educational reform, White hoped that, once established, a "worthy American University" would act as a nucleus from which liberally minded men of learning could extend their influence. Eliot saw the professions as, at best, the home of his potential rather than actual allies. The meager education of most doctors and lawyers, he declared in 1869, was giving the term "learned profession" a "sarcastic flavor."[59] A few years later University of Minnesota president William Watts Folwell described most law and medical schools as places of "acknowledged infamy."[60] Gilman thought that every sort of title was too easily acquired in America. In new areas any well-dressed man who looked capable of fighting became a "colonel"; those with more intellectual aspects became "judges." One-horse colleges dubbed themselves universities, and universities conferred honorary D.D.'s and LL.D.'s in "extravagant profusion."[61]

Even regular degrees in the United States smacked of debased coinage; in 1870 the nation had more institutions conferring baccalaureate and medical degrees than all of Europe. At his inaugural in 1868 President James McCosh of Princeton proposed that all the colleges in New Jersey form a board to confer baccalaureate degrees. In 1885 Gilman proposed that Columbia, Princeton, Johns Hopkins, and other elite institutions unite to confer degrees "on a uniform basis of merit and with uniform tests of proficiency." Gilman mandated outside examiners for Ph.D. candidates at Hopkins. Similarly, in his 1869 inaugural address at Harvard, Eliot predicted "great gain" if examining were separated from teaching, in the manner of Britain's ancient universities, where the colleges taught and the university examined.[62]

Competition

Disillusioned with public life, the pioneers distanced themselves from the sort of competitions—recitations and rank lists—by which collegians traditionally had prepared for public life. Since each recitation was a mini-examination, with each student's performance immediately assigned a numerical mark, little teaching actually occurred during a recitation. Lectures lacked an immediate examining component, but they were superior as instruments for communicating knowledge and were highly compatible with periodic written examinations. In contrast to recitations, which were notorious for encouraging regurgitation of the reading assignment, written examinations, at least in principle, could test for understanding, which the pioneers often equated with "power." A written examination could require the student to synthesize material in ways not possible during recitations, which typically were very brief.

Nearly any written examination would be longer than a recitation, and at Gilman's Johns Hopkins, course-ending examinations lasted six hours. Gilman took the added step of allowing students to substitute written examinations for courses. A student, that is, could sit for a written examination whenever he felt himself prepared, even at matriculation, with the result that a Hopkins undergraduate could acquire the baccalaureate degree in anywhere from one to four years. Similarly, Eliot argued that electivism would make it possible for Harvard students to graduate in three rather than four years if they chose to accelerate, for by the mid-1880s courses no longer had to be taken in any prescribed order.

In combination, electivism and written examinations did much to undermine the traditional competitions for college rank. In his inaugural address Eliot stated that "the college rank list reinforces higher motives." In context, however, this was a passing remark, accompanied by his acknowledging that "many excellent persons see great offense in any system of college rank" and his pointing to the "self-referential" attitudes that it encouraged in students as the "worst of rank."[63] To win high rank the student had to become absorbed with his position relative to that of other students rather than with knowledge. A student who became first scholar in his class resembled the soldier whose act of courage in combat led him to expect lifelong deference; Harvard traditionalists relished the thought that the first scholar would be so acknowledged throughout his life.[64]

The rank list was already living on borrowed time at Harvard when Eliot was inaugurated. The ardor of students for public recognition at graduations that were attended by state and sometimes national notables had sustained competition for college rank from the 1780s to 1830. Thereafter, competition for commencement parts became increasingly controversial among students themselves as the adoption of systems of numerical marks to determine rank stripped them of any voice in rank and therefore challenged what had always been the half-mythic student view that they generously acknowledged each other's merit. In addition, marking systems like Quincy's Scale of Comparative Merit became fiendishly complicated with the gradual introduction of written examinations, lectures, and electives. Starting in the 1840s, the Harvard faculty engaged in interminable wrangling over establishing equivalencies between required and elective studies, between subjects, whether required or elective, in different departments, between attendance at recitations and at lectures, and between the same subjects taught in different years (e.g., freshman Latin versus sophomore Latin), all to maintain the Scale of Comparative Merit.[65]

Triggered by the absurdity of efforts to reconcile the traditional scale of marks with the new pedagogy, a reaction was setting in at Harvard. Starting in 1869, students could gain honors at graduation for achievement in a subject, and while this left the final rank list intact, it created an alternative route to honors. Eliot approved this, but few students took the option; his steady expansion of electivism discouraged concentrations. Many instructors stopped marking recitations at all, recitations were fading in the face of competition from lectures, and the range of electives was expanding to the point where electives were no longer competing with required courses. By 1874–75 nearly all required courses had been pushed into the freshman year. In his annual report for 1879–80 Eliot announced that recitations had "well-nigh disappeared."[66] In 1886 a faculty-student committee reported what had been obvious for some time: the marking system was unsuited to the elective system. Different instructors marked on different scales (one perversely awarded a grade less than zero); some courses were difficult, others were "snaps." The same report described new regulations that required each instructor to classify his students into one of five groups, using whatever method he wished.

Because marks were no longer required, students could not know their relative rank within each group. As a result, a faculty committee reported, "the rank list disappears," and it became impossible to trace "the fate of the first and second scholars" after graduation. Starting with the class of 1888, Harvard initiated a new system of graduation honors: *cum laude, magna cum laude, summa cum laude*. Based on categories of achievement as measured by course grades, this system overcame Eliot's objection to the self-referential character of the ranking system, for in principle any number of students could achieve a *cum, magna,* or *summa.*

The new system of honors was open to the objection that students taking different courses could not be compared with each other. George Birkbeck Hill, an Oxonian who visited Harvard in 1893, observed that under the elective system, honors depended on an average of marks in the sixteen courses required for graduation, but "whether a student has stood at the summit of sixteen mole hills or sixteen mountains matters not a whit."[67] Appalled that at Harvard the ablest and dullest students took the same courses, Hill thought that American colleges needed a better "classification" of their students in the form of a clear distinction between their "classmen" and their "passmen." Hill shared the British love of intense competition between social peers. In contrast, the roots of many American colleges in radical, seventeenth-century Protestantism left a tenacious legacy of concern for bringing their weakest students up to a passing mark rather than heaping honors on their best. A proposal in 1909 by Yale president Arthur Twining Hadley to introduce an Oxford-style distinction between pass and honors degrees was narrowly rejected by the faculty and then thumpingly rejected by the Alumni Advisory Board on the grounds that Yale's job was to educate the passmen, not reward the classmen.[68]

That academic competition aroused little interest among undergraduates at elite colleges was widely acknowledged. Woodrow Wilson complained in 1909 that the undergraduate "side-shows"—fraternities, secret societies, intercollegiate sports—had "swallowed up the circus, and those who perform in the main tent must often whistle for their audiences, discouraged and humiliated." Wilson attributed student indifference to academic achievement to the "rapidly augmenting" numbers of collegians whose parents were very wealthy and who "felt little spur to rise above mediocrity."[69] Yet the competitive instincts of turn-of-the-century undergraduates were keen; they vied with each other for campus editorships, starting positions on athletic teams, and selection by student societies that competed to enlist the campuses' Big Men, and they proclaimed that campus competitions were truly democratic because the social position of a student's family did not determine his success in campus activities.

By 1900, however, college men were viewing the pursuit of academic rank as an activity suited to college women or to the "greasy grinds" of their own sex. The fictional Dink Stover, protagonist of Owen Johnson's *Stover at Yale* (1911), is quickly introduced by his peers to the "game" of maneuvering for a tap by a senior society. Sucked into the game, Dink learns to calculate the contributions of different sports and different positions on each team to securing a tap, next decides that he does not want to play the game, and in the end discovers that his earnest sincerity and disdain for snobbery pays off with a tap from Skull and Bones. Johnson carried Dink through many escapades, but never once did he depict Dink attending a class. Johnson may have been taking some authorial license with reality, but in 1902 a Yale faculty committee gathered some revealing evidence of the declining prestige of academic distinction. Traditionally, students who ranked high in marks had been awarded commencement appointments consonant with their class rank and had been prime candidates for selection by elite student societies. Hadley himself had been valedictorian and hence top scholar in his class of 1876. Of thirty-four valedictorians from 1861 to 1894, only three had failed to be elected to a junior fraternity and only eight to a senior society. After 1894, however, top scholars were no more likely than the average student to secure taps for elite societies, which meant not likely at all.[70]

Eliot, Gilman, and White showed little interest in spurring students to compete with each other. Traditionally, educators had trusted the student community and its "solidarity" to prevent competition from descending into destructive rivalries. Self-starters in college, Eliot, Gilman, and White valued a student's self-direction more than the group consciousness forged by common experiences. Their embrace of electivism included a belief that choice itself was educative, the best of all preparations for real life. In their mature view, the ancien régime of daily recitations, daily marks, and prizes based on minute distinctions between students on the grounds of "scholarship" was petty and juvenile, more likely to defeat real scholarly inquiry than to spur it. When they spoke of "manliness," they meant the resoluteness that enabled an individual to make the movers and shakers of society take his ideas seriously, not athletic glory or Dink Stover's belief in fair play and rewards honestly won in college societies.

Their emphasis on self-direction led Eliot, Gilman, and White to view written examinations as measures of what a student had learned rather than as a way to separate the wheat from the chaff or to calibrate the purity of the wheat. Marks and grades were scarcely acceptable topics of discussion among Johns Hopkins undergraduates.[71] Such was Eliot's commitment to the educative value of choice that he concluded that students who chose to waste their college years should be free to do so. Under Eliot, Harvard's requirements for graduation ranged from negligible to modest. Until 1893–94 a student could obtain the bachelor's degree by passing with a C in one-fourth of his courses each year, a requirement that makes the storied Gentleman's C look more like a Gentleman's D. Then the requirement was raised to one-half Cs, and to two-thirds in 1901–2.[72] Eliot never complained about the severity of Harvard's entrance examinations, which, although rejecting only around 15 percent of applicants, had the reputation of being the most difficult in the nation. Strict monitoring at the gate followed by laissez-faire was his approach. Eliot believed that electivism would encourage students to pursue their special interests and that the satisfaction of students' interests would be its own reward. In 1888 he turned down a proposal by the Overseers to attach additional marks of recognition to academic excellence beyond the awarding of *cum*, *magna*, or *summa* at graduation.

Yet by 1900 evidence was mounting that Harvard undergraduates were abusing their freedom. A faculty committee in 1899–1900 reported that more than half of the undergraduates in the class of 1898 elected little or nothing beyond elementary courses and that fewer than 30 percent of them had taken more than half of their courses in one department. In 1903 another faculty committee set off what the Harvard community recognized as a "bombshell" under the elective system when it reported, on the basis of more than 1,700 responses to a questionnaire, that undergraduates were spending only about half the time on each course that the faculty had been assuming. Students joked that electivism had turned the Faculty of Arts and Sciences into the "Faculty of Larks and Cinches."[73]

Eliot was not inclined to worry about abuses of the elective system, a complacency shared by the pioneers' students who went on to become leading educators. For example, as a Cornell student, David Starr Jordan had absorbed White's preference for student freedom. Jordan's views on grading were also shaped by Matthew Arnold's opinion, shared by a growing number of professors, that choice itself was educative and that culture was a process of self-harrowing and growth whose acquisition could never be reduced to numbers.[74] When he moved to Stanford from Indiana University in 1891, Jordan oversaw marking procedures that initially were slack and that developed Orwellian features: first, a bottom-loaded provision to classify undergraduates as "excellent," "passed," "conditioned," or "failed"; then a faculty vote in 1892 abolishing "excellent"; next, at Jordan's prompting, a requirement that some comment on the quality of a student's work be quietly included in a report to the registrar, to be consulted only by interested parties; and finally, in 1903 a decision to translate these comments into A, B, C, or D but to inform students only whether they had passed or failed.[75] Similarly, under the influence of James Burrill Angell, who shared White's distaste for the daily monitoring of students, Michigan had a three-tiered system—passed, not passed, and failed—until 1907, after which the university's desire for a chapter of Phi Beta Kappa led it gradually to introduce an excellent-to-failed letter-grade system.[76]

Bridges

Sharing many ideals, the pioneers nevertheless faced the same problem: how exactly were universities to extend their public influence? White dreamed of a great national university that would provide a magnet for the "educated public," the sort of people who subscribed to the *Nation* and the *Popular Science Monthly* and who attended meetings of the ASSA. But the idea of establishing a national university had been taken more seriously in George Washington's day than in later years. America's "educated public" was a fuzzier notion than England's Oxbridge honors graduates or Germany's *Bildungsbürgertum*. Eliot's dismissal of the "learned professions" as an oxymoron was not quite fair. Movements were afoot to tighten admission to the professions. For example, the American Bar Association (ABA), founded in 1878 as an outgrowth of meetings of the ASSA and composed of elite lawyers, explicitly sought to attach "the presumption of merit" to the legal profession.[77] But of the first twelve ABA presidents, only three had attended law schools, and until the 1920s the ABA, most of whose members had entered the profession by apprenticeship rather than law schools, rejected all measures aimed at privileging the admission of law-school graduates to the bar. Instead, it relied on strengthening bar examinations and prodding states to specify a period of law study, either apprenticeship or law school, before admission. This approach met with some success but at a glacial pace; as late as 1917 no state required lawyers to have attended law school and several did not even require high-school graduation as a prerequisite for practicing law.[78]

Believing that the professions were becoming the key forces in American society, Eliot tacked toward the only open water. He would raise the standards of professional education at Harvard and then count on Harvard's prestige to gain allies within the professions.[79] In effect, he wanted to stratify the professions by the educational credentials of their members. Eliot often changed his mind, but never about the need to construct professional education on the foundation of liberal education in order to establish a modern natural aristocracy. Before 1869 no Harvard president had ever chaired a meeting of its medical faculty. Harvard's medical school remained an essentially for-profit institution whose professors directly collected student fees (the same "money relation" that had angered Eliot at the Lawrence School). The medical school's academic requirements could charitably be described as negligible: a student could obtain the M.D. by passing 60 percent of his courses in each of two annual series of lectures, the second an exact replica of the first, and passing a brief oral exam. Insisting that medicine was a science and not, as many leading physicians still contended, an art, Eliot succeeded in placing Harvard's medical professors on salary, instituted a three-year sequence of progressively arranged lectures in 1871, and forced the medical school to require that all courses be passed for the medical degree.[80]

Eliot's contributions to legal education resulted in equally dramatic changes. As late as 1869–70, anyone who attended Harvard's law school for eighteen months was entitled to the bachelor of law degree without examination, a policy Eliot found "humiliating."[81] A graduate of Harvard's college and law school, Christopher Columbus Langdell, appointed Dane Professor of Law by Eliot in 1870, became the law school's first dean in the following year and quickly instituted a three-year course and examinations.

Langdell was just the sort of man to attract Eliot's attention. He was known in the profession for his knowledge of legal principles, not for his courtroom performances. Sharing Eliot's association of professional knowledge with science, he introduced the case method, which called upon students to reason to legal principles from evidence drawn from the study of appellate decisions, and he identified fully with Eliot's plan for reforming the legal profession.[82] In Langdell's eyes, the nineteenth-century history of the American legal profession was the story of declension, which began when Jacksonian-era legislatures had reduced law to the status of an ordinary calling. In contrast, European governments often employed lawyers as prestigious civil servants, and even England, which did not, maintained the distinction between barristers and attorneys. In the absence of privileging lawyers as higher civil servants or the barrister/attorney distinction, Langdell believed, the burden of elevating the American legal profession would have to fall on university law schools.[83]

A few decades would elapse before Harvard law graduates would carry the case method to other law schools, but the case method, with its premium on nimble students and artful teachers who could tease out the implications of appellate decisions, made law school more attractive to college graduates, who saw it as preferable to apprenticeships in which would-be lawyers, when not sweeping the floor, spent a lot of time copying documents and reading commentaries on the law. When Harvard restricted admission to its law school to college graduates in 1896, a measure which Eliot had favored from the start and which he implemented in the medical school in 1901, 80 percent of its law students already were college graduates.[84]

None of these changes occurred in a vacuum. Between 1870 and 1914 some fifteen thousand Americans, most with the medical degree in hand, undertook some form of serious medical study at universities in Germany, Austria, or German-speaking Switzerland, with the peak in the 1870s and 1880s.[85] Just as German-trained doctors were separating themselves from the pack of all-purpose healers, lawyers in firms that dealt with corporate and tax issues were distancing themselves from lawyers who prepared documents and pled whatever cases came their way.[86]

These developments contributed significantly to the eventual success of Eliot's reforms, but nothing to his original vision of reform. The reform of professional education became the primary objective of Eliot's early years as president, a period in which he was not under any external pressure to take the path he chose. The same was true of Gilman. Although financial problems delayed the opening of Johns Hopkins's medical school until 1893, from the start of his presidency Gilman had envisioned a medical school whose students would be college graduates equipped with the basic sciences. Before the opening of its medical school, the profession to which the Johns Hopkins University contributed the most was the academic profession.

In 1870 Yale's William Graham Sumner complained that "there is no such thing as yet at Yale as an academic career."[87] Yale was slowly changing, but the recitation system so esteemed by Noah Porter discouraged the drawing of distinctions among professors even on the basis of teaching, for in recitations only the students performed. At Harvard, although he gradually phased out recitations, Eliot made no special effort to recruit eminent scholars until he began to feel competition from Johns Hopkins. His system of free electives led him to hire more, rather than necessarily luminous, professors to teach the expanded range of courses required by electivism. Political economist Charles Dunbar and historian Henry Adams were known primarily as journalists when hired by Eliot. Adams and Eliot's cousin Charles Eliot Norton, the first American professor of art history, came from well-connected Boston families, a matter of no small importance to Eliot. Self-taught in art history, a knowledge of which he picked up mainly on trips abroad for the Boston import firm that employed him, Norton was best known as a cofounder of the *Atlantic Monthly* and writer on political topics. Norton and the others would go on to distinguished scholarly careers, but they were hired as reliable gentlemen loyal to Harvard rather than as scholars.

Gilman's position was different. The Johns Hopkins University had no alumni to appease. Hopkins's endowment of $3.5 million, an enormous sum in the 1870s and seven times Cornell's original endowment, gave Gilman the means to fulfill his dream of the university as an institution in which most students already possessed college degrees and became apprentices to brilliant minds. In his inaugural address Gilman announced his intention to hire brilliant men and to promote them "because of their merit to successive posts, as scholars, fellows, assistants, adjuncts, professors and university professors." Research encouraged calibration of the faculty's merits by the quantity and quality of its scholarship.[88] In 1883 the Hopkins trustees established a clear distinction between professors and associate professors.[89] During the 1890s faculty members across the nation responded to intensifying demand for their services by calling for more clearly articulated procedures for promotion and retention.[90] An especially high degree of professional consciousness marked Hopkins's faculty (which would spearhead the establishment of the American Association of University Professors—AAUP—in 1915), and its graduate students spread Gilman's ideas across a broad range of American colleges and universities.

The contours of the American professorate were slowly articulated after 1880. During the 1890s courts inclined strongly to the old-fashioned view that professors were employees subject to arbitrary dismissal by trustees, who claimed a right to appoint their friends and relatives to professorships.[91] Politics, religion, and regional loyalties continued to govern hiring practices at most institutions. Yet the seeds of the modern professorate, sown at Johns Hopkins in the 1880s, were germinating. Decades before the establishment of the AAUP, American academics had successfully forged more accessible university hierarchies in higher education by capitalizing on increasing acceptance of the need for specialized knowledge. In European universities one professor typically represented an entire field, (e.g., modern history) and was likely to head a research institute staffed by apprentices and assistants. In this type of hierarchy, rising to full professor was an unrealistic expectation for most Ph.D.'s. In contrast, the structure of even elite university departments in the United States accommodated the aspiration of every Ph.D. to become a professor by establishing himself as a specialist in a subfield. European departments resembled pyramids; American departments looked like train stations, with parallel tracks entering and exiting.[92]

The annual conferences of the elite Association of American Universities (AAU, 1900) became forums in which officials and professors at leading universities debated issues that scarcely had existed two decades earlier. Did offering fellowships to attract graduate students deprive a professor of "the legitimate and noble emulation to win young disciples on his merits," as G. Stanley Hall maintained in language that smacked of essential merit and was fast becoming quaint, or was it a defensible way to attract the most promising students to the best-equipped institutions, as most younger professors argued? To what extent should market considerations determine salaries? Was it seemly to meet outside offers, a practice routine in corporations, or would this simply generate fishing expeditions and, as one discussant put it in words that remind us of the professorate's still narrow ethnic and religious base, a lot of "Jewing up and Jewing down"? Was merit to be measured by research or teaching or service, or some combination of all three?[93]

AAU members disagreed on these issues, but there were elements of consensus. Most professors were wary of a strict application of market principles, partly because they saw themselves more as public benefactors, as men who put knowledge to public good, than as businessmen, and partly because they feared the indignity of making less than the football coach.[94] Few professors wanted any part of the military system of promotion by time in rank, but most were rank-conscious and opposed paying anyone at a lower rank more than anyone at a higher rank. Intra-rank differences were acceptable on the basis of merit so long as they were not *extreme*, an adjective that remained undefined. Resembling neither businessmen nor freelance professionals, professors, even if employed by private universities, thought of themselves as public servants, the traditional term for individuals who after 1870 were increasingly called civil servants.

Preferring institutional to essential merit, the pioneers admired the career soldier, the physician who applied science more than art to healing, and the university-educated lawyer instructed in legal science. Each institutional type had its opposite: the politician-turned-general who relied on his charisma to inspire his troops; the advocate whose courtroom theatrics won cases and led him into politics; the doctor who touted his "genius" at curing the sick. White contributed to a similar shift in 1885 when he appointed Robert H. Thurston to head Cornell's Sibley College of the Mechanic Arts. In keeping with the wishes of its founder, the self-made Hiram Sibley, the "mechanic arts" connoted shopwork and reflected the values of engineers who had imbibed an entrepreneurial rather than professional self-consciousness in the shops that made steam engines and machine tools for businesses and who dominated the American Society of Mechanical Engineers (ASME, est. 1883). Shifting Sibley's focus to the lectern and classroom from the shop, Thurston made Sibley a leading university engineering school.[95]

The absorption of engineering education by engineering schools occurred gradually between 1870 and 1930. Like Eliot's reforms at Harvard, this change was boosted by developments in the larger society. By the mid-1890s large electrical equipment manufacturers like General Electric and Westinghouse had developed programs for giving engineering graduates practical experiences without exposing them to the world of shop culture, which was both highly personal and rough-and-tumble.[96]

Advocates of the university-centric model of professional preparation always invoked "science," instruction in abstract principles, to justify their project, and they always faced opposition from veterans of apprenticeships in law or medical offices or machine shops, who rallied under the banner of real-world experience. The debate resembled trains moving in opposite directions on parallel tracks. Advocates of experience appeared to have a lot working for them. "Experience" sounded democratic, closer to the common man, accessible to anyone, compatible with the American spirit of entrepreneurship and with the American understanding of merit. "Science" sounded elitist and, worse, dubious. If law was a science, why did judges disagree? If medicine was one, where was the evidence? Yet the advocates of university professional education had one thing in their favor. "Experience" consisted of countless individual experiences that, collectively, formed only a thin bond among practitioners. In contrast, the university model consisted of subjects, taught and examined in classrooms, that became the basis of universally applicable standards.

Standards and Certifying Institutions

Their eagerness to establish true universities led Eliot, Gilman, and White into an ever-widening circle of contacts with schools and colleges. So keen was Gilman's interest in Baltimore's public schools that he earned the admiration of a young reporter, Henry Louis Mencken.[97] White saw his plan for merit scholarships as both a way to deepen Cornell's pool of applicants and an inducement to New York's high schools to raise the level of their instruction in subjects that were acceptable for college admission. During the 1890s Eliot deluged public educators with a flood of proposals to push high-school subjects into the upper elementary grades and to strengthen high-school instruction in science.

In the absence of even an accepted definition of a college, colleges varied as much as lower schools. In 1900 a college diploma could signify much or laughably little. In 1908 roughly two-thirds of the nation's colleges spent less than $20,000 a year on instructional salaries, while 12 percent spent more than $100,000 and 1.4 percent over $500,000.[98] Recognizing the vast differences in quality among colleges, Eliot arbitrarily imposed a basis for classifying applicants for Harvard Law School when in 1893 he published a list of colleges whose graduates would be admitted to the law school without examination. A graduate of an unlisted college faced more than the inconvenience of an entrance examination; he was classified as a special student and could graduate only if his law school average was at least fifteen points higher than that required of regular students. Eliot intended his list as an inducement for college graduates to attend the law school, but his move immediately landed him in a nasty controversy with Catholic colleges, none of which made his original list.[99]

The absence of standards in higher education pushed Eliot into this clumsy move. His stated rationale—that Catholic colleges drew their professors from the clergy—was true. But because the same was true of many non-Catholic colleges that made his list, Eliot's move appeared to be based on religious prejudice. The same absence of standards characterized college admissions. Individual professors in the small number of colleges that required entrance examinations set the entrance exam in their own subjects, usually without conferring with each other. The "chaotic diversity" of college entrance examinations had long concerned Eliot. Such diversity tightened the connection between individual feeder schools and individual colleges, especially in required subjects like Latin—a student preparing for Princeton's entrance examination in Latin would be at sea if confronted by Harvard's—and made it very difficult for public high-school students, the young men whom Eliot saw as recruits for the natural aristocracy, to prepare for college entrance examinations. In the 1890s Eliot and Nicholas Murray Butler played key roles in establishing the College Entrance Examination Board (CEEB, 1899; later the College Board).[100]

Initially, the institutional membership of the CEEB included only a small number of private colleges and universities. The vast majority of American colleges, including several prestigious eastern colleges, admitted students from approved high schools without examination; this was the so-called certificate system.[101] Promising a steady flow of applicants, the certificate system nevertheless had critics, who complained that it allowed high schools to dictate acceptable subjects, including vocational ones, to the colleges. Further, the criteria for acquiring the status of an "approved" high school varied widely and often boiled down to whether the principal of a high school seeking certification was an alumnus of the college offering certification and shared the college's denominational preference.[102] The CEEB itself was a characteristically American innovation, a private body with public influence. A college could make whatever use of the CEEB's examinations it chose. (The audience at an 1899 conference erupted in laughter when Eliot, responding to a complaint by the president of Lafayette College that the proposed CEEB examinations would prevent the admission of the scholastically challenged sons of wealthy trustees, pointed out that Lafayette would be free to admit only students who failed the examinations.)[103] Yet over time the influence of the CEEB would become significant.

Along with Jordan, Butler, Hadley, and Harper, Eliot also served as one of the original trustees of the Carnegie Foundation for the Advancement of Teaching (CFAT). Like the CEEB, CFAT belonged to the new class of agencies that certified the degree to which institutions met the presumption-of-merit standard. Established in 1905 to administer Andrew Carnegie's gift of $10 million for pensions for college teachers, CFAT immediately undertook to distill a standard definition of a *college* from the kaleidoscope of American *seminaries* and *collegiate institutions*. CFAT defined a college whose professors were eligible for Carnegie pensions as a private, nonsectarian institution that had at least six full-time professors, offered a four-year course in the liberal arts and sciences, and required at least four years of high-school preparation. The "Carnegie unit" came into existence to measure the sufficiency of the high-school preparation required for admission to college. Only fifty-two of the more than six hundred institutions of higher education listed by the U.S. Bureau of Education initially met these qualifications.[104]

The burden of defining these standards fell to Henry S. Pritchett, an astronomer whom Carnegie plucked from the presidency of MIT in 1906 to head CFAT. Carnegie expected his system of pensions to clean out the dead wood on faculties, but he linked this idea to his often stated desire to find the "exceptional man," the diamond in the rough. Without any formal schooling until he was ten, Pritchett himself actually was a diamond in the rough, a product of the mixture of self-teaching and sporadic contact with quasi-colleges so common in the nineteenth century. Pritchett's slaveholding family had migrated to Missouri in the 1830s. His father sold some slaves to attend an obscure college and some more to study astronomy at Harvard for a year, and eventually founded the Pritchett School Institute, a college of sorts from which Henry graduated in 1875.[105] Aware from experience of the vast range of education offered by colleges, Pritchett dedicated himself to institutionalizing best practices.

Institutionalizing best practices required a definition of *goodness*. In 1910 Edwin E. Slosson, a chemistry professor turned journalist, drew on a recent CFAT study to rank leading universities by the size of their annual instructional budgets. By this measure, Columbia ranked first, followed in order by Harvard, Chicago, Michigan, Yale, Cornell, Illinois, Wisconsin, Pennsylvania, California, Stanford, Princeton, Minnesota, and Johns Hopkins. Although seven universities that did not make the cut spent more on instruction than Johns Hopkins, Slosson contended that Hopkins had to make the list because it had always placed the greatest emphasis on the distinguishing feature of university education, "graduate work."[106]

Slosson's standard made it possible for lately arrived universities to enter the select circle, no small accomplishment in light of the prevailing custom of assessing colleges and universities by the fame of their graduates. He acknowledged that his readers would be surprised to find on his list universities about which they knew little, including Chicago and Stanford, each opened in the 1890s, and several state universities that had been founded on shoestring budgets and long denigrated for their land-grant origins. Slosson recognized other possible standards for assessing universities, such as the number of its graduates listed in biographical directories like *Who's Who* (first published in 1900). On balance, however, Slosson thought that the inclusion of a university's graduates in biographical directories said more about a university's antiquity than about its quality. In fact, he did not think that universities differed much in the quality of their undergraduates. "Men of exceptional ability," he wrote, "are pretty evenly distributed throughout the undergraduate body of the United States."[107] Every institution had good and bad teachers and more books than an undergraduate could read. "Anywhere he can learn more than he wants to."[108] The real difference lay in the quality of graduate instruction, which bore little relation to the public's estimate of universities and which was likely to change from year to year ("the removal of a single man from one institution to another may upset the balance of power").[109]

Slosson worried that talent was wasted in America because young men were ignorant of the gradations of quality among universities. He observed that the Carnegie Institution of Washington (CIW), whose presidency Gilman had assumed after resigning from Johns Hopkins, had been initially intended to discover the "diamonds in the rough, the mute inglorious Darwins buried in country colleges." But Slosson thought it significant that the CIW had shifted from the search for the "exceptional man" to supporting a few permanent scientific establishments. In effect, the CIW rewarded individuals who had been identified, in one scholar's words, "by the credentialing and promotional processes that were coming to serve as guidelines by which scientists recognized ability and accomplishment."[110] "Nowadays," Slosson concluded, "we put faith in institutions rather than in individuals, and our modern Medicis subsidize sciences instead of men of science."[111]

The objectives of reformers can be described in piecemeal terms—setting the minimal standards for the number of full-time faculty and the minimal time and prerequisites for professional study—but their underlying objective was to establish the "presumption of merit" in behalf of the graduates of the institutions that had absorbed the message of reformers. The idea that institutions could be relied on as certifiers of merit was a gradual development, yet revolutionary in its break with the ingrained idea that merit was best assessed by direct contact with the person whose merit was in question. Today we call this certifying role *credentialing*, and it has been portrayed by a considerable body of scholarly opinion as an essentially protective device by which established practitioners screen out competitors by elevating the educational thresholds for professions.[112] This way of comprehending credentialing misconstrues both the motives and the historical context of the reformers, who could count on the resistance rather than the support of well-established practitioners in the leading professions. It could scarcely have been otherwise, for the bearers of standards were not inventing new professions but upgrading existing ones that were clogged with practitioners educated the old way.

The drive for educational standards was ubiquitous between 1905 and 1915. The setting of institutional standards always involved publicizing the best practices already adopted by a minority of institutions and urging their wider acceptance. Abraham Flexner's 1910 *Report on Medical Education in the United States and Canada*, commissioned by CFAT, was the most famous example of publicizing the best practices and excoriating the worst. Born in 1866 in Louisville, Kentucky, to impoverished German Jewish immigrants, Flexner was admitted to Johns Hopkins as an undergraduate in 1884 on condition that he make up subjects in which his knowledge was deficient. Taking advantage of Gilman's rule that students could skip courses if they could pass examinations in those subjects, he studied classics and graduated in two years. His undergraduate experience shaped Flexner's ideal of education: serious students pursuing knowledge as apprentices to masters, without the irrelevancies of fraternities and secret societies or the stimulus of competition.[113] Influenced by Pritchett, whose biography he would later write, Flexner became a zealous and influential advocate of higher standards for American universities. His report on medical education bluntly proposed to euthanize American medical schools that failed to meet the standard of employing full-time professors, establishing laboratories to encourage faculty research, and affiliating with hospitals to encourage clinical training.

Yet the Flexner report was not quite the thunderbolt often portrayed. Starting with Eliot's reforms at Harvard in the 1870s, several medical schools had been moving for a generation in the direction favored by Flexner, and their graduates colonized and upgraded the faculties of other medical schools. By 1906 reformers had gained control of the American Medical Association's (AMA) Council on Medical Education, which in that year began to classify medical schools into four categories based on their graduates' performance on state medical examinations. (Flexner described this as "probably the first attempt made in America to rank institutions of higher education on some sort of qualitative basis.") Following the Flexner report, the AMA began to classify medical schools into three categories. A-list schools had large endowments, clinical facilities, preferably a teaching hospital under control of the medical school itself, and at least six full-time professors doing research in the basic sciences. B-list schools typically flunked one or more of these tests. C-list schools, requiring reorganization, included all proprietary schools. Between 1906, when the 162 medical schools in the United States accounted for nearly half of the medical schools in the world, and 1910, the number of American medical schools dropped to 131, and to 76 by 1930.[114] This contraction initially owed nothing to state licensing boards, which were dumping grounds for political appointees; in 1906 nongraduates of medical schools could obtain licenses to practice medicine in thirteen states. Rather, graduates of elite medical schools and their allies within the profession effected the shrinkage.

Representatives of elite professional schools also spearheaded the drive for higher standards in the legal profession. Elite law professors who followed Eliot in advocating possession of the baccalaureate for admission and a full-time, three-year course of study had to accommodate the remarkable proliferation after 1890 of a cheap alternative, the part-time, usually evening, law school.

In 1926 more than half of the law students in the nation were studying in part-time schools.[115] Some of these schools served women, who were excluded from elite law schools.[116] In Washington, D.C., the part-time schools served government clerks, and in all major cities they were favored by immigrants and their children, the sort of people who could rarely afford the opportunity costs of full-time law schools that also required some college education.[117] Between 1899 and 1929 a growing number of law schools nevertheless raised their standards by requiring two years of college for admission (from 2 schools in 1899 to 70 in 1927) and by requiring three years of full-time study for the LL.B. (from 47 schools in 1899 to 166 by 1927).[118]

This rise of educational standards reflected pressure from the Association of American Law Schools (AALS, 1900, founded to represent elite law professors). After 1920 pressure from the ABA's section on Legal Education and Admission to the Bar, headed by Elihu Root, pushed the ABA toward an insistence on higher educational standards, a cause it had long opposed. As secretary of war decades earlier, Root had overseen publication of Emory Upton's masterful study of American military policy; now he brought the same zeal for formal professional education to law. Root had close ties to Henry S. Pritchett; Root's older brother had taught at the Missouri school founded by Pritchett's father. With an impetus from Root, the ABA, and mounting anti-immigrant sentiment in the 1920s, state legislatures began to raise educational requirements for the legal profession. By 1932 seventeen states, up from six in 1928, required two years of college for admission to the bar.[119] By then the Depression was dealing a lethal blow to part-time law schools.

Standards created losers as well as winners. In the medical and legal professions the short-term effect of standards was to undermine professional schools that served women, African Americans, and recent immigrants. For example, in the wake of the Flexner report all but one of the nation's medical colleges for women closed.[120] In a society ridden with prejudice, standards nevertheless were not in themselves prejudicial. In 1926 the AALS expelled the white law schools of Vanderbilt University and the University of Mississippi for failing to require two years of college. Each school rebounded, met the standard, suffered a predictable loss of enrollment, and gained readmission. Similarly, the dictates of the ABA and AALS set the agenda for black law schools. After 1922, for example, Howard University's law school steadily raised its entrance requirements, expanded its library to meet the threshold set by the AALS, employed more full-time professors, and saw its enrollment drop. In 1931 Howard secured accreditation by the ABA and election to the AALS. Nor did standards exclude Jews, whose educational prospects were much more likely to be victimized during the 1920s by invocations of "character."[121] Over the long course the most numerous victims of standards were the sort of poor young men who had tried to escape manual work on farms and in shops during the nineteenth century by hitching their wagons to the stars of commercial professional schools of "acknowledged infamy."

The Gradual Triumph of Standards

The drive to elevate standards in higher education and the professions had its critics. Pointing in 1903 to "a Mandarin disease" that elevated badges and diplomas over "personality," inhibited the free development of talent, and fostered snobbery in higher education, William James slashed at the "Ph.D. Octopus."[122] He cited the case of a "very brilliant" student of philosophy who had secured an appointment teaching English literature in a college, only to be told after several years of excellent teaching that he needed to acquire a Ph.D. in philosophy and then to be informed that his dissertation needed "more technical apparatus." What angered James even more was that the quest for academic credentials drew mediocrities into graduate study like moths to light; imposing standards amounted to a war on brilliance in the name of deadening uniformity.

James's target, the Ph.D., was an import from Germany and it acquired resonance as a credential only late in the nineteenth century, but his argument was not new. Eliot's move to raise admissions requirements at Harvard's medical school had been attacked on the same grounds: since medicine was an inborn art rather than an acquired science, higher admissions standards might exclude "a genius in the art." James himself made it in just under the standards wire: he received his M.D. from Harvard in 1869 after a twenty-minute oral exam. Assuming that James underwent the usual procedure, he was examined by nine medical professors, and if five held up white rather than black cards after the exam, Harvard had just given birth to a new medical doctor.

James's sympathy for genius had deep roots in the nineteenth century's ideal of the self-taught man, like Abraham Lincoln. In England, Francis Galton's *Hereditary Genius* (1869) gave a certain scientific cachet to this ideal by insisting that inborn talent would rise above any circumstances. In elevating a species of folk wisdom to the status of science, Galton initiated a prolonged debate among savants about the relative contributions of nature and nurture to the production of eminent scholars. In 1903 James McKeen Cattell, among the most important American contributors to the nurture side of this debate and editor of *Science*, had undertaken to prepare a list of one thousand significant living American scientists by asking researchers in each of twelve fields of science to compile an order of merit in his field. The fact that Cattell asked experts in each field for their ratings was itself revealing, since it required physicists to rate physicists and anatomists to rate anatomists, rather than the sort of cross-field comparisons invited by "genius." (In later editions of Cattell's directory this had the unintended effect of underrepresenting those who worked across fields, like biochemists and astrophysicists.) In 1906 these one thousand scientists became the asterisked entries in the first edition of Cattell's larger directory of around four thousand active American scientists, *American Men of Science* (subsequent editions, with the same misleading title since some women were included, appeared in 1910, 1921, 1928, 1933, 1938, and 1944, the year of Cattell's death).[123]

Cattell's was not the first order of merit in American science. Chartered by Congress in 1863 as an advisory body, the National Academy of Sciences (NAS) conferred honor on scientists by electing them to its membership. But because it had only fifty founding members and generally restricted the election of new members to vacancies created by resignation or death, the NAS was small—forty years after its founding it would still have fewer than one hundred members—and it had a reputation for mutual back-scratching when it came to elections. More important, Cattell's announced goal for compiling his directory was to identify the parameters of scientific productivity. Identify the circumstances that surrounded eminent scientists, and the production of such individuals would be speeded up, he argued. Cattell's researches into eminent scientists led him to reject heritability in favor of environment, by which he meant proximity to scientific institutions and opportunities for education in science.

Where James saw standards as trampling genius, Cattell and others praised them for substituting calibrated units of measurement for *personalism* (aka the personal equation)—the assessment of people or institutions on the basis of the assessor's personal impressions, often formed by direct contact. Standard-setters were not free of self-interest—the psychologist Cattell shoehorned psychologists into *American Men of Science* despite his field's marginality—and establishing measurements often required collating the assessments offered by numerous persons. But the final assessment strove for impersonal judgment. In starring "men of science," Cattell relied on experts in different fields. In developing performance scales for school subjects, E. L. Thorndike assembled experts to establish standards of good penmanship. Frederic Lyman Wells, a psychologist who taught at Barnard, asked his students to state their preferences for individual stories written by Edgar Allan Poe and then, using the methodology popularized by Cattell in *American Men of Science*, published *A Statistical Study of Literary Merit* (1907), in which he rated leading American authors on ten qualities (e.g., charm, euphony, clarity, originality, wholesomeness).[124] Wells's approach bears comparison with that of Poe himself, whose "The Literati of New York City" (1846) had created a publishing sensation with its often barbed portrayals of contemporary authors. Poe supplemented his (usually negative) assessments of other writers with analyses of their handwriting, which he assumed expressed their character and which always reinforced his opinion.[125] Wells's approach, collating several independent assessments and breaking down literary excellence into discrete components (charm, euphony, et al.) aimed to avoid the holistic assessments of his peers that Poe so relished and the controversy that Poe welcomed.

Various motives explain these attempts at accurate ranking, but most boil down to two: disillusion with the traditional bases of establishing hierarchies and a desire for efficiency. These motives reinforced each other. Thorndike turned to performance scales after publishing his study of attrition in the public schools, and he collaborated with Leonard P. Ayres, who also had investigated attrition, on the handwriting scale. Thorndike's stated goal was to increase "efficiency" in education, by establishing, for example, a point beyond which it was a waste of time to attempt to improve a child's handwriting. This made sense, especially in view of his and Ayres's evidence that most children never reached the eighth grade. Like Edwin Slosson, Cattell believed that the decentralized character of higher education, combined with the lingering belief that genius would triumph over any circumstances, created a lot of waste in the identification and utilization of talent. Establishing impersonal standards that punctured myths would speed up the production of American scientists.

The gradual triumph of standards raises what the king of Siam would have called a "puzzlement." Why? And why did the new standards take the (expensive) form they acquired, with professional education mounted on top of college education? The reformers benefited from the fact that they were attacking attitudes and views but nothing like an organized system. They did not impose mediocrity, as James feared; rather, they defined minimal expectations. Any institution was free to raise its own requirements. Indeed, it is a little misleading to speak of the imposition of standards, for legislatures played very little role in raising educational standards. Initiatives were nearly always the work of private groups that could compel no one. Further, advocates of higher standards found allies among the graduates of the very institutions whose low standards they targeted. Complaining about Cornell's slow pace in requiring the bachelor's degree for entry into its law and medical schools, M. Carey Thomas, an 1877 graduate of Cornell and the future president of Bryn Mawr College, remarked that "it is a foregone conclusion that the graduates in law and medicine of Cornell University must in time come to rank far below the graduates of Columbia, Harvard, and Johns Hopkins."[126]

Moreover, raising standards did not displace the sons of the traditional clients of prestigious universities; the alumni "howl" factor was mute. "American democracy," Flexner observed, "objects to sieves."[127] To be sure, standards acted as sieves, but compared with rigorous entrance examinations followed by reams of letters of rejection, standards acted less visibly and personally. The Gentleman C might flunk out of Harvard Law School in the 1920s, but he experienced little difficulty getting in; the school did not require a "meritorious" college transcript until 1930. During the 1920s academic pressures intensified *within* elite law and medical schools much more than pressure to gain admission to these schools.[128] Measured by the years of preparatory education demanded, the requirements for admission to law schools and medical schools rose steadily, but so did enrollments in secondary and higher education. In the four decades after 1890 the American population doubled while the number of students in higher education rose by a factor of ten. By 1937 more than half of the nation's medical schools required at least three years of college preparation, a stipulation met in that year by 92 percent of the applicants admitted to medical schools. During the interwar years most applicants for law and medical schools who met the stated requirements gained admission.

There were exceptions. Admissions committees assumed that African Americans were mentally inferior to whites and discouraged their applications. Women faced quota restrictions even in medical schools nominally open to them. Elite law and medical schools also applied quotas to Jews throughout the interwar years. In the early 1940s three out of every four non-Jewish applicants to medical schools gained entry but only one of every thirteen Jewish applicants. But standards did not initiate the exclusion of these groups from elite professional education, for they had never been welcomed. In fact, Harvard Law School would not admit women until 1950.[129]

In a nation whose government could never be relied on to enforce merit-based hierarchies, the pioneers and their successors transformed higher education and the professions of law, medicine, and engineering. In their own eyes, they were doing for the nation what the nation's government would have accomplished were it not so dependent on popular consent.

7

SQUEEZE PLAY

Merit in Government

Three decades after the death of the last pioneer of higher education, Charles W. Eliot, in 1926, the sociologist C. Wright Mills argued in *The Power Elite* (1956) that a "political directorate," the part of the power elite that concerned itself with politics, ran the United States. Much of the debate stirred by Mills focused on his contention that the elites in business, the military, and government were interlocking, that their members thought sufficiently alike to appoint each other to positions of power. They had attended the same prep schools and colleges, socialized in the same clubs, and putted on the same greens. Few attended to Mills's other main contention: the power elite lacked "meritorious ability."[1] It was composed of second-raters with inherited wealth and ascribed status. True, its members often possessed glittering educational credentials. They had passed from Groton, St. Mark's, or Lawrenceville to Harvard, Yale, or Princeton, along the way joining the Fly or Porcellian clubs at Harvard or their equivalents at Yale or Princeton. They then moved on to elite law schools. But their educations merely sealed their social status; the power elite owed more to its social credentials than to its intellectual achievement.

Members of the power elite were well connected in business or the military but transients in government. What made outsiders' capture of high appointive offices possible was the vacuum created by the absence of a "genuine bureaucracy" in the civilian government. But by a genuine bureaucracy Mills meant something more than an obsession with petty rules. He followed the early twentieth-century German sociologist Max Weber, who had described *bureaucracy* as the "most efficient" type of organization. A true bureaucracy awarded rank to experts whose knowledge and skills had been attested to by qualifying examinations, sanctioned merit-based careers in the form of ladders up the hierarchy of skill and achievement, vested authority in the office more than in its occupant, and rewarded the type of person who could segregate his personal opinions from his official duties.[2]

Experts, Managers, and Public Administration

Mills's ruminations on bureaucracy had several contexts. The most immediate was President Dwight D. Eisenhower's purge of Democrats from the higher civil service in 1953 (hence Mills's repeated references to golf). Mills also referred to the need for an "administrative corps" of expert bureaucrats who could "judge carefully" the consequences of alternative policies and survive changes in administrations. Authorities on public administration, "public administrationists," had advanced this ideal during the 1930s, and it was still pulsating in the mid-1950s. One component of it lay in detaching governance from politics. In 1888 Edward Bellamy's utopian novel, *Looking Backward,* described a plan of elections—the high officers in Boston's industrial army in the year 2000 are elected by the retired members of each branch of industry—that freed government from politics. Because only the retired members vote, no one casting a vote can gain a personal benefit from the outcome of elections. Elections become spontaneous expressions of the nation's "gratitude towards its high officers" and rewards for their merit.[3] A year earlier Woodrow Wilson had called for a "science of administration which shall seek to straighten the paths of government, to make its business less unbusiness-like, to strengthen and purify its organization, and to crown its duties with dutifulness." (Wilson's essay proved retroactively seminal: no one paid it much attention until after public administration established itself as an academic field and then it became canonical.)[4] A work more directly influential on advocates of public administration, who were coming on the scene after 1900, was *Politics and Administration* (1900) by Frank Goodnow, a professor of administrative law at Columbia University.

Goodnow sounded what would become a familiar theme for public administrationists by expressing doubts about whether legislatures could command either the competence or the unity of purpose to implement the popular will. The issues confronting government once had been broadly ethical and within legislative competence—for example, how to distribute the public lands, determine voter qualifications, or delineate church-state relations. Now governments engaged in more technical activities such as regulating the professions or organizing agricultural research. Public administrationists agreed that legislatures should continue to define broad public objectives, such as building a highway system, but in order to avoid pork-barreling and logrolling, administrators within the executive branch should decide where the roads were to run and how much should be spent on them. Modern administration called not only for experts but for coordinators and facilitators who would survey needs and resources and plan strategies of implementation. Skill for this sort of work was more likely to be found in the executive branch than in legislatures, which public administrationists tended to view as natural hosts of special interests. In *The Promise of American Life* (1909) the journalist Herbert Croly proposed what amounted to Plato's Guardian Class in the form of councils of experts in law or finance, who would assist state governors in drafting laws. In 1914 Croly went further and laid out the value of a "permanent expert administration" similar to the British system, in which the executive changes but the administration persists.[5]

Experts, facilitators, and coordinators were not the makers of revolutions, but Philip Dru, the protagonist of Colonel Edward House's eponymous novel of 1919 who triumphs over political and military enemies, proclaims himself "Administrator of the Republic" and decrees a host of Progressive measures: a graduated income tax, women's suffrage, and the establishment of intelligence tests for physicians. He also rewrites the federal and state constitutions to eliminate judicial review. With the money saved by applying his machete to courts and judges, Dru then can offer high salaries to attract the best men into government.[6]

Public administration in twentieth-century America did not follow the path of either Col. House's Administrator of the Republic or C. Wright Mills's expert "administrative corps." Proposals similar to Mills's aroused the interest of professors and politicians after 1930 and eventually received an embodiment of sorts in the Civil Service Reform Act of 1978. Professors and politicians nevertheless had conflicting agendas. The former envisioned a higher civil service, selected and advanced by academic merit, as an American counterpart to civil-service elites in Europe; politicians, including several presidents, saw it as a way to make the federal bureaucracy more responsive to their wills. Predictably, the politicians rather than the professors got their way, but with the passing of time, both sides stumbled into fields strewn with obstacles.

These obstacles included scholastic egalitarianism, a legacy of equal rights. This deeply embedded way of thinking viewed access to both public employment and public schooling as a birthright of American citizens. By 1883, when Congress passed the Pendleton (Civil Service Reform) Act, this tradition had solidified into the twin beliefs that "average" Americans could be assumed to be familiar with the "common" branches of knowledge ("common schools" and "public schools" were interchangeable terms) and that any examination for entry into the public service was acceptable only to the extent that it tested common knowledge. At first glance, this position would seem to have excluded hiring experts, individuals who by definition possessed uncommon bodies of knowledge. In principle and often in practice, however, employing a multitude familiar with the "common branches" and a few experts did not create conflict. Rather, especially during the New Deal, bitter disputes developed over more subtle issues. First, were experts in public employment to be given responsibilities beyond their specialties? Second, were governmental appointing agencies to be allowed discretion to select experts not merely on the basis of their experience and/or academic credentials but also on the basis of the *prestige* of their academic credentials? Advocates of the latter approach preferred higher education to experience as the basis of selection, and they viewed the quality (or prestige) of an institution of higher education as a marker of the intellectual brilliance of its graduates. Seeking to carve out expansive "careers" in the civil service for the best and the brightest graduates, they favored meritocratic selection. Ironically, they discovered that the most formidable obstacles to establishing civil-service careers based on meritocratic selection arose from the mentality that had established merit systems at all governmental levels in the wake of the Pendleton Act.

American thinking about the civil service was profoundly shaped by the revulsion against the very practices that distinguished the United States from all other advanced nations between the 1830s and the 1880s, the partisan distribution of public appointments known as the spoils system.

Killing the Spoils

Just as Eliot, Gilman, and White had opposed the commercialization of knowledge and trusted impersonal standards over the "personal equation," public administrationists urged the application of disinterested scientific principles to government. The public administrationists and the pioneers shared a zeal for merit systems and civil-service reform. All of the pioneers had ties to the National Civil Service Reform League (NCSRL) and through it to the genteel reformers of the Gilded Age, the self-styled Independents and "Best Men." These were men like E. L. Godkin, the Irish-born editor who had launched an influential weekly, the *Nation*, in 1865, and the editor George William Curtis, who at White's invitation became a nonresident professor at Cornell. Well-educated patricians, the Best Men had launched the New York Civil Service Reform League in 1877 and the NCSRL in 1881, and they had inspired the latter's numerous auxiliaries from Boston to San Francisco. Styling themselves Liberal Republicans, they had sought to unseat Ulysses Grant in 1872; in 1884 many of them, the so-called Mugwumps, left the Republican Party to back Grover Cleveland.

The motives that inspired the introduction of merit systems in Europe during the course of the nineteenth century had little relevance to the situation of American civil-service reform. In contrast to Prussia, civil-service reform in the United States did not embody an alliance between a monarchy and a self-conscious middle-class to restrict the power of a nobility.[7] In contrast to Britain, where first the Chartist movement and then the European Revolutions of 1848 impressed the reformers with the need to solidify the gentry's domination of politics by selecting the fitter members of their class for public service through rigorous and competitive written examinations, the American reformers did not envision the civil service as a likely career for the offspring of gentry families.[8] Rather, the abuse targeted by American reformers was vast in extent but narrow in scope: the rewarding of party activists with routine government jobs. In Britain and in America, merit was the alternative to patronage, but the primary beneficiaries of patronage in Britain had always been the well-connected members of the gentry and nobility (including their poor relations), a patronage of notables. This feature of Britain's public service had given it the reputation of a foundling hospital for the dissolute sons of the gentry. In America the partisan spoils system mainly favored little people, whose influence arose from their party loyalty more than their family rank. Attacking a perversion of aristocracy, the British reformers installed difficult "literary" examinations that tested knowledge of the Oxbridge honors curriculum, while their American counterparts, leaving all higher posts to partisan appointment, relied on examinations that tested elementary-school knowledge. Writing to a British acquaintance in 1895, Theodore Roosevelt, then head of the United States Civil Service Commission (USCSC) established by the Pendleton Act, observed the "curious" fact that although the British examinations, even for postal clerks, were far more difficult than their American counterparts, British reformers were charged with "being too democratic and leveling," in contrast to American reformers, who were charged "with being bureaucratic and tending to create an aristocracy of office holders."[9] Visiting the United States in 1904, Max Weber was told that Americans preferred "having people in office we can spit upon, rather than a caste of officials who spit upon us, as is the case with you."[10] In 1882 Godkin assured Americans that the merit system contemplated by the Pendleton bill would not create an "office-holding aristocracy" because the American version of reform would stamp the civil service as unsuited to "the active, busy, and adventurous sorts." One might as well try to form an aristocracy out of college professors or schoolteachers, he alleged.[11]

A second distinctive feature of the American context of reform lay in the legacy of republicanism. Before 1840 the primary argument against the partisan distribution of office had been its invitation to despotism rather than to corruption or inefficiency. The focus of critics of partisan appointments had always been on *executive* patronage, on how the threat of dismissal would undermine the "manly" independence of representatives of the people. As political parties came to be accepted as legitimate voices of the people—a development in motion during the 1820s and solidified after 1840—civil-service reformers came to fear that, without some limits, executive patronage threatened to devour the parties themselves. Reformers now saw their main task as to slice sufficiently into the cancer created by the spoils system to enable the parties to return to what the leading reformer Dorman B. Eaton, who drafted the Pendleton Act, called their "true function" of debating major national issues.[12] What enraged reformers was that the spoils system degraded politics by turning the federal government into a brokerage for job seekers.[13]

Reformers also complained about fraud and waste. In an exposé of waste in the New York Customhouse and Post Office,[14] Eaton related how the postmaster of New York City found hundreds of sacks of long-neglected mail, including a package clearly addressed to the vice-president of the United States, strewn about the main post office. The patronage system created an incentive to multiply offices in order to fill them. Each patronage appointee was required to contribute an "assessment," anywhere from 2 to 10 percent of his salary, to his party, and was expected to campaign for his party. In effect, he had two jobs. The system's waste aroused support from businessmen for civil-service reform but also raised a question. How would success on written examinations raise the level of honesty or competence in the federal service? Even Godkin doubted that written examinations would measure competence, and he echoed the prevailing view in the 1870s and 1880s that character and integrity could be measured only by "personal inspection."[15]

The best argument that reformers could mount for the capacity of written examinations to measure character was that performance would require studious habits, a sign of moral probity.[16] Skeptics plausibly responded that performance on written examinations mainly measured opportunities for schooling, which everyone conceded were unevenly distributed across the nation.[17] Even for those who believed that written examinations assessed competence, there was an alternative to the "open, competitive examinations" dictated by the Pendleton Act in the form of pass examinations. Dating to the 1850s in the federal service, pass examinations tested the "fitness" of civil servants to hold the jobs they owed to patronage and were popular with Stalwarts, the wing of the Republican Party led by Roscoe Conkling that was less inclined than the rival Half-Breeds toward civil-service reform.

Restricted to individuals who already held federal patronage jobs, pass examinations were convenient ways to assess an officeholder's knowledge of his or her job duties. In Britain, John Stuart Mill urged open, competitive examinations for the public service on the grounds that such examinations would select the best possible person for a post and not merely assess the competence of a current officeholder.[18] But Americans showed no interest in this argument. From the American perspective, pass examinations left the spoils system intact, and it was this system, and not its beneficiaries, that required execution.

Ironically, although critics of the system long had targeted the potential of executive patronage to undermine the republic, presidents were among the main victims of the spoils system, for under the system Congress proposed and presidents disposed. A member of Congress would nominate candidates whom presidents were expected to appoint in return for the congressman's support on policy issues. Aside from taking up an inordinate amount of the president's time and outraging factions in his party whenever their nominees were not appointed, the system, while effectively stripping the president of control over his rank-and-file appointees, left him vulnerable whenever scandals blew up. Some of these problems also affected congressmen. Representative James A. Garfield complained in 1870 that patronage issues consumed one-third of the time of congressmen, and that was before the federal service doubled in size between 1871 and 1881.

By the time Congress turned to serious consideration of the reform bill proposed by Senator George H. Pendleton of Ohio, George McClellan's running mate in 1864, some kind of civil-service reform had become inevitable. With their potent connections to the press, a helping hand from the corruption scandals of the 1870s, and public outrage at the assassination of President Garfield in 1881 by a disappointed office seeker and self-described Stalwart, reformers had generated enough public anger at the spoils system to arouse Congress. No one could measure the size of the Independent vote, but the extremely close presidential elections of 1876 and 1880 made it risky to ignore. Congressional and state elections in 1882 yielded some spectacular examples of the power, real or perceived, of the reform vote, including the landslide election of Buffalo's reform Democrat mayor, Grover Cleveland, to the governorship of New York.[19]

Most national elected officials nevertheless saw civil-service reform as an issue requiring delicate positioning by both parties. If anyone needed reminding, Pendleton's own career indicated how a wrong move at the wrong time could break a political career. Given Republican dominance in the civil service—no Democrat had been elected president since 1856—some Democrats hoped to delay reform until after the 1884 election, which they expected to win, and then massacre Republican appointees. Pendleton had jumped the gun, and Ohio Democrats made him an early casualty of the Pendleton Act by refusing to renominate him for the Senate in 1884, effectively ending his political career. As the party long in power, Republicans had much to lose from reform, especially the abolition of compulsory political assessments proposed by Pendleton's bill, but they were eager to reclaim the Independent vote, which they reasonably saw as a naturally Republican bloc that had been alienated by corruption under Republican regimes.[20]

The congressional debates over reform in 1882 and early 1883 revealed wide support for some sort of reform but uncertainty over which path to choose. Some proposed a more extensive reliance on pass examinations; others favored requiring partisan nominees for jobs to take open, competitive examinations before appointment; still others supported the full package, embodied in the Pendleton bill, of open, competitive examinations for entry-level positions, promotion by examination (not necessarily open or competitive), the establishment of a civil-service commission, and the abolition of compulsory political assessments. In the end, the bill was enacted with only modest congressional opposition. Its strongest backers came from urban areas in the Northeast that contained large federal installations, mainly post offices and customhouses, the locations of the most highly publicized examples of wasteful government.[21]

Requiring open, competitive examinations for entry-level positions, the Pendleton Act dealt a potentially lethal blow to the spoils system by stripping executives of the main incentive to dismiss an occupant of an office: replacement by a party loyalist. At the same time, the limited scope of the Pendleton Act dampened the objections of congressmen who were doubtful about the need for the full package. In response to complaints from southerners and westerners about their underrepresentation in the federal service, the law required the apportionment of appointments by population among the states, the territories, and the District of Columbia. It also confirmed an 1865 law that had given preference to soldiers discharged for wounds or sickness incurred in the line of duty (veterans' preference).

The Best Men attacked veterans' preference, which was gradually translated into a mountain of point bonuses on examinations, as a violation of the merit principle. But the merit system and veterans' preference were bound together in both the federal government and the states: states with merit systems also led the way in legislating veterans' preference.[22] Inasmuch as the adoption of merit systems resulted less from a widely shared commitment to merit in the abstract than to the desire of politicians to reduce their own discretion in making nominations, there was no inconsistency here. Adhering to rules and procedures, civil-service commissions were charged with preventing incursions by spoils rather than with promoting any specific definition of merit. As long as the legislative basis for veterans' preference was clear and consistently applied, courts showed no disposition to interfere. Resting on the legal establishment of a class of beneficiaries and justified as a reward for services to the nation (hence a form of merit), veterans' preference was not susceptible to the charge of political favoritism, which usually focused on individuals who benefited from their personal political connections, the "personal equation."[23]

The Pendleton Act abolished required political assessments throughout the federal civil service (the parties then turned to fund-raising), but otherwise left the nation with a dual system, part merit and part patronage. It applied only to rank-and-file executive positions that had been or would be "arranged into classes." Arrangement into a class meant grouping similar positions, hence the *classified* service, a term used interchangeably with "positions under the merit system" and the "competitive service" in the late nineteenth century.[24] At the passage of the law, only clerical positions in Washington had been so arranged, with a specified salary attached to each class, but the Pendleton Act also stipulated that subordinate offices in the larger post offices and customhouses, well-known nests of partisan activity, be arranged into classes as well. Neither party was willing to sacrifice all patronage, partly because neither could predict the political balance of power after the next election; limits on reform gave politicians a hedge against electoral uncertainty.[25]

In an area not controlled by the Pendleton Act, Congress used its control over positions subject to senatorial confirmation to retain its control over heads and assistant heads of departments in Washington, and a vast number of comparatively minor "field" offices, including most postmasters, deputy collectors of customs and internal revenue, registrars and receivers in land offices, district attorneys and marshals, commissioned officers in the Coast and Geodetic Survey, and officers in the foreign and consular services. Congress could establish these "excepted" categories either by its silence or expressly by statute. Presidential executive orders also excepted categories of workers and designated individuals, in the latter case on the grounds that the person excepted possessed a "special fitness" for the position. Even if the USCSC smelled a rat, as it often did, it could do little because its powers were mainly advisory.[26]

Not all excepted positions were controlled by spoilsmen. Some departments and bureaus, like the Internal Revenue Service and Census, were seen as fair game for partisanship.[27] Others, including the Coast and Geodetic Survey and the Public Health Service, much less so. Congress accepted the need for competent technical experts in government, and during the 1890s the USCSC began to administer "non-assembled" examinations, which were noncompetitive assessments of academic credentials and experience, in order to select technical specialists in departments like Agriculture and in the Coast and Geodetic Survey and Public Health Service. In practice, specialists were selected on merit and became part of what was generally called the "noncompetitive" service.[28]

These federal agencies were comparatively unaffected by the politics of patronage, but patronage was never far from the surface in congressional debates.

For example, in 1913, during an acidic congressional debate over a tariff bill's exemption of a variety of revenue agents from the classified service, Republican Reed Smoot mocked the Democrats' support for the exemption as no more than an assertion that "we want the offices and we intend to have them." Hoke Smith of Georgia parried this thrust by questioning whether examinations measured fitness. Republicans then pounced on a more vulnerable, or perhaps just more honest, target: a New Jersey Democrat who blandly acknowledged that while he would never recommend a person merely because he was a Democrat, neither would he ever nominate someone for any office, however insignificant, unless he was a Democrat.[29]

Despite the persistence of patronage, the proportion of federal positions under the merit system rose from 10.5 percent in 1883 to 51.2 percent in 1903 to 75.0 percent in 1930, a more than sevenfold increase that was probably well beyond the expectations of the congressmen who voted for reform in 1883. It is tempting to think that so dramatic an increase reflected growing partisan acceptance of the idea that a public service whose gate was guarded by open, competitive examinations would be a better service, but there is little evidence for this. The first Democrat elected president in nearly three decades, Grover Cleveland was under terrific pressure from his party to purge Republican officeholders. Never a full-blooded civil-service reformer—he disliked the Best Men for their self-righteousness—Cleveland nevertheless believed in a public-spirited rather than partisan civil service. He spent wearying hours reviewing the credentials of nominees, and at the start of his second term kept a Republican, Theodore Roosevelt, as head of the USCSC. All his idealism earned was a near revolt in his party, which forced him to backtrack. By the end of his first term he had replaced three-fourths of federal civilian employees.[30] Nevertheless, by the end of his nonconsecutive two terms in 1897, Cleveland had extended the merit system to cover over 45 percent of all federal civilian positions. No subsequent president would match Cleveland in bringing so high a proportion of federal employees under the system.[31]

Rather than a broad acceptance of the principle of open, competitive examinations, the main cause of this extension of the merit system lay in a mixture of partisanship and presidential ambitions. In either case, the procedure was the same, blanketing or "covering" by executive order. For example, a president failing renomination by his party or defeated for reelection would protect his own partisan appointees by moving their positions into the merit system. Nearly three-fourths of Cleveland's first-term extensions of the merit system occurred after his defeat in 1888, and over 90 percent of his Republican successor Benjamin Harrison's extensions were similarly lame-duck appointments. In 1908 Theodore Roosevelt blanketed more than fifteen thousand fourth-class (small town) postmasterships in the solidly Republican states north of the Ohio River and east of the Mississippi. By then Roosevelt knew he would be succeeded by fellow Republican William Howard Taft, so he was not saving these positions from an impending Democratic purge. Roosevelt's use of blanketing reflects the second motive behind the extension of the merit system: to diminish the influence of his own party's leaders and to substitute what Stephen Skowronek has called an "executive-centered reconstitution of civil administration in its place."[32] From the start of his presidency Roosevelt had sought to gain control over the civil service, less to protect it from raids by spoilsmen—he skirted the merit system when it suited his purpose[33]—than to make the civil service a servant of the president. His executive orders sharply restricted even voluntary political activity by civil servants and imposed gag orders by promising dismissal for any civil servant who sought to advance his career by lobbying Congress.[34]

Changing the Guard

The Best Men's interest in civil-service reform waned in the 1890s, when both the membership and numbers of reform leagues contracted. In the early 1900s a new crop of reformers was coming on the scene, and by the 1920s the concerns of the Gilded Age reformers had been supplanted by those of public administrationists. Compared with the earlier generation, the new generation was much less interested in purifying partisan politics and much more inclined to describe the nation's problems as administrative rather than political.

Hostile to the parties, the new generation was typified by Charles A. Beard, the historian; Frederick A. Cleveland, university professor, expert on public finance, and activist for municipal reform; W. W. Willoughby, who held a doctorate in politics from Johns Hopkins and whose career included positions with the U.S. Labor Department, the government of Puerto Rico, the Census Bureau, and Princeton University; and Robert S. Brookings, a St. Louis businessman with a deep pocket and a passionate commitment to founding public policy on scientific research. Whereas the Gilded Age reformers had equated efficiency with economy and had expected economy to flow from stripping the parties of control over routine public jobs, the younger generation placed economy within the framework of the scientific analysis of all government operations. The older generation edited periodicals, wrote essays, and delivered lectures. The younger one garrisoned new research bureaus like the New York Bureau of Municipal Research (BMR, founded 1906); the Institute for Government Research (IGR, founded 1916), similar to the BMR but with a national focus; and the Brookings Institution (founded 1927). Staffers and supporters of these institutions slid noiselessly among research institutions, government service, and universities.[35] Their interest was initially pricked by books like Lincoln Steffens's *The Shame of the Cities* (1904) and the cause of municipal reform, but their attention gradually shifted to national issues, especially after 1910, when President William H. Taft plucked Cleveland from the BMR to head his Commission on Economy and Efficiency (Goodnow and Willoughby also worked on this commission). Willoughby would later become the first director of the IGR, the forerunner of the Brookings Institution, and he would continue to push for an executive budget, an objective finally reached when Congress, which had brushed aside most of the Taft Commission's recommendations, responded to huge wartime deficits by passing the Budget and Accounting Act of 1921.

The concept of public administration as a definable discipline was largely the creation of this generation.[36] Among the first textbooks in the field were those written by Leonard D. White, a University of Chicago professor of public administration who combined an academic career with government service. (He would head the USCSC from 1934 to 1937.)[37] Public administrationists agreed that administration had become the "heart" of government and that there existed principles of administration common to all large enterprises.[38] Public administrationists owed an intellectual debt to the scientific management movement. Its founder, Frederick W. Taylor, had been more interested in the shop floor than the front office, but he had predicted that scientific management would increase the need for managers.[39]

Public administration also drew concepts from contemporary theories about the role of management in business. Harvard's Charles W. Eliot had envisioned business eventually joining the ranks of the professions, and in the 1920s Wallace Donham, dean of Harvard's Graduate Business School, advanced the idea, later popularized by Gardner Means, Adolph A. Berle Jr., and James Burnham, that "effective responsibility" in American business had passed from the founding generation of capitalists to a new class of managers (a functional distinction roughly parallel to that between politics and administration).[40] Donham saw this new class as a meritocratic elite winnowed from the inept by the business process, whereas in government, politics perverted the selection process. The Pendleton-era reformers had taken it for granted that businesses managed their personnel better than governments; no business would last long if it based hiring and firing on election results. After World War I the preference for business methods gained momentum. Corporate executives working in wartime planning agencies had abundant opportunity to contrast business efficiency with government chaos. Among these executives were Walter S. Gifford, future president of the American Telephone and Telegraph Company, who had served as executive director of the War Industries Board, and Chester I. Barnard, Gifford's mentee, future president of New Jersey Bell, and by the 1940s the leading American theorist of management.

Although management theorists wrote mainly about business, they viewed the principles of management as applicable to all large organizations, including governments. *Onward Industry!* (1931), by James D. Mooney of General Motors, discovered identical principles of management in the modern corporation, the Roman Catholic Curia, and the Ottoman bureaucracy.[41] Henri Fayol, a French mining engineer, colliery manager, and management theorist with a wide following in America, attributed his own success to his ability to coordinate the diverse subdivisions of his businesses, not to any personal qualities. Lower-level employees, he argued, possessed technical skill, but the manager required a higher administrative ability, which, in addition to coordination, included planning, organizing, commanding, and controlling.[42] With a few emendations, Americans turned this into a tidy acronym, POSDCORB. Generations of public administration students "learned that public executives plan, organize, staff, direct, coordinate, report, and budget."[43]

Administering Merit

Public administrationists construed the impressive extension of the merit system in the Cleveland through Taft administrations as the unfolding of a historical inevitability, but subsequent events would jar them. One source of their later anxiety lay in the huge expansion of veterans' preference after World War I. Under the Pendleton Act, classified positions had to be filled "by selections according to grade from among those graded highest" on competitive examinations. Appointing officers could select a candidate from an "eligible list" of those graded highest. In 1888 the USCSC had established a lower passing grade for veterans, 65 rather than 70, and then authorized the jumping of veterans who passed with a grade of 65 (or higher) to the head of the eligible list in order of grade. Then, in 1919, Congress extended veterans' preference to all honorably discharged veterans and their widows, regardless of disability, and to the wives of disabled veterans.[44] This opened the gates to the 4.5 million World War I veterans and to all veterans honorably discharged in peacetime. In the wake of the 1919 legislation the number of preference claims acted on by the USCSC rose from 600–900 a year to 60,000–70,000 a year. At the onset of the Depression a disabled veteran who scored 60 on the examination would be boosted by the bonus to 70 and would then jump over a nonveteran who had scored 100.[45] At the height of the Depression over 30 percent of appointees to the classified service were preferred veterans. Similar trends affected the states, with the difference that states often extended veterans' preference to promotions.

Public administrationists routinely attacked veterans' preference, but they never dented it and ultimately they could do little more than document its extent and ruefully compare the generosity of American provisions for veterans with the more limited accommodations made in Europe.[46] In their attacks on veterans' preference, public administrationists had the backing of feminists. Although the widows of veterans and the wives of disabled veterans were eligible for preference, the vast majority of beneficiaries were men. Veterans' preference was not the only obstacle confronting women who competed for civil-service jobs. Under laws dating to the Pendleton era, division chiefs and other appointing officers, while required to choose from a list of eligibles as determined by examination, could specify the sex of those considered for appointment. Until 1932 the USCSC maintained separate male and female lists of eligibles to facilitate sex-based selection and the gender-typing of civil-service jobs. In that year, under pressure from reformers whose lodestar was wider applicant pools to identify merit, the two lists were merged. But the merger exposed women to competition from veterans. As the Depression deepened, the quest by veterans for public-service jobs intensified and the unfairness of compelling women to compete with this privileged class prompted a return to separate registers in 1934.

Another development that aggravated public administrationists, who became the most vocal advocates of the merit system during the first half of the twentieth century, lay in the increasing difficulty of removing classified civil servants. Nothing in the Pendleton Act prohibited the removal of a civil servant, but the Gilded Age reformers expected that open, competitive examinations would shrink removals by eliminating their main incentive and that the probationary period required by the act would sort out the remaining bad apples. The result would be to substitute a public-spirited civil service for one composed of quick-footed entrepreneurs whose loyalty was to their party and who sought private advantages from public jobs. What the reformers did not foresee was that the law would turn classified employees into a self-interested faction that invoked the merit system to secure better pay and job protection. Whether they owed their positions to success on competitive examinations or to blanketing, federal civil servants became an increasingly unionized and potent lobby from the 1890s to the 1930s.[47]

Although the federal government did not allow aggrieved employees to petition the USCSC for redress until the 1940s, classified employees secured close to ironclad job protection much earlier. This occurred mainly because persistent conflicts between the president and Congress limited the scope of executive authority. Between 1890 and 1910, federal employees, especially postal workers, formed unions, which often brought them into conflict with department heads and with Theodore Roosevelt's desire for control over the federal bureaucracy. As an increasingly potent bloc of voters, federal employees had leverage with members of Congress in each party. In response to Roosevelt's various gag orders, which threatened dismissal of federal workers who appealed over the heads of their supervisors to Congress for pay increases or other benefits, Congress in 1912 passed the Lloyd–La Follette Act, which stipulated that removals in the classified service occur only "for such cause as will promote the efficiency of said service and for reasons given in writing." Although the act allowed an examination of witnesses and formal proceedings only at the discretion of the appointing officer, and thus seemingly upheld the power of supervisors, in practice this provision became a dead letter.[48] In the vast federal bureaucracy the "appointing power" was usually understood to refer to the cabinet-level department head, not the immediate supervisor in a bureau or agency.[49] "Circumlocution and delay" characterized any attempt to remove or discipline classified civil servants.[50]

Urban governments also had difficulties getting control of merit systems. Reform-minded mayors were less insulated than elected federal officials from political machines, which proved effective at skirting merit-system rules. Investigating Chicago's public service in the mid-1920s, Leonard D. White found that politically connected applicants secured jobs as temporary workers exempt from the merit system and did so again and again, until they effectively became permanent.[51] As late as 1972, 40 percent of Chicago's municipal employees were "temps"; although limited by law to serving for 180 days, some had served for twenty years.[52] Not surprisingly, municipal employees often took it for granted that merit was just a facade and that jobs and promotions depended on politics. Since the exercise of political influence violated civil-service law, employees, like the shiftless stenographer who announced that she took only two letters a day "because I don't feel like doing any more," greeted crackdowns with charges that they were politically motivated.[53]

The obstacles in the path of attempted removals were the flip side of the obstacles that restricted the discretion of supervisors to promote the meritorious. The common thread lay in the distrust that permeated the applications of merit. Public administrationists were torn between their desire to reward merit with promotions and, reflecting the legacy of the spoils system, their disinclination to give supervisors much discretion on the grounds that discretion might open the door to political favoritism. The issue of promotions was especially thorny. The Pendleton Act stated that no person could be promoted unless he passed an examination of some sort or was shown to be exempt. In 1910 a NCSRL committee chaired by Charles W. Eliot urged tying promotions throughout the federal service to examinations. Except for a small number of positions requiring technical expertise in the Coast and Geodetic Survey and the Department of Agriculture, however, the federal service made little use of examinations for higher posts. Examinations were cumbersome to administer each time a vacancy arose. Excepting the State Department and, to a lesser degree, the Department of Agriculture, most high posts were outside the classified service and hence not subject to examinations.

Despite this, public administrationists remained committed not only to the principle of merit but to the ideal of careers in the public service. As they understood it, careers required opportunities for promotion up internal ladders. Theodore Roosevelt had avowed the same goal, and in the early 1900s the USCSC began to explore ways to identify applicants with the potential to win promotions. In 1911, when there were few mental tests of any sort and no group tests, the annual report of the USCSC stated that it was reasonable to expect "a certain degree of general intelligence" from clerks in different departments. With this goal in mind, the USCSC revised an existing test in which applicants were asked to write a letter. In the new format the test required the arrangement of a loose statement of facts of around five hundred words into a logical and compact paragraph of one hundred fifty words.[54] The perceived success of the U.S. Army's testing program during World War I led the USCSC to open a dialogue with the emerging testing industry in the early 1920s.[55] The commission experimented with intelligence tests, as did several state and municipal civil services.

But intelligence tests were vulnerable to the same charge that long had clouded scholastic examinations for public employment: their lack of clear relevance to job duties. Whatever public administrationists might think, the public still measured the civil service by the number of jobs it provided, a view buttressed by the expansion of veterans' preference during the 1920s. Veterans' organizations had a special loathing of IQ tests because they were not graded on a 0–100 scale to two decimal places, which was the basis of all veteran-preference legislation. Intelligence tests quickly came under ferocious attack from veterans and other groups, and the USCSC backed off.[56] If fitness for a specific job was to be the standard, then the ideal test was the one that best simulated the job. Even before American entry into World War I in 1917, psychologists were trying to devise tests that predicted job performance, and these were widely available during the 1920s. The federal government borrowed and adapted some of these tests, such as a test for mail carriers that measured short-term memory for place-names.[57] Such job-specific tests were a comparatively uncontroversial way to winnow the pool of applicants for entry-level positions. State and municipal civil services also made use of job-specific tests for promotion. In contrast to entry-level aptitude tests, which aimed to establish the likely fit between an inexperienced candidate and the job sought, promotion examinations called for specific knowledge of rules and procedures ("What official body issues permits to generate combustible gases?"), and they proved to be a nutrient for cram schools.[58]

The most practical of all tests was job experience itself. Two investigators of New York City's civil service reported in 1937 that the relative weighting of experience and education in the allocation of well-paying public jobs was so tilted toward experience that recent college graduates were at a severe disadvantage in securing them.[59] The federal government weighed academic credentials in its nonassembled examinations for technical experts, mainly in the Coast and Geodetic Survey and the Department of Agriculture, but even in these instances experience was more heavily weighted than credentials. Any effort to expand the role of academic credentials was likely to trigger outbursts against aristocracy. In the 1920s public administrationists did not consider stratifying civil services by educational attainment (length of schooling) an available option.

In this climate of opinion, many jurisdictions, including most federal agencies, preferred to hinge promotions on some mixture of efficiency ratings and seniority rather than on competitive examinations or educational credentials.[60] Public administrationists preferred a light weighting of seniority and a heavy one for efficiency ratings, the reverse of the weightings preferred by most public employees, trade unions, and industrial workers, who favored seniority and its cousin experience as the criteria easiest to identify and least subject to manipulation.[61] Objections to rating scales were legion, but most boiled down to the argument that rating scales invited favoritism. Supervisors could easily smuggle their personal or political dislikes into rating scales. Even if they did not, some supervisors rated high, others low, and all were subject to the halo effect.

Confronted with objections to rating scales, most public administrationists followed authorities on personnel management in business by urging improved rating scales and training for raters to eliminate favoritism. The usual technique was to load the scale with ever more traits to be rated. Public administrators especially praised the rating scale devised by J.B. Probst, chief examiner of the St. Paul, Minnesota, Civil Service Bureau, which rated eleven different traits. Leonard D. White, who usually spoke for the public administrationist mainstream, was skeptical. Not enough was known about the traits that contributed to efficiency, he stated. In his widely influential *Introduction to the Study of Public Administration*, White also identified a larger problem: the spoils system's legacy of distrust, which continued to permeate public service in the United States. White was especially struck by the differences between the American rating scales and procedures in Britain: "American practice tends to develop elaborate devices to correct the untrustworthy judgment of superiors; English practice contents itself with general judgments of superior officers."[62]

The same legacy of distrust also blunted the efforts of public administrationists to increase opportunities for promotion by opening competition for vacancies to civil servants located far from the unit where the vacancy occurred. In order to ensure deep applicant pools and broad opportunities for promotion, White proposed pooling all civil-service positions—federal, state, and local—within a metropolitan area, or, alternatively, pooling all positions within a single branch of the civil service in a state (e.g., police). His precedents included teachers, whose certificates qualified them for positions in different locales, and city managers, who moved from locale to locale throughout the nation. Public administrationists would advance versions of this proposal, especially on the federal level, for the next fifty years, often in the form of an elite "senior" civil service, modeled on Britain's Administrative Class, whose members moved through different posts as part of an apprenticeship in government.

In the 1920s, however, the obstacles in the path of any such proposal were formidable. White, who completed a study of Chicago's municipal employees in 1924–25, had already identified one impediment: civil servants themselves valued security and predictability more than transfers and promotions. In principle, Chicago's municipal employees whose score placed them high on the eligible list had a cornucopia of opportunities for promotion, often involving transfers, throughout the city's public service. This was just the sort of system that White and other public administrationists favored. It was closed in the sense that only city employees could take the examinations—a desirable feature in White's eyes because it restrained the morale-busting practice of bringing in political favorites from the outside for higher posts—but open in the range of possibilities it offered. But, White found, in practice it did not work. Employees routinely waived possibilities for promotion, sometimes to avoid new and challenging duties, sometimes under pressure to make way for a political favorite.[63] The "ceaseless competition with the hope of brilliant success" that characterized industry (as White thought) had little appeal for government workers.[64] This combination of disinclination and political pressure "virtually nullified" Chicago's system of competitive examinations for promotion, he concluded.[65]

One aspect of Chicago's public service that especially dismayed White lay in the persistence of political influence despite the city's pioneering adoption of position classification, an idea backed by both public administrationists and public-employee unions. A species of scientific management, position classification aimed to solve an old problem, the loose fit between the descriptions of public jobs and their actual duties. Before the 1920s classes of positions were defined more by their salaries than their duties. For example, at the passage of the Pendleton Act, clerical positions in Washington were classified by a thirty-year-old law into positions paying $1200, $1400, $1600, or $1800 a year, with no job descriptions attached to any of these salary pegs.[66] This method of appropriation, known as the statutory roll, persisted in congressional appropriations into the early 1920s. So did an alternative, known as the lump-sum appropriation, which allowed the administrator of an agency to allot salaries so long as he did not exceed the appropriation.[67] In the absence of classification of jobs by duties, a supervisor could slide a favorite into a higher salary, perhaps with a fancier title as a fig leaf. In 1920 there were 583 different titles for executive-branch civil servants in Washington.[68] Much the same was true in the states. An investigation in Pennsylvania turned up an "auditor" who was essentially a typist and a tabulating-machine operator who was described as a "statistician."[69]

Position classification promised to restrain the covert influence of patronage and to ensure "equal pay for equal work" by a sequence of steps: describing the exact duties, responsibilities, and qualifications for each position; grouping horizontally (across departments) all positions with similar descriptions into homogenous "grades"; and layering grades on top of each other into "classes" on the basis of ascending duties and qualifications. Chicago initiated position classification in 1912, and the idea spread quickly to jurisdictions elsewhere in Illinois and to other states with merit systems. The USCSC had been calling for position classification since 1902, and in 1912 Congress authorized it to establish a Division (later Bureau) of Efficiency to develop a system of efficiency ratings on the premise that salaries would be standardized by job description.[70] The report of the Joint Committee on Reclassification of Salaries established by Congress in 1919—it hired former BMR staffer and future urban planner Robert Moses as an "acknowledged expert"—led to passage of the Classification Act of 1923, which established five distinct federal "services": custodial; clerical-mechanical; clerical-administrative-fiscal (CAF); subprofessional; and professional and scientific. These were loose categories. (For example, the CAF service lumped together everyone doing office work.)[71] But within each service there were many grades and classes, and pay scales partially overlapped across the several services.[72] The act also created a Personnel Classification Board to review job allocations made by department heads.[73]

Within the federal government, position classification had the support of employee unions, which saw it as a way to recoup salary lost to postwar inflation, and feminists, who viewed it as a way to overcome blatant sex discrimination. Both groups were soon disappointed, for Congress saw it primarily as an economy measure, a means of scaling down allegedly inflated job descriptions. Women were among the main victims of the act, since many of the important jobs that they were performing, including actually doing the work of statisticians, were reduced to suit their low salaries. By making job descriptions rather than the personal qualities of an office's occupant the basis of pay and promotion, position classification limited merit-based promotion. In principle, position classification was supposed to open lines of promotion by making workplace hierarchies more transparent.[74] But White, who approvingly compared a well-run bureaucracy to a machine,[75] acknowledged that position classification "was intended to put an end to personal treatment and is constructed on the ideal of dealing with positions and not with individuals."[76] Under the old system, supervisors were able to reward employees with spot promotions, like brevets in the army, merely by changing their titles. In contrast, the rules governing position classification usually required that "employees shall enter at the lowest grade of a class, skipping none of the intermediate points."[77] White conceded that this created a difficulty for "the superior employee," for supervisors could not legally distinguish between employees of the same grade on the basis of merit even though their range of proficiency might be great.

Position classification was representative of the Progressive Era drive to curtail the favoritism and personalism on which so many existing hierarchies were founded and to establish seemingly unarguable measures of competence. It did not take reformers long, however, to recognize that it was a straitjacket.[78] Its damaging effects were restrained only by its difficulty of implementation, which led different jurisdictions to adopt it at widely varying paces. Chicago established position classification in 1912, but another forty years passed before Philadelphia adopted the practice. The vast federal bureaucracy was notably sluggish in implementing position classification. The 1923 Classification Act applied only to departments in Washington. Not until 1949 did a new Classification Act extend the system to the field (outside Washington) services, which accounted for most of the growth of the federal bureaucracy during the 1930s and 1940s. With the onset of the Depression and the New Deal, position classification in the federal bureaucracy became a shambles.

The Public Merit Project

The New Deal had profound but conflicting effects on the federal bureaucracy. The number of executive branch employees rose, especially in the field services and outside the classified service. Most of the New Deal's emergency agencies were exempted from civil-service rules on the grounds that emergencies required specialists even when no job description existed. The proportion of federal civilian employees in the classified service dropped from 80 percent in 1933 to 60.5 percent in 1936.[79] Suspicion that President Franklin D. Roosevelt was reviving the spoils system by the liberal distribution of patronage in agencies established outside the merit system—such as the Tennessee Valley Authority (TVA), Works

Progress Administration (WPA), and Public Works Administration (PWA)—was sufficiently keen, especially after FDR's intervention in the congressional elections of 1938, to prompt passage in 1939 of the first Hatch Act, which prohibited even voluntary political activity by federal employees.

This was one side of the story. On the other side, the New Deal inspired well-educated young men and women to enter government service. One beneficiary of this idealism was the Foreign Service, established in 1924 by the Rogers Act's merger of the existing consular and diplomatic services and surfeited with outstanding applicants from elite colleges during the 1930s.[80] By the end of the 1930s the Foreign Service was widely hailed as the government's shining example of a "career" service. Whether other government agencies would follow its path aroused considerable discussion. A 1939 report on the prospects for engineers in the federal service defined a career as "a course of life, employment, or profession that offers possibilities for advancement or honor" and "increase in power, opportunity to do research, increase in professional or public prestige or both, personal publicity, foreign travel, [and] military rank or other incentive." This report also described the army, the navy, and the Foreign Service as the only government employments that currently held forth the prospect of careers to "a major degree," while acknowledging the possibility of careers in the Coast and Geodetic Survey, the Bureau of Standards, and the Bureau of Reclamation "in a lessening degree."[81]

In principle, a career so defined was a meritocratic status system. Initial entry depended on rigorous selection by examination, but thereafter careerists expected a high degree of paternalistic protection by the government in exchange for loyalty to the service, with most promotions coming within the service and in due course for satisfactory performance.[82] Theodore Roosevelt had complained in 1895 that a "certain fluidity" in the American character prevented young men from looking to the civil service for careers; they did not want to be tethered to a single desk or job. But as put forward during the 1930s, a career system connoted rank in the service rather than the job, similar to the armed forces and the Foreign Service. In these services the rank of officers did not depend on their duty assignment; officers routinely were moved from post to post with no change in rank. So understood, a career in the government service was a far cry from the sort of entrepreneurial trajectories of antebellum officeholders who zigzagged between elective and appointive office in their pursuit of power and prestige. Was it equally distant from the merit system? In 1937 a presidential advisory committee recommended that the existing merit system evolve into a career system.[83]

For convenience, I call the development of the merit system into a career system the Public Merit Project. This project differed from the objectives of the Pendleton-era reformers, who had far more interest in killing the spoils system than in improving the quality of public employees. It was also distinct from the early public administrationists' dream of a civil service stacked with nonpartisan experts with specialties in recognized sciences. The Public Merit Project bore more resemblance to C. Wright Mills's "genuine bureaucracy," a public service that drew the best and brightest from higher education into policy planning. The project would persist for the rest of the twentieth century, but it would repeatedly run afoul of two institutions its supporters held in low regard: existing merit systems and politics.

Any attempt to nudge the merit system toward a career system faced three obstacles. First, the federal government's intensifying demand for scientists and professionals during the 1930s was primarily for specialists rather than for freelancers who ranged between jobs and among departments. This demand strengthened the association between rank and job description in the federal service, and it was concentrated in a narrow band of departments. A study of "junior professional" appointees—those appointed to the lowest grade of the professional and scientific service—from January 1935 through March 1939 disclosed that more of these junior professionals were employed by the Department of Agriculture, typically as agronomists, agricultural surveyors, foresters, and soil scientists, than in all other federal departments and agencies combined.[84] Second, although pressure was mounting to privilege academic credentials in civil-service hiring, especially in the professional and scientific service, overt moves to recruit specialists from universities triggered hostility from specialists who owed their positions to experience. In 1939 the USCSC introduced an examination for "junior professional assistant" (JPA) that was open only to college graduates and college seniors.[85] The outcome was conflict. On one side stood older scientists and engineers, who labeled the requirement undemocratic, called for continuing the practice of allowing candidates to substitute experience for credentials, and insisted that examinations for senior positions be restricted to solving the "practical problems arising in every-day work on the job."[86] On the other side, consulting engineers, the National Research Council, A.T.& T., Chrysler Motors, university engineering and agricultural colleges, and various societies representing social scientists called for a deemphasis on experience, for broadly gauged examinations that would test "ability to learn" and grasp of scientific fundamentals, and for interviews to assess "personal qualities."[87]

The third obstacle to developing a career system out of the merit system arose from the tenacity of the view that any move to inject more flexibility into the merit system—for example, by hiring university graduates whose glittering academic credentials easily met the "presumption-of-merit" test—would be unfair to those with less glowing credentials and would reopen the door to spoilsmanship.

Tension between career and merit systems came to a head over the status of federal lawyers. In 1938 FDR's Executive Order No. 7916 blanketed some twenty-four thousand hitherto exempt positions into the classified service.[88] In the past, federal civil servants had welcomed the job protection that accompanied blanketing, but No. 7916 aroused opposition, especially from federal lawyers, and FDR postponed its application pending an investigation headed by Supreme Court justice Stanley Reed. The status of federal lawyers was destined to provoke a major split on the Reed Committee. In 1938 more than two-thirds of government lawyers worked outside the classified service (Justice, the Veterans' Administration, the Securities and Exchange Commission, and Treasury were their main roosts). In contrast to scientists and engineers, whose academic backgrounds were usually non-elite and often land-grant colleges, elite law schools provided a disproportionate number of federal lawyers, who were attracted to the New Deal by what USCSC head Samuel H. Ordway called the "social significance" of their jobs and who did much of the New Deal's most important work by matching the courtroom performance of the private lawyers retained by corporations. As unclassified employees, these young lawyers did not enjoy the protection of the merit system, but they could be hired without consideration of veterans' preference and apportionment and their academic credentials and government experience made them attractive candidates for positions in private firms.[89]

In 1939 an advisory committee chaired by Philadelphia lawyer Henry W. Bickle and including future secretary of state Dean Acheson recommended against blanketing unclassified lawyers into the classified service. In the eyes of the advisory committee, the procedures for hiring lawyers under the merit system, aside from their glacial pace, were tilted toward mediocrity. The advisory committee cited the fact that the top thirty-three candidates on a register of eligibles for the post of junior attorney in the Federal Communications Commission were disabled veterans, ten of whom would have failed the written examination used to rank the eligibles had it not been for the veterans' bonus. The advisory committee recommended instead the establishment of a Committee on Government Lawyers, consisting of the chief legal officers in the various departments and agencies that extensively employed lawyers. This committee would be charged with compiling an unranked register of eligibles on the basis of candidates' high school, college, and law school records, combined with personal interviews. The advisory committee made little effort to disguise its preference for snaring young graduates of elite law schools: candidates for the register had to apply within three years of law school graduation, and no one could remain on the register beyond age thirty. In a revealing aside, the advisory committee dismissed the value of letters of recommendation except when written "by persons whose judgment is known and respected by the examiners," a view, the committee quickly acknowledged, that would favor graduates of prestigious law schools. Final selection from the unranked register would then be left to the chief legal officers of departments and agencies.[90]

These recommendations won the backing of solicitors and general counsel in several federal agencies and departments. The arguments for an unranked register were legion, but at their core lay the belief that the merit system was for mediocrities. The practice of restricting promotion to those on lower rungs of the ladder meant that anyone sufficiently patient to wait for a vacancy would eventually be promoted despite "average attention to the job and average intelligence," with a consequent "deadening effect on the energy and mental agility of members of the staff."[91] The counterattack on these views enlisted a sprinkling of federal legal officers and a bloc of representatives from the USCSC, the American Bar Association, the recently founded and left-wing National Lawyers Guild (many of whose members were drawn from the underside of law schools), and the testing industry. These groups argued that only the absorption of federal lawyers into the classified service would end partisanship and favoritism, that existing written examinations for entry onto ranked registers could be improved, that anyone who thought that veterans' preference could be skirted by keeping lawyers outside the merit system grossly underestimated the vigilance and power of veterans' organizations, and that equality of opportunity required competitive examinations for recruitment and promotion.[92]

The final report of the Reed Committee recommended "inducting" all members of the professional and scientific service, including lawyers, into the merit system, except those exempt by statute. On the surface this looked like a victory for the USCSC and the merit system, the more so because the Ramspeck Act of 1940, passed during the committee's deliberations, removed most remaining statutory obstacles to the extension of the classified system. But this recommendation failed to disguise the committee's division over the plan for an unranked register. Most of the lawyers on the committee favored the proposal for an unranked register (dubbed Plan A), supplemented by a proposal for a Committee on Government Lawyers to work with the USCSC and the testing industry to devise a new entry-level examination. These lawyers then blithely pronounced this plan to be compatible with absorbing lawyers into the classified service. This stance elicited a sharp dissent from Leonard D. White, who had served on the Reed Committee, and Ben D. Wood, an authority on testing. Both rallied around Plan B, the application of existing civil-service procedures to lawyers. To these dissenters, Plan A, with its dismissal of ranked registers, opened the door to every form of pressure and discrimination—"political, racial, religious, regional, professional, academic, and personal"—and hence was incompatible with the ideals of the merit system.[93]

Unable to resolve its internal split, the Reed Committee punted and asked FDR to choose between Plans A and B. He chose Plan A but then ordered the establishment of a Board of Legal Examiners within the USCSC to draw up regulations governing the recruitment, examination, and promotion of federal lawyers. Although the linchpin of Plan A was the unranked register, FDR left the door open to ranking by a more sophisticated exam. Next, reflecting Wood's influence, the new board produced a four-hour multiple-choice test, which included a standard intelligence test, legal knowledge, and history and public affairs. White, who had never been comfortable with the idea that law was too delicate a flower to submit to mass testing, admired the examination.

Along with a high passing score, the sort of test that the board produced, combining intelligence with knowledge of history and public affairs, could have produced an unranked list that nevertheless favored the most academically talented candidates. At the same time, such a list would not have overtly privileged graduates of elite law schools. But there was a catch. Because the examination had been devised on the assumption that government lawyers would be inducted into the classified service, the list of eligibles, while not overtly ranked, was subject to apportionment among the states (required by the Pendleton Act). This requirement led to the establishment of much higher passing scores in large states like New York than in smaller ones such as Wyoming. With American entry into World War II, younger lawyers joined the armed forces, the examination was taken mainly by older lawyers, and the range of law schools represented on the register was very broad. This was not what the advocates of an unranked register had initially envisioned. They had favored Plan A to recruit the top graduates of the most prestigious law schools into government service. But Congress had the final say. Amid wartime conditions the Board of Legal Examiners collapsed when in 1943 Congress declined to fund it (previously, it had been funded out of existing USCSC appropriations). With some exceptions, federal lawyers remained outside the classified service.

Word Games

The issues that wracked the federal service during the New Deal were far from the issues considered by framers of the Pendleton Act. The Best Men defined merit as the opposite of partisan favoritism. They had not conceived of reform as a means to bring well-educated people like themselves into government jobs; they did not equate merit with bodies of knowledge or skills that would improve governance; and they did not follow European practices by aligning tiers of the civil service with tiers of the educational system. All of them would have been happy to see better men, high-minded and cultured men, go into politics, but they knew that competitive examinations, even if they tested only common-school attainments, provoked enormous controversy in the United States. An elite, career civil service selected by rigorous examinations bore an uncomfortable resemblance to the "permanent office-holding class" that William Jennings Bryan pronounced (on accepting the Democratic nomination in 1896) "not in harmony with our institutions."[94] An act calling for fixed seven-year terms for all federal employees under the merit system passed both houses of Congress in 1912, only to be vetoed by President William H. Taft.[95]

By the 1930s the sharpening of the politics/administration distinction was providing a rationale for the Public Merit Project. In 1935 Leonard White wrote a glowing account of Britain's civil service, including its elite Administrative Class of mobile senior civil servants and permanent undersecretaries, who were selected for their academic brilliance, who could look forward to high state honors that were beyond the ken of American bureaucrats, and who held rank in the service rather than the job.[96] Four years earlier political scientist Walter Rice Sharp had familiarized Americans with the examinations for the foreign service and for the Ministry of Finance in France. These French examinations were public events that lasted for days and were effectively open only to graduates of the École Libre des Sciences Politiques.[97] The 1927 examination for the foreign service, held at the Quai d'Orsay, required oral expositions of irredentism in Europe, the formation and evolution of Britain's dominions, Serbia since 1869, and the Irish Question since 1815. Even for comparatively minor positions like chief clerk (*re-dacteur*) in the postal service, the French examination lasted seven to eight hours. An American observer wrote that this examination "almost always presupposes a knowledge of literature and philosophic criticism which few candidates for similar appointment in America would be likely to possess."[98]

Virtually alone among advanced nations, the United States had never possessed the sort of tiered and articulated system of higher education that in European nations facilitated direct passage from a university to a job in a prestigious civil service or, as in France, a ricochet from the higher civil service to a corporate boardroom. Their tradition of equal rights led most Americans in the 1930s to continue to gag at the thought of a British- or French-style higher civil service. As a member of a presidential commission observed, many in Congress would view "the separation of our Federal employees into classes of distinction" as "un-American."[99] Public administrationists who rallied behind the Public Merit Project faced an added problem. Governments often hired university graduates with technical and scientific specialties as experts. But no government—federal or state—viewed administration as an expert specialty nor did any even distinguish administrative work from clerical tasks like processing claims. Public administrationists, who mainly nested in schools and departments of public administration, were providing a professional education for which, as yet, no profession existed.

The New Deal provided a way out of this dilemma, for the proliferation of New Deal agencies like the WPA and TVA that reached into state and local affairs gave resonance to their view that government and administration were components of a single national fabric and that administration, far from being a mere noun to describe the myriad activities required to implement policy, signified a field of knowledge requiring special training. Experts in the science of administration would form the core of an American higher civil service.[100]

Supporters of the Public Merit Project cited Britain's higher civil service as their lodestar, but they prudently rationalized this preference in language free of terms like "higher" and "class." Rather, they crusaded for a higher civil service under the banner of "administrative management," a term that became familiar in the wake of FDR's appointment in 1936 of the Committee on Administrative Management, headed by Louis Brownlow (a former city manager) and including former BMR head Luther H. Gulick and the University of Chicago's Charles Merriam, who had been instrumental in introducing position classification to Chicago's civil service in 1912 and who had later used his influence to have White appointed head of the USCSC in 1934. The main outgrowth of this committee's report was the Reorganization Act of 1939, which created the Executive Office of the President, a milestone in the long-term shift of reform focus from the legislature to the executive.[101] The same committee saw executive reorganization as an opportunity to piggyback the ideal of a career service on top of the merit system.

Compared with the British, who defended the Administrative Class by bluntly distinguishing between directing and routine work,[102] Americans had to deploy circumlocutions like administrative management and to claim that the routine administration of public affairs had already created such a class in all but name.[103] In 1935 White called for distilling an "administrative corps" from federal civil servants who in his eyes were already engaged in such high-level management that, for all practical purposes, they had become indispensable to policy formation. He envisioned such a corps as mobile shock troops that could be deployed wherever needed, and he contended that such a corps, rigorously selected and replenished, would rival the faculties of leading universities in its prestige. These shock troops would gather information from different bureaus and agencies; coordinate federal, state, and local initiatives; explain the consequences of different policies; and thus indirectly advise political appointees—the department secretaries and assistant secretaries—on policy. These enlarged duties would be smuggled into the federal service under titles like *aide* or *business manager* to avoid the appearance of establishing a distinct class of upper civil servants. The theory of administrative management borrowed terms common in corporate management theory, where the distinction between directing and doing was well established.[104] In government, however, the directors were not the executives of a corporation but elected officials and their appointees; everyone else was a doer. Public administrationists were trying to carve out a directing role for doers. In the long run, their enterprise was doomed.

Postwar

The ideal of a higher civil service as a career service integrated with the merit system nevertheless gained momentum after World War II with a burst of proposals for establishing an elite civil service. These proposals were initially driven by the perceived need to raise the pay of high-level federal civil servants, which had lagged during the war. With support from the so-called first [Herbert] Hoover Commission on government reorganization, Congress passed a new classification act in 1949. This law consolidated most of the occupational services created by the 1923 Classification Act into a new General Schedule (G-S); it also established the "supergrade" positions (GS-16 through GS-18). Although primarily a response to the wartime pay squeeze, the establishment of the supergrades provided a basis for implementing the ideal of an elite corps of mobile civil servants who would hold a commissioned rank rather than a stipulated job. In 1955 the Task Force on Personnel and Civil Service, headed by the ubiquitous Leonard D. White and attached to the so-called second Hoover Commission, called for the establishment of a senior civil service (SCS), whose members were to be selected from the supergrades and be available for transfer to any department.[105]

The proposed SCS quickly became snarled in politics. Facing two decades of Democratic appointees, Dwight D. Eisenhower campaigned in 1952 against the "entrenched" bureaucracy, and in March 1953 he issued a controversial executive order that established a Schedule C hiring authority, outside the merit system, for positions "of a confidential or policy determining character."[106] It did not take much imagination to realize that Eisenhower appointees under Schedule C could gain effective tenure within the civil service under the wing of the proposed SCS, which he supported. The SCS also encountered opposition from the bureaucrats whom it was intended to benefit. Some argued that the thousand or so existing supergrades already constituted a SCS, albeit without commissioned rank; the incumbent supergrades feared the humiliation of being passed over for the SCS or, if selected, being bounced from post to post.[107] Unions of federal workers complained that the SCS proposal was just a front for an attack on the civil service. As the first Republican president in two decades, Eisenhower had a less sinister objective: he backed the proposed SCS to make the federal bureaucracy more responsive to his will.[108]

Nothing came of the proposed SCS, but the controversy it sparked signified a growing reversal of positions on civil-service reform. During the 1930s public administrationists portrayed the idea of a higher civil service as a way to enhance the power of civil servants against revolving-door political appointees; after 1952 the same idea was put forth as a way to make the federal bureaucracy more responsive to the will of elected officials and their appointees. Changes in party control of the executive branch led to renewed calls for a politically responsive bureaucracy. For example, after his election to the presidency in 1968, Richard M. Nixon proposed the establishment of a Federal Executive Service (FES) that would allow up to 25 percent of its members to be political appointees. Under this proposal, career men and political appointees in the FES would work on three-year renewable contracts. If his contract was not renewed, the career civil servant could accept reassignment to a GS-15 position or retirement, fallbacks not open to the FES's political appointees. Much like Eisenhower, Nixon viewed reform of the civil service in the name of merit as a wedge for making it more responsive to his policies.[109]

The FES never made it into law, but attempts to introduce a facsimile of Britain's Administrative Class persisted into the last quarter of the twentieth century. By then, however, events and ideas had dashed the public administrationists' dream of a career higher civil service marked by internal recruitment, nonpartisanship, and rewards for meritorious achievement. At the very time when C. Wright Mills was calling for a truly meritorious federal bureaucracy, the Cold War was spurring the executive branch to bypass the rigidities of the federal bureaucracy by establishing "think factories" like the Rand (for Research and Development) Corporation that could recruit the best talent into the federal service without going through the laborious procedures required by civil-service rules.[110]

At the same time, the administration/politics distinction, the basis for civil-service reform between 1900 and 1950, was collapsing. Led by Herbert A. Simon, future Nobel laureate in economics, political scientists inclined to the behaviorist analysis of politics were concluding that all administration involved decision making about policy. If decision making and not administration was the real stuff of government, it was worth studying in its own right, which is exactly what political scientists were starting to do.[111] Public administration, among the most prestigious subdivisions of political science during the interwar years,[112] had become one of the least prestigious, a kind of intellectual backwater, by the 1960s. Increasingly, government bureaucracies came to be seen as runaway locomotives with agendas that included neither the efficient implementation of policy nor responsiveness to political direction.[113] Party allegiance might sometimes determine the policy orientations of federal bureaucrats, Simon and his colleagues wrote in 1950, but professional allegiances were probably more important in shaping bureaucratic orientations; "agriculture, the labor movement, the personnel movement—these and many others have had their particular ideologies and have indoctrinated their professional groups with these ideologies."[114] For the new realists like Simon, public administration was itself an ideology, distinguished by its normative preference for merit-based career civil services and distrust of political interference with government bureaucracies.

8

MERIT IN CRISIS

During the last five to six decades the ideal of merit has come under withering criticism on the grounds that it is incompatible with other principles of the
Founding: equal rights and popular consent. Critics have argued that because we
cannot choose our parents or our IQs, even the fairest application of merit-based
selection cannot overcome the legacies of birth. Yet Americans had spent the better part of two centuries devising ways to reconcile merit with equal rights and
popular consent. Equal rights meant citizens' equal right to advancement on the
basis of merit. Rather than condemn the Bank of the United States on economic
grounds, for example, Jacksonian Democrats attacked it for violating equal rights
by giving advantages to the few that were not available to the many. In a republic
based on popular consent, it has been important not only that citizens advance
by merit but that they are seen by other citizens as doing so. Lacking quantitative
measures of merit at the Founding, Americans detected its presence by the absence of such opposites as advancement by blood lines, nepotism, legal privilege,
and, as John Adams warned, mere popularity. Where citizens claimed equality,
nevertheless, the basis of distinctions had to become unarguably transparent, an
objective that eventually led Americans to devise number-obsessed systems for
ranking people: Sylvanus Thayer's merit system at West Point, Josiah Quincy's
Scale of Comparative Merit, report cards in public schools, and the employee rating scales of the twentieth century. In the 1920s advocates of scientific personnel
management insisted that corporations publicize their procedures and post their
flow charts for promoting workers from one job to another on the assumption

that passed-over employees would be less likely to complain if they could see how the system operated. At the same time, American economists were embracing marginal-productivity theory and its promise to explain small wage differences on the basis of small differences in productivity.

The need to secure popular consent to the policies of the republic's government has often trimmed the scope of merit. Recall Benedict Arnold's outrage when he was victimized by the Baltimore Resolution's requirement of regional apportionment of major generals. A century later, civil-service reformers wrote a state apportionment system into the Pendleton Act. By then, regional quotas had come to be accepted as necessary safeguards of the republic. Quota systems were in no sense merit systems, but to the extent that they safeguarded a republic based on advancement by merit, they safeguarded merit.

Although quota systems fall into the category of necessary evils, equal rights and popular consent have often conspired to shape the means of identifying and rewarding merit. The American penchant for multiple-factor theories of intelligence provides one illustration of this. There are many more. The antebellum public school reformers, for example, envisioned that the exercise of ability and effort within reach of the average child would secure a reward, promotion to the next grade. Civil-service reformers set examinations based on the "common branches" that everyone was expected to know. Thus, universal free education was thought to create opportunities for citizens unimaginable in nations where the dreaded "office-holding aristocracy" controlled entry into the public service. In the twentieth century, advocates of a higher civil service modeled on those of Britain and France encountered resistance to privileging educational credentials possessed only by the few.

All of this helped to align merit with equal rights and popular consent, values present at the Founding. But none of it obliterated barriers to advancement based on accidents of birth—race, ethnicity, sex, religion, region, and social class—that were woven into the fabric of American society in 1940, significantly defining the boundaries of the communities in which Americans lived and constraining free movement in most spheres of activity, including the higher rungs of the occupational ladder to which the most ambitious and fortunate Americans aspired. A few examples suffice. In 1940 most investment banks in New York City were either White Anglo-Saxon Protestant (e.g., Brown Brothers Harriman) or Jewish (e.g., Lehman Brothers). Harvard Law School did not admit women. Of 1,755 female attorneys in New York City in 1956, only twelve worked in large law firms. Columbia did not promote Ruth Benedict, author of *Patterns of Culture* (1934), to full professor until 1948, the year *after* she had been elected president of the American Anthropological Association. African Americans were nearly invisible in Wall Street law firms. Jews were grossly underrepresented in the professorate during the interwar years, and Republicans were still unwelcome in the southern professorate unless they taught at black colleges.

Indeed, race, ethnicity, and wealth long sorted applicants into tiers of higher education. Segmentation based on accidents of birth characterized the hierarchies within American higher education that were becoming more deeply engraved during the interwar years. For example, the Ivies mainly competed with each other for students, the vast majority of whom came from privileged families. At the apex, Harvard, Yale, and Princeton had long attracted extremely wealthy and well-connected students. In 1939 the median annual income of male graduates of Harvard, Yale, and Princeton over age forty was $8580, compared with $4640 for other Ivy League colleges, $4270 for selective eastern colleges, $3970 for the Big Ten, and $4240 for all colleges.[1] Unless one supposes that Harvard, Yale, and Princeton graduates were twice as smart and/or twice as well educated as even other Ivy graduates, an assumption defying all evidence and reason, one must conclude that the former entered college with exceptional wealth and connections. Fear that Jewish entrants would drive its traditional Knickerbocker clients to other Ivies was Columbia's main spur to its restrictions on Jews.[2] The privileging of wealth did not stop with graduation from an elite college. Elite university professional schools privileged graduates of elite colleges.

Low-prestige universities that provided instruction in law or engineering or business nevertheless offered the same degrees as the elite professional schools. Americans tended to associate "college" or "law school" with economic success, a view reinforced by racial, ethnic, and religious segmentation. For example, urban Catholic universities staked out a sphere for themselves in professional education during the interwar years. Enrollments in Catholic colleges and universities rose nearly fivefold between 1916 and 1940.[3] Catholic colleges could take Catholic families for granted as a source of applicants. Catholic colleges fed Catholic law schools, which in turn fed Catholic law firms.

Colleges had their scholarships, but none provided a free ride and many carried denominational, racial, or geographical restrictions.[4] Shortly after ascending from Harvard's Chemistry Department to its presidency in 1933, James Bryant Conant proposed endowing National Scholarships for the promising graduates of public high schools, especially in the Midwest and Far West, who would not otherwise consider Harvard. By 1940 Conant was describing the program in Jeffersonian terms as a way to advance a "classless society" ruled by merit rather than privilege.[5] Prodded by Henry Chauncey, an assistant dean who, thanks to Conant's sponsorship, became a future president of the Educational Testing Service (ETS), Conant required competitors for National Scholarships (and only them) to take the Scholastic Aptitude Test (SAT, now the Scholastic Assessment Test), which a former army tester had devised in 1926. Admission to Harvard nevertheless continued to favor applicants from wealthy and prominent families. Conant scarcely glimpsed the financial constraints on college attendance.[6] He never intended to exclude the Preppies, Clubbies, and Gentlemen Cs— groups that included many of Harvard's benefactors and the sitting American president—from admission to Harvard.[7] As late as 1941 Harvard admitted over 90 percent of its final applicants.[8]

Only someone with a gift for self-deception could ignore the retreat of these kinds of segmentation since 1940. Within recent memory, the chief of the investment bank of Merrill Lynch was an African American, and the head of Goldman Sachs, a Protestant, grew up on a small farm in Illinois. Among the latter's successors was a Jew who grew up in public housing in New York City, sold hot dogs at Yankee stadium as a boy, and went on to Harvard for college and law school. Indeed, for many long-excluded groups, higher education has been the highway to success. With rare exceptions, in 1900 law offices in New York City were closed to Jews. Barriers to Jews practicing law were much lower by the mid-1950s, a reflection of a 54 percent jump in Jewish enrollment in Ivy League colleges since 1940.[9] Within universities, smart women are no longer confined to nursing, education, and home economics. Women now head several leading universities. They currently earn 57 percent of bachelor degrees and 58 percent of graduate degrees. The idea that talent is becoming more important to the success of corporations than capital has a special attraction to career-oriented women.[10]

Testing and the Rise of Meritocracy

Within the last five to six decades merit has been equated, more than ever before, with measures of intellectual agility and academic achievement. Boosted by the growth of the testing industry, the Cold War, rising college applications, and the ambitions of college administrators to achieve national reputations for their institutions, American higher education became increasingly selective in the late 1950s. McGeorge Bundy, Boston blueblood and National Security Advisor under Presidents Kennedy and Johnson, remembered that during his school days at Groton in the 1930s all save the incorrigibly stupid and lazy could get into any college they wanted.[11] In 1952 Harvard College accepted two of every three applicants; by 1960 it was rejecting more than two of every three. Similarly, Stanford admitted more than three-fourths of its applicants in the early 1950s; by the early 1960s it was rejecting three-fourths.[12] Pressure to gain entrance to elite professional schools also mounted. Representative of the trend, the law school of the University of California, Berkeley, accepted 70 percent of its 352 applicants in 1954 but only 34 percent of 1,988 applicants in 1968.

Standardized tests for intelligence, notably the SAT, significantly affected this heightened selectivity. The SAT had long been popular among public educators because it promised to distinguish superior intellects from those who were merely well educated.[13] In 1944 the number of public-school students taking the SAT exceeded the number from independent schools for the first time. Americans had a history of devising tests for different kinds of intelligence and aptitudes, but with the heightened selectivity of admissions, the SAT became the colleges' selective tool of choice.

Professional schools also came to rely more on standardized tests for admission. Created by the ETS and in use by 1948 at the most prestigious law schools, the Law School Admission Test (LSAT) enabled law schools to close the "revolving door" created by a combination of easy entry followed by mass expulsions for academic deficiencies. One wheel that long had driven the revolving door was the difficulty of comparing transcripts from different colleges. In effect, this was like comparing apples not just with oranges but with pears, cherries, and bushels of honeysuckle. We have seen in Chapter 6 how this situation led Harvard to create its first- and second-list colleges, with the divisive results that attended a move by an elite Protestant university to put the newly arrived in their places. In time, the fuse ignited by a few law schools in the postwar decade set off reforms elsewhere, so that by 1970 selectivity in admissions with few subsequent expulsions became the norm at well-regarded but non-elite law schools.

In sum, brains and academic achievement came into fashion. There was money to be made catering the IQ/SAT banquet. Stanley Kaplan built his SAT tutoring business in the 1950s, to the displeasure of the ETS, which insisted that preparation for aptitude tests was time wasted. Books with titles like *College Begins at Two* (Isabelle P. Buckley, 1965) and *How to Raise a Brighter Child* (Joan Beck, 1967) brought wealth and fame to what Benjamin DeMott labeled "the Supergrow brainfood crowd."[14]

During the late 1960s and 1970s, however, a perfect storm blew up over *meritocracy,* a word coined by British sociologist Michael Young in his dystopian fantasy *The Rise of the Meritocracy* (1957), which described a society run by people born into neither wealth nor privilege but favored by high measured intelligence. Although the word caught on in America, the values that Young satirized were far more deeply embedded in British history. These are approvingly described by a graduate student named Michael Young, whose dissertation in progress starts with the reforms of the British civil service in 1870 and eventually breaks off in 2034 when the reader learns that a revolt against the meritocracy by "Populists" (lower-class workers allied with upper-class wives who have been radicalized by their consignment to their homes to nurture their high-IQ children) has broken out and that Young has been killed in riots, appropriately at Peterloo, before he could correct his manuscript.[15]

The real Michael Young's varied career had immersed him in Labour Party issues, and he knew by heart the story of British plans to use examinations to identify the talented children of the working class for free places in grammar schools, the type of schools that educated children for prestigious white-collar work and for universities. England's Education Act of 1944 terminated fees for public secondary education and instituted comprehensive high schools, but within a tripartite framework (grammar, technical, and comprehensive schools) with outcomes determined by educational streaming and examinations. Young favored making American-style comprehensive schools the dominant component of English education, but he believed that the Labour Party, despite its nominal commitment to comprehensive schools, would not jettison merit for equality because of its commitment to substituting merit for privilege and its adherence to the British belief in the intrinsic superiority of one person to another.

The society described, without humor or irony, by the fictional Michael Young in 2033–34, reached disturbing heights of nastiness: wealthy parents with dull children paid premiums to adopt working-class children with high IQs; children with high IQs nagged their parents to be retested so as no longer to embarrass them; corporate higher-ups who traditionally had treated their smarter subordinates with respect demanded outsized bonuses now that they were the smartest people in the room. The United States seemingly lacked all the elements of Young's story: no publicly recognized history of nepotism or inherited status as a problem; no Eleven Plus examinations; no English-style "grammar stream"; and an unflappable confidence that as long as opportunities for betterment remained open, no real conflict could arise between merit and equality. In the late 1950s and early 1960s Americans like John Gardner witnessed what were at best weak and reversible steps toward American meritocracy. In *Excellence* (1961) Gardner— president of the Carnegie Corporation of New York, future secretary of Health, Education, and Welfare (under Lyndon Johnson), and founder of Common Cause—conceded that Americans were paying more attention to intelligence. For example, gifted children, who had been exiled to the wilderness after 1930 "by an almost savage rejection of any measures" designed for them, had once again become a favorite subject of psychologists and educators.[16] Mental ability, Gardner recognized, was coming into fashion, but he saw its path strewn with booby traps: the legacy of Progressive educators like Marietta Johnson, a favorite of John Dewey, who proclaimed in 1929 that "any school in which one child may fail while another succeeds is unjust, undemocratic, and uneducational";

the practice of automatic promotions in school regardless of a child's performance; and the American lack of candor about individual differences in ability. Gardner compared the typical response of a teacher in England to a child who fumbled a question—sit down because "you are not up to this"—with the typical American response—"you need to study harder."[17]

Gardner had read *The Rise of the Meritocracy*, but the "ocracy" in meritocracy implied rule, or at least domination. Gardner was sure that the intellectually excellent neither ruled nor dominated America. They scarcely knew who they were. In Gardner's eyes, the real problem in the United States arose from popular indifference to gradations of intelligence and academic achievement. Ordinary Americans complacently assumed that effort counted more than brains in getting ahead, that schooling contributed to success by inculcating pleasing personality traits, and that education's main value lay in transmitting skills useful for self-advancement, a process of transmission that any educational institution could accomplish about as well as any other. In America, equality became the basis of academic mediocrity.[18] Indeed, since the late nineteenth century several writers had tried to persuade Americans that academic achievement really counted in getting ahead, but it was a difficult sell. Various studies of business elites, while establishing that the usual suspects (Harvard, Yale, Princeton, Columbia, MIT) contributed a disproportionate number of corporate higher-ups among those who had attended college, also documented that a high proportion of business leaders, up to half in some studies, had never attended college.[19]

Gardner also saw no American equivalent to Young's Populists on the horizon. America would remain the land of the second chance, because more academic sorting occurred at ages 18–20 (late bloomers were a familiar sight in colleges) than at 15.[20]

He expected that the American tradition of self-culture would salve the psychological wounds wrought by meritocracy; those less favored in the IQ lottery would have opportunities to pursue excellence in fields (art, music) that did not require high IQ. Finally, unlike Britain, the United States had no ruling class or even a power elite. It resembled, in the words of Vienna-born sociologist Suzanne Keller, a pack of cards, with an ace in each suit.[21]

Meritocracy and Modernization

America would continue on its meritocratic path, Gardner thought, because of the requirements of modernization rather than because the meritocrats were well organized or influential.[22] To American social analysts of the 1950s and early 1960s, nothing seemed more inevitable than society's increasing reliance on experts with specialized knowledge. Gardner's America might indulge in nostalgia for Main Street, but as early as 1920 Sinclair Lewis had placed the Ford car at the center of Gopher Prairie. The United States, the home of mass society and mass culture, was not the land of John Ruskin, William Morris, or Aldous Huxley, nor was it the home of Michael Young, who for decades had warned that modernization threatened England's social fabric.[23] The one accepted test of the American social system was how much mobility it provided, not how well it guarded local traditions.

Gardner identified a benign meritocracy in the making. Guided by the seeming imperatives of modern society, the American meritocracy targeted entrenched privilege far less than the mediocratizing tendencies of the adolescent peer culture.[24] These were the targets of three notable meritocratic initiatives of the 1950s: Early Admission, Advanced Placement (AP), and the National Merit Scholarship Corporation (NMSC). The original purpose of Early Admission was to allow exceptional male students to defer military induction until they had completed two years of college. AP's goal was to encourage the acceleration of gifted high-schoolers into college. Both initiatives aimed at liberating smart young people from the militant anti-intellectualism of the postwar Life Adjustment movement, which urged that public high schools adopt adjustment-to-marriage courses, driver's education, and more vocational courses as ways to ease the passage of teenagers to adulthood rather than to higher education.

Established in 1955 to arouse public respect for intellectual talent, the NMSC sought to expand college enrollments by intensifying the motivation of young people to attend college.[25] The structure of competition for National Merit Scholarships, with several rounds and the liberal award of "letters of recognition," was explicitly designed to popularize academic achievement among high-school students, who were assumed to be averse to it in the absence of special prodding. John M. Stalnaker, who headed the NMSC, turned competition for the scholarships into a planned "scholarama."[26]

The foregoing initiatives arose in the context of the manpower-planning movement, which gained momentum during the Cold War and which was permeated by the view that modernization necessarily intensified society's need for smart people. Manpower planners churned out studies of the likely demand for scientific and technical manpower,[27] but most planners quickly recognized that fluctuations in the economy occurred too quickly and unpredictably to warrant the federal government's assumption of responsibility for aligning educational and training programs with expected demand. Most concluded that the safest course was to ensure "a continuous stream of college trained people."[28]

Calls for widening the stream of college-educated manpower fit snugly into the agenda of a circle of educational planners, a rough equivalent of the New Deal's

Brain Trust but with less glittering academic credentials. These planners started in the 1930s to call for federal policies to encourage more young people to attend college as a way to reduce unemployment. After World War II they broadened their agenda to embrace the permanent expansion of college enrollments in the name of democracy, an objective to be pursued primarily by expanding public junior colleges (in contrast to four-year colleges, junior colleges maintained robust enrollments during the Depression). George F. Zook, who made the cover of *Time* magazine in 1933 as U.S. Commissioner of Education and who headed the American Council on Education (ACE) from 1934 to 1950, typified the marriage between educational planning and democratizing higher education. For Zook, who had worked his way through the University of Kansas driving a hearse, mass higher education meant vocational education, preferably carried on in junior colleges. In 1947 a commission appointed by President Harry S Truman and chaired by Zook issued an influential report, *Higher Education for American Democracy*, which proposed to raise average educational attainment to fourteen years (i.e., through the first two years of college) and assigned the main burden of democratizing higher education to junior colleges, which it renamed "community colleges."[29]

Although upon enrollment most students in junior colleges expressed an intention to transfer to four-year colleges, a majority did not. Zook and his allies had called for junior colleges to jettison their transfer function and to adopt the rather inelegantly named "terminal function." Zook also hoped that four-year colleges would start to offer two-year terminal (vocational) programs. After 1970, critics with New Left sympathies flayed community colleges and especially their "terminal function" for diverting the dreams of their many students who enrolled intending to transfer to four-year colleges only to find that they had been dumped in marginal institutions, the Uriah Heeps of higher education, to prepare for low-prestige occupations.[30] But in Zook's day the debate centered on whether, as the Truman report assumed, the economy could absorb a better-educated work force. In 1949 Harvard economist Seymour Harris attacked this assumption. When Harris spoke of demand, he meant current job vacancies, with wages signifying the intensity of demand. Citing evidence that labor contracts were awarding bricklayers $27 a day while teachers in several states averaged $27 a week, he detected no evidence of rising demand for brainworkers.[31] Harris's pessimism echoed the view, widely held during the 1930s, that the American economy was stuck on a permanent plateau and would never attain the robust growth that marked the half-century before 1930. That the colleges produced more graduates than the economy could absorb into jobs suited to their expectations became an integral component of this "mature economy" thesis.

Yet Harris the neo-classical economist and Zook the manpower planner were talking past each other. In tune with the manpower movement, Zook envisioned a future of bottomless demand for educated manpower. So did Eli Ginzberg, a self-described "skeptical economist" who questioned the neo-classical assumption that price signals would maintain equilibrium between supply and demand.[32] By midcentury Ginzberg's view that specialists would inevitably create the need for more specialists was resonating more widely than Harris's pessimism about demand for educated manpower. As late as 1940, federal policies to encourage college enrollments were advanced mainly as ways to keep young people off the unemployment rolls and attracted no more than mild interest. The Selective Service Act of 1940 did not offer draft deferments to collegians as such, and during World War II draft boards were notoriously impervious to requests for the exemption of scientists, even those working on the Manhattan Project.[33] But during the war, psychologists mounted evidence that soldiers with higher educational attainment were better soldiers who were more likely to complete training programs and less likely to go AWOL.[34] With the backing of Vannevar Bush, a science administrator who in 1945 famously described science as "the endless frontier," after World War II Zook lobbied for draft deferments for collegians, an objective achieved in 1951. The Selective Service System effectively became the nation's principal manpower planning agency.[35]

The Cold War ensured that the ripple effect of the manpower movement would be huge. As a by-product of the movement, sundry foundations and commissions launched investigations during the 1950s into the institutional, developmental, and familial correlatives of superior ability, especially scientific ability, all in the hope of maximizing the supply and utilization of ability. A conception of intelligence as a fan-like distribution of many factors rather than a pyramid topped by Charles Spearman's g guided this quest for "educated manpower." The manpower movement did much to popularize the need not just for educated manpower but for a lot of it. This need became a rallying cry for virtually anyone who wanted to expand any kind of education. Calls for the discovery of talent quickly overflowed the banks of IQ to soak up all sorts of special aptitudes and abilities.

The manpower movement left a significant imprint on the closest American approximation to Young's *Rise of the Meritocracy*, Daniel Bell's *Coming of Post-industrial Society: A Venture in Social Forecasting* (1973). Bell had coined *post-industrial society* in 1962 when he was engaged in the academic cottage industry of planning for the twenty-first century. Bell proclaimed that the "post-industrial society, in its initial logic, is a meritocracy. Differential status and differential income are based on technical skills and higher education."[36] Bell did not think that the United States had become a meritocracy, nor did he quite say that it would become one. Rather, meritocracy was an "ideal type," like Max Weber's conception of bureaucracy, an analyst's construct of a coherent pattern among diverse changes. Bell nevertheless identified meritocratic tendencies in his own society, not only in the spread of universities but also in the form of changes in the social structure, specifically the great increase in Americans engaged in the professions, science, technology, and the creation of knowledge. These changes signified rising demand for certain types of people, and although he foresaw some speed bumps, he expected the future to accentuate present patterns.

In Bell's hands, meritocracy sounded egalitarian and participatory. Pointing to the nonprofit "systems research and development" corporations that had sprung up in the postwar decade, he described the nearly unimaginable complexity of the knowledge society: corporations like Rand, the Lincoln Laboratory of MIT, MITRE (MIT Research and Engineering), and the Systems Development Corporation (spun off from Rand), sometimes housed in universities or run by consortia of universities but with intricate ties to the Department of Defense, the Atomic Energy Commission, the National Aeronautics and Space Administration, the National Science Foundation, the National Institutes of Health, and other government departments and agencies, not only employing but also training squadrons of educated people to manage and program computers relevant to air defense, the organization of health services, and more. As Bell observed, the structure of the knowledge industry, especially its R&D component, was overturning the received wisdom, "as drawn from Max Weber and accepted by most students of stratification," that the model of organization most suited to modern conditions was a pyramidal bureaucracy marked by functional specialization and by a hierarchy based on recruitment, selection, and promotion according to impersonal technical criteria.[37]

The Reserve of Ability

Abraham Flexner once observed that Americans did not like "sieves" in the form of selection procedures focused on eliminating the unworthy.[38] Rather, like Conant, who merely sought to sprinkle Harvard's run-of-the-mill applicants with some future natural aristocrats, they preferred to select "in" rather than "out." The American approach to an issue that aroused the interest of educators on both sides of the Atlantic after World War II illustrates the same propensity. American and European educators justified striking increases in enrollments in higher education after 1945 and especially after 1960 on the grounds that the traditional methods of identifying individuals capable of absorbing higher education severely underestimated the pool of talent, or "reserve of ability."[39] Superficially, the American and European projects were similar; substantively, they differed.

Discussions of untapped talent in Europe arose in connection with moves to widen educational opportunity by modifying the dual structure of European schooling, which had developed with compulsory education during the nineteenth century. Schools known as elementary (or "primary") provided basic education for working-class children through the compulsory years. Secondary schools, such as the English grammar school, the French *lycée*, and the German *Gymnasium*, perpetuated centuries-old traditions of classical education and provided a qualitatively superior education for pupils from childhood through adolescence. There were national differences across Europe,[40] but none fundamentally changed the duality of nineteenth-century European education. All of this contrasted with the United States, where public secondary education developed as a successive stage of elementary education.

European reforms during the first half of the twentieth century sought to open access for talented working-class children to the sort of academic education that led to higher education and the prestigious professions. Historian Fritz Ringer has identified this approach as the "progressive" measure of merit. In a perfectly progressive system, as Ringer defines it, the children of workers would attend university in the same proportion that their parents' occupations formed a percentage of the total work force.[41] As long as universities practice selection by merit, this never happens. But European educators, geneticists, and social scientists increasingly doubted that the lopsided class distribution of university students (50–80 percent from professional and upper managerial families versus 1–2 percent from farm families) reflected the distribution of intelligence. During World War II, intelligence tests were often conducted on conscripts, long after the differentiation effected by the class-based school system had occurred, and it seemed likely that the lower IQs of working-class youth merely reflected their early termination of schooling. The idea that schooling could increase IQ won converts to the proposition that an expansion of education could occur without compromising standards of excellence. World War II boosted the progressive measure, especially on the Continent. Educators recognized that their nations, devastated by the war, had witnessed the desertions of their working classes to parties of the far right and left during the interwar years. Restoring social harmony now seemed to require policies to realize the progressive measure.

In contrast to Europeans, who equated the reserve of ability with a pool of untapped intellectual talent, buried by the class system, which could be directed into the academic stream of secondary education and then to universities, Americans thought of it as a pool of high-school graduates who had just enough cognitive ability to graduate from *some* institution of higher education, including a junior college, but who chose not to apply. This was a plausible approach in the American context, and several studies documented the existence of just such a pool.[42]

It was idle to speculate about the suppressive effect on IQ of an overtly dual school system because the United States did not have one; further, a cadre of educators, including George F. Zook, had long argued that reducing the expense of college by constructing more nonresidential and vocationally oriented junior colleges and streetcar universities would spur enrollments. Finally, higher education conjured up far less unified and coherent images in the United States than in Europe—Conant wrote that to a European the diversity of colleges and universities in the United States "must seem a chaotic nightmare"—yet many Americans reverenced higher education in any form as a passport to success for their children.[43] In sum, educational planners wanted to keep the students coming, regardless of where they were going, and they were much less inclined than their European counterparts to accept social class as a determinant of educational outcomes.

All of these assumptions and values permeated the Truman Commission's report. Although several adherents of the multiple-factor theory of intelligence served on the commission, it rested its case for expanding college enrollments on an IQ-type test, specifically the Army General Classification Test (AGCT), which had been administered to ten million inductees during World War II. Since the AGCT data included the highest year of schooling attained by each test taker at induction, it became possible to determine the lowest AGCT test score typical of those who had completed a given grade of schooling. On this basis the commission concluded that 49 percent of the American population had the ability to complete fourteen years of schooling and 32 percent to complete college. Accordingly, the commission proposed a program of federal scholarships to increase enrollments in higher education, which had stood at 1.5 million in 1940, to at least 4.6 million in 1960.[44]

The Effects of Class

Many of the educational initiatives of the 1950s were vulnerable to the indictment that they were smokescreens to disguise class-based interests. Advocates of manpower planning and the emerging postindustrial society subordinated the influence of class to that of modernization; modernization theory made meritocracy sound foreordained. Attaching little weight to class as a determinant of educational outcomes, the Truman Commission's report implied that, with a dollop of grease on its tracks, higher education could accelerate social mobility. Yet a brigade of postwar social analysts saw the opposite: American society resembled a tar pit in which prospects for raising educational attainment and speeding upward mobility were negligible. By no means was this outlook the property of the left during the 1950s. Its leading advocate derided Marxism and in a conservative decade reached a wide audience. The self-described "social anthropologist" W. Lloyd Warner became famous in the 1940s and 1950s for calibrating the fine gradations—upper uppers, lower uppers, upper middles, lower middles, upper lowers, lower lowers—that marked the pecking orders in "Yankee City" (Newburyport, Massachusetts), and he found comparable levels of stratification in places like "Hometown" and "Jonesville." Warner's community studies familiarized the reading public, really for the first time,[45] with the finally calibrated language of class.

Warner equated class with "social class," a concept similar to "socio-economic status" that conflated a person's social position based on measures of income, wealth, and occupation with how he was assessed by others on the basis of his education, ethnicity, religion, clubs, and source of income (salary, wages, inheritance). He argued that millions of Americans were gripped by a sort of false consciousness. They might think of themselves as having risen in status because they owned cars, houses, and televisions. Studies of blue-collar workers in the early 1950s documented the American disposition to associate class and status with material possessions.[46] But Warner alleged that he knew better; he told them that their status superiors saw the knives sticking out of their backs. He even devised an "Index of Status Characteristics" to "permit men and women better to evaluate their social situations and thereby adapt themselves to social reality and fit their dreams to what is possible."[47] Social class, despite its reflection of the subjective impressions of others and regardless of whether the person assessed was aware of it, left an indelible mark on its victims. Such was its weight that "the lives of many are destroyed because they do not understand the workings of social class."[48]

The charge that American social thought in the 1950s underestimated the significance of class as a tool of analysis obviously does not fit Warner. After he moved from Harvard to the University of Chicago in 1935, Warner's new colleagues included Robert J. Havighurst and Allison Davis, the latter a coauthor of the Warner-directed study of the South's caste system *Deep South* (1941). In 1945 Havighurst and Davis collaborated on a pioneering study of how children of different social classes performed on different test items. This research helped to persuade mainstream sociologists that the correlation between IQ and social class was better explained by cultural deprivation than by genetic determinism.[49] Indeed, in Warner's view, social class fundamentally determined the experiences of schoolchildren. Middle-class teachers expected little from lower-class children, even the ones who showed academic ability. If they found low-status children taking Latin, they failed them and chased them back onto the vocational track, and if they discovered high-status children on the vocational track, they quickly elevated them to the college-preparatory track. Warner, who wrote in 1944 that "the educational system may be thought of as an enormous complicated machine for sorting and ticketing and routing children through life," foreshadowed the New Left's indictment of schooling as an agent of "social sorting" and "social reproduction."[50]

Although Warner saw himself as stripping the veil from society to reveal the oppressive effects of its inner machinery, his analysis of social class had deeply conservative implications. On one hand, Warner and his coauthors cited Jefferson's ideal of a natural aristocracy of talent as their inspiration. Because "our status system" maintained people of inferior ability and training in responsible jobs, our task was to find "people of talent" and encourage them "to rise from lower social levels" by increasing the number of scholarships for poor children to attend college. Abundant evidence indicated that only a small fraction of students with IQs over 110 from families of low socio-economic status attended college, but Warner maintained that only a tiny fraction of students from poor families, 2–3 percent, could escape the tentacles of class sufficiently to benefit from scholarships to four-year colleges. Warner's reasoning speaks volumes about postwar social analysis. The objective of the scholarship program was to "increase the amount of social mobility without increasing it too much." Without a certain amount of social mobility, Americans would no longer "stick together" and "play the game." On the other hand, "too much social rise and fall would produce a chaotic society in which few would care to cooperate socially with others because the rewards would be so fleeting."[51] In his best-seller *The Organization Man* (1956) William H. Whyte credited Warner with establishing among educators "one of the principal ideological bases" for their belief that "rather than tantalize themselves with aspirations," most students "should adjust to the fact of a fairly fixed social system."[52]

Warner's conservatism pulsated through mainstream social analysis during the 1940s and 1950s. One tenet of his conservatism, shared by many other social analysts, stemmed from his understanding of how statuses came into existence. His studies of Australian aborigines in the 1920s had persuaded him that even primitive societies had status-based hierarchies (the organizers of hunting expeditions outranked spear carriers) and that statuses were neither deliberately created nor assigned by the will of the powerful. Rather, they arose from a largely subconscious social consensus. As the product of a social consensus, statuses became "bonding" beliefs, views that gave coherence to society. Bonding beliefs might be mythical, but they were nevertheless indispensable to social cohesion. Puncturing them would destroy communal "solidarity," roil social relationships, and create the disorientation that Emile Durkheim, the pioneering French sociologist to whom Warner dedicated *Democracy in Jonesville* (1949), labeled *anomie*.

Durkheim also influenced Talcott Parsons, a young Harvard faculty member who in the late 1930s conducted an informal seminar whose members included Kingsley Davis and Wilbert Moore, two sociologists who would collaborate in 1945 on a widely cited essay, "Some Principles of Stratification." Davis and Moore argued that social inequality, far from resulting from the purposive exercise of power by the privileged, was "an unconsciously evolved device by which societies ensure that the most important positions are conscientiously filled by the most qualified persons." Rather than overt conflict, an inarticulate consensus about which positions were important, the rules governing access to them, and the rewards necessary to attract the best people forged the essentially painless inequality of all societies.[53] In sum, stratification functions to keep society running smoothly. Neither the rich nor powerful create class distinctions. Like Daniel Bell's postindustrial society, social stratification arises from faceless forces, independently of anyone's intention.

Yet by the mid-1950s, Warner, who had spent his early career debunking the idea that fluidity marked American society, was reversing his course. His community studies had documented the presence of motionless hierarchies in the towns and cities he selected. His local informants told him that their communities had once been open to achievement by those of humble origins but that the channels of upward mobility had become clogged.[54] Evidence that "blocked" mobility was becoming the norm forced Warner to confront a problem. For America's stratified society to remain stable, some mobility would have to take place. Stability ultimately rested on a consensus about values, and American values included the dream of success, the expectation that superior ability would be rewarded with greater wealth. Americans awarded higher status to one who had risen a great social distance to an office than to one of equal ability who inherited the office.[55] This dream of success was just the sort of bonding belief necessary for social cohesion.

To reconcile his view of American society as stable with his recognition that the unrealistic success myth sowed instability, Warner turned to the study of social mobility. His starting point was to dismiss the relevance of his own studies of Yankee City by acknowledging that research for them had been conducted during the Depression, when opportunities were scarce, and that his research design had failed to count the most mobile Americans, those who left their communities as young men. To share new insight into postwar trends, Warner and James C. Abegglen published two books in 1955: *Occupational Mobility in American Business and Industry*, aimed at an academic audience, and *Big Business Leaders in America*, designed for a popular audience.[56] Warner and Abegglen analyzed over 8,300 responses to a questionnaire they sent to more than fifteen thousand business leaders drawn from the 1952 edition of *Poor's Register of Directors* and then compared their results with those of Frank Taussig's business elite (described in

Chapter 5), which had been drawn from the 1928 edition of the same volume. Gripped by a Cyclops-like focus on heredity, Taussig had sought to prove that the American occupational hierarchy provided a snapshot of the distribution of merit. If sons of carpenters occupied lower rungs on the ladder of occupations than sons of big businessmen, big businessmen obviously were smarter than carpenters. Two decades later the grip of hereditarianism on American social science was much weaker. Talcott Parsons spoke for many social scientists when he wrote in 1937 that the nature/nurture controversy was irrelevant to his own work.[57] No longer could social analysts assume that social hierarchies provided a window onto the distribution of ability. Rather, they investigated whether elites were being invigorated by fresh blood from below.

Neither Warner nor other investigators of business elites could find much evidence of circulation. For example, Warner and Abegglen's data demonstrated that the 1952 business elite was as likely as Taussig's 1928 elite to be recruited from the sons of business leaders. Indeed, members of the 1952 elite cohort who were sons of large business owners were even more likely than their counterparts in the 1928 elite (60 percent versus 41 percent) to work in the same firm as their fathers. Other investigators of business elites found much the same. "No merit system can be expected to work perfectly," Mabel Newcomer averred, but inasmuch as "wealth and social status are all but indispensable conditions of success, the group from which top talent is chosen is restricted indeed."[58]

Investigators nevertheless wrestled an upbeat conclusion from their unpromising evidence by identifying a historical, self-enacting trend toward advancement by merit that was rooted in the "rationalization" and "professionalization" of business. Pouncing on the datum that the proportion of business leaders who were sons of major executives or large owners decreased in large firms between 1928 and 1952, Warner and Abegglen concluded that because large firms increasingly recruited their executives from training programs rather than kinship connections, the future seemed to "augur well for continued openness in the American business system."[59] Similarly, Newcomer construed a modest rise in the proportion of the fathers of business leaders in 1950 who were sons of laborers over their counterparts in 1900 and 1925 (5.4 percent versus 2.9 and 3.1 percent, respectively) as evidence that family influence was giving way to individual achievement. She set this conclusion within a larger framework of the professionalization of business, an inexorable trend that, starting with the severance of ownership from control, pointed toward a future of respect for rules and greater reliance on educational credentials in corporate America. "A college degree," she concluded, "has become more important than great wealth and easier to obtain."[60]

The studies published in the 1950s by Warner, Newcomer, and others illustrate how even the most data-obsessed investigators wore ideological blinkers.

Taussig's hereditarianism had gone out of fashion, but Warner and the others saw everything from a new, and equally dogmatic, perspective. As Seymour M. Lipset and Reinhard Bendix observed in 1959, investigators of social mobility sought evidence "to reinforce the social base of American ideological egalitarianism."[61] In the United States the social base of egalitarianism meant the American Dream, the prospects for climbing the ladder. As Conant, who had become a self-described Cold Warrior by 1947, urged, the nation had to put its philosophical house in order and identify the values that distinguished it from the Soviet Union. In the context of the Cold War, even those who questioned the Dream like Warner found ways to project it into the future.

The idea of an inexorable march toward corporate rationalization and professionalization reminds one of Bell's divination of a coming postindustrial society. In each case, the future promised greater reliance on advancement by impersonal criteria, including educational attainment and specialized knowledge. To suggest a long-distance connection, one is also reminded of a circle of reasoning evident in the early days of the republic: republican ideals are more conducive than monarchal ideals to advancement by merit; America is a republic; hence it will favor advancement by merit as long as it adheres to its republican principles.

Of course, there was a difference between the discourse about merit in the early republic and that of the 1950s: that of the early republic featured a thesaurus of maintenance; that of the 1950s invoked the language of forecasting. Forecasting always runs the danger of disappointing midwives of the future. Some prominent social commentators of the 1950s saw no evidence of a meritocratic and public-spirited corporate elite. In *The Organization Man* William H. Whyte portrayed corporate executives as intellectual lightweights who selected trainees on the basis of personality tests designed mainly to eliminate nonconformity. In an appendix Whyte told trainees how to cheat on these tests by interring any hint of intellectual curiosity: be sure to say that you would rather go bowling with the guys than read a book.[62] In *The Power Elite* (1956) C. Wright Mills maintained that climbing the ladder in business did not evidence merit because corporate higher-ups got ahead by getting along. They took their cues from Dale Carnegie (*How To Win Friends and Influence People*, 1936) rather than Andrew Carnegie.[63]

Merit as Ideology

In late nineteenth-century Britain the invocation of merit became an ideology—a value that triggered political action—for those, mainly on the political left, who advocated replacing privilege with merit, especially the sort of scholastic ability that sparkled on examinations. Labour Party intellectuals took up the cause of

merit-based selection for free places in grammar schools. Michael Young recognized that although it was enacted by a coalition government headed by a
Conservative, England's Education Act of 1944, which continued the Eleven Plus
examination to sort students into grammar, technical, or comprehensive schools,
was at heart a Labour Party measure.

For a long time, America remained an ocean apart from this discourse. Although merit was an ideal of the Founding of the republic, Americans found it
much more difficult than the British to see intellectual cultivation as a component of political leadership, or academic brilliance as a passport to offices of preferment. Formidable barriers to equal educational opportunity existed but did
not arouse controversy comparable to Britain's. For example, the different tiers of
higher education during the 1930s resembled ships passing in the night. Pressure
for systemic change was negligible. Nearly all reformers of higher education during the interwar years roosted within the tier they tried to reform. For example,
Frank Aydelotte, a former Rhodes Scholar and president of Swarthmore College
from 1921 to 1940, introduced an honors program modeled on the Oxbridge
tutorial system and adopted by a small number of elite institutions. The most
publicized pressure for change came from educators who demanded wider access
at the bottom of the system, the public junior colleges and "post-secondary" education, but the change sought was mainly to standardize the product, so that, for
example, public junior colleges became more similar to each other. In the South,
segregation kept white and black colleges in separate spheres, but it did not exclude efforts to upgrade black colleges within the framework of white supremacy.

The remarkable rise in high-school enrollments between 1890 and 1930 contributed to this essentially voluntary and painless process of differentiation by
creating an enormous pool of potential collegians. By 1940 the proportion of
18–21-year-olds enrolled in American colleges (14.6 percent) vastly exceeded
that in Britain, Germany, and France (respectively, 3.6, 3.9, and 2.6 percent). Inasmuch as neither the federal nor state governments assigned students to colleges,
it was up to the colleges to identify and tap their applicant pools. To secure a reliable flow of applicants, colleges spent a lot of time identifying their clienteles and
"missions" but without aiming to elevate their place in the hierarchy of higher
education.

The event that pushed the American discourse about merit toward issues that
had been higher on the European than American agenda was the publication
of James S. Coleman's *Equality of Educational Opportunity Study* (the Coleman
Report, 1966). The Coleman Report was occasioned by an obscure provision
in the Civil Rights Act of 1964 that mandated a study "concerning the lack of
availability of equal educational opportunities for individuals by reason of race,
color, religion, or national origin." To his surprise (in fact, utter shock), Coleman,

who surveyed four thousand schools and nearly 600,000 students, found little difference between white and black schools when it came to physical plant, curricula, and teacher characteristics. Yet a significant gap between white and black achievement scores, present in the first grade, notably widened by the twelfth grade. Coleman's data indicated that differences in expenditures on schools had relatively little effect on outcomes as measured by academic achievement. The one school characteristic that did show a relationship to scores on achievement tests was the presence of children from affluent families. In sum, schooling appeared to be overrated as an anti-poverty tool.[64]

The Coleman Report triggered what Daniel Bell called "the most extensive discussion of social policy in the history of American sociological debate."[65] Once Coleman had pried off the lid, a geyser of policy alternatives spewed in the late 1960s and 1970s. Concerned about the negligible number of African American students in their student bodies and prodded by student protest, colleges took several tacks to accommodate the demands of African American students, including combining aggressive recruitment policies with remedial and enrichment education. This approach faltered in the 1970s as it became clear that remedial and enrichment programs had failed to reduce the achievement gap (as measured by test scores and grade point averages) between white and black students. For a brief period, most notably at the City University of New York, that historical Mecca of meritocracy, administrators gave Open Admissions a try. But this tack was extremely controversial at a time when more colleges and universities than ever before were striving for "excellence." Open Admissions also angered white ethnics, who feared that it would depreciate their own college degrees.

By the end of the 1970s advocates of race-conscious admissions were turning to increasing minority representation by a less rigorous application to prospective African American students of the established instruments of academic selection: high-school grade point averages and SAT scores.[66] This approach brought what critics denounced as "reverse discrimination" and "racial quotas." Affirmative action in the form of racial preference in favor of blacks flew in the face of New Frontier liberalism's insistence on color-blind justice, aroused negligible support from civil-rights organizations, and has consistently received negative reviews in public opinion polls. Yet its scope steadily widened in both workplaces and colleges in the late 1960s and 1970s. Urban and campus riots created a sense of urgency to increase black representation in workplaces and student bodies. Officials charged with implementing the Civil Rights Act of 1964 spoke the language of color-blindness while adopting policies to produce color-conscious results. In so doing, they were aided by Section 2000-e of Title VII of the act. This section stated that while it was not unlawful for an employer to administer a "professionally developed ability test" to employees as long as it was not designed, intended, or used to discriminate, a test that produced an "adverse impact" (later called "disparate impact") on protected groups, regardless of its intent, would be unlawful unless the employer could demonstrate the test's consistency with "business necessity."

These were striking changes. Sociologist John David Skrentny has described overt racial preference as a third rail of American politics that threatened death to anyone who touched it. Yet the shift from color-blind to color-conscious policies occurred swiftly, aroused little debate (as Daniel Bell observed), and was largely completed by 1971, when in its landmark *Griggs v. Duke Power*[67] decision the Supreme Court unanimously ruled that a North Carolina company violated Title VII when it instituted an IQ test and a requirement for a high-school diploma for intra-plant job transfers (Duke traditionally confined black workers to custodial jobs). Accepting that Title VII aimed at equal employment opportunity, the Court decided that the plaintiff did not have to show discriminatory intent; it was enough that requirements had a disparate impact on black workers.

As *Griggs* indicated, racial preference was initially applied to workplaces, where advocates saw it as a remedy for generations of policies that overtly and covertly excluded blacks. Probably the best-known workplace application of racial preference, the Philadelphia Plan's call for explicit racial hiring goals in the late 1960s, occurred in the skilled building trades, traditionally dominated by white father-and-son unions. In workplaces racial preference conflicted with color-blind justice but usually not with merit, because validated tests that could pass legal scrutiny did not exist for most jobs. As several petitions and briefs filed in *Griggs* pointed out, the questions on the IQ-type test deployed by Duke Power were ludicrously inappropriate for industrial jobs.

In sum, the first round of conflict over affirmative action ended without an engagement of the issue—racial preference versus merit—that would eventually preoccupy the courts. Despite this, there were legacies that would influence later debate over affirmative action: an emerging consensus that racial preferences were at times necessary to offset discriminatory practices (to the surprise of many liberals, Richard M. Nixon initially supported the Philadelphia Plan); a willingness to use percentages of minority hires as a measure of progress, regardless of whether they were called quotas or goals; and the so-called 80 Percent Rule, used to define a "substantially different rate of selection in hiring, promotion, or other employment decisions which work to the disadvantage of members of a race, sex, or ethnic group." Although formulated in 1971 as a measure of hiring and promotion practices that did not depend on examinations, this rule would later be used to establish that a competitive examination for a job that resulted in a selection rate of less than 80 percent of a protected group violated Title VII.

The foregoing supports Skrentny's view that affirmative action was implemented, mainly as a form of crisis management, before it was debated. Racial preference and merit eventually came into conflict in higher education, but critics who denounced affirmative action for violating the principle of basing admission to college on merit faced an obvious problem. Admission to college had never been based solely on academic or intellectual criteria. Even at super-selective Harvard in the 1970s, alumni children, or "legacies," were five times more likely to gain admission than nonlegacies. A German analyst of American higher education wrote in 1978 that "probably in no other highly industrialized country are the privileged so blatantly favored in admission to higher education as in the U.S."[68] And not just those privileged by wealth. Admissions committees have long construed athletic skill, musical talent, religious denomination, and place of residence as legitimate criteria by which to assess applicants. Reflecting the American view that a college education is as important for the social as for the intellectual skills it imparts, committees' desire for a "well-rounded" entering class has complemented the American preference for selection in rather than selection out. Small wonder, then, that as federal court decisions in the cases of *Regents of the University of California v. Bakke* (1978),[69] *Hopwood v. State of Texas* (1996),[70] *Grutter v. Bollinger* (2003),[71] and *Gratz v. Bollinger* (2003)[72] indicate, the flash points of affirmative-action controversies usually have ignited over admission to medical and law schools, where intellectual criteria are paramount, rather than colleges.

These decisions left a trail of reversals of lower court rulings, often by split votes, with an unusually large number of justices writing concurring and dissenting opinions and, in testament to the courts' ambivalence, each party to the suit claiming victory. In *Bakke* the Supreme Court established that race could be considered in admissions decisions so long as "fixed quotas" were not used. Bakke left undecided the constitutional scope of racial preferences. In *Hopwood* the Fifth Circuit Court of Appeals barred the University of Texas Law School, which had been using a quota system to ensure admission of minimum numbers of black and Mexican American applicants, from considering race in admissions to overcome past injustices or to achieve a diverse student body. The U.S. Supreme Court declined to review *Hopwood* because the university had abandoned the objectionable quota system, but in *Grutter* the Supreme Court essentially voided *Hopwood* by affirming that race could be used to achieve diversity as long as quotas were not used. In *Gratz*, decided the same day as *Grutter*, the Court invalidated an undergraduate admissions policy because it resembled a fixed quota system by automatically assigning twenty points to each applicant from an underrepresented minority group. In sum, the Supreme Court has not killed racial preferences, but neither do justices want their noses rubbed in them, for they have frequently voided explicit, number-fixated quotas and set-asides.

If we inquire what is wrong with quotas, we are led to the tenacious American view that desert is an integral component of merit, a key prop of Americans' reconciliation of merit with equal rights. A quota system for admission to colleges and professional schools would be the most effective and convenient way to achieve "diversity," which has become the courts' rationale for race-conscious admissions. But quotas imply that a group defined by an ascriptive trait (race) has an ipso facto entitlement to preferential treatment, an idea that violates the belief, ingrained since the Founding, that in America rewards *must* be based on merit.

The legal status of affirmative action has been much cloudier than that of veterans' preference, which is sometimes cited as a precedent.[73] Although veterans' preference amounted to a group entitlement, in principle all of its beneficiaries at its inception fit the category composed of wounded and disabled veterans. In contrast, the beneficiaries of affirmative action were under no obligation to demonstrate that they had been disadvantaged by racism, and with each passing year (we are approaching the fiftieth anniversary of the Civil Rights Act of 1964) claims to disadvantage become less persuasive. From a working-class background, Cheryl Hopwood, a single mother with a severely disabled child who outscored favored groups on the scholastic measures required for her admission to law school, would appear to be more deserving than the anonymous blacks and Mexican Americans admitted over her without any consideration of their desert. On the other hand, veterans' preference has been corrupted by its deployment in partisan politics, so that its original purpose as a desert is mostly lost. Veterans' preference currently finds itself in the position of having few friends beyond its beneficiaries but facing a secure legal future. In contrast, although racial preferences have a large squad of cheerleaders, especially in higher education, their constitutional status is likely to remain cloudy.

Applied to higher education, affirmative action has rested partially on the assumption that racial preferences that increase black enrollments in selective and highly selective colleges and professional schools would contribute to racial equality. Ironically, whether increasing educational opportunities for minorities would increase their social opportunities was becoming a hotly contested issue even as affirmative action was making inroads into higher education. For several decades, a battalion of economists, sociologists, and educators has questioned the link between more schooling and higher earnings that had been forged at the turn of the 1960s by human-capital theory, which built on the idea that education, especially higher education, was better understood as an individual and social investment than as a consumer good. It resembled buying stock in a company more than purchasing a car. Around 1960 future Nobel laureates Gary

Becker and Theodore Schultz were amassing a mountain of evidence that earnings in maturity increased with higher levels of educational attainment.[74] Becker recalled having been taught as a graduate student at the University of Chicago in the early 1950s that rising educational attainment had caused a decline in the rate of return on schooling between 1900 and 1940.[75] But he was more impressed by the quantity and quality of the data pointing to a rising rate of return since 1940.

Human-capital theory complemented the hopeful liberalism of the early 1960s. A reader of Becker's *Human Capital* (1964) would conclude that more investment by government in raising average educational attainment would contribute to narrowing starting-line inequalities. The economic return to college graduates was notably higher than to high-school-only graduates even when differences between the two groups in IQ and parental socio-economic status were controlled for. Rooted in differences in ability, inequalities of outcomes would persist, but they would lessen because diplomas signified genuine additions to knowledge, skills, and traits. The "distribution of earnings," Becker wrote, "would be exactly the same as the distribution of ability if everyone invested the same amount in human capital."[76] Preparing the second edition of *Human Capital* (1975), Becker had to contend with scores of recent studies contending that employers used educational attainment as a device to select applicants whom they expected (without evidence) would be more productive, so that only a small part of the earning's differentials from education could be attributed to education per se. Becker responded that it made no difference whether education paid because employers used it merely as a surrogate for productive workers or because it imparted the knowledge and skills that made workers more productive.

Actually, it *did* make a difference, and for reasons that cut to the heart of the debate over merit during the closing decades of the twentieth century. The conflict between human-capital theorists and their critics raised a fundamental issue: did college graduates merit their long-term economic rewards because they brought superior skills, energy, and character traits (e.g., tenacity) to their jobs, or were they rewarded merely for answering "present" at the college roll call? In the latter case, their economic reward amounted to little more than a ratification of the high socio-economic status of their parents. But it was ridiculous to imagine that employers would pay a premium for college graduates if the graduates' qualifications amounted to a sheepskin, Becker countered, or that they would pay the taxes to support a "horrendously expensive" system of college education.[77] His tone was dismissive, but among the economists Becker cited as advancing this "signaling" (aka credentialing or screening) argument were Nobel laureates Kenneth Arrow and Joseph Stiglitz. Between the first and second editions of Becker's book there had been a run on the human-capital theory bank.

The Attack from the New Left

The New Left led the charge. Committed to egalitarianism without the Old Left's preoccupation with socialism and laws of inevitable historical development, the New Left took a distinctive approach to education. In composite form, its views can be summarized as follows. Even within a system of education marked by a reasonable approximation of universal access, schooling at all levels in the United States has been and continues to be manipulated by the interests of social classes. Decades earlier W. Lloyd Warner had trumpeted the impact of class- and culture-based ideologies on education, but within the framework of the Parsonian idea that social differences arose inevitably from the requirements of social order. More competent people were selected to do the more important jobs in all societies from the United States to the Soviet Union and beyond. Stratification theorists of the 1940s like Kingsley Davis and Wilbert Moore had a propensity for the passive voice (people "were selected"). In New Left thinking, talk of individuals selected for "assigned" roles fatally neglected the intragroup conflict that permeated social institutions and the role of class-based ideologies in shaping all selection processes. *Class* did not necessarily mean the industrial proletariat; rather, reflecting the influence of C. Wright Mills (an inspiration to the New Left), class was defined by how much power a group wielded. Ideology was a means by which the powerful defended their position, usually by invoking seemingly consensual ideals, like the requirement that a society select its most competent people to discharge its most important jobs. In a break with the British tradition that endorsed merit as a means of eradicating explicit and well-recognized class barriers, the New Left added merit and meritocracy to this ideological stew. Celebrating meritocracy, especially by linking it to the emerging "post-industrial" society described by Daniel Bell, naturalized and rationalized social domination by those who were good at taking tests and acquiring advanced degrees.[78]

The economic downturn of the early 1970s and the sudden appearance of unemployed Ph.D.'s boosted critics of human capital and of the irresistible advance of Bell's postindustrial society and prompted a spate of books like Ivar Berg's *Education and Jobs: The Great Training Robbery* (1970).[79] Berg found little evidence that employers rated their better-educated employees as more productive than their less educated ones. Rises in educational attainment did not occur because jobs required more knowledge but because, in a society saturated with holders of diplomas, employers could screen job applicants merely by decreeing that applicants for jobs formerly filled by high-school graduates now had to possess college degrees.

In the early 1970s MIT economist Lester Thurow supported the signaling argument by emphasizing that most workers, rather than acquiring marketable bodies of knowledge and skills before applying for jobs, acquired their skills on the job. For entry-level jobs, employers ranked the queue of applicants on the basis of background characteristics, mainly educational credentials, rather than job skills. Diplomas were proxies for the presumed intelligence and maturity that would reduce the employer's expense in training new workers.[80] Human-capital theory continued to assume that employers would not pay a premium for credentials without some evidence that they were receiving a return greater than the premium.[81] In contrast, Thurow concluded that as the proportion of the male labor force with at least some college education grew, the college-educated were forced to accept lower-paying jobs, from which they displaced those with less education.

Just below the surface of this debate lay a more important issue. Even if schooling paid a rate of return, could it change the distribution of income? The New Left shifted the debate over equality of educational opportunity away from the old-fashioned concern with how many children attended school and how long they stayed there to what happened to them when they exited. The message of Christopher Jencks's influential *Inequality* (1972)[82] was that "in the search for economic equality schooling is a red herring. It only diverts attention from the real issue of direct income redistribution."[83] Jencks acknowledged that IQ and parental socio-economic status strongly influenced educational attainment, which correlated positively with occupational status. But he added that these parameters accounted for only a small part of income differences within occupations. Even if the environmental differences that contributed to differences in test scores and educational attainment were equalized, the result would have little effect on income differences. Those who sought greater economic equality in the United States should look directly to redistribution policies rather than education.[84]

In Jencks's view, luck and chance played a much greater role than intelligence in causing income inequality, which was as great as ever.[85] Breaking with Michael Young and Daniel Bell, he divined no trend toward meritocracy. Inasmuch as American society was not stratified by intelligence, invoking meritocracy to rationalize income inequality made no sense. An egalitarian fundamentalist, Jencks also objected to meritocracy because it instilled competitive values. There was something "perverse and sadistic," he wrote in 1968, "in trying to make America more competitive than it already is."[86] By his measure, it approached a moral evil to encourage a talented lower-class youth to attend Harvard and thereby be exposed to the competitive rat race.[87]

It would require a guess to decide which position—Jencks's hostility to competition and mobility or his fixation on income equality—put him more outside mainstream thinking. There was little in the history of American public policy or

law to indicate that Americans had a keen interest in using public policy to redis-
tribute income.[88] Jencks's position, however, resonated with scholars in Europe,
who were concluding that the demonstrable rise in access to selective levels of
education (e.g., British grammar schools, European universities) since 1945 had
not led to greater equality between the educational attainment of the middle and
working classes. Middle-class children continued to outperform working-class
children on tests of ability and to be disproportionately represented in the selective schools that led to universities and to positions in the professions, finance,
and government.[89]

At the time of *Inequality*'s publication, the French sociologist of education
Raymond Boudon was completing the manuscript of a book (soon translated
and published as *Education, Opportunity, and Social Inequality: Changing Prospects in Western Society*) that introduced American academics to the wider di-
mensions of the inequality controversy. Boudon's data indicated that despite a
significant lessening of inequality of educational opportunity (IEO) in Western
societies since 1945, inequality of social opportunity (ISO) had changed little.
Seeking an explanation, Boudon cast a net enmeshed with stratification theory.
The tenacity of what W. Lloyd Warner had called "social class" ("social heritage"
in Boudon's language) impressed Boudon with the difficulty faced by children
in overcoming the psychological effects of parental socio-economic status. The
child with lower socio-economic status who chose a general rather than a vocational curriculum stood a good chance of losing his friends. Education, it turned
out, provided a social safety net for those on top; its porous mesh, however, did
little to propel to the top those who started on the bottom.[90]

Most American readers of Boudon probably had not read *Reproduction in
Education, Society and Culture*, by Pierre Bourdieu and Jean-Claude Passeron,
which, although published in France in 1970, did not come out in English until
1977. Yet they may have heard of *cultural capital*, a term popularized by Bourdieu.
Cultural capital consisted of the store of terms and phrases mastered by those
who controlled access to prestigious positions in the government, business, and
the professions and who used their mastery to keep the culturally deprived in
their places. Although hidden from sight, the real function of schooling was to
persuade the excluded of the legitimacy of their exclusion and the winners of academic competitions "that they have themselves chosen and won" their places.[91]
As Bourdieu expressed it in Gallic language in 1984: "there is no way out of the
game of culture."[92]

To cite cultural information as "capital" and cultural acquisition as a cause of
social inequality sounded vaguely Marxist or at least un-American. America was
the land of self-improvement and the home of the fill-in-the-bubble test, not the

land of *No Exit* and French civil-service examinations that called for essays on the Balkan Question.[93] Yet Bourdieu pointed to articles by Jencks and other Americans as evidence that Americans were finally getting over American exceptionalism. For the transatlantic Left of the 1970s, getting over American exceptionalism meant getting over the idea that education could enhance social equality.

Human-capital theorists found themselves on the conservative side of debates about merit, but paradoxically, they sounded more like the Old Left of the interwar years, which envisioned merit as a highway to equality for the deserving. Recall that Becker stated that if everyone invested the same amount in human capital, the distribution of earnings would exactly correspond to the distribution of abilities. Becker equated this formulation to one made in 1931 by the famed British socialist R. H. Tawney: equal opportunity "obtains in so far as, and only in so far as, each member of a community, whatever his birth or occupation or social position, possesses in fact, and not merely in form, equal chances in using to the full his natural endowments of physique, of character, and of intelligence."[94] Tawney was laying down conditions to make equal opportunity more than a daydream. It did no more good to tell a young man that all positions were open to him than to tell a tadpole that he might someday start to croak, or to hail the decline of caste even as class was replacing it.[95] Similarly, Coleman talked of "effective" equality of opportunity,[96] and Becker expected that investment in education would give practical meaning to equality of opportunity.

To Each His Deserts

By 1975 merit had become the bogeyman of egalitarians in much the way aristocracy and plutocracy had in earlier times. The index of John Rawls's widely influential *A Theory of Justice* (1971) contained an entry for *meritocracy* but none for *aristocracy* or *plutocracy*. More to the point, Rawls, as his critics observed, thought that merit did not belong in a consideration of distributive justice. Inequalities in wealth or authority were justifiable only to the extent that they benefited everyone and, in particular, the least advantaged members of society. Only if this were the case could those either well endowed or more fortunate in their social position expect the willing cooperation of others, argued Rawls. In Rawls's words, his conception of justice "prevents the use of the accidents of natural endowments or the contingencies of social circumstances as counters in the quest for political and economic advantage."[97] Basically, Rawls exorcised moral desert from distributive justice; when it came to wealth, income, and the good things in life, no one deserved anything.[98]

Americans have a long history of seeking ways to ensure that citizens receive economic rewards that closely approximate their productive contributions. Present at the Founding, this objective persisted through Jacksonian attacks on monopoly to the recent past, when feminists raised the flag of "comparable worth."[99] Nearly everyone thought that the economic rewards that flowed to the winners in a fair competition were merited because they rewarded the improvement of one's natural talents that flowed from diligence and exertion. True, competition was not always fair. In business, gamesters and speculators were always trying to get something for nothing. Political parties tilted the playing field and sometimes thrived on corruption. Sexism and racism poisoned fairness. But because America was a republic ruled by the ballot box and an ever widening electorate, these challenges to just deserts could be overcome.

Or so it was thought, and the thought became deeply ingrained. Americans are much more likely than Japanese and Swedes to equate a fair economic system with one in which pay depends on ability.[100] The decline of the proportion of the work force engaged in manufacturing nevertheless complicated the ideal of desert. Situations in which wages directly reflected productivity were becoming hard to find.[101] Challenges to desert were developing even before the decline of manufacturing. To talk about a worker's desert assumed that he had freedom of choice. Nineteenth-century economists imagined the worker could control his destiny by improving his skills, choosing his vocation, and rationally entering contracts. Decades before John Rawls launched his philosophical attack on desert, however, events were eroding the foundations of this assumption. The Depression strengthened unions, which would demonstrate time and again that the "laws" of wages were subject to negotiation, and it led to increased employment in government, where pay scales had been set by statutory decree even before 1929.

One authority Rawls cited on the subject of desert was the University of Chicago economist Franklin H. Knight, specifically his article "The Ethics of Competition," first published in 1923. Knight tasked himself with demolishing the prevailing view among economists that those whose production satisfied wants, especially the "lower" and more fundamental wants, deserved a greater share of the social dividend. Knight linked this view to "the competitive system," laissez-faire, individualism, Adam Smith, and the classical economists, but he summarized it in a sentence that reads like a textbook definition of the theory of marginal productivity: "A freely competitive organization of society tends to place every productive resource in that position in the productive system where it can make the greatest possible addition to the total social dividend as measured in price terms, and tends to reward every participant in production by giving it the increase in the social dividend which its co-operation makes possible."[102] Knight found this formulation defective. It presupposed a society of freely contracting individuals, but many in the society—minors, the aged, and the vast majority of adult women—were not free contractual agents. Even the unencumbered male in the prime of life is a product of the economic system, which forms his desires, and the political system, which often enacts laws skewed toward the well positioned. Individuals do not necessary satisfy their lower wants before their higher ones and rarely think rationally about their needs.

Knight's goal was to sever desert from economics. Foreshadowing Rawls, Knight contended that the value of a good or service ultimately depended on demand, which lacked any moral content and which had no claim to a superior share of the social dividend, "except to the extent that the capacity [to furnish the product] itself is the product of conscientious effort."[103] (On this count, Rawls went further by arguing that effort formed no basis for desert because effort depended so much on natural aptitudes.) No one, Knight argued, could seriously claim that "competence," as measured "by the price system, corresponded to ethical merit." There is no basis for thinking that "it is more meritorious merely to be different from other people than to be like them."[104] "The Ethics of Competition" was republished in 1935 as part of a collection of Knight's essays selected by a committee of four economists, two of whom, Milton Friedman and George Stigler (University of Chicago graduate students at the time), would become Nobel Prize laureates in economics. Friedman and Stigler both became champions of free-market capitalism and accepted marginal-productivity theory, but each followed Knight in questioning the theory as an ethical system based on desert. Friedman defended the free market because it contributed more to the sustained growth of per capita income by releasing energies and risk taking, not because it rewarded individuals according to their deserts.[105]

In 1975 Lester Thurow observed that economists' interest in efficiency had trumped their interest in equity since the 1950s.[106] Like Friedman, many defenders of free-market capitalism have gradually moved away from linking economic rewards to marginal productivity and toward a defense of freedom as a good in itself,[107] or, alternatively, a defense based on capitalism's efficiency.

The Swinging Pendulum

Although advocates of human capital had never satisfactorily described the component of schooling that induced employers to pay more for increments of it, the closer one approaches the year 2000, the less one reads about credentialing or schools as mere agents of social reproduction. The initiative passed to advocates of human capital. Their studies turned up evidence that more schooling, even increments too small (a few months) to result in any credential, had higher returns than less schooling.[108] By 1990, in addition, it had become clear that the glut of educated manpower that developed in the early to mid-1970s and that resulted in books like R. B. Freeman's *The Overeducated American* (1976)[109] was a transient artifact of a sudden spurt in the number of college graduates combined with the surge of baby boomers into the job market. Between 1979 and 1986 the "wage premium" for college graduates rose very sharply, exceeding anything found in the earlier data.[110] At the same time, rising concerns about foreign competition and American economic decline led policymakers to identify educational deficits as the cause of decline.

The 1983 publication of *A Nation at Risk: The Imperative for Educational Reform*, written by President Ronald Reagan's National Commission on Excellence in Education, initiated one of those periodic self-purgations in which Americans exorcise their failures, in this case educational failures, in a kind of ritualistic reenactment of the Puritan covenant. The report noted that between 1963 and 1980 average SAT scores dropped more than fifty points in the verbal section and nearly forty points in the math section. Rising concern about the decline of America's economic competitiveness with other nations gave *A Nation at Risk* its electrical charge. The "educational foundations of our society," the report proclaimed in ominous language, "are presently being eroded by a rising tide of mediocrity that threatens our very future as a Nation and a people." It warned that "if an unfriendly foreign power had attempted to impose on America the mediocre educational performance that exists today, we might well have viewed it as an act of war."[111]

A Nation at Risk fathered President George W. Bush's "No Child Left Behind" program. This program, however, dealt with only a small segment—failing schools—of the concerns raised by *A Nation at Risk*, and it shifted the blame for failing schools from the larger culture to teachers. In recent decades we have been submerged with proposals to make the pay of our public-school teachers, such as it is, depend on their performance in the classroom, which is to be measured by the scores of their pupils on standardized achievement tests. Although schoolchildren are tested more than ever before, under No Child Left Behind teachers alone receive failing grades.

A Nation at Risk was the work of a presidential commission on education that had experts on tap but never on top. When experts first came on the political scene in the early 1900s, they were seen as nonpartisan reporters of the truth. Politicians did not necessarily defer to experts, but they conceded that experts were disinterested in the sense that they had nothing to lose if their advice was ignored. As the reach of federal policy has extended into education, health care, and the family, research has become vastly more politicized than in 1900 or 1950.

There are red and blue think tanks, and indeed think tanks in several shades of each color. The New Left alleged that professions of disinterestedness arise from self-interested and class-based motives. Increasingly, conservatives have also questioned the authority and judgment of professionals. Bureaucrats have demanded that colleges and universities assess the "value" that they "add" to each student over the course of four years, although no one has identified a way to establish a baseline, the student's "value" on entry. (Professors seek to find out what our students have learned in courses by administering what are known as final examinations, but these appear not to count as measures of "value added.") Everyone, it seems, wants a foolproof guarantee that he is getting value back for his money. The results often are risible. In a predictably brief experiment at the start of the 1980s, North Carolina attempted to factor "number of tickets written" into merit raises for state troopers.[112]

As the following excursion into the federal government's personnel policies since the 1970s illustrates, the increasing valence of performance evaluation has combined with declining selectivity at the gate.

Obituary for the Public Merit Project

During the New Deal, academics specializing in public administration and their allies within the federal government unfurled the Public Merit Project: attracting talented college graduates into the federal government and putting them in positions where they could do the most good. Entry-level examinations that tested for intellectual ability and hence promise were components of this project, which was closely linked to the ideal of internal recruitment: the best and the brightest would enter public service if they perceived opportunities for advancement that were not blocked by political appointees. The Public Merit Project rested on the assumption that to establish careers for the talented required minimizing partisan influence within the classified service.

The Civil Service Reform Act (CSRA) of 1978 fulfilled another long-standing objective of supporters of the Public Merit Project by establishing a higher civil service, the Senior Executive Service (SES). Unlike its stillborn predecessors, the Senior Civil Service (SCS, Eisenhower) and the Federal Executive Service (FES, Nixon), the SES was born alive and with much fanfare. It was open to federal executives holding GS-16 through GS-18 positions; members would hold rank in the SES and would be available for transfer wherever needed. In reaction to President Richard M. Nixon's attempt to manipulate the civil service for political ends, the CSRA limited the proportion of political appointees in the SES to 10 percent and promised senior career executives who entered the SES enhanced performance incentives, including ranks like "distinguished" and "meritorious" executive, annual performance bonuses, and sabbaticals. It also replaced the U.S. Civil Service Commission with two new agencies, a Merit Systems Protection Board (MSPB) and the Office of Personnel Management (OPM), whose head was to advise the president on personnel.

All of this reminds us of the ideals that Leonard D. White had preached from the 1930s until his death in 1958. There was, however, a key difference. White conceived of a higher civil service as a merit-embodying class of executives who would supervise themselves. Eisenhower and Nixon viewed it as a way to make the federal bureaucracy more responsive to politicians. President Jimmy Carter had a different objective: to make the federal bureaucracy more responsive to the work ethic. The problem with the merit system, Carter said, was that there was no merit in it.[113]

Having run for president against the inside-the-beltway establishment, Carter took civil-service reform more seriously than any predecessor since Andrew Jackson. But the civil service Carter inherited differed from the one taken over by Jackson. On the one hand, Carter could try to impose his will without being charged with "executive despotism," the mantra of the National Republicans and Whigs in the 1830s. On the other hand, the merit system, which had become a form of tenure in office long before 1978, limited his freedom of action. Before the CSRA, executives in the high GS grades were evaluated by a system of service ratings prescribed by a 1950 law, which required agencies to establish performance appraisal systems with three summary ratings: Outstanding, Satisfactory, and Unsatisfactory. Lacking rewards and, in practice, punishments, this system had long been derided. Observing that 98 percent of all ratings under the law were Satisfactory (this would rise to 99 percent by 1977) and that the law's provisions for interminable appeals negated any incentive to give an employee an Unsatisfactory rating, a government commission in 1953 described the rating system as a burdensome process of making perfunctory judgments. The Federal Salary Reform Act of 1962 drew some link between pay and performance by requiring determination of an "acceptable level of competence" to determine eligibility for "within grade increases" (WGIs) that had been laid out by the Classification Act of 1949. But in practice WGIs became automatic.

To engineer more individual responsibility into the merit system, the CSRA legislated a version of Peter Drucker's Management by Objectives (MBO). The pay of managers and supervisors in the GS-13 to GS-15 grades (called GM employees) was now more closely tied to their performance in meeting objectives deemed "critical" to their agencies. Under the new merit pay system, GM employees were guaranteed only half of their "comparability" (with the private sector) pay increases; the other half was held back as a pool for merit raises. Federal employees in the so-called supergrades (GS-16 to GS-18) who became members of the SES signed contracts by which they surrendered some of the protections of the merit system in return for the prospect of bonuses for meritorious performance. But dissatisfaction with the new system sprouted quickly, and accounts of its effects read like obituaries. Members of the SES were angered when Congress failed to fund incentive pay at the expected level. Forty percent of the career executives who had converted to the SES left the government between 1979 and 1983, most to retire.[114] Managers and supervisors in the GS-13 through GS-15 grades (the GM employees) quickly discovered a glitch: many of those rated Fully Successful were receiving merit pay increases that failed to match the annual "comparability" raises for nonmanagers (called GS employees) in the same grades.[115] Congress fixed the glitch in 1984 with a new Performance Management and Recognition System (PMRS). PMRS established greater consistency across agencies and between GM and GS employees at the price of reducing the flexibility of the merit pay system. Under PMRS, employees rated Fully Successful were guaranteed their comparability raises. The PMRS also stipulated that employees rated Outstanding receive a minimum raise of 2 percent of base pay.[116]

Merit pay increasingly resembled the guest everyone sought for a dinner party who then behaved so egregiously as never to be invited back. As originally envisioned, only 1 or 2 percent of employees under merit pay would be rated outstanding or its equivalent, but by 1990, in an example of what is known in personnel circles as the "consequence sensitivity error," over 30 percent of GM employees were rated Fully Successful and in 1993 Congress removed the mandatory 2 percent raise.[117] Rumors circulated that some agencies were gaming the system by rotating the Fully Successful rating among their GM employees. With rating inflation, GM employees began to regard a rating of Fully Successful (as opposed to Exceeded Fully Successful) as a slap in the face, and in 1991 a blue-ribbon panel formed to assess the effects of PMRS proposed a return to a two-grade rating system, Satisfactory or Unsatisfactory. Nothing came of this, and a study conducted by the National Research Council failed to turn up any evidence that pay-for-performance stimulated improved government services. In 1993 Congress, confronted with rating inflation, imposed statutory limits on cash awards for exceptional achievement by GM employees, revoked the mandatory 2 percent raise for GS employees rated Outstanding, and then let PMRS expire.[118]

Implementing merit pay in the federal government faced special problems created by the government's size, its legalistic environment, the absence of a product or profit to measure, the transparency (compared with business) of its pay procedures, and the strengthening of interest groups and weakening of political parties. The CSRA itself ran to 128 pages, compared with 5 for the Pendleton Act, and most sections of the 1978 law bore the imprint of interest groups that had grown vastly more powerful since 1883, when the only interest groups that really counted were called the Republican Party and the Democratic Party. The CSRA, as one scholar observed, resembled a Christmas tree, decorated with promised benefits for career civil servants and elements designed to bring in powerful constituencies, including civil-rights groups, the veterans' lobby, and unions of federal workers.[119]

The politicizing of the career civil service was becoming routine in the 1970s and 1980s. One study indicated that most careerists who planned to exit the SES were motivated less by interference with their political neutrality than by policy differences with political appointees.[120] Some public administrationists have wondered aloud why a politicized career civil service should enjoy the benefits of the merit system, but the public's main concern in recent decades has been the performance of the federal bureaucracy, specifically its cost-effectiveness, rather than the degree of its politicization.[121]

This preoccupation with cost-effectiveness has often made politicians sound like business-school professors extolling the virtues of Management by Objectives (MBO), Total Quality Management (TQM), "reengineering," "customer satisfaction," "worker empowerment," and "managing for results." In the 1990s this managerial emphasis took the form of "reinventing government," a slogan taken from the title of a 1992 best-seller by David Osborne, a journalist, and Ted Gaebler, a former city manager.[122] The strong showing of maverick independent Ross H. Perot in the 1992 presidential election (19 percent of the popular vote) persuaded President Bill Clinton of the political value of committing his administration to attacking waste in public programs. In March 1993 Clinton asked Vice President Albert Gore to conduct a six-month review of the federal government, called the National Performance Review (NPR), to identify opportunities for cost-cutting. The outcome was a blizzard of studies, under the general title of *Creating a Government That Works Better & Costs Less.*[123] In 1994 Congress passed the National Performance and Results Act, which mandated pilot projects relevant to reinvention.[124]

A striking feature of reinvention proposals, many of which were implemented at the federal, state, and local levels, lay in their indifference to the government-reorganization proposals put forward by commissions since the 1930s. Raising the quality of government personnel had long been an integral component of plans to improve the operations of government. The CSRA had the same goal; the SES was expected to make career service more attractive by giving high-level career civil servants more flexibility and performance incentives. In contrast, the thrust of the NPR was that as long as departments and agencies found ways to deliver services less expensively, raising the quality of their personnel was not a priority and may not have really mattered. Reinvention effectively shifted focus from managers to management. Herbert N. Jaspers, a management consultant with extensive experience in the federal government, complained to a House committee in 1995 that the reinvention movement treated managers as if they were the "virtual enemies of good government."[125] Most reformers in the Progressive and New Deal eras agreed that the road to "good government" ran through "better government personnel." The reinvention movement did not propose, of course, "worse government personnel," but the movement illustrated how growing distrust of institutions and the professions has led to substituting surveillance of performance for the identification of ability.

Starting with the Supreme Court's decision in *Griggs,* pressure from the judiciary and civil-rights activists has crumbled two more blocks in the foundation of the Public Merit Project: the deployment of mental tests, tests for ability, to increase the efficiency of public service personnel and the use of examinations to recruit superior college graduates into executive positions in the public service. Neither of these initiatives was among the objectives of the Pendleton-era reformers. Rather, they primarily arose during the New Deal era. Once they looked like magic bullets; by the 1990s they looked like broken arrows.

In the wake of *Griggs,* the Urban League challenged the legality of the Federal Service Entrance Examination (FSEE), introduced in 1954 for junior-level applicants for managerial, professional, and technical operations. In keeping with the ingrained aversion to examinations, like those for higher civil services in Europe, that assessed a candidate's grasp of the sorts of cultural information likely to be learned only in elite academic institutions, the FSEE consisted of ninety-five objective questions designed to measure reading comprehension and ability to reason quantitatively in solving problems with numbers. Proportionately, far more whites than blacks passed the examination.[126] The League asked for evidence that those who failed the examination would have performed more poorly in the federal service than those who passed. Especially when it came to tests for employment, the testing community had long relied on "predictive validity" as a measure of a test's validity, its conformity to something real. A test could meet the standard of predictive validity if its results conformed to criteria—reading comprehension, ability to reason quantitatively—believed by the employer to be relevant to the job.[127] But if the employer had to show, as the Urban League demanded, that someone who performed poorly on the test and then was given the job anyway would fail at it, the bar for a test's validity was being set at a dizzying height. Inasmuch as performance on the job could be measured only by evaluative ratings, which in the federal service nearly always meant satisfactory or better, the government faced a hopeless task.

That the government failed to recognize that the task was hopeless is evidenced by its response to the Urban League's challenge.[128] After extensive consultation with the testing industry aimed at eliminating bias in the questions, the USCSC devised a new screening test for college graduates, introduced in 1974 and now called the Professional and Administrative Career Examination (PACE).[129] The government still did not recognize that the bomb dropped by *Griggs* had a delayed fuse. Not until 1978 did it begin to assemble sample evidence on the proportion of white, black, and Hispanic test takers to achieve the cut-off score of 70 for eligibility (respectively, 42 percent, 5 percent, and 12.9 percent).[130] By then, the Equal Employment Opportunity Commission and the Departments of Labor and Justice had agreed on guidelines to establish "adverse impact." Any examination to select federal employees for eligibility lists that resulted in a selection rate of less than 80 percent of members of any racial, ethnic, or gender group was deemed to have an "adverse impact" on that group and hence violated Title VII. After Angel G. Luevano led a class action suit on behalf of blacks and Hispanics against OPM director Alan Campbell in 1979, the Justice Department chose not to contest the suit. PACE was abolished in 1982.

In 1990 OPM introduced the Administrative Careers with America (ACWA) test as the long-awaited replacement for PACE.[131] But applicants for entry-level administrative federal positions did not have to take ACWA. A grade-point average of 3.2 or better from any college was an acceptable substitute. Only one component of ACWA, which consisted of multiple-choice questions to assess vocabulary, reading comprehension, and arithmetical reasoning, conformed to the usual meaning of an examination. The remainder, called the Individual Achievement Record (IAR), required candidates to respond to questions about their individual achievements and successes. As an OPM brochure explained, the IAR assessed "how well you have made use of your opportunities."[132] This was not quite the same as asking applicants to name their favorite color, but it was close. In 1994 the examination component of ACWA was essentially terminated; only the IAR remained.[133]

The U.S. government terminated PACE because the examination had an adverse impact on blacks and Hispanics: the Justice Department decided it would lose a case brought under Title VII of the Civil Rights Act of 1964. In 2009, on the other hand, the U.S. Supreme Court ruled in *Ricci v. DeStefano*[134] that the city of New Haven, Connecticut, violated Title VII when it discarded the results of examinations administered in 2003 for promotion to lieutenant and captain in its Fire Department on the grounds that the tests had resulted in a disparate impact (of the 118 firefighters who took the tests, the passing rate for blacks was one-half that for whites).[135] The lead plaintiff, Frank Ricci, a dyslexic white firefighter, paid a friend to read to him in preparation for the test, which he passed. Writing for the majority of five justices, Justice Anthony Kennedy stated that "fear of litigation alone cannot justify an employer's reliance on race to the detriment of individuals who passed the examinations and qualified for promotions." Kennedy assigned the burden of proof to the city of New Haven, which had discarded the results of a test it had sanctioned without providing any evidence that the tests were insufficiently job-related. In future cases the lead plaintiff might well be a black or Hispanic who insists that the employer prove that the test was job-related. Justice Kennedy deprecated "fear of litigation" as a defense, but fear of litigation is likely to have a chilling effect on the use of employment tests.

The State of Merit in the Union

Arguably, the foregoing bodes ill for merit in government. For several decades, the federal government sought to tie pay to merit as identified by performance evaluations. On a parallel track, it attempted to screen applicants for jobs by improved examinations. With a shove from the courts, it then lost interest in "better government personnel." Although these generalizations fairly describe the chain reaction of fiascos that followed the CSRA, the government did not sever its lines of access to talented people. The Public Merit Project rested on the belief that the best and the brightest, selected and promoted on the basis of impersonal criteria, should be recruited into a civil-service hierarchy of positions stratified by education and measured intelligence. This belief resembled C. Wright Mills's notion, itself indebted to Max Weber, of a "genuine" bureaucracy. Yet as Daniel Bell recognized, since 1950 the "knowledge society" and its huge R&D component has overturned the conviction, fundamental to the Public Merit Project, that the model of organization most suited to modern conditions is a Weberian bureaucracy. Whenever it chooses, the federal government can draw on the immense intellectual resources of people who are paid to create knowledge in universities, think tanks, and corporations like Rand and its numerous progeny.

The substitution of self-evaluation (the Individual Achievement Record) for tests that at least *aimed* at objectivity has likely cost the federal government in the form of lost efficiency. After all, the prohibited tests screened applicants for white-collar jobs in which reading comprehension and an ability to draw relationships among test items would appear to have relevance. But the collapse of the Public Merit Project signifies more than a bureaucratic loss of efficiency. It reminds us of the competing projects that the federal government has taken on, including the quest for egalitarian outcomes in a stratified society. Thus, we come face to face with the erosion of belief in the idea that people can be assessed by standards independent of their personal experience.

Over the course of American history, those who have invoked merit—the Men of Merit we met in Chapter 1, the mental testers described in Chapter 5, the pioneering university leaders encountered in Chapter 6, and the public adminis-trationists who embraced the politics/administration distinction and, following Leonard D. White, called for a higher civil service—have invariably linked the ideal to *disinterest*, a word that most people, including those who should know better, now seem to think means apathy or boredom. In sum, the ideal of merit has been bound at the hip with another ideal, objectivity, "that noble dream," in the words of historian Peter Novick.[136] Novick's magisterial study examined both the assertions and criticisms of historians' claims to belong to a truth-telling profession, and he concluded that "the evolution of historians' positions on the objectivity question has always been closely tied to changing social, political, cul-tural, and professional contexts."[137]

At each stage, dissenters have questioned the profession of objective disin-terest put forth by adherents of merit. In 1787–88 antifederalists conceded the Men of Merit's achievements and ability but insisted that even these paragons were not above self-interest. In the 1840s Whigs skewered George Bancroft's bid to base promotions in the navy on merit as a back door to smuggling more Democrats into high officer ranks. In retrospect, we can see, as some contem-poraries recognized, that such items on the early IQ tests as asking test takers to name the city in which Cornell University was located or the line of work in which Christy Mathewson excelled were laughably culture-bound. Herbert Simon later bashed the politics/administration distinction on the grounds that all administration is political and ideological. Reacting against Jacksonian-era laws mandating the election of judges, bar associations began in the late nine-teenth century to encourage the establishment of boards to assess the qual-ifications of candidates for state judgeships. Some states continued to elect judges, but increasingly, voters had to choose from a select list of qualified candidates.[138] Such arrangements are still on the books, but in recent decades judicial appointments by merit-selection boards have come under withering attack, usually for their alleged liberal bias.

Novick declined to predict the next turn of the wheel, whether toward an invigorated objectivism or a resurgent subjectivism. Prudence should make us wary of forecasting the future direction of the ideal of merit in the American republic, for it has bobbed and weaved many times. But it now seems to be on the defensive, if not on its back.[139]

Merit is under siege in our society not only from the relativism that long has permeated the intelligentsia. It is also being subverted by a popular culture in which high-decibel blogs and reality television offer not just visibility but also the prospect of fame and fortune to people who nominate themselves for the spotlight. If everyone can be famous, we ask, does anyone deserve fame? Pouring "a little merriement upon this solemn subject of Aristocracy," John Adams asked Thomas Jefferson the same question in November 1813. Which is more astonishing, Adams wondered: the pride, vanity, artifice, low cunning, avarice, and unbounded ambition exhibited by aristocrats in all nations, or the stupidity with which the multitude "not only become their Dupes, but even love to be Taken in by their Tricks."[140] Adams, recall, was engaging in a futile attempt to persuade Jefferson that the latter's "natural aristocracy" (composed of talent and virtue) was an empty bag, for a talent in Adams's view was any attribute that, regardless of its desert, received a reward. To clinch his case, he invoked (without naming) the recently notorious Lady Hamilton, the beauty who walked the streets of London "with a baskett of Cabbage, Sprouts, Dandlions and Spinage on her head" until Sir William Hamilton took notice, made her a lady, and transported her to the court of Naples, where she famously caught the eye of Horatio Nelson. "This Lady not only causes the Tryiumphs of Copinhagen and Trafalgar," wrote Adams, "but seperates Naples from France and finally banishes the King and Queen from Sicilly."[141]

The American republic, once thought (except by those as sharp-eyed as Adams) to be a stranger to the seductive power of show and display, would later invent the public-relations industry, the internet, the blog, and social networking. Indeed, Adams's "aristocrats" sound like our "celebrities," who can draw on far mightier machines of publicity than George Romney's brush could provide for Emma Hamilton.[142] In principle, identifying merit demands a screening for valued traits, for no one could judge his own merit, as George Washington recognized. Celebrities, however, are ranked only by the attention they succeed in attracting, while bloggers screen themselves. *Time* named "You" its 2006 "person of the year," and Lady Gaga ends her performances by crooning, "Don't go away loving me, go away loving yourself." The land of instant celebrity is also the land of self-esteem. American schoolchildren lag on achievement tests but lead the world in self-confidence. Collegians study less than they did a half-century ago but receive higher grades. States have cut their support for public universities since the end of the Cold War, but universities are investing more in football stadiums and basketball arenas, and they appear to have developed a penchant for hiring coaches who look good on television. Each year the line between achievement and media-hyped publicity becomes fuzzier.

Although many Americans doubt that advancement is based on merit, most still affirm that it should be. A similar generalization can be made about democracy. Most Americans doubt that their vote really counts and suspect that powerful offstage interests shape policy more than do the voters, but nearly all of them defend government by popular consent. Today merit and consent, each an ideal of the Founding, nevertheless provoke different reactions. Evidence of the failings of popular consent scarcely ruffles the ideal, while evidence of the difficulties encountered in implementing merit provokes derision of the ideal. I view this as unfortunate. Throughout the course of our history, invocations of merit have served many hitherto excluded groups in their demand for equal rights. Critics of merit would do well to contemplate the alternatives.

MERIT, EQUALITY, CONSENT

This book has argued that advancement by merit was among the founding principles of the American republic and that its history is best understood within that context. In contrast to France, where revolutionaries would urge that careers be opened to talents, the Whig gentry that led the American Revolution in most states did not raise the banner of merit to rally groups excluded from governance by factitious social distinctions. Rather, its members thought that in a colonial society lacking a hereditary aristocracy, careers had long been open to talents, that their families had earned their social rank, and that their own luminous contributions to the Revolution had not only validated their claims to high office as a reward for their merit but also established a republic that by its nature guaranteed merit-based advancement to all citizens.

As an ideal of the Founding, advancement by merit nevertheless emerged in harness with equal rights and popular consent, principles of the Founding with potential to conflict with merit. Merit implies difference, while equality suggests sameness. Merit implies selection on the basis of a standard by one higher up of another lower down, a view potentially in conflict with the ideal that republican citizens consent to decisions that affect their lives. In the 1970s the New Left saw merit and equality as locked in necessary conflict. More often than not, Americans have reconciled merit with other principles of the Founding, but in ways that have influenced their understanding of merit. For example, in a capitalist republic founded on equal rights and popular consent, it became especially important to establish that ordinary working people, who could not plausibly look to public office as a reward, could gain economic rewards proportionate to their talents and efforts. Although this principle flowed naturally from the founding view, shared by many Europeans, that America was distinctive in its capacity to reward industry, it faced constant challenges in the form of changes in commerce, finance, and manufacturing that made it more difficult to establish the exact relationship between economic activity and rewards. Still, the relationship had to be established. It was no accident that Americans embraced scientific methods for measuring small differences in productivity or that American economists of the early twentieth century embraced marginal-productivity theory with more unanimity than did economists in Europe, where the theory originated.

The ways in which Americans have managed selection, especially selection by examinations, also illustrates their need to harmonize merit with other principles of the Founding. Viewing republics as naturally receptive to advancement by merit, the Founding Generation saw no need to establish a system of examinations to select its successors. Americans have repeatedly derided attempts to re-create such a class by means of a British- or French-style system of examinations to select a governing elite. Often they have acted as if examinations were essentially pedagogical agents, designed to help students learn rather than to sort the wheat from the chaff. Public educators long balked at the notion that schools engaged in social sorting at all, and even when they accepted the selective/sorting role of public schools, they devised tests that promised to assist citizens in finding unsuspected abilities within themselves, what I have called "selection in" rather than "selection out." No nation has matched or even approached the American penchant for devising tests for a multitude of aptitudes, abilities, and personality traits. Mental or psychological tests appealed to Americans because these tests promised to reveal an individual's inner qualities that might otherwise be disguised by social appearances. In a nation whose values were antithetical to assuming that a citizen's social trajectory was fixed by his birthright, the promise of mental tests to forecast destinies was irresistible.

Americans have usually reconciled merit with equality by translating equal rights as *equal opportunity* to gain rewards proportionate to one's abilities and efforts. What is often unappreciated is just how deeply embedded has been the American penchant for *increasing* the number of rewards in order to satisfy popular aspirations. Just as Americans incline to reward unremarkable achievements with high-sounding if oxymoronic job titles ("assistant head coach"), the theaters in which they have competed with each other have been marked by a very wide diffusion of rewards. This has not always occurred by design. The Constitution did not adopt federalism in order to diffuse rewards, but federalism made it possible for someone whose ambitions were blocked in one jurisdiction to skip to another, where the rules were different, and it bred an entrepreneurial approach to seeking office. Although the Men of Merit worried at the Founding that the republic would fail to provide them with the "loaves and fishes" of offices garnished with popular deference, in reality Americans fought their revolution with thirteen state armies and one national army, each with its own reward structure. After the Revolution, federalism continued to create numerous channels of entry into public life. Including elective and appointive office, the traditional professions, and the pre-Pendleton civil service, public life was a capacious sphere in which to seek distinction, the more so because entry did not require passing examinations or possessing educational credentials.

Federalism also facilitated direct recourse to politics by those unable to secure advancement by the rules of the institution in which a benefit was sought. Today a university that evades the process of peer review to seek a congressional earmark is abandoning the principle of selection by merit as we understand it. In the nineteenth century, however, the relationship between merit and politics was more nuanced. For example, during the Civil War, Americans relied on a small regular army in which promotion depended on seniority and a much larger volunteer army in which political connections could carry a man a long way. In retrospect, we almost reflexively classify pulling political strings as the opposite of merit. But many Americans argued during the Civil War that the road to military promotions that ran through politics was likely to reward excellent officers, for a capacity for leadership would carry politicians and generals alike farther than a pedantic knowledge of issues and tactics. As the Prince de Joinville observed during the Civil War, the belief that any American could succeed at any task without special training was a deeply embedded American value, so much so that Americans ignored evidence to the contrary. In 1860 the American political system rewarded certain kinds of behavior, such as taking risks and seeking advancement outside normal channels, which quickly came to be seen as meritorious traits.

The foregoing examples illustrate how features of the republic, initially designed for other purposes, have facilitated the diffusion of rewards and shaped the American understanding of the components of merit. At times, however, Americans have structured competitive forums with the specific design of increasing the number of rewards. Arising from equal rights, popular aspirations to advance in the world have shaped the nature of hierarchies (ladders of achievement) in America. Whether in government, business, education, or the professions, hierarchies do not acquire their form from some necessary response to socio-economic forces; rather, they reflect political and cultural values. The values explain why the shape of hierarchies differs from one nation to another. For example, the public-school reformers of the nineteenth century organized the promotion of pupils from grade to grade not merely for the sake of efficiency but also to habituate the young to competitions in which modest but widely diffused rewards predictably followed the exercise of average ability and effort. In the late nineteenth century, American educators departed from the German university model by adopting a departmental structure that allowed each faculty member to rise to full professor on the basis of his specialty.

None of this changes the fact that merit has come under withering fire in the last three to four decades. It is derided by those who have risen by merit. Professors blast meritocracy; judges denounce tests. Ordinary Americans still value merit, most evidently by changing their behavior to conform to its requirements. The ideal of merit has encouraged ambition, self-improvement, self-denial, and, more basically, the belief that Americans can gain control over their lives. Although these values currently enjoy little respect from social scientists, most Americans today endorse them as preferable to such alternatives as advancement by luck or birthright.

Luck and birthright, of course, *do* matter. Do they matter more than merit in the distribution of rewards? In truth, the answer to this question lies in the eye of the beholder rather than in any finely calibrated scale that purports to weigh the factors leading to rewards. It is like asking whether the glass is half full or half empty. Recall that Stephen Decatur's first biographer, S. Putnam Waldo, attributed Decatur's achievements to his "positive merit" but acknowledged that misfortune could shatter his most judicious plans. Misfortune did more than shatter Decatur's plans. It killed him; he died in a duel in 1820. But none of this mattered to Waldo, for Decatur's "active worth" could never be erased by misfortune. Even in death he retained his "positive merit."

Our own society is more likely to see the glass as half empty, in the sense that pundits incline to substitute luck for merit as an explanation of achievement. Indeed, achievements and heroes leave us cold. As we have seen, to doubt the achievements of the great has been part of our republic's fabric since the Revolution seeded "jealousy" (suspicion) as a national trait. Throughout our national history, suspicion has clouded claims to distinction based on merit. It is the price we pay for embracing merit as a republican ideal.

Notes

INTRODUCTION

1. Quoted in Willard S. Randall, *Benedict Arnold: Patriot and Traitor* (New York: William Morrow, 1990), 189.

2. Quoted in Willard M. Wallace, *Traitorous Hero: The Life and Fortunes of Benedict Arnold* (New York: Harper, 1954), 126.

3. The change outlined in this paragraph is best described by Holly Brewer, *By Birth or Consent: Children, Law, and the Anglo-American Revolution in Authority* (Chapel Hill: University of North Carolina Press, 2005).

4. Louis Hartz, *The Liberal Tradition in America: An Interpretation of American Political Thought since the Revolution* (New York: Harcourt, Brace, 1955).

5. Harold Rugg, "Is the Rating of Human Character Practicable?" *Journal of Educational Psychology* 12 (1922), 427.

6. Quoted in Charles C. Binney, *The Life of Horace Binney* (Philadelphia: J. B. Lippincott, 1903), 73.

7. Stephen Jay Gould, *The Mismeasure of Man* (New York: W. W. Norton, 1981); Nicholas Lemann, *The Big Test: The Secret History of the Meritocracy* (New York: Farrar, Straus, and Giroux, 1999); John Carson, *The Measure of Merit: Talents, Intelligence, and Inequality in the French and American Republics, 1750–1940* (Princeton, N.J.: Princeton University Press, 2007). One other comparative study bears noting: Sheldon Rothblatt's admirably balanced *Education's Abiding Moral Dilemma: Merit and Worth in the Cross-Atlantic Democracies, 1800–2006* (Oxford: Symposium Books, 2007). Rothblatt's "worth" corresponds roughly to what is commonly referred to as character, a trait whose role in assessing merit has shrunk.

1. REPUBLIC OF MERIT

1. David Ramsay, *An Oration on the Advantages of American Independence* (Charleston, S.C., 1778), 2–3. Ramsay's view was widely echoed at the Founding. His fellow South Carolinian Charles Pinckney claimed in 1788 that since "mediocrity of fortune" was the leading feature of American national character, the American government "knows no distinctions but those of merit or talents." See Jonathan Elliot, ed., *The Debates in the Several State Conventions on the Adoption of the Federal Constitution*, 5 vols. (1888; New York: B. Franklin, 1974), 5:323.

2. David Ramsay, "The History of the American Revolution," in *American Political Writing during the Founding Era, 1760–1805*, 2 vols., ed. Charles S. Hyneman and Donald S. Lutz (Indianapolis: Liberty Press, 1983), 2:725.

3. Quoted in James L. Huston, *Securing the Fruits of Labor: The American Concept of Wealth Distribution* (Baton Rouge: Louisiana State University Press, 1998), 39.

4. An excerpt from a London magazine, reprinted in the *Maryland Gazette* (Oct. 11, 1745), gives a clear idea of the connotations of merit and its opposites. The article complained that Britain had failed to promote naval officers by merit, "abilities and experience alone," as evidenced by their "Character and Reputation." Rather, promotion had depended on adherence to Whig or Tory principles, on "connexion" to "Men of Interest

in a Borough" or to "Brothers or Relatives of Members of Parliament" or to "Members of Parliament themselves," or to the sons, acquaintances, or relatives of noblemen, or even to "Noblemen themselves."

5. Edward M. Spiers, *The Army and Society, 1815–1914* (London: Longman, 1980), 1–25; Eric Robson, "Purchase and Promotion in the British Army in the Eighteenth Century," *History*, n.s., 36 (1951), 57–72. In the Royal Navy an officer's appointment to lieutenant depended on his family connection; a promotion to higher ranks depended on the amount of influence he could command. See Michael Glover, *Wellington's Army in the Peninsula, 1808–1814* (New York: Hippocrene Books, 1977), 22.

6. Charles H. Firth, *Cromwell's Army*, 2nd ed. (London: Methuen, 1912), 40–42; Ian Gentles, *The New Model Army in England, Ireland, and Scotland, 1645–1653* (Oxford: Blackwell, 1992), 103–6.

7. The assumption that Purchase ensured an officer corps dominated by the sons of the landed gentry was probably erroneous but nevertheless deeply ingrained; see Hew Strachan, *Wellington's Legacy: The Reform of the British Army, 1830–1854* (Manchester, U.K.: Manchester University Press, 1984), 110–11.

8. Harold J. Perkin, *The Origins of Modern English Society, 1780–1880* (London: Routledge and K. Paul, 1972), 46.

9. Colin Bonwick, *English Radicals and the American Revolution* (Chapel Hill: University of North Carolina Press, 1977), 4–5, 19–22, 262.

10. James Burgh, *Political Disquisitions: An Enquiry into Public Errors, Defects, and Abuses*, 3 vols. (London, 1775; New York: Da Capo Press, 1971), 2:82, 85, 88.

11. John Trenchard and Thomas Gordon, *Cato's Letters*, ed. Ronald Harowy, 4 vols. in 2 (Indianapolis: Liberty Fund, 1995), 338–43.

12. Burgh, *Political Disquisitions*, 3:34.

13. J. E. Lendon, *Empire of Honour: The Art of Governance in the Roman World* (Oxford: Clarendon Press, 1997), 30–36.

14. Trenchard and Gordon, *Cato's Letters*, 384.

15. Eric Foner, *Tom Paine and Revolutionary America* (New York: Oxford University Press, 1976), 95–96, 217.

16. Richard Price, *Political Writings*, ed. D. O. Thomas (Cambridge: Cambridge University Press, 1991), 145. Radical Whiggery comes into sharper focus when it is contrasted with Adam Smith, who held it in contempt. Smith was sure that America, like all countries, had a "natural aristocracy" that Britain could manipulate to its advantage by giving the colonists seats in Parliament. This would turn their heads from the "paltry raffle of colony faction" to the "great prizes" to be won from the wheel of "the great state lottery of British politicks." Quoted in Donald Winch, *Adam Smith's Politics* (Cambridge: Cambridge University Press, 1977), 155.

17. See also Durand Echeverria, *Mirage in the West: A History of the French Image of American Society to 1815* (Princeton, N.J.: Princeton University Press, 1957), 70–74, 147–50; Michael Kraus, "America and the Utopian Ideal in the Eighteenth Century," *Mississippi Valley Historical Review* 22 (1936), 487–504.

18. Quoted in Tim Blanning, *The Pursuit of Glory: Europe, 1648–1815* (New York: Viking, 2007), 92.

19. Theodore Sedgwick, *Public and Private Economy*, 3 vols. (New York, 1836–39; Clifton, N.J.: A. M. Kelley, 1974), 1:234.

20. Quoted in Bernard Bailyn, *The Ordeal of Thomas Hutchinson* (Cambridge, Mass.: Harvard University Press, 1974), 180.

21. John A. Ragosta, *Wellspring of Liberty: How Virginia's Religious Dissenters Helped Win the American Revolution and Religious Liberty* (New York: Oxford University Press, 2010), 43–70.

22. H. J. Habakkuk, "England," in *The European Nobility in the Eighteenth Century*, ed. A. Goodwin (London: A. & C. Black, 1953), 1–3, 12; J. H. Plumb, *Sir Robert Walpole: The Making of a Statesman* (Boston: Houghton Mifflin, 1956), 6–15, 25–27; Hans-Eberhard Mueller, *Bureaucracy, Education, and Monopoly: Civil Service Reform in Prussia and England* (Berkeley: University of California Press, 1984), 228; Samuel Clark, *Class, State, and Status: The Rise of the State and Aristocratic Power in Western Europe* (Montreal: McGill University Press, 1995), 158–60, 203–5, 283.

23. Quoted in Bernard Bailyn, *The Origins of American Politics* (New York: Knopf, 1968), 131.

24. Quoted in ibid., 132. Studies of colonial leadership have given credence to Colden's generalization. See Jessica Kross, "'Patronage Most Ardently Sought': The New York Council, 1665–1775," in *Power and Status: Officeholding in Colonial America*, ed. Bruce Daniels (Middletown, Conn.: Wesleyan University Press, 1986), 231; Edward M. Cook Jr., *The Fathers of the Towns: Leadership and Community Structure in Eighteenth-Century New England* (Baltimore: Johns Hopkins University Press, 1976), 185–90; Joy Gilsdorf and Robert Gilsdorf, "Elites and Electorates: Some Plain Truths for Historians of Colonial America," in *Saints and Revolutionaries: Essays on Early American History*, ed. David Hall, John Murrin, and Thad Tate (New York: W. W. Norton, 1984), 235–39; Jack P. Greene, "The Growth of Political Stability: An Interpretation of Political Development in the Anglo-American Colonies, 1660–1760," in *The American Revolution: A Heritage of Change*, ed. John Parker and Carol Urness (Minneapolis: Associates of the James Bell Ford Library, 1975), 26–52.

25. James K. Martin, *Men in Rebellion: Higher Government Leaders and the Coming of the Revolution* (New Brunswick, N.J.: Rutgers University Press, 1973), 29–30.

26. J. H. Elliott, *Empires of the Atlantic World: Britain and Spain in America, 1492–1830* (New Haven, Conn.: Yale University Press, 2006), 163–64.

27. Quoted in Ronald K. Snell, "Ambitious of Honors and Places: The Magistracy of Hampshire County, Massachusetts, 1692–1750," in Daniels, *Power and Status,* 18–19.

28. Edmund Morgan, *American Slavery, American Freedom: The Ordeal of Colonial Virginia* (New York: W. W. Norton, 1975), 288–89.

29. Quoted in Snell, "Ambitious of Honors and Places," 18.

30. John Adams, "A Defence of the Constitutions of the United States of America," in *Works of John Adams*, 9 vols., ed. Charles F. Adams (Boston, 1851), 4:380, 382.

31. Pauline Maier, *The Old Revolutionaries: Political Lives in the Age of Samuel Adams* (New York: Knopf, 1982), 292.

32. Quoted in Samuel E. Morison, "Precedence at Harvard College in the Seventeenth Century," *Proceedings of the American Antiquarian Society*, n.s., 42 (1932), 375.

33. Benjamin Peirce, *A History of Harvard University* (Cambridge, Mass., 1833), 309.

34. Quoted in ibid., 309.

35. Quoted in Morison, "Precedence at Harvard College," 376.

36. The earliest studies of the system, the first by Franklin Bowditch Dexter in 1893 and the next by Samuel Eliot Morison in 1932, agreed that "dignity" passed primarily through the student's father rather than his mother, siblings, or other relatives. In his multivolume continuation of John Langdon Sibley's memorials of Harvard graduates, Clifford K. Shipton discovered another crucial piece of the puzzle: the prestige or standing of a father's civil office, not his wealth or social standing as such, determined precedence. Franklin Bowditch Dexter, "On Some Social Distinctions at Harvard and Yale before the American Revolution," *Proceedings, American Antiquarian Society*, n.s., 2 (1893–94), 38–39; see also Clifford K. Shipton, *Biographical Sketches of Those Who Attended Harvard College in the Classes 1756–1760* (vol. 14 of *Sibley's Harvard Graduates* [18 vols.]) (Boston, 1968), 533 (volumes in this series hereafter cited as *Sibley/Shipton Harvard Graduates*).

The civil office criterion explains why Samuel Adams, class of 1740, was ranked toward the top of his class while his cousin John was ranked in the middle third. Samuel's father, a mere maltster, held a commission as a justice of the peace, while John's father, although a church deacon and militia officer, did not.

37. Melyen's letter is printed in John L. Sibley, "Catalogues of Harvard University," *Proceedings of the Massachusetts Historical Society* 8 (1864–65), 35. See also *Sibley/Shipton Harvard Graduates*, 4:299.

38. *Sibley/Shipton Harvard Graduates*, 8:689.

39. Virginia DeJohn Anderson, *New England's Generation: The Great Migration and the Formation of Society and Culture in the Seventeenth Century* (Cambridge: Cambridge University Press, 1991), 95–96.

40. Winthrop, "A Modell of Christian Charity" (1630), in *Winthrop Papers*, vol. 2, ed. Marjorie Gutheim (Boston: Massachusetts Historical Society, 1931), 282.

41. Morison, "Precedence at Harvard College," 383–91.

42. *Sibley/Shipton Harvard Graduates*, 9:48. On prizes, see Peirce, *History of Harvard University*, 103.

43. See Dexter, "On Some Social Distinctions," 56; *Sibley/ Shipton Harvard Graduates*, 13:162, 10:418–19, and 8:314–16.

44. This case involved the rankings of two students, Samuel Phillips Jr., the future founder of Phillips Academy, Andover, and Daniel Murray. Phillips's father pressured the college's government to elevate his son a notch above Murray on the grounds that he held the more prestigious title of Justice of the Peace and of the Quorum; see Cook, *Fathers of the Towns*, 151; Frederick S. Allis Jr., "The Education of Samuel Phillips, Jr., Founder of Phillips Academy," *Publications of the Colonial Society of Massachusetts* 59 (1982), 46–47. Inasmuch as Phillips became a staunch Whig while the Murrays became Loyalists, this case may have been connected to the brewing Imperial Crisis.

45. The student, David Avery, was a former carpenter's apprentice who eventually became a missionary to the Indians; see Franklin B. Dexter, *Biographical Sketches of the Graduates of Yale College*, 6 vols. (New York: H. Holt, 1885–1912), 3:305–9.

46. Peirce, *History of Harvard University*, 309.

47. James Harrington, *The Commonwealth of Oceana; and, A System of Politics*, ed. J. G. A. Pocock (Cambridge: Cambridge University Press, 1992), 23; Pocock, "Machiavelli, Harrington, and English Political Ideologies in the Eighteenth Century," *William and Mary Quarterly*, 3 ser., 22 (1965), 548–83; Pocock, "The Classical Theory of Deference," *American Historical Review* 81 (1976), 516–19.

48. Richard Bushman, "Corruption and Power in Provincial America," Library of Congress Symposia on the American Revolution, *The Development of a Revolutionary Mentality* (Washington, D.C.: Library of Congress, 1972), 63–91.

49. Ellen E. Brennan, *Plural Office-Holding in Massachusetts, 1760–1780* (Chapel Hill: University of North Carolina Press, 1945), 25–35; Bailyn, *Ordeal of Thomas Hutchinson*, 48–54.

50. Quoted in Martin, *Men in Rebellion*, 38.

51. Morris to Horatio Gates, Oct. 30, 1776, in *Letters of Members of the Continental Congress*, 8 vols., ed. Edmund C. Burnett (Washington, D.C.: Carnegie Institution of Washington, 1921–36), 2:135; hereafter cited as *LMCC*.

52. John Witherspoon to Horatio Gates, Oct. 30, 1776, in Burnett, *LMCC*, 2:138; Willard M. Wallace, *Traitorous Hero: The Life and Fortunes of Benedict Arnold* (New York: Harper, 1954), 268.

53. W. W. Abbot, ed., *Papers of George Washington*, Revolutionary War Series, 20 vols. (Charlottesville: University Press of Virginia), 1:62 n. 1; Jonathan G. Rossie, *The Politics of Command in the American Revolution* (Syracuse, N.Y.: Syracuse University Press,

1975), 27; Louis C. Hatch, *The Administration of the American Revolutionary Army* (New York: Longmans, Green, 1904), 7.

54. Adams, *Works of John Adams*, 1:263.

55. Abbot, *Papers of George Washington*, Revolutionary War Series, 1:160.

56. Douglas Adair, "Fame and the Founding Fathers," in *Fame and the Founding Fathers: Essays by Douglas Adair*, ed. Trevor Colbourn (New York: W. W. Norton, 1974), 9.

57. J.R. Pole and Jack P. Greene have described an "expansive sense of self-worth" as a hallmark of colonial America; see Pole, *American Individualism and the Promise of Progress* (Oxford: Oxford University Press, 1990), 6, 8, 12–14, 17, and Greene, *Pursuits of Happiness: The Social Development of Early Modern British Colonies and the Formation of American Culture* (Chapel Hill: University of North Carolina Press, 1988), 195.

58. Quoted in George W. Greene, *The Life of Nathanael Greene*, 3 vols. (New York, 1871), 2:315; for background on this controversy, see Burnett, *LMCC*, 5, xxi–xxii.

59. Charles Royster, *A Revolutionary People at War* (Chapel Hill: University of North Carolina Press, 1979), 147. See also Caroline Cox, *A Proper Sense of Honor: Service and Sacrifice in George Washington's Army* (Chapel Hill: University of North Carolina Press, 2004).

60. Greene to John Adams, June 2, 1776, in Greene, *Life of Nathanael Greene*, 2:423.

61. Abbot, *Papers of George Washington*, Revolutionary War Series, 2:55; see also Rossie, *Politics of Command*, 27.

62. John Adams to George Washington, June 19, 1775, in Abbot, *Papers of George Washington*, Revolutionary War Series, 1:9, 12.

63. Burnett, *LMCC*, 2:261–62.

64. Ibid., 265.

65. Quoted in Wallace, *Traitorous Hero*, 126.

66. Quoted in Charles C. Sellers, *Benedict Arnold: The Proud Warrior* (New York: Minton and Balch, 1930), 87. For a full review of this controversy, see Willard S. Randall, *Benedict Arnold: Patriot and Traitor* (New York: William Morrow, 1990), 327–31. John Adams wrote in 1790 that whenever a junior officer is promoted over a senior, "it almost invariably happens that the superseded officer feels his heart broken by his disgrace." See Adams, "Discourses on Davila," in Adams, *Works of John Adams*, 6:247.

67. James Lovell to William Whipple, Aug. 11, 1777, in Burnett, *LMCC*, 2:445.

68. George Washington to the President of Congress, Dec. 23, 1777, in *The Writings of George Washington*, 14 vols., ed. Worthington C. Ford (New York, 1890), 6:260–62.

69. Washington to the President of Congress, Dec. 20, 1780, in ibid., 2:71.

70. Adams, "Defence of the Constitutions," in Adams, *Works of John Adams*, 4:581. On Adams's shifting views of natural aristocracy, see John R. Howe, *The Changing Political Thought of John Adams* (Princeton, N.J.: Princeton University Press, 1966), 141–42, 158–59.

71. Adam Smith, *The Theory of Moral Sentiments*, ed. D. D. Raphael and A.L. Macfie (Oxford: Clarendon Press, 1975), 50–58.

72. Adams, "Discourses on Davila," in Adams, *Works of John Adams*, 6:250, 253.

73. On the eve of reform in 1832, 658 members sat in the House of Commons, of whom 513, a number that had not changed for 150 years, sat for England and Wales; see Edward Porritt, *The Unreformed House of Commons* (1903; New York: A. M. Kelley, 1963), 1:86.

74. Elliot, *Debates in the Several State Conventions*, 2:246, 277. Smith fits Saul Cornell's description of the "plebeian" antifederalist, more worried about rule by a homegrown "natural aristocracy" than concentration of excessive power in the federal government; see Cornell, "Aristocracy Assailed: The Ideology of Backcountry Anti-Federalism," *Journal of American History* 76 (1990), 1148–72.

75. Smith's language, echoed by other antifederalists, drew on the English radical Whigs' distrust of "the great." *Cato's Letters* formed a favorite mine for citations by antifederalists with this outlook. See "An Address to the New Hampshire Ratifying Convention, Feb., 1788," in *The Complete Anti-Federalist*, 7 vols., ed. Herbert J. Storing (Chicago: University of Chicago Press, 1981), 4:244–45 n. 6.

76. Elliot, *Debates in the Several State Conventions*, 2:256.

77. James T. Flexner, *The Young Hamilton* (Boston: Little, Brown, 1978), 21.

78. Charles Page Smith, *James Wilson: Founding Father, 1742–1798* (Chapel Hill: University of North Carolina Press, 1956), 159–68.

79. Max Farrand, ed., *Records of the Federal Convention of 1787*, rev. ed., 4 vols. (New Haven, Conn.: Yale University Press, 1937), 1:376.

80. Ibid., 1:302.

81. Ibid., 1:375, 380. Citing the younger William Pitt, who had become prime minister in 1783 at age 24, Wilson even opposed a motion to fix the minimum age for members of the House of Representatives at 25.

82. Farrand, *Records*, 1:285, 381–82.

83. Wilson, "Lectures on Law," in *The Works of James Wilson*, 2 vols., ed. Robert G. McCloskey (Cambridge, Mass.: Harvard University Press, 1967), 2:593.

84. Wilson, "Lectures on Law," 595. "The wreath of honour," Wilson wrote, should never be removed from those temples "around which it has been meritoriously placed." Quoted in Jean-Marc Pascal, *The Political Ideas of James Wilson, 1742–1798* (New York: Garland, 1991), 109. Wilson's language ("the love of reputation and the fear of dishonour are, by the all gracious Author of our existence, implanted in our breasts for purposes the most beneficent and wise") often echoed that of Adam Smith and John Adams, but without the conclusion that the multitude applauded the wrong qualities; that might happen in Europe but not in the American republic. See Wilson, "On the Natural Rights of Individuals," in McCloskey, *Works of James Wilson*, 2:593.

85. Farrand, *Records*, 2:284. Mason was scarcely a champion of popular government, but he was angered by the insistence of Men of Merit like Charles Pinckney, a cousin of General Charles C. Pinckney, on the need for honors and emoluments attached to office, a stance that Mason construed as evidence of their self-interest and hence, in republican terms, lack of virtue.

86. Mason would have gone further by making congressmen ineligible for state and federal offices during the duration of their terms; see Robert A. Rutland, ed., *The Papers of George Mason, 1725–1792*, 3 vols. (Chapel Hill: University of North Carolina Press, 1970), 3:913.

87. See the House debate over the removal power on June 17, 1789, in *Annals of the Congress of the United States*, 1st Congress, 1789–91, 1:458–59.

88. Leonard D. White, *The Federalists: A Study in Administrative History* (New York: Macmillan, 1948), 19–25.

89. Cassius [Aedanus Burke], *Considerations on the Society or Order of the Cincinnati* (Philadelphia, 1783), 3. On Burke's career, see John C. Meleney, *The Life of Aedanus Burke: Revolutionary Republican in Post-revolutionary South Carolina* (Columbia: University of South Carolina Press, 1989).

90. Burke, *Considerations on the Society*, 9–10.

91. Elliot, *Debates in the Several State Conventions*, 2:246, 277.

92. Cathy D. Matson and Peter S. Onuf, *A Union of Interests: Political and Economic Thought in Revolutionary America* (Lawrence: University Press of Kansas, 1990), 155.

93. After 1810 the federal government occasionally administered examinations to assess the competence of army and navy surgeons and officers, but no one appears even to have thought of using examinations to select civilian employees of the federal

government; see Leonard D. White, *The Jeffersonians: A Study in Administrative History, 1801–1829* (New York: Macmillan, 1951), 363–64.

94. John M. Murrin, "Escaping Perfidious Albion: Federalism, Fear of Aristocracy, and the Democratization of Corruption in Postrevolutionary America," in *Virtue, Corruption, and Self-Interest: Political Values in the Eighteenth Century*, ed. Richard K. Matthews (Bethlehem, Pa.: Lehigh University Press, 1994), 103–47.

95. Farrand, *Records*, 1:388. This was a slap at Mason, who, elected to the Virginia House in 1758, tired of the legislative routine after two terms and returned to private life.

96. This was consistent with views Madison expressed during the federal convention; see Farrand, *Records*, 1:136. It was also consistent with the position he took in *The Federalist* No. 10. Although his defense of a large republic on the grounds that it would multiply the number of interests has often been (mis)interpreted as a justification of a kind of interest-group liberalism in which multiple factions merely canceled each other out, Madison consistently associated large electoral districts (more likely in a large than in a small republic) with facilitating the election of disinterested First Characters whose conspicuous reputations would free them from dependence on small factions. He wrote in No. 10 that in a large republic "the suffrages of the people being more free, will be more likely to center on men who possess the most attractive merit."

97. Merrill Jensen, ed., *Documentary History of the First Federal Elections*, 4 vols. (Madison: University of Wisconsin Press, 1976), 1:302–3 (hereafter cited as *DHFFE*); see also Saul Cornell, *The Other Founders: Anti-Federalism and the Dissenting Tradition in America, 1788–1828* (Chapel Hill: University of North Carolina Press, 1999), 148. Madison earlier had defended the small size of the House of Representatives on the same ground; see Gary J. Kornblith and John Murrin, "The Making and Unmaking of an American Ruling Class," in *Beyond the American Revolution: Explorations in the History of American Radicalism*, ed. Alfred F. Young (DeKalb: Northern Illinois University Press, 1993), 56; David F. Epstein, *Political Theory of the Federalist* (Chicago: University of Chicago Press, 1984), 96.

98. *DHFFE*, 1:246, 274, 469; 2:125; 3:209, 210, 232–33. Federalists used similar arguments to defend the election of U.S. senators by state legislatures; see *DHFFE*, 2:125.

2. MERIT AND THE CULTURE OF PUBLIC LIFE

1. David Ramsay, *An Oration on the Advantages of American Independence* (Charleston, S.C., 1778), 2. Contemporaries recognized Ramsay's address as a major document of the Revolution; Hezekiah Niles reprinted it in his *Principles and Acts of the Revolution in America* (Boston, 1822).

2. Ronald P. Formisano, *The Transformation of Political Culture: Massachusetts Parties, 1790s–1840s* (New York: Oxford University Press, 1983), 11–14.

3. Catullus, No. III, Sept. 29, 1792, in *Selected Writings of Alexander Hamilton*, ed. Morton J. Frisch (Washington, D.C.: American Enterprise Institute, 1985), 379.

4. Joanne B. Freeman, *Affairs of Honor: National Parties in the New Republic* (New Haven, Conn.: Yale University Press, 2001), 69–74; Ron Chernow, *Alexander Hamilton* (New York: Penguin, 2005), 529–30.

5. Jon E. Lendon, *Empire of Honour: The Art of Governance in the Roman World* (Oxford: Clarendon Press, 1997), 36.

6. Andrew S. Trees, *The Founding Fathers and the Politics of Character* (Princeton, N.J.: Princeton University Press, 2004), 47–49.

7. Harold C. Syrett, *Papers of Alexander Hamilton*, 27 vols. (New York: Columbia University Press, 1961–87), 3:139.

8. David G. Allen et al., eds., *Diary of John Quincy Adams*, 2 vols. (Cambridge, Mass.: Harvard University Press, 1981), 2:212, 218.

9. Quoted in Carl Prince, *The Federalists and the Origins of the U.S. Civil Service* (New York: New York University Press, 1977), 4.

10. [Noah Webster], *The Revolution in France, Considered in Respect to Its Effects* (New York, 1794), 49–50.

11. Syrett, *Papers of Alexander Hamilton*, 22:87–146. See also Robert Gough, "Officering the American Army, 1798," *William and Mary Quarterly*, 3 ser., 43 (1986), 460–71.

12. Syrett, *Papers of Alexander Hamilton*, 22:92–93, 125–29.

13. Ibid., 22:90–93.

14. Ibid., 22:99.

15. James Madison to Thomas Jefferson, Oct. 25, 1797, in *The Republic of Letters: The Correspondence between Thomas Jefferson and James Madison, 1776–1826*, 3 vols., ed. James Morton Smith (New York: W. W. Norton, 1995), 2:993–94.

16. He made a special plea for his brother-in-law, Rensselaer Schuyler, who sought a captaincy of cavalry. After confessing to McHenry that Schuyler had committed "imprudences which have been painful to his father" (former major general Philip Schuyler), Hamilton justified his recommendation on the ground that the father needed consolation; see Syrett, *Papers of Alexander Hamilton*, 22:88.

17. Hans Rosenberg, *Bureaucracy, Aristocracy, and Autocracy: The Prussian Experience, 1660–1815* (Cambridge, Mass.: Harvard University Press, 1958), 213–21; Hans-Eberhard Mueller, *Bureaucracy, Education, and Monopoly: Civil Service Reform in Prussia and England* (Berkeley: University of California Press, 1984), 228. Provincial aristocrats often supported examinations in order to trim the power of courtiers; see Dominic Lieven, *The Aristocracy in Europe, 1815–1914* (New York: Columbia University Press, 1992), 1–4. In turn, educational requirements in the civil service drove the differentiation of German educational institutions; see Detlef K. Müller, "Systemization: The Case of German Secondary Education," in *The Rise of the Modern Educational System: Structural Change and Social Reproduction, 1870–1920*, ed. Detlef K. Müller, Fritz Ringer, and Brian Simon (Cambridge: Cambridge University Press, 1987), 22–24. The dependence of the portion of the German middle class on civil service employment obtained through educational credentials led Germans to distinguish this *Bildungsbürgertum*, a group with no real counterpart in the United States, from the economic middle class, the *Wirtschaftsbürgertum*; see David Blackbourn, "The German Bourgeoisie: An Introduction," in *The German Bourgeoisie: Essays on the Social History of the German Middle Class from the Late Eighteenth to the Early Twentieth Century*, ed. Blackbourn and Richard J. Evans (London: Routledge, 1991), 4–5.

18. On Paterson, see John E. O'Connor, *William Paterson: Lawyer and Statesman, 1745–1806* (New Brunswick, N.J.: Rutgers University Press, 1979), 51.

19. James T. Flexner, *Young Hamilton* (Boston: Little, Brown, 1978), 26.

20. Hamilton to James Bayard, Jan. 16, 1801, in *Alexander Hamilton and Thomas Jefferson*, ed. Frederick C. Prescott (New York: American Book Co., 1934), 167.

21. Joel Barlow, *Advice to the Privileged Orders in the Several States of Europe* (1792; Ithaca: Cornell University Press, 1956), 54.

22. Carl Prince, "The Passing of the Aristocracy: Jefferson's Removal of the Federalists, 1801–1805," *Journal of American History* 57 (1970), 563–75.

23. Lester J. Cappon, ed., *The Adams-Jefferson Letters*, 2 vols. (Chapel Hill: University of North Carolina Press, 1959), 2:338, 398–99.

24. Cappon, *Adams-Jefferson Letters*, 2:372.

25. Adams, "Discourses on Davila," in *Works of John Adams*, 9 vols., ed. Charles F. Adams (Boston, 1851), 6:244. Adams added these words to his annotated copy of "Davila" in 1812.

26. For Madison's early ruminations about public opinion, see Colleen A. Sheehan, "The Politics of Public Opinion: James Madison's 'Notes on Government,'" *William and Mary Quarterly*, 3 ser., 49 (1992), 609–27.

27. Tunis Wortman, *A Treatise Concerning Political Enquiry and the Liberty of the Press* (1800; New York: Da Capo, 1970), 66, 121.

28. John Taylor, *An Inquiry into the Principles and Policy of the Government of the United States*, ed. Roy F. Nichols (New Haven, Conn.: Yale University Press, 1950), 58.

29. Ibid.

30. John M. Murrin, "Escaping Perfidious Albion: Federalism, Fear of Aristocracy, and the Democratization of Corruption in Postrevolutionary America," in *Virtue, Corruption, and Self-Interest: Political Values in the Eighteenth Century*, ed. Richard K. Matthews (Bethlehem, Pa.: Lehigh University Press, 1994), 103–47.

31. Steven C. Bullock, *Revolutionary Brotherhood: Freemasonry and the Transformation of the American Social Order, 1780–1840* (Chapel Hill: University of North Carolina Press, 1996), 108; see also Dorothy A. Lipson, *Freemasonry in Federalist Connecticut* (Princeton, N.J.: Princeton University Press, 1977), 41, 232.

32. Quoted in Bullock, *Revolutionary Brotherhood*, 149.

33. Quoted in Michael F. Holt, *Political Parties in America: Political Development from the Age of Jackson to the Age of Lincoln* (Baton Rouge: Louisiana State University Press, 1992), 96.

34. R. Kent Newmyer, *Supreme Court Justice Joseph Story: Statesman of the Old Republic* (Chapel Hill: University of North Carolina Press, 1985), 30–31.

35. Christopher McKee, *A Gentlemanly and Honorable Profession: The Creation of the U.S. Naval Officer Corps, 1794–1815* (Annapolis, Md.: Naval Institute Press, 1991), 300.

36. S. Putnam Waldo, *The Life and Character of Stephen Decatur*, rev. ed. (Middletown, Conn., 1821), 290–91. For precursors of this conception of merit in antiquity, see Arthur W.H. Adkins, *Merit and Responsibility: A Study in Greek Values* (Chicago: University of Chicago Press, 1975), 32–35, 40, 332.

37. Gaines was promoted to major general three weeks after Scott, but Scott's promotion was a brevet (temporary) promotion. During the course of the controversy each man challenged the other to a duel. On the death of General-in-Chief Jacob Brown, an exasperated John Quincy Adams passed over both men to elevate a colonel, Alexander Macomb, whereupon Scott announced that he would not be bound by Macomb's orders and sought to have him arrested.

38. William B. Skelton, *An American Profession of Arms: The Army Officer Corps, 1784–1861* (Lawrence: University Press of Kansas, 1992), 200, 34–67.

39. Dorothy B. Goebel, *William Henry Harrison: A Political Biography* (Indianapolis: Indiana Library and Historical Society, 1926), 137–39. For more examples of this agile careerism in the army and its sometimes catastrophic effect on military operations, see Robert S. Quimby, *The U.S. Army in the War of 1812* (East Lansing: Michigan State University Press, 1997), 19–22, 25–26, 37–47.

40. Daniel R. Coquilette, "Justinian in Braintree: John Adams, Civilian Learning, and Legal Elitism, 1758–1775," *Publications of the Colonial Society of Massachusetts* 62 (1984), 362–63, 366, 376.

41. John Morgan, *A Discourse upon the Institution of Medical Schools in America* (Philadelphia, 1765).

42. Gerald Gawalt, "Sources of Anti-lawyer Sentiment in Massachusetts, 1740–1840," *American Journal of Legal History* 14 (1970), 285.

43. For example, as late as 1770 only 20 percent of Yale graduates entered the legal profession; by 1800 more than half did; see Christopher Grasso, *A Speaking Aristocracy: Transforming Public Discourse in Eighteenth-Century Connecticut* (Chapel Hill: University of North Carolina Press, 1999), 435.

44. Eric Christianson, "The Emergence of Medical Communities in Massachusetts, 1790–1794: The Demographic Factors," *Bulletin of the History of Medicine* 54 (1980), 69;

Thomas N. Bonner, *Becoming a Physician: Medical Education in Great Britain, France, Germany, and the United States, 1750–1945* (New York: Oxford University Press, 1995), 175.

45. Quoted in Gawalt, "Sources of Anti-lawyer Sentiment," 291. On the status of European (but not British) lawyers as government officers, see Blackbourn, "German Bourgeoisie," 5.

46. Donald M. Scott, "The Popular Lecture and the Creation of the Public in Mid-Nineteenth-Century America," *Journal of American History* 66 (1980), 798.

47. Daniel H. Calhoun, *Professional Lives in America: Structure and Aspiration, 1750–1850* (Cambridge, Mass.: Harvard University Press, 1965), 56.

48. William G. Rothstein, *American Medical Schools and the Practice of Medicine: A History* (New York: Oxford University Press, 1987), 49.

49. Emmet F. Horine, *Daniel Drake (1785–1852): Pioneer Physician of the Midwest* (Philadelphia: University of Pennsylvania Press, 1961), chaps. 4–12.

50. Ibid., 129–31.

51. Joseph F. Kett, *The Formation of the American Medical Profession: The Role of Institutions, 1780–1860* (New Haven, Conn.: Yale University Press, 1968), 86–94.

52. Peter D. Hall, "The Social Foundations of Professional Credibility: Linking the Medical Profession to Higher Education in Connecticut and Massachusetts, 1700–1830," in *The Authority of Experts: Studies in Theory and History*, ed. Thomas L. Haskell (Bloomington: Indiana University Press, 1984), 118.

53. Peter Karsten, *The Naval Aristocracy: The Golden Age of Annapolis and the Emergence of American Navalism* (New York: Free Press, 1972), 4–6.

54. At the Founding, appointments rather than removals had seemed the likeliest route to illicit executive influence on legislatures, though Hamilton (*The Federalist*, No. 76) was typical in pointing to the Constitution's Article I, Section 6, as a safeguard.

55. Jefferson's removals were notably more extensive than he implied by calling them "moderate." See Carl Prince, "The Passing of an Era: Jefferson's Removals of the Federalists," *Journal of American History* 57 (1970), 563–75.

56. [Thomas Hart Benton], *Thirty Years' View, or a History of the Working of American Government for Thirty Years, from 1820 to 1850*, 2 vols. (New York, 1854), 1:161.

57. Ibid.

58. Ibid., 80–82.

59. Cited in Leonard D. White, *The Jeffersonians: A Study in Administrative History, 1801–1829* (New York: Free Press, 1951), 388. Madison and Quincy Adams responded in similar terms to the law (389). See also Madison to Jefferson, Dec. 10, 1820, in Smith, *Republic of Letters*, 3:1826. Cormorants provided public men with their favorite metaphor for office seekers; see Allan Nevins, ed., *The Diary of John Quincy Adams, 1794–1845* (New York: Longmans, Green, 1928), 234.

60. Harry Ammon, *James Monroe: The Quest for National Identity* (Charlottesville: University Press of Virginia, 1990), 494–95.

61. Jackson to Waightstill Avery, Aug. 12, 1788, in *Correspondence of Andrew Jackson*, 7 vols., ed. John S. Bassett (Washington, D.C.: Carnegie Institution of Washington, 1926–35), 1:5.

62. On Jackson's career in the Tennessee militia, see Bassett, *Correspondence of Andrew Jackson*, 1:xii–xiii.

63. Jackson to William Cocke, Nov. 9, 1797, in ibid., 1:40.

64. Jackson to Samuel Swartwout, Feb. 22, 1825, in Bassett, *Correspondence of Andrew Jackson*, 3:289. On the ideal of the president or presidential candidate as a Mute Tribune of the people, never overtly seeking office, see M. J. Heale, *The Presidential Quest: Candidates and Images in American Culture, 1787–1812* (London: Longman, 1982), 9–23.

65. Sevier to Jackson, May 8, 1797, in Bassett, *Correspondence of Andrew Jackson*, 1:31.

66. For a now classic description of sponsored mobility, see Ralph Turner, "Sponsored and Contest Mobility and the School System," *American Sociological Review* 25 (1960), 855–67.

67. Robert V. Remini, *Andrew Jackson: Volume 2, The Course of American Freedom, 1822–1832* (Baltimore: Johns Hopkins University Press, 1981), 79.

68. Michael Wallace, "Changing Conceptions of Party in the United States: New York, 1815–1828," *American Historical Review* 74 (1968), 454, 458 n. 12. In 1826 a writer in the *Albany Argus,* the organ of Van Buren's Regency, conceded that the "fatal rock" on which the democratic elements in New York had foundered was "an undue attachment to individuals." When Van Buren thought of notables who used parties as tools for personal ambition, De Witt Clinton's name sprang first to his mind; Clinton, nominally a Republican, had run for the presidency in 1812 essentially as a Federalist.

69. Paul R. Frothingham, *Edward Everett: Orator and Statesman* (Boston: Houghton Mifflin, 1925), 10–23.

70. Everett to McLean, Oct. 7, 1828, in "Use of Patronage in Elections," ed. Worthington C. Ford, *Proceedings of the Massachusetts Historical Society*, 3 ser., 1 (1907–8), 391.

71. Ibid., 361.

72. Ibid., 376.

73. Richard John, *Spreading the News: The American Postal System from Franklin to Morse* (Cambridge, Mass.: Harvard University Press, 1995), 211.

74. Ibid., 65–69.

75. Daniel Webster, "The Appointing and Removing Power," in Webster, *The Writings and Speeches of Daniel Webster*, 16 vols. (Boston: Little, Brown, 1903), 7:184.

76. Quoted in Robert V. Remini, "Election of 1832," in *History of American Presidential Elections, 1789–1968*, ed. Arthur M. Schlesinger Jr. (New York: McGraw-Hill, 1971), 559.

77. Webster, "Appointing and Removing Power," 184.

78. Ibid. In this speech Webster also called for repeal of the Tenure of Office of Act of 1820, a good illustration of how Jackson's removals shifted attention to executive despotism.

79. [Benton], *Thirty Years' View*, 1:81–83.

80. Preston Farrar to Henry Clay, Feb. 19, 1841, in *Papers of Henry Clay*, ed. Robert Seager II (Lexington: University Press of Kentucky, 1988), 9:501.

81. Milo M. Quaife, ed., *The Diary of James K. Polk during His Presidency, 1845 to 1849*, 4 vols. (Chicago, 1910; New York: Kraus Reprint, 1970), 2:201–2, 279 n. 1, 280–81, 314–15, 339, 3:136.

82. "Excerpt from a Speech by John Bell, 1835," in Schlesinger, *History of American Presidential Elections*, 4:639.

83. "Introductory," *American Review: A Whig Journal of Politics* 1 (1845), 8–9. See also Willie Mangum's comments on Van Buren cited by M. J. Heale, *The Making of American Politics, 1750–1850* (London: Longman, 1977), 160.

84. William Holland, *The Life and Opinions of Martin Van Buren, Vice-President of the United States* (Hartford, Conn., 1835), 80.

85. In 1849 a conservative analyst lamented that few Americans any longer recognized that men of "vast intellect and upright character" had a "divine right" to the presidency. See "Grimke on Free Institutions," *North American Review*, n.s., 69, no. 145 (1849), 453.

86. Leonard D. White, *The Jacksonians: A Study in Administrative History, 1829–1861* (New York: Macmillan, 1954), 350.

87. Carl R. Fish, *The Civil Service and the Patronage* (1904; New York: Russell and Russell, 1963), 233.

88. White, *Jacksonians*, 349–51; see also John Bell to Gov. Letcher, Jan. 13, 1841, in *The Life of John J. Crittenden*, ed. Chapman Coleman (1871; New York: Da Capo, 1970), 13.

89. Lilian Handlin, *George Bancroft: The Intellectual as Democrat* (New York: Harper and Row, 1984), 206–7. As McKee has observed, the tendency of civilians (like Bancroft) to argue for merit-based promotion and for naval officers to prefer seniority went back to the 1790s; see McKee, *Gentlemanly and Honorable Profession*, 276–77.

90. Bassett, *Correspondence of Andrew Jackson*, 3:xi.

91. Calhoun, *Professional Lives in America*, 56, 26.

92. The declining frequency of conflicts over filling medical professorships can be traced in Otto Juettner, *Daniel Drake and His Followers: Historical and Biographical Sketches* (Cincinnati: Harvey Publishing Co., 1909).

93. Skelton, *American Profession of Arms*, 195–96.

3. SMALL WORLDS

1. Philip H. Burch Jr., *Elites in American History: The Federalist Years to the Civil War*, 3 vols. (New York: Holmes and Meier, 1981), 1:240–41. Of major cabinet and diplomatic officers from 1789 to 1861, 66.7 percent were college graduates and another 9.5 percent had some college education. There were fluctuations from administration to administration in the proportion of college graduates holding high places, but no clear trend over time. The administration with the highest percentage of college graduates was that of Franklin Pierce (1853–57, 88.9 percent), a proportion even higher than the average for the Federalist presidents, Washington and Adams (73.8 percent). For data on the extremely high proportion of graduates of the College of New Jersey who held prominent positions in public life, see James McLachlan, *Princetonians, 1748–1768: A Biographical Directory* (Princeton, N.J.: Princeton University Press, 1976), 673–75; John Maclean, *A History of the College of New Jersey, from Its Origin in 1748 to the Commencement of 1854*, 2 vols. (Philadelphia, 1877), 1:357–63. See also Frank E. Kobon, "The Educational Levels of the Jacksonians," *History of Education Quarterly* 7 (1967), 515–20.

2. Charles A. McCaughey, "The Transformation of American Academic Life, 1821–1892," *Perspectives in American History* 8 (1974), 263–64.

3. Edmund S. Morgan, *The Gentle Puritan: A Life of Ezra Stiles* (New Haven, Conn.: Yale University Press, 1962), 384; see also Charles A. Bristed, *Five Years in an English University*, 2nd ed. (New York, 1852), 386.

4. Franklin B. Dexter, ed., *The Literary Diary of Ezra Stiles*, 3 vols. (New York: C. Scribner's Sons, 1901), 3:227 n. 1, 403. Mary L. Smallwood scoured the records of the colonial colleges and could find no similar grading system; see Smallwood, *An Historical Study of Examinations and Grading Systems in Early American Universities* (Cambridge, Mass.: Harvard University Press, 1935). Nor could she find evidence of a similar system between 1785 and 1813, when Yale began a system of numerical marks. In all of the colleges seniors were orally examined before graduation, but this "senior examination" was widely derided as a "solemn farce." See Edward P. Cheyney, *History of the University of Pennsylvania, 1740–1940* (Philadelphia: University of Pennsylvania Press, 1940), 86; Morgan, *Gentle Puritan*, 93.

5. Josiah Quincy, *The History of Harvard University*, 2 vols. (Cambridge, Mass., 1840; New York: Arno Press, 1977), 2:280.

6. Yale introduced quarterly oral examinations for all classes in 1761, the same year in which it first instituted sanctions for "grossly defective" students. See Brooks M. Kelley, *Yale: A History* (New Haven, Conn.: Yale University Press, 1974), 71. A comparable system of quarterly examinations began at Princeton in 1762. See also David Humphrey, *From King's College to Columbia, 1746–1800* (New York: Columbia University Press, 1978), 162, 303–4; Walter C. Bronson, *The History of Brown University, 1764–1914* (Providence, R.I.: The University, 1914), 103.

7. Sheldon S. Cohen "The Turkish Tyranny," *New England Quarterly* 47 (1974), 564–83.

8. Quoted in Henry Adams, "Harvard College, 1786, 1787," in Henry Adams, *Historical Essays (1891)* (New York: Hildesheim, 1973), 101.

9. Quoted in Adams, "Harvard College," 97.

10. *Autobiography of William H. Seward, from 1801 to 1834; with a Memoir of Him by Frederick H. Seward* (New York, 1877), 34.

11. Maclean, *History of the College of New Jersey*, 1:334, 2:161.

12. Theodore R. Crane, *Francis Wayland: Political Economist and Educator* (Providence, R.I.: Brown University Press, 1962), 34–35. When Wayland surveyed the American "collegiate system" in 1842, he was struck by the near absence of such rewards; see Francis Wayland, *Thoughts on the Present Collegiate System in the United States* (Boston, 1842; New York: Arno, 1969), 95–96. Some prize competitions persisted in the colleges. For example, Yale continued to award its Berkeley prizes for excellence in Latin, but these were long open only to resident graduates; by 1839, when Charles Astor Bristed sought to win one, they had been opened to undergraduates, but Bristed noted that only one student presented himself for the competition; see Bristed, *Five Years in an English University*, 376–77.

13. [William Austin], *Strictures on Harvard University, by a Senior* (Boston, 1798), 17.

14. M. Halsey Thomas, ed., *The Diary of Samuel Sewall, 1674–1729*, 2 vols. (New York: Farrar, Straus and Giroux, 1973), 2:525, 568–69, 693, 720, 924. A surviving commencement sheet indicates that a master's candidate gave the valedictory in 1730; see John Noble, "An Old Harvard Commencement Performance," *Publications of the Colonial Society of Massachusetts* 6 (1899–1900), 275.

15. As late as 1821 Yale's enrollment included thirty-one resident graduates, but the number dropped to four in 1826–27 and to virtually none in the 1830s; see George W. Pierson, *A Yale Book of Numbers: Historical Statistics of the College and University, 1702–1976* (New Haven, Conn.: Yale University Press, 1983), 5.

16. James McLachlan, "The *Choice of Hercules*: American Student Societies in the Early Nineteenth Century," in *The University in Society*, 2 vols., ed. Lawrence Stone (Princeton, N.J.: Princeton University Press, 1974), 2:473–89.

17. Samuel L. Knapp, *American Cultural History, 1607–1829* (originally titled *Lectures on American Literature* [New York, 1829]; Gainesville, Fla.: Scholars' Facsimiles and Reprints, 1961), 113, 163–88, 207–8.

18. "Harvard College Records, II," *Publications of the Colonial Society of Massachusetts* 16 (1925), 868; Benjamin Peirce, *History of Harvard University* (Boston, 1833), 241–44; Morgan, *Gentle Puritan*, 364.

19. For Harvard's equivalent of these societies, see Sheldon Cohen, "Harvard College on the Eve of the American Revolution," *Publications of the Colonial Society of Massachusetts* 59 (1982), 178.

20. [Anson D. Morse], *Student Life at Amherst College* (Amherst, Mass., 1871), 18–21. In 1828 Amherst College's Athenian Society owned twelve hundred volumes, a remarkable number given that the college had been founded only three years before. Morse found the Amherst literary societies' expenditures on books for their libraries "almost incredible."

21. Adams, "Harvard College," 113. Syllogistics also declined at Yale and for the same reason: they afforded little opportunity for students to display their learning and eloquence; see Christopher Grasso, *A Speaking Aristocracy: Transforming Public Discourse in Eighteenth-Century Connecticut* (Chapel Hill: University of North Carolina Press, 1999), 403.

22. Adams, "Harvard College," 113; David G. Allen et al., eds., *Diary of John Quincy Adams*, 2 vols. (Cambridge, Mass.: Harvard University Press, 1981), 2:37. Quincy Adams described the "good parts" as two English orations and two poems. Poems do not appear to have had a fixed position in the hierarchy, and a commencement might well pass without one.

23. Peirce, *History of Harvard University*, 241–43; "Harvard College Records, II," 868. The pressure for exhibitions at Harvard came from its Overseers, who introduced them in 1761 to excite "an emulation to excel in eloquence and oratorical attainment" and to render the scholars "ornaments to the College and an honor to their Country." Previously, the word "exhibition" had been employed at Harvard exclusively to signify a cash award on the basis of need or a student's kinship to the donor to help the student defray expenses; thereafter, it signified a public oratorical performance, staged biennially or quarterly, by sophomores, juniors, and seniors.

24. Quoted in Kemp P. Battle, *History of the University of North Carolina, 1789–1868*, vol. 1 (Raleigh, N.C.: Edwards and Broughton, 1907), 432. This quotation was from a newspaper account of North Carolina's 1837 commencement.

25. Quoted in William Nelson, ed., *Documents Relating to the Colonial History of the State of New Jersey*, 33 vols., 1 ser., 26 (1904): 524. Abundant evidence points to the attendance of the high and mighty at commencements. For example, Ezra Stiles recorded the presence of Connecticut's governor and four congressmen at Yale's 1791 commencement; see Dexter, *Literary Diary of Ezra Stiles*, 3:402; Grasso, *Speaking Aristocracy*, 408. Commencements at the University of Georgia became virtual political caucuses, where "governors were made and unmade, political principles concocted and published, and animosities aroused and developed, which sometimes boded no good for the innocent by-standing University"; see E. Merton Coulter, *College Life in the Old South, as Seen at the University of Georgia* (Athens, Ga., 1928), 144. The political value of commencements was not lost on even fledgling colleges; Dickinson College's trustees compelled the college to stage a commencement in 1787 even though it had held classes for less than a year; see Charles C. Sellers, *Dickinson College: A History* (Middletown, Conn.: Wesleyan University Press, 1973), 15–16.

26. Allen, *Diary of John Quincy Adams*, 2:265 n. 9. This quotation is from the *Massachusetts Centinel* of July 21, 1787. The *Boston Gazette*'s account (July 23) of the commencement was even more direct in its attack on John Adams, observing that "it is truly singular to see certain people whose whole importance has been created by the partiality of their countrymen, affect to decry the merits of a democracy because forsooth they cannot be noblemen."

27. Joseph F. Kett, *The Pursuit of Knowledge under Difficulties: From Self-Improvement to Adult Education in America, 1750–1990* (Stanford, Calif.: Stanford University Press, 1994), 18.

28. Charles Irons, "Public Men and Public Universities: State Schools in the Antebellum South" (M.A. thesis, University of Virginia, 1999), 15; R. D. W. Connor, comp., *A Documentary History of the University of North Carolina, 1776–1799*, 2 vols. (Chapel Hill: University of North Carolina Press, 1957), 2:3, 12, 17–18, 32, 35–36, 109–10.

29. Lowell H. Harrison, "A Young Kentuckian at Princeton, 1806–1810: Joseph Cabell Breckenridge," *Filson Club Historical Quarterly* 38 (1964), 296. Joseph's father, John Breckenridge, was attorney general under Jefferson.

30. S. Weir Mitchell, ed., "Historical Notes of Dr. Benjamin Rush, 1777," *Pennsylvania Magazine of History and Biography* 27 (1903), 140.

31. Thomas J. Wertenbaker, *Princeton, 1746–1896* (Princeton, N.J.: Princeton University Press, 1896), 207–8. The plan foundered because the more numerous Cliosophics voted themselves all the desirable parts.

32. Samuel Tyler, *Memoir of Roger Brooke Taney, LL.D.* (Boston, 1872), 49–50.

33. M[aximilian] La Borde, *History of South Carolina College* (Philadelphia, 1874), 33.

34. Philip A. Bruce, *History of the University of Virginia*, 5 vols. (New York: Macmillan, 1920), 2:142–43.

35. Battle, *History of the University of North Carolina*, 468.

36. Allen, *Diary of John Quincy Adams*, 2:136 n. 1, 205, 220–21.

37. Quoted in Samuel E. Morison, *Harvard College in the Seventeenth Century*, 2 vols. (Cambridge, Mass.: Harvard University Press, 1936), 2:374.

38. Henry D. Sheldon, *Student Life and Customs* (New York: D. Appleton, 1901), 123–24.

39. [William Henry Channing], *Memoir of William Ellery Channing*, 3 vols. (Boston, 1848), 1:49–50.

40. Allen, *Diary of John Quincy Adams*, 2:226 n.1.

41. Ibid., 2:265 n. 9.

42. Claude M. Fuess, *Daniel Webster*, 2 vols. (Boston: Little, Brown, 1930), 1:51.

43. William Stickney, ed., *Autobiography of Amos Kendall* (1872; New York: P. Smith, 1949), 65.

44. Samuel E. Morison, "The Great Rebellion at Harvard College and the Resignation of President Kirkland," *Publications of the Colonial Society of Massachusetts* 27 (1928), 81–83; the occasion of the Gorham Rebellion was the expulsion of a popular student, William Gorham, who refused to perform an assigned part in the junior exhibition at a time when the junior class was in an uproar over the college government's appointments for the exhibition and the suppression of a student antislavery society. See [Morse], *Student Life at Amherst College*, 95–96. The Gorham Rebellion led to a sharp decline in Amherst's enrollments; see William S. Tyler, *A History of Amherst College . . . from 1821 to 1891* (New York, 1895), 86–96; Colin B. Burke, *American Collegiate Populations: A Test of the Traditional View* (New York: New York University Press, 1982), chap. 1.

45. Whether faculty practiced this sort of favoritism, the belief that they did was nearly universal; see George F. Whicher, ed., *Remembrance of Amherst: An Undergraduate's Diary, 1846–1848* (New York: Columbia University Press, 1946), 40.

46. Quoted in Ernest John Knapton, "The Harvard Diary of Pitt Clarke, 1786–1791," *Publications of the Colonial Society of Massachusetts* 59 (1982), 239; [Austin], *Strictures on Harvard University*, 5–6, 9–10, 15–20. On Dennie's undergraduate degradation (which demonstrates that Harvard continued the main punishment of the social-precedence system decades after it had abolished the system), see Arnold Ellis, "Joseph Dennie and His Circle," *Bulletin of the University of Texas*, No. 40, Studies in English, No. 3 (1915), 35–36. Enraged by his degradation, Dennie described Harvard as "that sink of vice, that temple of dullness, that roost of owls."

47. [David Phineas Adams][?], "Notions of Genius at Harvard," in *The Federalist Literary Mind*, ed. Lewis P. Simpson (Baton Rouge: Louisiana State University Press, 1962), 112–15; see also [John Pierce], "A College Rake," in Simpson, *Federalist Literary Mind*, 118. These essays appeared in the Federalist literary organ, the (Boston) *Monthly Anthology*, respectively in 1804 and 1803.

48. Charles Francis Adams, *Diary*, 2 vols., ed. Aïda DiPace Donald and David Donald (Cambridge, Mass.: Harvard University Press, 1964), 1:250–51, 242–43. Similarly, in arguing that a nation's literature reflected its genius, Samuel Lorenzo Knapp wrote that literature is "the transcript of the head and heart of man"; see Knapp, *American Cultural History*, 31, 29.

49. Jonathan Messerli, *Horace Mann: A Biography* (New York: Knopf, 1972), 44.

50. *Autobiography of William H. Seward*, 47.

51. William D. Snider, *Light on the Hill: A History of the University of North Carolina at Chapel Hill* (Chapel Hill: University of North Carolina Press, 1992), 31.

52. Stickney, *Autobiography of Amos Kendall*, 26, 46.

53. Knapton, "Harvard Diary of Pitt Clarke," 308. On the history of Phi Beta Kappa, see Richard N. Current, *Phi Beta Kappa in American Life: The First Two Hundred Years* (New York: Oxford University Press, 1990), 53, 58. The anti-Masonic outburst in the 1820s led to attacks on Phi Beta Kappa. In 1831 several Harvard Kappans, including John Quincy

Adams, Joseph Story, and Alexander Hill Everett, gathered in Boston to debate whether Phi Beta Kappa elections should continue to require unanimity. Adams insisted on unanimity on the principle that anything less would turn PBK into a "mere" literary society rather than a league of friends. He lost on this issue when a three-fourths rule was voted in; see Charles Francis Adams, ed., *Memoirs of John Quincy Adams, Comprising Portions of His Diary from 1795 to 1848*, 12 vols. (Philadelphia, 1876), 8:390–91.

54. Stickney, *Autobiography of Amos Kendall*, 59, 42–46.

55. Ibid., 32–33.

56. Ibid., 67.

57. Ibid.

58. Steven J. Novak, *The Rights of Youth: American Colleges and Student Revolution, 1768–1815* (Cambridge, Mass.: Harvard University Press, 1977), 1.

59. Ashbel Green, *Life of Ashbel Green* (Philadelphia, 1849), 344, 361, 391.

60. Morison, "Great Rebellion," 81–83.

61. Charles C. Wall, "Students and Student Life at the University of Virginia, 1825–1861" (Ph.D. dissertation, University of Virginia, 1978), 250–65.

62. James L. Morrison Jr., "*The Best School in the World*": West Point in the Pre–Civil War Years, 1833–1866 (Kent, Ohio: Kent State University Press, 1986), 87–89; Stephen E. Ambrose, *Duty, Honor, Country: A History of West Point* (Baltimore: Johns Hopkins University Press, 1966), 65–67, 72–73.

63. Ticknor's enthusiasm for Thayer's system included a trip to West Point in 1826 to observe a four-hour oral examination of cadets; see George S. Pappas, *To the Point: The United States Military Academy, 1802–1902* (Westport, Conn.: Praeger, 1993), 163–64.

64. Robert A. McCaughey, *Josiah Quincy, 1772–1864: The Last Federalist* (Cambridge, Mass.: Harvard University Press, 1974), 148; Andrew P. Peabody, *Harvard Reminiscences* (1888; Freeport, N.Y.: Books for Libraries Press, 1972), 30–31. Harvard tutors had marked recitations during the 1820s but on different scales amid charges of favoritism. Peabody, a student at Harvard during the 1820s, noted that final honors were conferred by a vote of the faculty, "without any documentary evidence on which the vote could be based." But he added that the older faculty members displayed a good deal of "judicial skill" and "tact" in deciding "the final distribution of honors, so that their decision commonly received the assent of students who were not themselves disappointed." He added, however, that there were "frequent instances" in which individual students were "sorely aggrieved." Obsessed with eliminating partiality, Quincy not only imposed a uniform marking scale but also insisted that he see each tutor's daily marks so that there would be no collusion among the tutors. Peabody observed that Quincy's system "was so formed as to leave hardly any room for even unconscious favoritism." See also Edmund Quincy, *Life of Josiah Quincy of Massachusetts* (Boston, 1869), 440–41. The Harvard University Archives contains an untitled three-volume manuscript listing of the numerical marks of all students between 1827 (before the initiation of Quincy's scale) and 1875.

65. David F. Allmendinger Jr., *Paupers and Scholars: The Transformation of Student Life in Nineteenth-Century New England* (New York: St. Martin's Press, 1975), 122–24; Battle, *History of the University of North Carolina*, 531–32; [Ezekial C. Belden], *Sketches of Yale* (New York, 1843), 84, 75; La Borde, *History of South Carolina College*, 337–38. It is conceivable, but unlikely, that marking systems were responses to larger enrollments. Enrollments rose at established colleges after 1800. Harvard, which awarded an average of 35 B.A. degrees a year in the 1720s and 39 in the 1790s, awarded an average of 58 in the 1820s and 57 in the 1830s. In proportional terms this represents a significant rise, but in absolute terms only a modest one. Yale, by 1835–36 the largest American college, enrolled only 413 students in that academic year. Between 1813, when Yale began to keep enrollment statistics and introduced the marking of recitations, and 1820, its average annual enrollment

was 271 and its graduating classes under 100. See Harvard University, *Quinquennial Catalogue of the Officers and Graduates, 1636–1925* (Cambridge, Mass.: Harvard University Press, 1925); *Catalogue of the Officers and Graduates of Yale University, 1701–1915* (New Haven, Conn.: Yale University Press, 1916); Pierson, *Yale Book of Numbers*, 4. What can be said is that enrollments in all colleges fluctuated jaggedly from year to year, especially when a rebellion had given the college a bad reputation. Princeton granted a record number of 54 B.A. degrees in 1806, but the expulsion of 125 students after a student mutiny left it with a graduating class of 35 in the following year; see Maclean, *History of the College of New Jersey*, 2:72, 80.

66. Quoted in Arthur H. Cole, ed., *Charleston Goes to Harvard: The Diary of a Harvard Student in 1831* (Cambridge, Mass.: Harvard University Press, 1940), xiii. For an informative description of how Yale's marking system worked, see Laura H. Moseley, ed., *Diary of James Hadley, 1843–1852* (New Haven, Conn.: Yale University Press, 1951), 240. Hadley recorded that he and other professors spent the morning of June 17, 1851, assigning senior appointments, and "in no one instance did we disturb the order of the marks; the only difficulty was to draw the line."

67. Quoted in McCaughey, *Josiah Quincy*, 167.

68. Oxford also introduced more rigorous examinations in the early 1800s. In contrast to Cambridge, the Oxford examinations were public and viva voce. See V. H. H. Green, "Reformers and Reform in the University," in *The History of the University of Oxford: Volume V, The Eighteenth Century,* ed. L. S. Sutherland and L. G. Mitchell; T. H. Ashton, general ed. (Oxford: Clarendon Press, 1986), 623–27.

69. Peter Searby, *A History of the University of Cambridge, 1750–1870,* vol. 3 of *A History of the University of Cambridge,* ed. Christopher N. L. Brooke (Cambridge: Cambridge University Press, 1997), 158–63. Oxford had a similar system of fellowships, but it moved more slowly than Cambridge toward merit-based rewards; see "Oxford University Commission," *North American Review* 76 (1853), 369–96.

70. Quoted in Searby, *Cambridge*, 96.

71. Ibid., 182.

72. Bristed, *Five Years in an English University*, 67.

73. The religious test was a requirement for the B.A., which was a requirement for winning a fellowship but not for sitting for the Tripos. As a share of a Cambridge college's endowment ("foundation"), a fellowship belonged to its winner, similar to the way a commission in the Royal Army belonged to its purchaser; so a share could be mortgaged. See Searby, *Cambridge*, 95.

74. Ibid., 160.

75. Francis Galton, *Hereditary Genius: An Inquiry into Its Laws and Consequences* (New York, 1870), 18–19.

76. On the fate of the proposals by Ticknor and George Bancroft, see David B. Tyack, *George Ticknor and the Boston Brahmins* (Cambridge, Mass.: Harvard University Press, 1967), 109–10, 122–23; George S. Hilliard, ed., *Life, Letters, and Journals of George Ticknor* (Boston, 1869), 362–64; on Quincy's opposition to sectioning by proficiency, see McCaughey, *Josiah Quincy*, 173.

77. The 50 percent policy was first printed in the Harvard commencement program of 1842; see Charles C. Smith, "Commencements at Harvard, 1803–1848," *Proceedings of the Massachusetts Historical Society*, 2 ser., 5 (Jan. 1890), 168–253. Amherst graduated an average of 38.5 students a year from 1822 to 1871, of whom an average of 24.7 received an appointment. There were pronounced fluctuations from year to year, but not over time, which suggests that the Amherst government used the allotment of parts from year to year as an instrument of discipline (i.e., by threatening an unruly class with a niggardly allotment); see [Morse], *Student Life at Amherst College*, 81. Probably the main reason

for restricting the number of parts in American colleges, however, lay in the congestion produced by too many eager participants. For example, when Charles W. Eliot (future president of Harvard) graduated from Harvard in 1853, there were forty-four commencement speeches plus five musical interludes. In 1850 the University of Georgia placed a ten-minute limit on speeches, with a 25-cent fine for each minute over the limit. See George P. Schmidt, *The Liberal Arts College: A Chapter in American Cultural History* (New Brunswick, N.J.: Rutgers University Press, 1957), 101–2.

78. Andrew Hilen, ed., *The Letters of Henry Wadsworth Longfellow*, 6 vols. (Cambridge, Mass.: Harvard University Press, 1967), 1:124.

79. Whicher, *Remembrance of Amherst*, 25, 258.

80. [Lyman Hotchkiss Bagg], *Four Years at Yale* (New Haven, Conn., 1871), 584. Bagg cited this as "another illustration of the mystery which surrounds a man's stand to the very end of the course."

81. Ambivalence partly reflected the persistent belief that talent in itself deserved no reward. Thus Rev. Samuel Knox wrote in 1799 that "the youth possessed of the best natural genius and yet averse to application merits no public approbation, at least in the same degree as the proficient by means of extraordinary diligent exertions." Although "some prizes might be conferred . . . for sudden and extraordinary efforts of genius, yet the general object of them should be understood by the student as a reward for that proficiency which arises from habits of perseverance and industry." See Knox, "An Essay on the Best System of Liberal Education," in *Essays on Education in the Early Republic*, ed. Frederick Rudolph (Cambridge, Mass.: Harvard University Press, 1965), 346.

82. Quincy, *History of Harvard University*, 2:398.

83. Tyack, *George Ticknor*, 123.

84. Quoted in Mark A. De Wolfe, *The Life and Letters of George Bancroft*, 2 vols. (New York: C. Scribner, 1908–9), 1:129.

85. Bristed, *Five Years in an English University*, 67; Peter Searby described Bristed as "the most perceptive critic of early Victorian Cambridge"; see Searby, *Cambridge*, 103.

86. Bristed, *Five Years in an English University*, 389.

87. Ibid., 391.

88. Wayland, *Thoughts on the Present Collegiate System*, 37–48, 41.

89. Smith, "Commencements at Harvard, 1803–1848," 238.

90. Quoted in Kenneth Cameron, ed., *Thoreau and His Harvard Classmates: Henry Williams' Memorial of the Class of 1837* (Hartford, Conn.: Transcendental Books, 1965), 96.

91. The Gorham petition is in the Amherst College Library. In 1837 all but three Brown University seniors declined their degrees "because the competitive system of commencement parts impressed them as appealing to 'the unworthy passions of the heart.'" See Bronson, *History of Brown University*, 235. For background on the Gorham Rebellion, which involved several issues that had simmered during the 1830s, see Tyler, *History of Amherst . . . , 1821 to 1891*, 86–96.

92. W.S. Tyler, *History of Amherst College during Its First Half-Century, 1821–1871* (Springfield, Mass., 1873), 252–53.

93. Robert F. Lucid, ed., *The Journal of Richard Henry Dana, Jr.* (Cambridge, Mass.: Harvard University Press, 1968), 1, 23, 25.

94. Having taken two years off to complete his famous book, he joined the class of 1837 and was ratcheted down a few notches because he had not competed with that class for all four years.

95. Sheldon, *Student Life and Customs*, 117. For a comparable development at Yale, see [Bagg], *Four Years at Yale*, 405–20.

96. [Bagg], *Four Years at Yale*, 690.

4. MAKING THE GRADE

1. Daniel Vickers, "Competency and Competition: Economic Culture in Early America," *William and Mary Quarterly*, 3 ser., 47 (1990), 3, 12; Jack P. Greene, *The Intellectual Construction of America: Exceptionalism and Identity from 1492 to 1800* (Chapel Hill: University of North Carolina Press, 1993), 175.

2. Rex Burns, *Success in America: The Yeoman Dream and the Industrial Revolution* (Amherst: University of Massachusetts Press, 1976), vii.

3. Joel Barlow, *Advice to the Privileged Orders in the Several States of Europe* (London, 1792, 1795; Ithaca: Cornell University Press, 1956), 105–6.

4. [Joseph Cogswell], "Principle of Emulation," *North American Review* 43 (1836), 497, 502–3, 510–11.

5. David Hogan, "Modes of Discipline: Affective Individualism and Pedagogical Reform in New England, 1820–1850," *American Journal of Education* 99 (1990), 22–28.

6. "Fallacies in Education," *Massachusetts Teacher* 1 (Jan. 15, 1848), 21, and 1 (Feb. 1, 1848), 3.

7. Alexis de Tocqueville, *Democracy in America, Part the Second*, Henry Reeve text, revised by Francis Bowen, intro. by Phillips Bradley (1840; New York: Vintage, 1990), 228.

8. William M. Gouge, *A Short History of Paper-Money and Banking in the United States*, 4th ed. (New York, 1840), 31.

9. Freeman Hunt, *Worth and Wealth: A Collection of Maxims, Morals, and Miscellanies for Merchants and Men of Business* (New York, 1856), 182.

10. [Moses Y. Beach], *The Wealthy Citizens of New York* (1845; New York: Arno Press, 1973), 4. See also Edward Pessen, "Moses Beach Revisited: A Critical Examination of His Wealthy Citizens Pamphlets," *Journal of American History* 58 (1971), 415–26 and esp. 415 n. 1.

11. John S. Ezell, *Fortune's Merry Wheel: The Lottery in America* (Cambridge, Mass.: Harvard University Press, 1960), 160.

12. George Wilson Pierson, *Tocqueville in America* (1938; Baltimore: Johns Hopkins University Press, 1996), 71n.

13. Edward Balleisen, *Navigating Failure: Bankruptcy and Commercial Society in Antebellum America* (Chapel Hill: University of North Carolina Press, 2001), 3, 124; see also James D. Norris, *R. G. Dun & Co., 1841–1900: The Development of Credit Reporting in the Nineteenth Century* (Westport, Conn.: Greenwood, 1978), 5–9.

14. Joyce Appleby has written that the economy became a template of society in the early republic; see Appleby, *Capitalism and a New Social Order: The Republican Vision of the 1790s* (New York: New York University Press, 1984), 50; see also J. R. Pole, *The Pursuit of Equality in American History* (Berkeley: University of California Press, 1978), 119.

15. William Manning, *The Key of Liberty: The Life and Democratic Writings of William Manning, "A Laborer,"* ed. Michael Merrill and Sean Wilentz (Cambridge, Mass.: Harvard University Press, 1993), 136.

16. The American creed of equal rights, which required governments to treat everyone the same, was less compatible with measures to alleviate indigence than the principle, embraced by some British radicals, that wealth transfers were justified by the greater happiness given to a poor person than to a wealthy one by the transfer; Richard Pankhurst, *William Thompson, (1775–1833): Pioneer Socialist* (London: Pluto Press, 1991), 21–22, 27, 33–34, 36. See also Mark Blaug, *Ricardian Economics: A Historical Study* (Westport, Conn.: Greenwood Press, 1973), chap. 6; Joseph Dorfman, *The Economic Mind in American Civilization, 1606–1865*, 5 vols. (New York: Viking, 1946–59), 2:687–88.

17. Keith Hope, *As Others See Us: Schooling and Social Mobility in Scotland and the United States* (Cambridge: Cambridge University Press, 1984), 261.

18. Ibid., 251.

19. John Taylor, *An Inquiry into the Principles and Policy of the Government of the United States*, ed. Roy F. Nichols (New Haven, Conn.: Yale University Press, 1950), 485.

20. Quoted in James H. Huston, *Securing the Fruits of Labor: The American Concept of Wealth Distribution, 1765–1900* (Baton Rouge: Louisiana State University, 1998), 34.

21. Theodore Sedgwick Jr., *Public and Private Economy*, 3 vols. in 1 (1836–38; Clifton, N.J.: A. M. Kelley, 1974), 1:228.

22. Rush Welter, *The Mind of America, 1820–1860* (New York: Columbia University Press, 1975), 166–67.

23. James D. Richardson, comp., *Messages and Papers of the Presidents, 1789–1897*, 10 vols. (Washington, D.C.: Printed by authority of Congress, 1897), 2:591.

24. For all his ire at the Paper Aristocracy, John Taylor argued that universal suffrage created a universal temptation to acquire political power for selfish reasons. The problem lay in human nature; see Taylor, *Constructions Construed and Constitutions Vindicated* (Richmond, Va., 1820), 71. With this in mind, Rush Welter wrote that Jacksonian thinkers, even as they extolled the virtuous republic of farmers and artisans, often betrayed "a deeply pessimistic view of human nature, in that they assumed that all men would do evil if they were given the political opportunity to do so." See Welter, *Mind of America*, 92.

25. John L. O'Sullivan, "American Aristocracy," *United States Magazine and Democratic Review* 8 (Aug. 1840), 116.

26. Quoted in Welter, *Mind of America*, 91.

27. Ibid., 292.

28. Raymond Culver, *Horace Mann and Religion in the Massachusetts Public Schools* (New Haven, Conn.: Yale University Press, 1929), 128; Welter, *Mind of America*, 286–90.

29. Herbert Ershkowitz and William G. Shade, "Consensus or Conflict? Political Behavior in the State Legislatures during the Jacksonian Era," *Journal of American History* 58 (1971), 610–11.

30. Welter, *Mind of America*, 284–85.

31. Whigs cited South America as a place with abundant land and resources but mostly devoid of prosperity, equality, and self-sufficiency; see Francis Bowen, *American Political Economy* (New York, 1870), 65.

32. *Fifth Annual Report of the* [Massachusetts] *Board of Education, Together with the Fifth Annual Report of the Secretary of the Board*, 1841 (Boston, 1842), 85–86.

33. Ibid., 81–120; Maris A. Vinovskis, "Horace Mann on the Economic Productivity of Education," in Vinovskis, *Education, Society, and Economic Opportunity: An Historical Perspective on Persistent Issues* (New Haven, Conn.: Yale University Press, 1995), 92–105. In 1863 John D. Philbrick, a leading Boston school official, wrote that Mann's report had done more than anything within the previous twenty-five years "to convince capitalists of the value of elementary instruction as a means of increasing the value of labor"; quoted in Merle Curti, *The Social Ideals of American Educators* (1935; Totowa, N.J.: Littlefield, Adams, 1970), 113.

34. Ira Mayhew, *Means and Ends of Universal Education* (New York, 1857), 256–58, 270–78.

35. Edward Cannan, *A History of the Theories of Production and Distribution in English Political Economy from 1776 to 1848* (London: P. C. King, 1924), 208; Mark Blaug, *Ricardian Economics: An Historical Study* (New Haven, Conn.: Yale University Press, 1954), 45–51, 144–45, 153–59.

36. John McVickar, *Outlines of Political Economy* (New York, 1825); Dorfman, *Economic Mind*, 2:518.

37. See Michael Hudson's introduction to E. Peshine Smith, *A Manual of Political Economy* (New York: Garland Press, 1974), 19.

38. Luther Hamilton, ed., *Memoirs of Speeches and Writings of Robert Rantoul, Jr.* (Boston, 1854), 139. Horace Mann expressed a similar view a decade later; see *Twelfth Annual Report of the* [Massachusetts] *Board of Education, Together with the Twelfth Annual Report of the Secretary of the Board, 1848* (Boston, 1849), 67–68.

39. Francis Wayland, *The Elements of Political Economy* (Boston, 1845), 50–52, 173. In 1841 Alonzo Potter, who in the following year coauthored *The School and the Schoolmaster* with Mann's ally George B. Emerson, offered a similar view in his *Political Economy* (1841; New York, 1876), 93–94.

40. Daniel W. Howe, *The Political Culture of the American Whigs* (Chicago: University of Chicago Press, 1979), 73, 77–78; Michael F. Holt, *The Rise and Fall of the American Whig Party* (New York: Oxford University Press, 1999), 26–32; Welter, *Mind of America*, 105–13, 191–92.

41. The best guide to the moral ideals of antebellum Unitarianism is Daniel W. Howe, *The Unitarian Conscience: Harvard Moral Philosophy, 1815–1861* (Cambridge, Mass.: Harvard University Press, 1970).

42. Culver, *Horace Mann and Religion*, 127–28, 134, 135–37; Vinovskis, "Horace Mann," 96–97.

43. Quoted in Jonathan Messerli, *Horace Mann: A Biography* (New York: Knopf, 1972), 200.

44. Horace Mann, "The Necessity of Education in a Republican Government," in *Life and Works of Horace Mann*, 5 vols., ed. Mary P. Mann (Cambridge, Mass., 1865-67), 2:177. In a similar vein, Horace Bushnell wrote in 1827 that "real merit has very little to do with political elevation. That one has outstripped another in the race does not mean that he is more worthy of the nation's confidence, but that he has been more successful in his schemes of ambition." See [Mary A. Bushnell Cheney], ed., *Life and Letters of Horace Bushnell* (New York: C. Scribner's Sons, 1903), 49.

45. James McLachlan, *American Boarding Schools: A Historical Study* (New York: Charles Scribner's Sons, 1970), 172.

46. Hogan, "Modes of Discipline," 22–28.

47. Quoted in Isaac L. Kandel, *Examinations and Their Substitutes in the United States* (New York: Carnegie Foundation for the Advancement of Teaching, 1936), 26.

48. "Extracts from the Report on the Grammar Schools," *Common School Journal* 7 (1845), 290–304.

49. *Seventh Annual Report of the* [Massachusetts] *Board of Education, Together with the Seventh Annual Report of the Secretary of the Board, 1843* (Boston, 1844), 65–67.

50. George Minns, "Some Reminiscences of Boston Schools Forty-Five Years Ago," *Massachusetts Teacher* 26 (1873), 412–13.

51. Samuel Read Hall, "Emulation," *American Annals of Education* 2 (1832), 205; S. P. D., "Common Schools," *American Annals of Education* 2 (1832), 283. The Boston Latin School, before 1820 the city's only public high school, also allowed students to rise from lower to high benches on the basis of their daily performance; Henry F. Jencks, *The Boston Public Latin School, 1635–1880* (Boston, 1881), 12. Ellwood P. Cubberley dated the award of little certificates of merit to schoolchildren for progress in their studies to the 1820s; see Cubberley, *Public Education in the United States: A Study and Interpretation of American Educational History* (Boston: Houghton Mifflin, 1919), 222.

52. "New Haven," *Connecticut Common School Journal* 2 (1840), 232–33. For a general account of the monitorial school movement, see Carl F. Kaestle, ed., *Joseph Lancaster and the Monitorial School Movement: A Documentary History* (New York: Teachers College Press, 1973), 7–8, 168.

53. Jean H. Baker, *Affairs of Party: The Political Culture of Northern Democrats in the Mid-Nineteenth Century* (Ithaca: Cornell University Press, 1983), 92–94.

54. "Boston Monitorial Schools," *American Journal of Education* 1 (1826), 72–73; Barbara Finkelstein, *Governing the Young: Teacher Behavior and Popular Primary Schools in Nineteenth-Century United States* (New York: Falmer Press, 1989), 102; "Monitorial Instruction," *American Journal of Education* 1 (June 1826), 344, 346.

55. Kaestle, *Joseph Lancaster*, 7–8, 169. Another common monitorial device was to give each student a card indicating his rank in the class. After each recitation the students exchanged cards based on their performance, and at the end of the day the student with the number one card, which contained a picture, could take it home as a prize; see Jacqueline S. Rainier, *From Virtue to Character: American Childhood, 1775–1850* (New York: Twayne, 1996), 116.

56. Warren Burton, *The District School as It Was*, ed. Clifford Johnson (1833; New York, 1928), 72.

57. *Autobiography of William H. Seward, from 1801 to 1834, with a Memoir of Him by Frederick H. Seward* (New York, 1877), 23.

58. Charles Coon, *North Carolina Schools and Academies* (Raleigh, N.C.: Edwards and Broughton, 1915), 4–5, 50–51, 199–200, 399–400.

59. "Examinations and Exhibitions," *American Annals of Education* 4 (1834), 372–73; "Evils of Exhibitions of Public Speaking," *American Annals of Education* 4 (1834), 377; "Some Views in Regard to Exhibitions and Examinations," *Massachusetts Teacher* 17 (1864), 8–9.

60. Burton, *District School*, 142–43.

61. Mann wrote in 1845 that "our civil and social condition holds out splendid rewards for the competitions of talent, rather than motives for the practice of virtue." He added that the natural resources of the United States constituted "such glittering prizes, placed within reach of such fervid natures and such capacious desires," as to turn "every man into a competitor and an aspirant." See *Ninth Annual Report of the* [Massachusetts] *Board of Education, Together with the Ninth Annual Report of the Secretary of the Board* (Boston, 1846), 75, 72. Mann's language resembled that of his pastor, William Ellery Channing: "The exaltation of talent, as it is called, above virtue and religion, is the curse of the age. Education is now chiefly a stimulus to learning, and thus men acquire power without the principles which alone make it good. Talent is worshipped; but if divorced from rectitude, it will prove more a demon than a god." Quoted in Alonzo Potter, "The School," in Potter and Emerson, *School and the Schoolmaster*, 35. James McLachlan observed that in Federalist deferential America, "individual excellence threatened no one," but in egalitarian Jacksonian America, "the excellence of a particular individual threatened everyone." See McLachlan, *American Boarding Schools*, 172.

62. Michel Foucault, *Discipline and Punish: The Birth of the Prison*, trans. Alan Sheridan (New York: Pantheon, 1977), 182–83, 179–80. Foucault applied this phrase to the substitution of "discipline" (*surveiller*) for torture, vengeance, and public spectacle between 1760 and 1840.

63. "Evils of Exhibitions of Public Speaking," 375–78; see also "Examinations and Exhibitions," 372–77.

64. "Some Views in Regard to Exhibitions and Examinations," 7.

65. "The Credit System," *Massachusetts Teacher* 15 (1862), 5–7, 132–34. In 1848 an officer in the Royal Navy, Alexander Macnochie, advanced a proposal for a new system of prison discipline, which he called the "credit" or "mark" system. In place of fixed sentences, prisoners were to be given indeterminate sentences that would end when the prisoner had accrued a designated number of credits or marks for completing specified tasks. See Torsten Eriksson, *The Reformers: An Historical Survey of Pioneer Experiments in the History of Criminals*, trans. Catherine Djurklou (New York: Elsevier, 1976), 83–85. I have not found any reference to Macnochie's system in the writings of American school reformers, but the similarities are tantalizing. In each case the purpose was essentially reformative rather than punitive; credits or "merits" were to be accrued for good acts.

66. "Methods of Keeping Records of Attendance, Deportment, and Scholarship, and of Making Reports to Parents," *Massachusetts Teacher* 11 (1858), 17. It is likely that report cards were more widely used in public schools as women came to dominate their teaching staffs. As alternatives to the "immediate" reproof of infractions, usually a cuffing or flogging, report cards were highly compatible with the feminization of teaching.

67. [A.P. Stone], "School Records," *Massachusetts Teacher* 17 (1864), 58–65; S.G.B., "Weekly Reports in Schools," *Common School Journal* 2 (1840), 185–87; "Marking-Records," *Massachusetts Teacher* 11 (1858), 20–21; "Methods of Keeping Records," 16–19.

68. Quoted in William J. Shearer, *The Grading of Schools* (New York, 1899), 12.

69. Stanley K. Schultz, *The Culture Factory: Boston Public Schools, 1789–1860* (New York: Oxford University Press, 1973), 41–44; Cubberley, *Public Education in the United States*, 97–98.

70. Calvin E. Stowe, "Report on Elementary and Public Instruction in Europe," in *Reports on European Education*, ed. Edgar W. Knight (New York: McGraw-Hill, 1930), 312.

71. Carl F. Kaestle, *Pillars of the Republic: Common Schools and American Society, 1780–1860* (New York: Hill and Wang, 1983), 32.

72. Shearer, *Grading of Schools*, 23; Maris Vinovskis, David L. Angus, and Jeffrey Mirel, "Historical Development of Age Stratification in Schooling," in Vinovskis, *Education, Society, and Economic Opportunity*, 177–79; "School Palaces in Boston," *Massachusetts Teacher* 14 (1861), 290–91; "How Many Pupils to a School? How Many to a Teacher?" *Massachusetts Teacher* 12 (1859), 249–54.

73. "Report on the Condition of the Common Schools in Litchfield County," in *Sixth Annual Report of the Superintendent of Common Schools of Connecticut* (Hartford, Conn., 1851), 60.

74. "School Palaces in Boston," 290–94.

75. [Stone], "School Records," 60; C.H., "Sequence of Studies," *Massachusetts Teacher* 18 (1865), 211.

76. "Sequence of Studies," 211.

77. By 1871 the Boston school committee was describing promotion as a "right," at least in the context that it was unjust to keep a child in elementary school (and out of high school) a day longer than necessary; see *Annual Report of the School Committee of the City of Boston, 1871* (Boston, 1872), 18.

78. "American Institute of Instruction," *Massachusetts Teacher* 10 (1857), 485.

79. Henry Barnard, *Practical Illustrations of the Principles of School Architecture* (New York, 1854), 59.

80. James P. Wickersham, *School Economy* (1864; Philadelphia, 1867), 139.

81. "Common School Systems of Connecticut," *American Annals of Education* 2 (1832), 203.

82. George B. Emerson, "The Schoolmaster," in Potter and Emerson, *School and the Schoolmaster*, 517–18; see also George B. Emerson, "On the Motives to Be Addressed in the Instruction of Children," *Common School Journal* 1 (1839), 351.

83. Emerson, "Schoolmaster," 516, 518. A professor at the University of North Carolina proposed that each teacher inform the class about "fixed points of excellence" that were within reach of all pupils in the class. Under this plan all pupils could obtain first place—the top place of excellence—without experiencing feelings of personal triumph; see "Effects of Emulation," *American Annals of Education* 4 (1834), 354.

84. "American Institute of Instruction," 485.

85. My argument applies more to northern than to southern Whigs, but antebellum southern Whigs were far more likely than southern Democrats to support state systems of public education and factories.

86. American Fourierites, or Associationists, as they preferred to be called, shared this rejection of Jeffersonian harmony. Carl J. Guarneri writes that in the Fourierite phalanxes,

"Whig ideas about the rights of labor and capital and the harmony of interests were given mathematical precision. With community profits distributed in fixed ratios to labor, capital, and skill, each group would receive its due." See Guarneri, *The Utopian Alternative: Fourierism in Nineteenth-Century America* (Ithaca: Cornell University Press, 1991), 39. Whigs shared this preference of "association" made possible by regional manufacturing centers in which well-paid workers provided a robust market for local farmers and in which the density of population made graded schools possible; see Tony A. Freyer, *Producers versus Capitalists: Constitutional Conflict in Antebellum America* (Charlottesville: University Press of Virginia, 1994), 50.

87. Francis Adams, *The Free School System of the United States* (London, 1875; New York, Arno Press, 1969), 201–3. Adams was secretary of Britain's National Education League. For a similar view from the perspective of a continental European, see P. A. Siljeström, *Educational Institutions of the United States*, trans. Frederica Rowan (London, 1853; New York: Arno Press, 1969), 299–300. Siljeström observed that European schools were not "graded" in the American sense. American schools formed a "connected system" in that the course of instruction in a higher school was considered a continuation of that in the school just below it; European schools, on the other hand, were "classified" in the sense that each school constituted a separate system of instruction "adapted for various positions in life, and for the different classes of the people."

88. Jurgen Herbst, *The Once and Future School: Three Hundred and Fifty Years of American Secondary Education* (New York: Routledge, 1996), 61–66; Paul E. Belting, *The Development of the Free Public High School in Illinois to 1860* (Springfield: Illinois State Historical Society, 1919), 159–60, 183–84.

89. Edward Bellamy, *Looking Backward, 2000–1887* (Boston: Houghton Mifflin, 1917), 96.

90. Ibid., 125.

91. Ibid., 126–27.

92. David B. Tyack, *The One Best System: A History of American Urban Education* (Cambridge, Mass.: Harvard University Press, 1974), 47–49, 55–57.

93. Emerson E. White, "Examinations and Promotions," *Education* 8 (1888), 517–22. and "Several Problems in Graded School Management," *Journal of Proceedings and Addresses of the National Education Association* (1874), 254–57; "Examinations and Promotions," U.S. Department of the Interior, Office of Education, *Report of the Commissioner of Education, 1886–1887* (Washington, D.C.: GPO, 1888), 240–43; Agnes M. Lathe, "Written Examinations—Their Abuse and Their Use," *Education* 9 (1889), 452–56; Emerson E. White, "Promotions and Examinations in Graded Schools" in U.S. Bureau of Education, *Circular of Information, No. 7, 1891* (Washington, D.C.: GPO, 1891).

94. For example, in Easton, Pennsylvania, in 1880 there were 1,024 pupils in grades 1–3, 912 in grades 4–5, 236 in grades 6–8, and 195 in the high school; James Mulhern, *A History of Secondary Education in Pennsylvania* (Philadelphia: University of Pennsylvania Press, 1933), 568–69.

95. Ibid., 571.

96. Charles W. Eliot, "Can School Programmes Be Shortened and Enriched?" in Eliot, *Educational Reform* (New York: Century, 1901), 168. Eliot delivered this address in 1888.

97. Charles W. Eliot, "Undesirable and Desirable Uniformity in Schools," in Eliot, *Educational Reform*, 273–302. Eliot delivered this address in 1892. See also Kandel, *Examinations and Their Substitutes*, 31.

98. Charles W. Eliot, "Shortening and Enriching the Grammar-School Course," in Eliot, *Educational Reform*, 264.

99. Charles W. Eliot, "The Working of American Democracy," in Eliot, *American Contributions to Civilization and Other Essays and Addresses* (New York: Century, 1907), 92; in the same volume see Eliot, "Family Stocks in a Democracy," 135–38.

100. Ernest W. Huffcut, "Requirements for Admission to Professional Schools," in *Association of American Universities, Journal of Proceedings, Fourth Annual Conference, 1902*, 40.

101. This modern understanding of tracking was embodied in several tracking plans introduced around World War I; for a description, see Ellwood P. Cubberley, *Public School Administration*, rev. ed. (Boston: Houghton Mifflin, 1929), 452–57.

102. Edward L. Thorndike, "The Elimination of Pupils from School," in Department of the Interior, Bureau of Education, *Bulletin No. 4, 1907* (Washington, D.C.: GPO, 1908); Leonard P. Ayres, *Laggards in Our Schools* (New York: Russell Sage Foundation, 1909).

103. Ayres, *Laggards*, 159.

104. Ibid., 169.

105. Ibid., 199.

106. Ibid., 146; similarly, Cubberley wrote that "the boy who has twice failed promotion has probably been prepared to become a failure in life." Cubberley, *Public School Administration*, 438.

107. J. E. Cairnes, *Some Leading Principles of Political Economy, Newly Expounded* (London, 1874).

108. Quoted in Joseph F. Kett, "The Adolescence of Vocational Education," in *Work, Youth, and Schooling: Historical Perspectives on Vocationalism in American Education*, ed. Harvey Kantor and David Tyack (Stanford, Calif.: Stanford University Press, 1982), 96–97.

109. Kandel, *Examinations and Their Substitutes*, 6, 16. See also George Zook, "The Extent and Significance of the Junior College Movement," *Transactions of the Fifty-Sixth Annual Meeting of the Ohio College Association* (April 1927), 8–11.

110. Kandel, *Examinations and Their Substitutes*, 18–19.

111. Vinovskis, Angus, and Mirel, "Historical Development of Age Stratification," 188–92.

112. William S. Learned, *The Quality of the Educational Process in the United States and in Europe* (New York: Carnegie Foundation for the Advancement of Teaching, 1927), 22–23, 24–25, 28–32, 36–37.

113. James S. Coleman, *The Adolescent Society: The Social Life of Teenagers and Its Impact on American Education* (New York: Free Press of Glencoe, 1961), 317.

114. Joseph L. Henderson, *Admission to College by Certificate* (New York: Teachers College, 1912).

115. Harold S. Wechsler, *The Qualified Student: A History of Selective College Admission in America* (New York: John Wiley, 1977), 19–32, 105, 125–26, and chap. 10.

116. W. T. Root, "The Freshman Thorndike College Entrance Test: First Semester Grades, Binet Tests," *Journal of Applied Psychology* 7 (1923), 89–91. One qualification needs to be made. During the 1920s and early 1930s Columbia University used the intelligence test devised by E. L. Thorndike to restrict the admission of Jews, especially ones from New York City public high schools, whom Columbia admissions officers viewed as overachievers whose intellectual limits would be illuminated by mental tests.

117. W. B. Pillsbury, "Selection: An Unnoticed Function of Education," *Scientific Monthly* 62 (1921), 62–74.

118. Simon N. Patten, *The New Basis of Civilization* (New York: Macmillan, 1907), 95–118; Daniel M. Fox, *The Discovery of Abundance: Simon N. Patten and the Transformation of Social Theory* (Ithaca: Cornell University Press, 1967).

119. Charles H. Cooley, *Social Organization: A Study of the Larger Mind* (New York: C. Scribner's Sons, 1909), 116, 118.

120. Herbert Croly, *The Promise of American Life* (1909; New York: Macmillan, 1914), 206–7.

121. H. H. Powers, "Weakness and Dangers of Association," in *Political Economy, Political Science, and Sociology*, ed. Richard T. Ely (Chicago: University Association, 1899), 339.

122. Albert Shaw, "The Outlook for the Average Man in a Non-competitive Society," *Educational Review* 24 (1902), 109–34. On Shaw, see Lloyd J. Graybar, *Albert Shaw of the Review of Reviews: An Intellectual Biography* (Lexington: University Press of Kentucky, 1974).

5. THE SCIENTIFIC MEASUREMENT OF MERIT

1. Michael M. Sokal, "James McKeen Cattell and Mental Anthropometry," in *Testing and American Society, 1890–1934*, ed. Sokal (New Brunswick, N.J: Rutgers University Press, 1987), 34.

2. Bernard Norton, "Charles Spearman and the General Factor in Intelligence," *Journal of the History of the Behavioral Sciences* 15 (1979), 142–54; Charles Spearman, "General Intelligence Objectively Determined and Measured," *American Journal of Psychology* 15 (1904), 201–93; Godfrey H. Thomson, "General versus Group Factors in Mental Activities," *Psychological Review* 27 (1920), 173–90.

3. For details on the Binet-Simon scales and on Terman's revisions (his 1916 revision became the best known but it was not his first), see Raymond E. Fancher, *The Intelligence Men: Makers of the IQ Controversy* (New York: W. W. Norton, 1985), 70–78, 139–41. Philip H. Du Bois has provided a clear and thorough summary of the early history of mental testing; see his *A History of Psychological Testing* (Boston: Allyn and Bacon, 1970), 11–70.

4. Kathryn W. Linden and James D. Linden, *Modern Mental Measurement: A Historical Perspective* (Boston: Houghton Mifflin, 1986), 56–57.

5. Frank N. Freeman, *Mental Tests: Their History, Principles and Applications*, rev. ed. (Boston: Houghton Mifflin, 1939), 3. See also Paula Fass, "The IQ: A Cultural and Historical Framework," *American Journal of Education* 88 (1980), 431–58; Rudolph Pintner, *Intelligence Testing: Methods and Results*, new ed. (New York: Henry Holt, 1931), 190–215.

6. Florence Goodenough, *Mental Testing: Its History, Principles, and Application* (New York: Rinehart, 1949), 89.

7. For general studies of this orientation, see Loren Baritz, *Servants of Power: A History of the Uses of Social Science in American Industry* (New York: Wiley, 1965), and David F. Noble, *America by Design: Science, Technology, and the Rise of Corporate Capitalism* (New York: Knopf, 1977).

8. "Robert Mearns Yerkes," in *History of Psychology in Autobiography*, vol. 2, ed. Carl Murchison (New York: Russell and Russell, 1961), 388.

9. "Lewis M. Terman," in Murchison, *History of Psychology*, vol. 2, 297–332; Henry L. Minton, *Lewis M. Terman: A Pioneer in Psychological Testing* (New York: New York University Press, 1968), chap. 2.

10. "Edward Lee Thorndike," in *History of Psychology in Autobiography*, vol. 3, ed. Carl Murchison (New York: Russell and Russell, 1961), 266; "Lewis M. Terman," 323; Leila Zenderland, *Measuring Minds: Henry Herbert Goddard and the Origins of American Intelligence Testing* (Cambridge: Cambridge University Press, 1998), 342.

11. Definitions of intelligence abounded in the 1920s, but most connoted an ability to draw relationships among items. The connotations of ability differed from those of "capacity," long a synonym for ability but implying absorptive power.

12. In technical terms, researchers did not find sex differences in the "variability" of intelligence. This was important because in *The Descent of Man* (1871) Darwin had speculated that males in all species developed variations to attract females; in the case of intelligence, men would produce more dolts but also more geniuses. For attacks on the Darwinian legacy, see Lewis M. Terman, *The Measurement of Intelligence* (Boston: Houghton Mifflin, 1916); George W. Frasier, "A Comparative Study of the Variability of Boys and Girls," *Journal of Applied Psychology* 3 (1919), 151–55.

13. Francis Galton, *Hereditary Genius* (New York: D. Appleton, 1870), 18–21.

14. On how Galton's commitment to eugenics shaped his statistical theory, see Donald A. MacKenzie, *Statistics in Britain, 1865–1930: The Social Organization of Scientific Knowledge* (Edinburgh: University of Edinburgh Press, 1981), 52–68.

15. Francis Galton, "Hereditary Talent and Character," *Macmillan's Magazine* 12 (1865), 157–66 and 318–27. Galton later decided that he should have substituted "mental ability" for genius. Given the later direction of mental testing (toward the study of small deviations from the average), "genius" seems closer to Galton's intent. He thought that geniuses differed as much from average people as did idiots.

16. Galton, *Hereditary Genius*, 19.

17. Galton's methods are fully described in Nicholas Wright Gillham, *A Life of Sir Francis Galton: From African Explorations to the Birth of Eugenics* (New York: Oxford University Press, 2001), 158–65, and thoroughly critiqued in Ruth Schwartz Cowan, *Sir Francis Galton and the Study of Heredity in the Nineteenth Century* (New York: Garland, 1985), 3–10. Galton used "eminence" and "reputation" ("the opinion of contemporaries, revised by posterity") interchangeably; see *Hereditary Genius*, 37. "Because there exists no criterion for a just comparison of the natural ability of the different sexes," he wrote, he did not count women. See *Hereditary Genius*, 62. But on the next page he offered a different and probably more revealing explanation of his Victorian views about women: "the female influence is inferior to that of the male in conveying ability."

18. Darwin had speculated that acquired characters were transmitted by "gemmules," tiny particles that circulated in the blood and that picked up environmental influences. But Galton's experiments discredited this all-in-the-blood idea by demonstrating that gray rabbits whose blood had been mixed with that of white rabbits bore more grays, and not mongrels.

19. Cowan, *Galton*, 30–31. Galton intuitively believed that the embryos of children were contained in the embryos of their parents, but he included traits like zeal and vigor, components of "genius," in the embryo. Weismann disputed this. See Hamilton Cravens, *The Triumph of Evolution: American Scientists and the Heredity-Environment Controversy, 1900–1914* (Philadelphia: University of Pennsylvania Press, 1978), 35–38, 42–43.

20. Daniel J. Kevles, *In the Name of Eugenics: Genetics and the Uses of Human Heredity* (Cambridge, Mass.: Harvard University Press, 2004), 15.

21. Theodore M. Porter, *Karl Pearson: The Scientific Life in a Statistical Age* (Princeton, N.J.: Princeton University Press, 2004), 258.

22. Kevles, *In the Name of Eugenics*, 30–31.

23. Ibid. Pearson was the more sophisticated mathematician, but Galton had made the same argument on intuitive grounds; see Galton, *Hereditary Genius*, 32.

24. W. Baptiste Scoones, "Is Examination a Failure?" *Nineteenth Century* 25 (1889), 236–55.

25. Galton, *Hereditary Genius*, 40.

26. James McKeen Cattell, "Mental Tests and Measurements," *Mind* 15 (1890), 373–81.

27. F. Y. Edgeworth, "The Statistics of Examinations," *Journal of the Royal Statistical Society* 51 (1888), 599–635, and "The Element of Chance in Competitive Examinations," *Journal of the Royal Statistical Society* 53 (1890), 644–63.

28. Isaac L. Kandel, *Examinations and Their Substitutes in the United States*, Bulletin 28 (New York: Carnegie Foundation for the Advancement of Teaching, 1936), 33–34.

29. John Fulton, *Memoirs of Frederick A. P. Barnard* (New York: Macmillan, 1896), 369–72.

30. Max Meyer, "Experiences with the Grading System at the University of Missouri," *Science*, n.s., 33 (1911), 661–67; William T. Foster, "Scientific versus Personal Interpretation of College Credits," *Popular Science Monthly* 78 (1911), 388–408; I. F. Finkelstein,

The Marking System in Theory and Practice (Baltimore: Warwick and York, 1913); Daniel Starch, "Reliability and Distribution of Grades," *Science*, n.s., 38 (1913), 630–36; Florian Cajori, "A New Marking System and Means of Measuring Mathematical Abilities," *Science*, n.s., 39 (June 12, 1914), 874–81.

31. Geraldine Jonçich, *The Sane Positivist: Edward Lee Thorndike* (Middletown, Conn.: Wesleyan University Press, 1968), 396, 324–25. Standardized testing involved administering trial questions to a sample of the population with an eye to establishing a norm, an agreed-upon level of proficiency, usually 75 percent, that children of a certain age could be expected to reach. IQ tests were standardized, but the earliest applications of standardization in American schools involved achievement tests. In 1917, when schools were using very few IQ tests, there were more than two hundred standardized achievement tests in America public schools. See Paul Davis Chapman, *Schools as Sorters: Lewis M. Terman, Applied Psychology, and the Intelligence Testing Movement* (New York: New York University Press, 1988), 34.

32. Quoted in Jonçich, *Sane Positivist*, 324.

33. Edward L. Thorndike, *Individuality* (Boston: Houghton Mifflin, 1911), 8.

34. Jonçich, *Sane Positivist*, 322.

35. Fritz K. Ringer, *Education and Society in Modern Europe* (Bloomington: Indiana University Press, 1979); Ross McKibben, *Classes and Cultures: England, 1918–1951* (Oxford: Oxford University Press, 1998), 209–10, 216–17, 242–44, 268–69.

36. Gillian Sutherland, in collaboration with Stephen Sharp, *Ability, Merit and Measurement: Mental Testing and English Education, 1880–1940* (Oxford: Oxford University Press, 1984), chaps. 7, 8.

37. Quoted in Edward A. Krug, *The Shaping of the American High School, Volume 2: 1920–1941* (Madison: University of Wisconsin Press, 1972), 144.

38. Quoted in ibid.

39. Walter D. Scott, Robert Clothier, Stanley R. Mathewson, and William R. Spriegel, *Personnel Management: Principles, Practices, and Point of View*, 3rd ed. (New York: McGraw-Hill, 1941), 216; Daniel J. Kevles, "Testing the Army's Intelligence: Psychologists and the Military in World War I," *Journal of American History* 55 (1968), 569.

40. Scott et al., *Personnel Management*, 151.

41. Kevles, "Testing the Army's Intelligence," 566.

42. Ibid., 570.

43. Harold Rugg, "Is the Rating of Human Character Practicable?" *Journal of Educational Psychology* 12 (1921), 427.

44. Rugg, "Is the Rating of Human Character Practicable?" *Journal of Educational Psychology* 13 (1922), 82. Rugg's articles appeared in the November and December issues (vol. 12, 1921) and in the January and February issues (vol. 13, 1922) of this journal.

45. Edward L. Thorndike, "A Constant Error in Psychological Rating," *Journal of Applied Psychology* 4 (1920), 25–29.

46. Rugg, "Is the Rating of Human Character Practicable?" *Journal of Educational Psychology* 13 (1922), 38.

47. John Carson, "Army Alpha, Army Brass, and the Search for Army Intelligence," *Isis* 84 (June 1993), 287–96. The alpha tests are shown in Carl Brigham, *A Study of American Intelligence* (Princeton, N.J.: Princeton University Press, 1923), 3–31. For a description of the conditions under which the tests were administered, see Stephen J. Gould, *The Mismeasure of Man* (New York: W. W. Norton, 1981), 202–3.

48. Robert M. Yerkes, ed., *Psychological Examining in the United States Army*, National Academy of Sciences Memoir 15 (Washington, D.C.: GPO, 1920).

49. Clarence Yoakum and Robert M. Yerkes, comps. and eds., *Army Mental Tests* (New York: Henry Holt, 1920), 27.

50. Ibid., 22–23.

51. Brigham, *Study of American Intelligence*, 197–210.

52. Ibid., 89.

53. Yerkes, *Psychological Examining*, 820–22, 829.

54. Richard T. Ely, *An Introduction to Political Economy* (New York, 1889), 224–25.

55. Thomas N. Carver, *The Distribution of Wealth* (New York: Macmillan, 1904), 157.

56. Martin Bronfenbrenner, *Income Distribution Theory* (Chicago: Aldine-Atherton, 1971), 174.

57. Frank A. Fetter, *Economics*, 2 vols. (New York: Century, 1916), 1:183. In 1911 Henry Ludwell Moore, a pioneering Columbia econometrician who had studied under Pearson, sought to prove that the distribution of wages actually conformed to marginal-productivity theory and to the distribution of workers' meritorious qualities. Lacking much evidence about the actual distribution of wages, however, he had to rely on one study from France in 1893 and another from Massachusetts in 1905. See Moore, *Laws of Wages: An Essay on Statistical Economics* (New York: Macmillan, 1911), 78–79, 81–82, 86–99. For a critique of Moore, see George Stigler, *Essays in the History of Economics* (Chicago: University of Chicago Press, 1965), chap. 13.

58. Algie M. Simons, *Personnel Relations in Industry* (New York: Ronald Press, 1921), 93.

59. Frank Taussig, *Principles of Economics* (New York: Macmillan, 1912), 132, 134–38. Taussig presented this typology in a chapter on wage differences in a society marked by noncompeting groups, one in which custom and lack of access to capital constrained movement from tier to tier, and he wondered whether, in the absence of these constraints, pay would depend on ability. His answer (142) was guarded: physicians as a class would receive higher remuneration than mechanics only if it could be shown that the skills of physicians were in shorter supply than those required for a skilled trade. No one, he added, had shown that.

60. Ibid., 132.

61. In 1925 Terman used Taussig's 1912 classification of occupations to argue that the gifted children he studied had fathers who possessed superior intelligence; over 80 percent of the fathers belonged to Taussig's top two occupational groups. See Lewis M. Terman, *Genetic Studies of Genius, Volume 1: Mental and Physical Traits of a Thousand Gifted Children* (Palo Alto, Calif.: Stanford University Press, 1925), 64.

62. Terman's Stanford-Binet became the most frequently used test for assessing the validity of any other intelligence test; see Gould, *Mismeasure of Man*, 171.

63. Simons, *Personnel Relations in Industry*, 93.

64. Terman, *Genetic Studies of Genius, Volume 1*, 66–69.

65. Pitirim Sorokin, *Social Mobility* (New York: Harper Bros., 1927), 102–3.

66. Sorokin, *Social Mobility*, 309–11. Gosta Carlsson, "Sorokin's Theory of Social Mobility," in *Pitirim A. Sorokin in Review*, ed. Philip J. Allen (Durham, N.C.: Duke University Press, 1963), 123–39.

67. Sorokin, *Social Mobility*, 281; Barry V. Johnston, *Pitirim A. Sorokin: An Intellectual Biography* (Lawrence: University Press of Kansas, 1995), 35.

68. Sorokin, *Social Mobility*, 216–50.

69. Frank Taussig, *American Business Leaders: A Study in Social Origins and Social Stratification* (New York: Macmillan, 1932).

70. Taussig, *American Business Leaders*, 3.

71. Hugo Munsterberg, "Psychological Tests of Accident Prevention," *Electric Railway Journal* 39 (1912), 394–95; Munsterberg fashioned a simulator to test street railway motormen on their ability to foresee likely accident-causing situations. For a description of his device and subsequent refinements to it (Munsterberg died in 1916), see Morris S. Viteles, "Research in Selection of Motormen," Pts. 1 and 2, *Journal of Personnel Research* 4

(1925), 100–115, 173–99. Munsterberg's test for marine officers required candidates to sort a deck of cards bearing different letter combinations into appropriate piles; he thought that this test would measure candidates' ability to perceive a situation at a glance and respond to it. See H. L. Hollingworth, *Vocational Psychology: Its Problems and Methods* (New York: D. Appleton, 1920), 111–12.

72. Henry L. Gantt, *Work, Wages, and Profits*, 2nd ed. (New York: Engineering Magazine, 1919), 78; Sanford Jacoby, *Employing Bureaucracy: Managers, Unions, and the Transformation of Work in American Industry, 1900–1945* (New York: Columbia University Press, 1985), 91–93.

73. Donald G. Paterson, "The Scott Company Graphic Rating Scale," *Journal of Personnel Research* 1 (1922–23), 361–76.

74. On the origins of the Personnel Research Foundation, see Noble, *America by Design*, 230 n. 2.

75. This set of ideals explains the overlapping memberships characteristic of researchers in the personnel movement. They subscribed to vocational education, vocational guidance, industrial psychology, and testing; see C. S. Yoakum, "Basic Experiments in Vocational Guidance," *Journal of Personnel Research* 1 (1922), 18–34. In general, the movement flourished when labor markets were slack and employers could pick and choose, and it struggled in tight labor markets. The obvious exception is the Depression, when markets were so slack that little hiring took place.

76. Walter D. Scott and Robert Clothier, *Personnel Management* (Chicago: A. W. Shaw, 1923), 133–69. Like Scott, Clothier had worked for the CCP during World War I. Assuring their readers that workers would respond with contempt were they told that there was always room at the top for a good man, the authors insisted on the need for graphic depiction of promotion possibilities. None of the charts they exhibited indicated the possibility of promotion from the bottom to the top. What they did indicate was the line that could lead from, say, carpenter's apprentice to carpenter to foreman or from assistant draftsman through several steps to production supervisor. Significantly, they conceded that most jobs would be dead ends, but even so, they argued, such jobs needed to be examined to see whether some promotion opportunities, if only titular, could be squeezed out of them. Charts depended on "job analysis" and standardizing occupational descriptions, which were expected to eliminate pay inconsistencies within companies and thereby reduce internal disputes; see Jacoby, *Employing Bureaucracy*, 150.

77. Henry H. Goddard, *Human Efficiency and Levels of Intelligence* (Princeton, N.J.: Princeton University Press, 1920), vi–vii.

78. Eliot Frost, "What Industry Wants and Does Not Want from the Psychologist," *Journal of Applied Psychology* 4 (March 1920), 23–24.

79. Jacoby, *Employing Bureaucracy*, 95.

80. Katherine M. H. Blackford and Arthur Newcomb, *The Job, the Man, the Boss* (New York: Doubleday, 1914). For a representative attack on this approach from the personnel management movement, see Donald G. Paterson and Katherine E. Ludgate, "Blond and Brunette Traits: A Quantitative Study," *Journal of Personnel Research* 1 (1922), 122–27.

81. Hollingworth, *Vocational Psychology*, chap. 2.

82. Truman L. Kelley, "Principles Underlying the Classification of Men," *Journal of Applied Psychology* 3 (1919), 50–67; L. L. Thurstone, "Mental Tests for Prospective Telegraphers," *Journal of Applied Psychology* 3 (1919), 110–17; Clarence S. Yoakum, "Basic Experiments in Vocational Guidance," *Journal of Personnel Research* 1 (May 1922), 18–34.

83. L. L. Thurstone, "The Intelligence of Policemen," *Journal of Personnel Research* 1 (1922), 64–74.

84. Henry C. Link, *Employment Psychology* (New York: Macmillan, 1919), 27–29.

85. Ibid., 35.

86. Harry D. Kitson, "Height, Weight, and Salesmanship," *Journal of Personnel Research* 1 (1922), 289.

87. See Ruml's two articles: "The Need for Examination of Certain Hypotheses in Mental Tests," *Journal of Philosophy* 17 (1920), 57–61, and "Reconstruction in Mental Tests," *Journal of Philosophy* 18 (1921), 181–85.

88. Edward S. Jones, "Personality Terms Commonly Used in Recommendations," *Journal of Personnel Research* 2 (1924), 421–30.

89. Max Freyd, "Measurement in Vocational Selection," *Journal of Personnel Research* 2 (Oct. 1923), 236. Psychologists continued to debate nature versus nurture on a more abstract level in the 1920s, when the hereditarian Terman and the skeptic Frank N. Freeman conducted studies comparing the intelligence test scores of adopted children with their siblings. See Minton, *Terman*, 150–54. A difficulty lay in controlling for the differences between the home environments of natural and adoptive parents. The problem persists. See Sandra Scarr, *Race, Social Class, and Individual Differences in IQ* (Hillsdale, N.J.: Lawrence Erlbaum Associates, 1981), esp. part V.

90. "Intelligence and Its Measurement: A Symposium," *Journal of Educational Psychology* 12 (March 1921), 128.

91. Ibid., 127–33.

92. Edward L. Thorndike, "Intelligence and Its Uses," *Harper's Monthly* 140 (1920), 235.

93. See the symposium "Intelligence and Its Measurement," *Journal of Educational Psychology* 12 (March 1921), 139 (Steven Colvin), 143–44 (Beardsley Ruml), and 12 (April 1921), 206 (L. L. Thurstone) and 216 (M. E. Haggerty). See also Percival M. Symonds, "The Present Status of Character Measurement," *Journal of Educational Psychology* 15 (1924), 484–98. We should remember that marking systems in American colleges had long graded such components of character as obedience, punctuality, and diligence, with marks for these components counting in the student's final score. In England merit usually meant intellectual brilliance, with no special notice taken of character or "worth" in the final score. See Sheldon Rothblatt, *Education's Abiding Moral Dilemma: Merit and Worth in the Cross-Atlantic Democracies, 1800–2006* (Oxford: Symposium Books, 2007), chap. 2.

94. Frank N. Freeman, "Tests of Personality Traits," *School Review* 33 (1925), 95. "The correlations are not very high," Rudolph Pintner concluded after surveying more than sixty different studies of correlations between scores on intelligence tests and the academic grades of collegians. Most studies discovered correlations between .3 and .5. See Pintner, *Intelligence Testing*, 294, 302–4, 289. See also F. Edith Carothers, *Psychological Examinations of College Students*, Contributions to Education 46 (New York: Teachers College, 1922), 79; Robert T. Rock Jr., *A Critical Examination of Current Practices in Ability Grouping*, Catholic University of America, Educational Research Bulletins 4 (Washington, D.C.: Catholic Education Press, 1929), 60–62. Rock found huge differences in the correlations between intelligence tests and school marks. Measures of IQ obtained by different intelligence tests also differed, as did results of different achievement tests administered to the same group; he concluded that as many as one-quarter of pupils placed in ability groups by IQ were misplaced.

95. Heather A. Warren, "Character, Public Schooling, and Religious Education, 1920–1934," *Religion and American Culture* 7 (1997), 62–63; see also Warren, "The Shift from Character to Personality in Mainline Protestant Thought, 1935–1945," *Church History* 67 (1998), 537–55.

96. Mark A. May and Hugh Hartshorne, "Objective Methods of Measuring Character," *Pedagogical Seminary* 32 (1925), 58–65.

97. Percival M. Symonds, "The Present Status of Character Measurement," *Journal of Educational Psychology* 15 (1924), 484–99.

98. Quoted in Kenneth H. Clark, Robert Hogan, and Raymond Wolfe, eds., *Fifty Years of Personality Psychology* (New York: Plenum Press, 1993), 9.

99. Gordon W. Allport, "Personality and Character," *Psychological Bulletin* 18 (1921), 444.

100. Floyd H. Allport and Gordon W. Allport, "Personality Traits: Their Classification and Measurement," *Journal of Abnormal Psychology* 16 (1921), 8.

101. Ibid., 23.

102. Tamara Plakins Thornton, *Handwriting in America: A Cultural History* (New Haven, Conn.: Yale University Press, 1996), 139.

103. June E. Downey, *The Will-Temperament and Its Testing* (Yonkers, N.Y.: World Book, 1923), 57–58.

104. Ibid.

105. Richard S. Uhrbrock, *An Analysis of the Downey Will-Temperament Tests*, Contributions to Education 296 (New York: Teachers College Bureau of Publications, 1928), 63–64.

106. Allport and Allport, "Personality Traits," 6.

107. Ibid.

108. Hugh Hartshorne, Mark A. May, and F. K. Shuttleworth, *Studies in the Nature of Character*, 3 vols. (New York: Macmillan, 1928–30), 1:34.

109. The first volume was subtitled *Studies in Deceit*. The third, which included F. K. Shuttleworth as an author, was subtitled *Studies in the Organization of Character*. The six articles in *Religious Education* were published in book form by Hartshorne and May as *Testing the Knowledge of Right and Wrong* (n.p.: Religious Education Association, 1927).

110. Hartshorne, May, and Shuttleworth, *Studies in the Nature of Character*, 1:108.

111. Ibid., 1:379.

112. Goodenough, *Mental Testing*, 81.

113. Scott et al., *Personnel Management*, 3rd ed., 152.

114. "Sidney Leavitt Pressey," in *A History of Psychology in Autobiography*, vol. 5, ed. Edward Boring and Gardner Lindzey (New York: Appleton-Century-Crofts, 1967), 323.

115. Lester F. Ward, "Broadening the Way to Success," *Forum* 2 (1886), 340–50. For the story of this article's retitling, see Ward, *Applied Sociology: A Treatise on the Conscious Improvement of Society by Society* (Boston: Ginn, 1906), 141–43.

116. Charles H. Cooley, "Genius, Fame and the Comparison of Races," *Annals of the American Academy of Political and Social Science* 9 (1897), 331–32.

117. Walter Van Dyke Bingham, *Aptitudes and Aptitude Testing* (New York: Harper and Bros., 1937), 269.

118. Spearman later modified his theory to allow for what he called the "group" factors in intelligence; see Douglas Bray, *Issues in the Study of Talent* (New York: King's Crown Press, 1954), 23–24.

119. Michael Ackerman, "Mental Testing and the Expansion of Educational Opportunity," *History of Education Quarterly* 35 (1995), 279–300.

120. Dael Wolfle, Introduction to *The Discovery of Talent*, ed. Wolfle (Cambridge, Mass.: Harvard University Press, 1969), xii–xiii. In the same volume see J. P. Guilford, "Three Faces of Intellect," 107–32, and Philip E. Vernon, "Ability Factors and Environmental Influences," 279–304; see also Bray, *Issues in the Study of Talent*, 24; Quinn McNemar, "Lost: Our Intelligence, WHY?" *American Psychologist* 19 (1964), 872.

121. Wolfle, "Introduction," xii–xiii.

122. Charles Broadly and Margaret Broadly, *Know Your Real Abilities: Understanding and Developing Your Aptitudes* (New York: Whittlesey House, 1948).

123. Strictly speaking, the AAF tests assessed job aptitudes rather than PMAs. That is, they rested on the standard procedure of vocational psychologists: divide a job into its component activities and then devise tests to determine how well someone could perform

each activity. For a description of the AAF tests, see Frederick B. Davis, *Utilizing Human Talent: Armed Forces Selection and Classification Procedures* (Washington, D.C.: American Council on Education, 1947). What captured the attention of multiple-factorists was evidence of the validity of these tests, which in practice led to a blurring of the distinction between them and PMAs; see McNemar, "Lost: Our Intelligence," 873.

124. Quoted in Davis, *Utilizing Human Talent*, 40.

125. Ordway Tead, *Equalizing Educational Opportunity beyond the Secondary School* (Cambridge, Mass.: Harvard University Press, 1947), 10, 22.

126. John C. Flanagan, *Design for a Study of American Youth* (Boston: Houghton Mifflin, 1962).

127. Vernon, "Ability Factors and Environmental Influences," 282.

6. THE "PRESUMPTION OF MERIT"

1. Johns Hopkins University, *Celebration of the Twenty-Fifth Anniversary of the Founding of the University and Inauguration of Ira Remsen as President of the University* (Baltimore: Johns Hopkins University Press, 1902), 105.

2. Glenn D. Altschuler, *Andrew D. White: Educator, Historian, Diplomat* (Ithaca: Cornell University Press, 1979), 147.

3. Eliot said that coeducation was suited only to communities "that cannot afford anything better." Ibid., 104.

4. Abraham Flexner, *Daniel Coit Gilman: Creator of the American Type of University* (New York: Harcourt, Brace, 1946), 44–46.

5. Francisco Cordasco, *The Shaping of American Graduate Education: Daniel Coit Gilman and the Protean Ph.D.* (Totowa, N.J.: Rowman and Littlefield, 1973), 59.

6. Lawrence Veysey, *The Emergence of the American University* (Chicago: University of Chicago Press, 1965), 66–68, 118–19.

7. Kim Townsend, *Manhood at Harvard: William James and Others* (New York: W.W. Norton, 1996), 121–22.

8. For a nuanced discussion of distinctions between terms like "specialized knowledge" and "specialization," see Jon H. Roberts and James Turner, *The Sacred and the Secular University* (Princeton, N.J.: Princeton University Press, 1999), 85–87.

9. Simon Newcomb, "Abstract Science in America, 1776–1876," *North American Review* 122 (1876), 103.

10. Ralph W. Emerson, "Self-Reliance," in *Essays*, First Series (Washington, D.C.: National Home Library, 1932), 44.

11. Shirley W. Smith, *James Burrill Angell: An American Influence* (Ann Arbor: University of Michigan Press, 1954), 28–29.

12. James Bryce, *The American Commonwealth*, 2 vols. (London: Macmillan, 1888–91), 2:630–31.

13. [Thomas Wentworth Higginson], "Regular and Volunteer Officers," *Atlantic Monthly* 14 (1864), 348–57.

14. Samuel P. Huntington, *The Soldier and the State: The Theory and Politics of Civil-Military Relations* (Cambridge, Mass.: Harvard University Press, 1957), 28–30; William B. Skelton, *An American Profession of Arms, 1784–1861* (Lawrence: University Press of Kansas, 1992), 36.

15. James McPherson, *The Battle Cry of Freedom: The Civil War Era* (New York: Oxford University Press, 1988), 326. There was nothing new about this. West Pointers had long been angered by the practice, just as they were angered by the much greater ease in obtaining high rank in militias compared with the regular army; see Marcus Cunliffe, *Soldiers and Civilians: The Martial Spirit in America, 1775–1865* (1968; New York: Free Press, 1973), 131–32.

16. Gerald F. Linderman, *Embattled Courage: The Experience of Combat in the American Civil War* (New York: Free Press, 1987), 43–47.

17. E. B. Long, ed., *Personal Memoirs of U.S. Grant* (New York: Da Capo, 1982), 130.

18. Cunliffe, *Soldiers and Civilians*, 282.

19. Prince de Joinville, *The Army of the Potomac: Its Organization, Its Commander, and Its Campaign*, trans. William Henry Hurlbert (New York: Anson D. F. Randolph, 1862), 13. Joinville, an extremely astute observer, also recognized the connection between democratic politics and reliance on volunteers. Politicians like Daniel Sickles were good at raising regiments of volunteers and were rewarded with high rank in the army; see Thomas Keneally, *American Scoundrel: The Life of the Notorious Civil War General Dan Sickles* (New York: Doubleday, 2002), chap. 6.

20. Linderman, *Embattled Courage*, 170.

21. Upton's idea of professionalism also included promotion by ability, compulsory retirement of army officers at sixty-two, and interchange between staff and line officers to prevent the former from becoming mired in routine. He also thought that the Union had erred in 1861 when it chose not to disperse regular officers among volunteer units. See Steven Ambrose, *Upton and the Army* (Baton Rouge: Louisiana State University Press, 1964), 85–86, 104–5, 143–44.

22. Quoted in Huntington, *Soldier and the State*, 257.

23. Quoted in Peter S. Michie, *The Life and Letters of Emory Upton* (New York, 1885), 419. Whether Upton's suicide can be attributed to his despair about the often hostile reception of his ideas was debated at the time. He also experienced intense suffering from what may have been a brain tumor; see ibid., chap. 13.

24. Emory Upton, *The Military Policy of the United States* (Washington, D.C.: GPO, 1904), iii.

25. Huntington, *Soldier and the State*, 237–42; Philip C. Jessup, *Elihu Root*, 3 vols. (New York: Dodd, Mead, 1938), 1:242–43.

26. Donald Chisholm, *Waiting for Dead Men's Shoes: Origins and Development of the U.S. Navy's Officer Personnel System, 1793–1941* (Stanford, Calif.: Stanford University Press, 2001), 29–30, 363–64, 394–96.

27. Ibid., 274, 323–24.

28. Ibid., 461–66.

29. For a discussion of these connections, see Huntington, *Soldier and the State*, 257.

30. Ibid., 587, 588–92. In the early 1920s the secretary of war proposed a similar system, supplementing promotion by seniority with the rapid advance of a small number of highly able officers, for the army. The plan was not implemented, mainly because of skepticism about identifying in peacetime officers who would prove superior in warfare; see Huntington, *Soldier and the State*, 297.

31. Quoted in Henry James, *Charles W. Eliot: President of Harvard University, 1869–1909*, 2 vols. (Boston: Houghton Mifflin, 1930), 2:188.

32. [Charles W. Eliot], "The New Education: Its Organization, I," *Atlantic Monthly* 23 (1869), 216n.

33. Daniel C. Gilman, "Civil Service Reform," in Gilman, *The Launching of a University and Other Papers* (New York: Dodd, Mead, 1906), 341–50.

34. Andrew D. White, "Do the Spoils Belong to the Victor?" *North American Review* 134 (1882), 111–33.

35. Charles Dunbar, "Economic Science in America, 1776–1876," *North American Review* 122 (1876), 143.

36. William G. Sumner, "Politics in America, 1776–1876," *North American Review* 122 (1876), 55, 87.

37. Daniel C. Gilman, "Higher Education in the United States" (1893), in Gilman, *University Problems in the United States* (New York, 1898), 309.

38. Daniel C. Gilman, "The Characteristics of a University" (1886), in Gilman, *University Problems*, 93. Although Francis Galton later wrote that he should have substituted "ability" or "talent" for "genius" in the title of his famous book, his depiction of genius as irrepressible reflected the usual connotation of genius in the mid-nineteenth century. After 1880 Galton's American critic, the sociologist Lester Frank Ward, led a sustained attack on the prevailing "adoration of genius," arguing instead that progress depended on widening opportunities for education; see Ward, "Broadening the Way to Success," *Forum* 2 (1886), 342–43. Ward summarized his position in *Applied Sociology: A Treatise on the Conscious Improvement of Society by Society* (Boston: Ginn, 1906), 137–38, 241.

39. James, *Eliot*, 1:36–47.

40. Ibid., 1:101.

41. [Eliot], "New Education," 206; for background on the New Education, see Robert V. Bruce, *The Launching of Modern American Science, 1846–1876* (New York: Knopf, 1987), chap. 24.

42. Gilman, *Launching of a University*, 8–9.

43. Fabian Franklin, *The Life of Daniel Coit Gilman* (New York: Dodd, Mead, 1910), 75–79, 90.

44. Carl Becker, *Cornell University: Founders and the Founding* (Ithaca: Cornell University Press, 1944), 156–57. For the larger intellectual context of Tappan's proposals, see Julie A. Reuben, *The Making of the Modern University: Intellectual Transformation and the Marginalization of Morality* (Chicago: University of Chicago Press, 1996), 25–28, 34–35.

45. Thomas L. Haskell, *The Emergence of Professional Social Science: The American Social Science Association and the Nineteenth-Century Crisis of Authority* (Urbana: University of Illinois Press, 1977), 65–68.

46. Quoted in Flexner, *Gilman*, 40.

47. Edward Waldo Emerson and Waldo Emerson Forbes, eds., *Journals of Ralph Waldo Emerson*, 10 vols. (Boston: Riverside Press, 1914), 10:197.

48. Brooks M. Kelley, *Yale: A History* (New Haven, Conn.: Yale University Press, 1974), 237–38.

49. Noah Porter, *The American Colleges and the American Public* (New Haven, Conn., 1870), 29.

50. Ibid., 94.

51. Ibid., 95.

52. Ibid., 169.

53. Ibid., 170.

54. Louise L. Stevenson, *Scholarly Means to Evangelical Ends: The New Haven Scholars and the Transformation of Higher Education in America, 1830–1890* (New Haven, Conn.: Yale University Press, 1986), chap. 4.

55. On the decline of literary societies, see Kolon T. Morelock, *Taking the Town: Collegiate and Community Culture in the Blue Grass, 1880–1917* (Lexington: University Press of Kentucky, 2008), 3, 5, 7, 9, 140–41, 143, 243–55, 275–78.

56. Lewis S. Welch and Walter Camp, *Yale: Her Campus, Class-Rooms, and Athletics* (Boston, 1899), 15–16.

57. Porter, *American Colleges*, 142.

58. E. L. Godkin, "The Danger of an Office-Holding Aristocracy," *Century* 2 (1882), 291.

59. [Eliot], "New Education," 215n.

60. William W. Folwell, "The Minnesota Plan," in Folwell, *University Addresses* (Minneapolis: H. W. Wilson, 1909), 114–15.

61. Daniel C. Gilman, "The Use and Abuse of Titles," *North American Review* 140 (1885), 258–59; see also Gilman, "Honorary Degrees," *Nation* 5 (1867), 93.

62. "President Eliot's Inaugural Address," in *The Development of Harvard University since the Inauguration of President Eliot*, ed. Samuel E. Morison (Cambridge, Mass.: Harvard University Press, 1930), lxiii.

63. Ibid., lxvii.

64. Henry A. Yeomans, *Abbot Lawrence Lowell, 1856–1943* (Cambridge, Mass.: Harvard University Press, 1948), 22–23, 67.

65. Mary Smallwood, *An Historical Study of Examinations and Grading Systems in Early American Universities* (Cambridge, Mass.: Harvard University Press, 1935), 94.

66. Samuel E. Morison, *Three Centuries of Harvard, 1636–1936* (Cambridge, Mass.: Harvard University Press, 1936), 345–47.

67. George B. Hill, *Harvard College by an Oxonian* (New York, 1894), 242. For an identical assessment by another British observer, see Bryce, *American Commonwealth*, 2:555–56.

68. George W. Pierson, *Yale College: An Educational History, 1861–1921* (New Haven, Conn.: Yale University Press, 1952), 330.

69. Woodrow Wilson, "What Is College For?" in *Papers of Woodrow Wilson*, 69 vols., ed. Arthur Link (Princeton, N.J.: Princeton University Press, 1975), 19:344, 337–38.

70. Pierson, *Yale College*, 240–41.

71. Hugh Hawkins, *Pioneer: A History of the Johns Hopkins University, 1874–1889* (Ithaca: Cornell University Press, 1960), 249.

72. "College Studies," in Morison, *Development of Harvard University*, xliii–xlvi.

73. Ibid., xlv–xlvi.

74. Orrin L. Elliott, *Stanford University: The First Twenty-Five Years* (Palo Alto, Calif.: Stanford University Press, 1937), 70.

75. Ibid., 162–63.

76. Howard W. Peckham, *The Making of the University of Michigan, 1817–1967* (Ann Arbor: University of Michigan Press, 1967), 109.

77. Robert Stevens, *Law School: Legal Education in America from the 1850s to the 1980s* (Chapel Hill: University of North Carolina Press, 1983), 93.

78. Ibid., 25–28, 98.

79. Hugh Hawkins, *Between Harvard and America: The Educational Leadership of Charles W. Eliot* (New York: Oxford University Press, 1972), 85. Hawkins observes that during the first six years of his presidency Eliot devoted "his most persistent attention" to reforming Harvard's law, medical, and divinity schools.

80. Hawkins, *Between Harvard and America*, 61; Frederick C. Shattuck and J. Lewis Bremer, "The Medical School," in Morison, *Development of Harvard University*, 556–60.

81. Quoted from Eliot's annual report of 1875–76 in Roscoe Pound, "The Law School, 1817–1929," in Morison, *Development of Harvard University*, 498.

82. Stevens, *Law School*, 36, 38–39. The appointment of James Barr Ames as assistant professor of law in 1883 complemented Langdell's goals. Stevens credits Ames with creating the distinction within the legal profession between "academics" and "practitioners." Most lawyers continued to enter the profession through apprenticeship and to be socialized into its norms by professional experience, and even in Langdell's day many of those who attended law schools did so merely as supplements to apprenticeship. See William R. Johnson, *Schooled Lawyers: A Study in the Clash of Professional Cultures* (New York: New York University Press, 1978), 11, 24–25, 38.

83. *Annual Report of the President and Treasurer of Harvard College, 1880–1881* (Cambridge, Mass., 1888), 80–81.

84. Alfred Z. Reed, *Present-Day Law Schools in the United States and Canada*, Bulletin 21 (New York: Carnegie Foundation for the Advancement of Teaching, 1928), 132.

85. Kenneth Ludmerer, *Learning to Heal: The Development of American Medical Education* (New York: Basic Books, 1985), 32–38.

86. Oscar Handlin, "A Small Community," in Bernard Bailyn et al., *Glimpses of the Harvard Past* (Cambridge, Mass.: Harvard University Press, 1986), 98–99.

87. Quoted in Laurence Veysey, *The Emergence of the American University* (Chicago: University of Chicago Press, 1965), 6.

88. Given its small size, Johns Hopkins's preeminence in research is striking. Between 1896 and 1901 the university conferred 221 doctorates, followed by Yale (182), Chicago (176), Harvard (156), Columbia (127), Pennsylvania (125), and Cornell (94); see E.A. Birge, "Statistics Concerning the Migration of Graduate Students," in Association of American Universities, *Journal of Proceedings and Addresses of the Third Annual Conference, 1902*, 40.

89. Hawkins, *Pioneer*, 126–27.

90. Richard Hofstadter and Walter P. Metzger, *The Development of Academic Freedom in the United States* (New York: Columbia University Press, 1955), 454.

91. Ibid., 465–66.

92. John Higham, "The Matrix of Specialization," in *The Organization of Knowledge in Modern America*, ed. Alexandra Oleson and John Voss (Baltimore: Johns Hopkins University Press, 1979), 12.

93. For a full airing of these views, see the paper by John M. Stillman of Stanford, "Relation of Salary to Title in American Universities," and the discussion that followed in Association of American Universities, *Journal of Proceedings and Addresses of the Eighth Annual Conference, 1906*, 72–91.

94. Market principles nevertheless had received a notable boost in 1893, when, in a celebrated episode, William Rainey Harper lured the cream of Hall's faculty at Clark University to the University of Chicago.

95. Monte A. Calvert, *The Mechanical Engineer in America, 1830–1910* (Baltimore: Johns Hopkins University Press, 1967), 3–8.

96. Ibid., 277–81.

97. Flexner, *Gilman*, 13.

98. Carnegie Foundation for the Advancement of Teaching, *The Financial Status of the Professor in America and Germany* (New York: Carnegie Foundation for the Advancement of Teaching, 1908), 5–6. This study was based on 430 reporting institutions.

99. Hawkins, *Between Harvard and America*, 186–90. Harvard continued to distinguish "first-list" and "second-list" colleges for admissions to its law school. In 1924 a graduate of a first-list college needed to rank in the top three-fourths of his graduating class to gain admission, while a graduate of a second-list college had to rank in the top quarter. See Arthur E. Sutherland, *The Law at Harvard: A History of Ideas and Men, 1817–1967* (Cambridge, Mass.: Harvard University Press, 1967), 249.

100. Eliot is credited with the first proposal, in 1877, to establish a standard college admission board, which he also saw as a way to elevate and standardize secondary education; see Hawkins, *Between Harvard and America*, 177–78. Nicholas M. Butler, "How the College Entrance Examination Board Came to Be," in College Entrance Examination Board, *The Work of the College Entrance Examination Board, 1901–1925* (Boston: Ginn, 1926), 1–6; Wilson Farrand, "A Brief History of the College Entrance Examination Board," in ibid., 21–30; Claude M. Fuess, *The College Board: The First Fifty Years* (New York: Columbia University Press, 1950).

101. Joseph L. Henderson, *Admission to College by Certificates* (New York: Teachers College, 1912). The system bears comparison with an earlier development in Britain, where, starting in 1858, first Oxford and then Cambridge set examinations for endowed schools. This approach was consistent with the status of both universities as examining bodies (the

colleges taught, the university examined), with the British preference for examinations, and with the national hegemony of the ancient universities, something envied but never attained by Harvard and Yale. See R. J. Montgomery, *Examinations: An Account of Their Evolution as Administrative Devices in England* (Pittsburgh, Pa.: University of Pittsburgh Press, 1967), 45; John Roach, *Public Examinations in England, 1850–1900* (Cambridge: Cambridge University Press, 1971), 34–35; L. Wiese, *German Letters on English Education*, trans. and ed. Leonhard Schmitz (New York, 1879), 119–20.

102. W. Bruce Leslie, *Gentlemen and Scholars: College and Community in the "Age of the University," 1865–1917* (University Park: Pennsylvania State University Press, 1992), 219.

103. Butler, "How the College Entrance Examination Board Came to Be," 4–5.

104. Ellen Condliffe Lagemann, *Private Power for the Public Good: A History of the Carnegie Foundation for the Advancement of Teaching* (Middletown, Conn.: Wesleyan University Press, 1983), 37–39.

105. Abraham Flexner, *Henry S. Pritchett: A Biography* (New York: Columbia University Press, 1943), 9, 20–21.

106. Edwin Slosson, *Great American Universities* (New York: Macmillan, 1910), ix–x.

107. Ibid., 482.

108. Ibid., 483.

109. Ibid., 487–88.

110. Lagemann, *Private Power for the Public Good*, 54. The CIW gradually retreated from its search for "a few exceptional men," a policy inspired by Carnegie that led in practice to small grants to individuals. In a notable case, it pulled funding from the self-taught botanist Luther Burbank in 1909; see Nathan Reingold, "National Science Policy in a Private Foundation: The Carnegie Institution of Washington," in Oleson and Voss, *Organization of Science in Modern America*, 321–22.

111. Slosson, *Great American Universities*, 489.

112. For an influential Marxist version of this argument, see Magali Sarfatti Larson, *The Rise of Professionalism: A Sociological Analysis* (Berkeley: University of California Press, 1977), 239–43. See also Corinne Lathrop Gilb, *Hidden Hierarchies: The Professions and Government* (New York: Harper and Row, 1966), 191.

113. Flexner, *Gilman*, 80–82. "I never heard either President Gilman or any member of the academic staff," Flexner wrote (33), "urge that the supreme end of a college education is citizenship or character, the slogans under which modern inefficiency is cloaked."

114. For year-by-year data on the process of upgrading medical education, see N. P. Colwell, "Medical Education," in U.S. Department of the Interior, Bureau of Education, *Biennial Survey of Education, 1926–1928* (Washington, D.C.: GPO, 1929), 41–45.

115. Alfred Z. Reed, *Present-Day Law Schools in the United States and Canada* (New York: Carnegie Foundation for the Advancement of Teaching, 1928), 120–21.

116. Stevens, *Law School*, 83.

117. Ibid., 85 n. 15.

118. Reed, *Present-Day Law Schools*, 136.

119. In 1930 the ABA sponsored a new organization, the National Conference of Bar Examiners, which sought to persuade bar examiners to set examinations that resembled those of the better law schools.

120. This was not Flexner's intent. He thought that women made excellent doctors, and he trusted, prematurely, that coeducation in the surviving medical schools would bring women into the profession.

121. Roger Geiger, *To Advance Knowledge: The Growth of American Research Universities, 1900–1940* (New York: Oxford University Press, 1986), 132–33; Flexner, *Gilman*, 33. Jerold Auerbach discusses problems facing Jewish lawyers in Auerbach, *Unequal Justice: Lawyers and Social Change in Modern America* (New York: Oxford University Press, 1976),

184–88. A notable number of Jews graduated with outstanding records from elite law schools in the 1920s and 1930s, and several served in high positions in New Deal agencies despite overt prejudice. But elite law firms were usually closed to Jews, and also to Irish Catholics. This situation gradually changed after 1945.

122. William James, "The Ph.D. Octopus," in James, *Memories and Studies* (London: Longmans, Green, 1912), 334–43. This essay originally appeared in the *Harvard Monthly* in March 1903. For a similar argument, see David Starr Jordan, "The Making of a Darwin," *Science,* n.s., 32 (1910), 929–42.

123. For Cattell's description of his methods, see Cattell, "A Further Statistical Study of American Men of Science," *Science,* n.s., 32 (1910), 633–48, 672–88. By including psychology as a science and defining teaching, administration, and editing along with research as elements of "merit" (635), Cattell made room for himself in the galaxy of men of science.

124. Frederic L. Wells, *A Statistical Study of Literary Merit* (New York: Science Press, 1907).

125. Poe, "The Literati of New York City," in *The Complete Works of Edgar Allan Poe,* 17 vols., ed. James A. Harrison (New York: Thomas Y. Crowell, 1902), 15:1–4.

126. Quoted in Waterman T. Hewett, *Cornell University: A History,* 4 vols. (New York: University Publishing Society, 1915), 1:295–96. Margaret W. Rossiter has argued that "ejecting women in the name of 'higher standards' was one way to assert male domination over the burgeoning female presence." See Rossiter, *Women Scientists in America: Struggle and Strategy to 1940* (Baltimore: Johns Hopkins University Press, 1982), xvii. Rossiter presents persuasive evidence that males used existing standards and devised new ones to marginalize women in professional associations at a time when more women were securing Ph.D.'s (114 in 1924, 60 percent conferred by AAU universities). But the move for standards preceded the push by women into graduate school and had a different source.

127. Abraham Flexner, *Universities: American, English, German* (New York: Oxford University Press, 1930), 213.

128. On Harvard Law School's gradual elevation of its standards, see Sutherland, *Law at Harvard,* 167–249.

129. Kenneth M. Ludmerer, *Time to Heal: American Medical Education from the Turn of the Century to the Era of Managed Care* (New York: Oxford University Press, 1999), 60–64; Sutherland, *Law at Harvard,* 249–50. Sutherland records that 35 percent (200/575) of the class that entered Harvard Law School in 1925 flunked out after the first year. Harvard's policy of admitting graduates of "first-list" colleges who stood in the top three-quarters of their graduating class meant that some (theoretically, all) could have been in the bottom half. More than a few of these men went on to eminent careers. One thinks of Dean Acheson, a C student at Yale, admitted to Harvard Law School. The massacre of the entering class of 1925 probably reflected a new requirement that a student who failed a course could remain in school only if he had an average 5 percent higher than the passing grade or at least two Cs. This was a wasteful way to make room for better students, but prestigious professional schools, as Ludmerer observes, needed paying customers and had only negligible resources for financial aid.

7. SQUEEZE PLAY

1. C. Wright Mills, *The Power Elite* (New York: Oxford University Press, 1956), 361.

2. Ibid., 231, 66–68, 106–7, 128–29, 353–54, 360. For a critique of Mills's argument about the political directorate, the component of the power elite that concerned itself with politics, and especially of his idea that it was composed of outsiders, see David T. Stanley, Dean F. Mann, and Jameson Doig, *Men Who Govern: A Biographical Profile of Federal Political Executives* (Washington, D.C.: Brookings Institution, 1967), 40–41, 80–81. For someone who became an icon of the New Left, Mills had a strange enthusiasm for the

German bureaucracy's hierarchical and authoritarian features; see Max Lerner, *America as a Civilization* (New York: Simon and Schuster, 1957), 413.

3. Edward Bellamy, *Looking Backward, 2000–1887* (Boston: Houghton Mifflin, 1917), 192.

4. Woodrow Wilson, "The Study of Administration," *Political Science Quarterly* 56 (1887), 481–506. Wilson never followed up this essay, and debate continues about his intent. See John A. Rohr, "The Constitutional World of Woodrow Wilson," in *Politics and Administration: Woodrow Wilson and American Public Administration*, ed. Jack Rabin and James S. Bowman (New York: Marcel Dekker, 1984), 31–49. See also Phillip J. Cooper, "The Wilsonian Dichotomy in Administrative Law," in the same volume, 79–94.

5. Herbert Croly, *Progressive Democracy* (New York: Macmillan, 1914), 358.

6. Edward House, *Philip Dru, Administrator: A Story of Tomorrow, 1920–1935* (New York: B.W. Huebsch, 1919).

7. On the origins of this alliance, see Hans Rosenberg, *Bureaucracy, Aristocracy, and Autocracy: The Prussian Experience, 1660–1815* (Cambridge, Mass.: Harvard University Press, 1958); on its development in the nineteenth century, see David Blackbourn, "The German Middle Class: An Introduction," in *The German Bourgeoisie: Essays on the Social History of the German Middle Class from the Late Eighteenth to the Early Twentieth Century*, ed. David Blackbourn and Richard J. Evans (London: Routledge, 1991), 4–18; in the same volume see Michael John, "Between Estate and Profession: Lawyers and the Development of the Legal Profession in Nineteenth-Century Germany," 162–97. For American influence on the Japanese system of competitive examinations as it developed in the nineteenth century, see Ikuo Amano, *Education and Examination in Modern Japan*, trans. William K. Cummings and Fumiko Cummings (Tokyo: University of Tokyo Press, 1990), 3–8.

8. Hans-Eberhard Mueller, *Bureaucracy, Education, and Monopoly: Civil Service Reforms in Prussia and England* (Berkeley: University of California Press, 1984), 227, 236. On the British reforms, which began in the 1850s with the so-called Northcote-Trevelyan reforms of the India Service and which were extended to the Home Service in 1870, see Keith Hope, *As Others See Us: Schooling and Social Mobility in Scotland and the United States* (Cambridge: Cambridge University Press, 1984), 252–55.

9. Theodore Roosevelt to Edward Porritt, Dec. 1, 1896, in *The Letters of Theodore Roosevelt*, 8 vols., ed. Elting E. Morison (Cambridge, Mass.: Harvard University Press, 1951–54), 1:422.

10. Max Weber, "Politics as a Vocation," in *From Max Weber: Essays in Sociology*, trans. and ed. H. H. Gerth and C. Wright Mills (New York: Oxford University Press, 1946, 1958), 110. In the same volume see "A Biographical View," 18.

11. E.L. Godkin, "The Danger of an Office-Holding Aristocracy," *Century* 2 (1882), 291.

12. Quoted in Stephen Skowronek, *Building a New American State: The Expansion of National Administrative Capacities, 1877–1920* (Cambridge: Cambridge University Press, 1982), 54. A prominent New York lawyer, Eaton had succeeded George W. Curtis as head of the short-lived Civil Service Commission which Grant had established in 1871 and for which Congress declined further funding in 1874. Eaton also authored *Civil Service Reform in Great Britain: A History of Abuses and Reforms and Their Bearing on American Politics* (New York, 1881), which argued that the British example proved that a party system and civil-service reform were compatible.

13. Andrew D. White, "Do the Spoils Belong to the Victor?" *North American Review* 134 (Feb. 1882), 115–16, 119; John M. Gregory, "The American Civil Service System," *Journal of Social Science* 18 (May 1884), 180; Theodore Roosevelt to Rufus Dawes, Oct. 24, 1890, in Morison, *Letters of Theodore Roosevelt*, 1:236.

14. Dorman B. Eaton, *The "Spoils" System and Civil Service Reform in the Custom-House and Post Office at New York* (New York, 1881).

15. Godkin, "Danger of an Office-Holding Aristocracy," 292.

16. Eaton, "*Spoils*" *System*, 61. Eaton added (80) a novel twist, which probably underscored the desperation of reformers to find some way to link examinations to character: open, competitive examinations would give every applicant for office an incentive to expose the character defects of those who scored higher, and in this way examinations would prevent the appointment of moral defectives.

17. Versions of this argument were often voiced in Congress; see *Congressional Globe*, 42nd Cong., 2nd sess. (1871–72), 441–46, 458–63. Proposals during the Civil War to establish competitive examinations for entrance into the United States Military Academy ran into the same argument; see *Congressional Globe*, 38th Cong., 1st sess. (1864), 1055–57.

18. John Stuart Mill, "Reform of the Civil Service," in *Essays on Politics and Society: Vol. 18, Collected Works of John Stuart Mill*, ed. J.M. Robson (Toronto: University of Toronto Press, 1977), 207–11.

19. Cleveland's plurality was sufficiently huge to become the subject of attention during the congressional debate over the Pendleton bill (one congressman called it the largest plurality ever achieved by a candidate for office in any state and attributed it to the public's demand for civil-service reform). See *Congressional Globe*, 47th Cong., 2nd sess. (1883), 863; Allan Nevins, *Grover Cleveland: A Study in Courage* (New York: Dodd, Mead, 1933), 104–6.

20. Ari Hoogenboom, *Outlawing the Spoils: A History of the Civil Service Reform Movement* (Urbana: University of Illinois Press, 1971), 143–47, 237–44.

21. On the extension of merit systems, see Ronald L. Johnson and Gary D. Libecap, *The Federal Civil Service System and the Problem of Bureaucracy* (Chicago: University of Chicago Press, 1994), 33–37.

22. Ibid., 21; Commission of Inquiry on Public Service Personnel, *Better Government Personnel: Report of the Commission of Inquiry on Public Service Personnel* (New York: Whittlesey House, 1935), 93, 102–36; William C. Beyer, "Municipal Civil Service in the United States," in *Problems of the American Public Service*, ed. Carl J. Friedrich et al. (New York: McGraw-Hill, 1935), 85. Mayors in merit cities often were unsympathetic to their own merit systems and poked holes in them. In contrast, the United States Civil Service Commission, authorized by the Pendleton Act to enforce the law, at least had a turf-protection interest in guarding the merit portion of the federal system. See Beyer, "Municipal Civil Service," 94–95, 120–21.

23. John F. Miller, "Veteran Preference in the Public Service," in Friedrich et al., *Problems of the American Public Service*, 273–74.

24. Paul Van Riper, *History of the United States Civil Service* (1958; Westport, Conn.: Greenwood Press, 1976), 99 n. 6.

25. Johnson and Libecap, *Federal Civil Service System*, 55.

26. For the distribution of competitive and noncompetitive positions in the federal civil service as of June 30, 1917, see Lewis Mayers, *The Federal Service* (New York: D. Appleton, 1922), 82–84.

27. In 1923 the USCSC noted that the posts of deputy collectors of internal revenue, a numerous group, were widely viewed as "spoils for the victors in political contests"; see USCSC, "Examinations and Appointments," *Fortieth Annual Report of the United States Civil Service Commission, 1923* (Washington, D.C.: GPO, 1923), vii.

28. USCSC, *Twenty-Eighth Annual Report, 1911* (Washington, D.C.: GPO, 1912), 1–32.

29. *Congressional Record*, 63rd Cong., 1st sess. (1913), 3873–3886. For background on this debate, see Charles W. Eliot to Woodrow Wilson, Sept. 10, 1913, in *Papers of Woodrow Wilson*, 69 vols., ed. Arthur S. Link (Princeton, N.J.: Princeton University Press, 1978), 28:272.

30. Nevins, *Cleveland*, 235–36; Richard E. Welch Jr., *The Presidencies of Grover Cleveland* (Lawrence: University Press of Kansas, 1988), 57–61.

31. Johnson and Libecap, *Federal Civil Service System*, 56–57.

32. Skowronek, *Building a New American State*, 179.

33. Mostly by finding government jobs for friends or for those he admired, like the poet Edward Arlington Robinson; see Leonard D. White, *Trends in Public Administration* (New York: McGraw-Hill, 1933), 171–72; Mayers, *Federal Service*, 70–71.

34. White, *Trends in Public Administration*, 160–67.

35. Donald T. Critchlow, *The Brookings Institution, 1916–1952: Expertise and the Public Interest in a Democratic Society* (DeKalb: Northern Illinois University Press, 1985), 19–26, 41–42.

36. Dwight Waldo, *The Administrative State: A Study of the Political Theory of American Public Administration*, rev. ed. (New York: Holmes and Meier, 1984), 27.

37. Leonard D. White, *Introduction to the Study of Public Administration* (New York: Macmillan, 1926). Hereafter cited as *Public Administration*. Unless otherwise specified, subsequent citations are to this edition. See also William F. Willoughby, *Principles of Public Administration* (Washington, D.C.: Brookings Institution, 1927).

38. White, *Public Administration*, 6.

39. Judith Merkle, *Management and Ideology: The Legacy of the International Scientific Management Movement* (Berkeley: University of California Press, 1980), 69; Peri E. Arnold, *Making the Managerial Presidency: Comprehensive Reorganization Planning, 1905–1996*, 2nd ed. (Lawrence: University Press of Kansas, 1996), 35.

40. Walter G. Scott, *Chester I. Barnard and the Guardians of the Managerial State* (Lawrence: University Press of Kansas, 1992), 49.

41. Subtitled *The Principles of Organization and Their Significance to Modern Industry* (New York: Harper and Bros., 1931), xix, 15, 64.

42. Lyndall Urwick, "The Function of Administration, with Special Reference to the Work of Henri Fayol," in *Papers on the Science of Administration*, ed. Luther Gulick and Lyndall Urwick (New York: Institute of Public Administration, Columbia University, 1937), 115–30.

43. Scott, *Barnard*, 33; Luther Gulick, "Notes on the Theory of Organization," in Gulick and Urwick, *Papers on the Science of Administration*, 3–45. Donald F. Kettl has called Gulick's essay the field of public administration's "definitive catechism." See Kettl, *The Transformation of Governance: Public Administration for Twenty-First Century America* (Baltimore: Johns Hopkins University Press, 2002), 83.

44. K.C. Vipond, "Veterans' Preference," in President's Committee on Civil Service Improvement, *Documents and Reports to Accompany Report on Civil Service Imrovement*, 3 vols. in one (Washington, D.C.: GPO, 1941), 3:61.

45. Pressure from the USCSC led President Warren Harding to issue an executive order in 1923 which provided a ten-point bonus for disabled veterans who passed with a grade of 60 and a five-point bonus for nondisabled veterans who passed with a 65 but which also revoked the jumping provision. Pressure from veterans' organizations led to a new executive order in 1929 reinstating the jumping provision. Miller, "Veteran Preference," 250–51, 261–62, 276, table 1. The reinstatement of the jumping rule in 1929 led to a rise in the proportion of appointees who were veterans to one-third by 1933.

46. Miller, "Veteran Preference," 292–307.

47. The Lloyd–La Follette Act of 1912 recognized the right of federal employee unions to affiliate with national organizations. See Sterling D. Spero, *Government as Employer* (New York: Remsen Press, 1927), 45, 61, 151–80.

48. Jay M. Shafritz, *Public Personnel Management: The Heritage of Civil Service Reform* (New York: Praeger, 1975), 48.

49. Willoughby, *Principles of Public Administration*, 325.

50. Commission of Inquiry on Public Service Personnel, *Better Government Personnel*, 51; Mayers, *Federal Service*, 403. Although Congress in 1890 required department heads to report the number and salaries of employees under their supervision who "are below a fair standard of efficiency," in practice department heads submitted annual reports in which they reported that they had no employees below this standard. See Mayers, *Federal Service*, 505–7. A sign of the political power of federal employees lay in the difficulty of enforcing the Hatch Acts of 1939 and 1940, which placed severe restrictions on political activities by federal workers. Although the USCSC investigated hundreds of alleged violations of these laws, only a small fraction of the cases ended with removal. See Spero, *Government as Employer*, 48–49. One obstacle to removing federal workers was erected by the public administrationists themselves, who advocated a system of pensions for classified employees (Congress established such a system in 1920), only to find that the resulting harshness of the penalty—removal would deprive an employee of pension rights—fueled the reluctance to fire anyone.

51. Leonard D. White, *Conditions of Municipal Employment in Chicago: A Study in Morale* (Chicago: J. F. Higgins, 1925), 62–63.

52. Shafritz, *Public Personnel Management*, 52.

53. White, *Municipal Employment in Chicago*, 65. See also Spero, *Government as Employer*, 50; Leonard D. White, *The Prestige Value of Public Employment in Chicago* (Chicago: University of Chicago Press, 1929), 29, 50–51, 107, 148–49; George C. S. Benson, *Administration of the Civil Service in Massachusetts* (Cambridge, Mass.: Harvard University Press, 1935), 25; Willoughby, *Principles of Public Administration*, 324.

54. USCSC, *Twenty-Eighth Annual Report*, 47, 44.

55. Herbert A. Filer, "Progress in Civil Service Tests," *Journal of Personnel Research* 1 (1923), 484–520.

56. Benson, *Civil Service in Massachusetts*, 27–28; Leonard D. White, *Introduction to the Study of Public Administration*, 3rd ed. (New York: Macmillan, 1948), 355.

57. "New Mail Carriers Examination," USCSC, *Fortieth Annual Report of the United States Civil Service Commission, 1923* (Washington, D.C.: GPO, 1923), 105.

58. Benson, *Civil Service in Massachusetts*, 26–28; Wallace S. Sayre and Milton Mandell, "Education and the Civil Service in New York City," U.S. Department of the Interior, Office of Education, *Bulletin* No. 20, 1937 (Washington, D.C.: GPO, 1938), 19–22, 23, 25–27.

59. Sayre and Mandell, "Education and the Civil Service," 19–23; John M. Pfiffner, *Public Administration* (New York: Ronald Press, 1935), 173.

60. White, *Public Administration*, 277–78.

61. Ibid., 311.

62. White, *Trends in Public Administration*, 258–59.

63. White, *Municipal Employment in Chicago*, 56–57.

64. White, *Public Administration*, 259.

65. White, *Municipal Employment in Chicago*, 58.

66. Mayers, *Federal Service*, 47.

67. Lewis Meriam, *Personnel Administration in the Federal Government* (Washington, D.C.: Brookings Institution, 1937), 15.

68. Mayers, *Federal Service*, 182–83.

69. Clyde L. King, "How Shall the Salaries of State Employees Be Fixed?" *Annals of the American Academy of Political and Social Science* 113 (1924), 202–3. In the same volume, see also Richard H. Lansburgh, "Classification of Positions and Salaries in the Service of the State of Pennsylvania," 261–68.

70. White wrote in 1926 that classification "creates the condition out of which standards naturally spring." White, *Public Administration*, 281–82.

71. The law did not distinguish administrative work, which remained a vague concept during the 1920s, from clerical work; see Thomas A. DiPrete, *The Bureaucratic Labor Market: The Case of the Federal Service* (New York: Plenum Press, 1989), 113–16.

72. President's Committee on Civil Service Improvement, "Classification," *Documents and Reports*, 3 (part 1): 167.

73. Jay M. Shafritz, *Position Classification* (New York: Praeger, 1973), 13–22.

74. White, *Public Administration*, 282.

75. White titled chapter 3 of his *Public Administration* "The Administrative Machine."

76. Ibid., 287.

77. Ibid.

78. Willoughby, *Principles of Public Administration*, 254–55.

79. President's Committee on Civil Service Improvement, "Statistical Data," *Documents and Reports*, 3 (part 2): 1.

80. From 1936 through 1938, for example, 1,665 candidates took the Foreign Service's written examination. Of these, 287 passed and were allowed to take the Service's oral examination. Of the 273 who actually took the oral examination, 91 passed and 75 were appointed. The four principal sources of candidates who sat for the Foreign Service's examinations in 1932, 1937, and 1938 were Harvard (75), Georgetown (63), Princeton (48), and Yale (43). See President's Committee on Civil Service Improvement, "Administration of American Foreign Service Personnel," *Documents and Reports*, 3 (part 1): 122–23. See also J. Rives Childs, *American Foreign Service* (New York: Henry Holt, 1948), 9–13; Selden Chapin, "Training for the Foreign Service," in *The Public Service and University Education*, ed. Joseph E. McLean (Princeton, N.J.: Princeton University Press, 1949), 111; for background on the passage of the Rogers Act, see Warren F. Ilchman, *Professional Diplomacy in the United States, 1779–1939: An Administrative History* (Chicago: University of Chicago Press, 1961), chap. 4.

81. President's Committee on Civil Service Improvement, "Report of the Advisory Committee on General Engineering Field," *Documents and Reports*, 1:15.

82. Frederick C. Mosher, *Democracy and the Public Service* (New York: Oxford University Press, 1968), 143–45.

83. President's Committee on Administrative Management, "The Development of the Merit System into a Career System," *Report of the Committee, with Studies of Administrative Management in the Federal Government* (Washington, D.C.: GPO, 1937), 130–33. This essay appeared as an unsigned appendage to the final report. Its contents so closely mirrored what White had argued in *Government Career Service* (Chicago: University of Chicago Press, 1935) that I suspect White wrote it but was constrained from signing because he was head of the USCSC at the time.

84. Lewis B. Sims, "The Scholarship of Junior Professional Appointees in the Government Service," in President's Committee on Civil Service Improvement, *Documents and Reports*, 3 (part 2): figure 3, 115.

85. USCSC, "College-Level Examinations," *Fifty-Fifth Annual Report, 1939* (Washington, D.C.: GPO, 1940), 19.

86. President's Committee on Civil Service Improvement, "A Supplemental Brief on the Technical Employees in the Federal Civil Service," *Documents and Reports*, 2:116.

87. President's Committee on Civil Service Improvement, "Statement Prepared by the Organization of Professional Employees of the Department of Agriculture," *Documents and Reports*, 2:57–60; "Report of the Advisory Committee on General Engineering Field," *Documents and Reports*, 1:18; "Society of American Foresters, Forestry and the Civil Service," *Documents and Reports*, 3 (part 1): 98–100; in a revealing aside, the Reed Committee's Advisory Committee on Social Scientists and Economists remarked that its proposals "risked the criticism that it is governed by an academic fetish, that it desires to restrict the market, or that it is drumming up business for the graduate schools." See *Documents and Reports*, 1:39.

88. FDR made this move in response to recommendations from the President's Committee on Administrative Management, which proposed an extension of the merit system; see Barry D. Karl, *Executive Reorganization and Reform in the New Deal: The Genesis of Administrative Management* (Cambridge, Mass.: Harvard University Press, 1963), 199–203.

89. President's Committee on Civil Service Improvement, "Statement of the Executive Director on the Survey of the Legal Staffs in the Departments and Independent Establishments," *Documents and Reports*, 2:17–18, and "Report of the Advisory Committee on Lawyers," *Documents and Reports*, 1:1–14.

90. President's Committee on Civil Service Improvement, "Report of the Advisory Committee on Lawyers," *Documents and Reports*, 1:1–12.

91. President's Committee on Civil Service Improvement, "Memorandum re Extension of the Civil-Service Principle in a Public Law Office," *Documents and Reports*, 2:60.

92. For these critical responses, see President's Committee on Civil Service Improvement, *Documents and Reports*, 2:34–35, 41–46, 48–61, 62. The National Lawyers Guild was a magnet for radicals, female lawyers, labor lawyers, and, to a degree, graduates of low-prestige law schools; see Ann Fagan Ginger and Eugene M. Tobin, eds., *The National Lawyers Guild: From Roosevelt through Reagan* (Philadelphia: Temple University Press, 1988), 9–41.

93. *Report of the President's Committee on Civil Service Improvement*, 77th Cong., 1st sess. (1941), 43 and, generally, chap. 5.

94. Quoted in Mayers, *Federal Service*, 87.

95. Ibid., 87.

96. Leonard D. White, ed., *The Civil Service in the Modern State: A Collection of Documents* (Chicago: University of Chicago Press, 1930); White et al., *Civil Service Abroad: Great Britain, Canada, France, Germany* (New York: McGraw-Hill, 1935). On Britain's higher civil service in this period, see Gail Savage, *The Social Construction of Experience: The English Civil Service and Its Influence, 1919–1939* (Pittsburgh: University of Pittsburgh Press, 1996). See also Richard A. Chapman, *The Higher Civil Service in Britain* (London: Constable, 1970), 4–7. The benefits enjoyed by the top civil servants in Britain by the late 1940s included annual pay of £3500, an annuity of £1750 on retirement, and a lump sum (tax free) of £5250 at retirement. See H. Strue Hensel, "Problems of Structure and Personnel," in McLean, *Public Service and University Education*, 88–90.

97. Frederick C. Mosher, *Democracy and the Public Service* (New York: Oxford University Press, 1982), 38. See also Chapman, *Higher Civil Service in Britain*, 40.

98. Walter R. Sharp, *The French Civil Service: Bureaucracy in Transition* (New York: Macmillan, 1931), 157.

99. William F. Littlejohn, "Promotion and Transfer Opportunities and Methods in the Federal Civil Service," in President's Committee on Civil Service Improvement, *Documents and Reports*, 3 (part 2): 26.

100. Arthur W. MacMahon and John D. Millett, *Federal Administrators: A Biographical Approach to the Problem of Departmental Management* (New York: Columbia University Press, 1939), 140–41, 150. This idea had been foreshadowed by the report of the Commission of Inquiry on Public Service Personnel, *Better Government Personnel*. Not all public administrationists agreed. Lewis Meriam, a Brookings Institution staffer, blasted it on the grounds that differences between state and federal civil services and between any two jobs in the federal government ruled out the universal application of "administrative capacity." See Meriam, *Public Service and Special Training* (Chicago: University of Chicago Press, 1936), 23–24. See also Meriam, *Personnel Administration in the Federal Government* (Washington, D.C.: Brookings Institution, 1937), 25, 37. For the roots of Meriam's views in the Brookings Institution, see Waldo, *Administrative State*, 114.

101. Karl, *Executive Reorganization and Reform*, 29–30; Barry D. Karl, *Charles Merriam and the Study of Politics* (Chicago: University of Chicago Press, 1974), 118–20, 123–24;

Louis Brownlow, *The Autobiography of Louis Brownlow, Second Half* (Chicago: University of Chicago Press, 1955), chap. 26.

102. Chapman, *Higher Civil Service in Britain*, 33.

103. MacMahon and Millett, *Federal Administrators*, 12, 16, 27–28, 65, 134, 141, 290–303, 347–50. See also Lucius Wilmerding Jr., *Government by Merit: An Analysis of the Problem of Government Personnel* (New York: McGraw-Hill, 1935), 96–97.

104. William Lazonick, *Business Organization and the Myth of the Market Economy* (Cambridge: Cambridge University Press, 1991), 47–49; Jürgen Kocka, *White-Collar Workers in America, 1890–1940: A Social-Political History in International Perspective*, trans. Maura Kealey (London: Sage Publications, 1980), 125–26, 131–32, 141–46. Although Kocka concedes that by the 1930s white-collar, salaried work had greater prestige than blue-collar, wage work in the United States, he contends that American white-collar workers were much less inclined than their German counterparts to look to the civil service for models and to think of themselves as a privileged group. The real division in business, he argues, was between managers and all others. He also argues, persuasively in my view, that Americans tended to think of their social class as marked by their material possessions and by their skills rather than by the type of work they did.

105. Mark Huddleston and William W. Boyer, *The Higher Civil Service in the United States* (Pittsburgh, Pa.: University of Pittsburgh Press, 1996), 31–32. For a review of the second Hoover Commission's personnel recommendations, see Neil MacNeil and Harold W. Metz, *The Hoover Report, 1953–1955: What It Means to You as a Citizen and Taxpayer* (New York: Macmillan, 1956), chap. 2.

106. Van Riper, *History of the United States Civil Service*, 494–95.

107. Paul T. David and Ross Pollock, *Executives for Government: Central Issues in Federal Personnel Administration* (Washington, D.C.: Brookings Institution, 1956), 76–82.

108. Huddleston and Boyer, *Higher Civil Service*, 38–43.

109. Ibid., 83–92. Nixon thought that Eisenhower had failed to clean out the "Democrat-infested Federal bureaucracy"; see Harold Seidman, *Politics, Position, and Power: The Dynamics of Federal Organization*, 2nd ed. (New York: Oxford University Press, 1975), 107.

110. Daniel Bell, *The Coming of Post-industrial Society: A Venture in Social Forecasting* (New York: Basic Books, 1973), 323.

111. Simon's key work, *Administrative Behavior*, was first published in 1947. See also Herbert A. Simon, *Models of My Life* (New York: Basic Books, 1991), 55–63, and "The Proverbs of Administration," *Public Administration Review* 6 (winter 1946), 53–67. Examples of the new direction of political science include Richard Neustadt's *Presidential Power: The Politics of Leadership* (New York: Wiley, 1960), and Graham T. Allison's *Essence of Decision: Explaining the Cuban Missile Crisis* (Boston: Little, Brown, 1971).

112. In 1940 one-fifth of all doctorates in political science were conferred in public administration; see Kettl, *Transformation of Governance*, 9.

113. Ibid., 12–14; Gordon Tullock, *The Politics of Bureaucracy* (Washington, D.C.: Public Affairs Press, 1965), 2, 18, 22–23, 26, 42–43.

114. Herbert A. Simon, Donald W. Smithburg, and Victor A. Thompson, *Public Administration* (New York: Knopf, 1950), 320.

8. MERIT IN CRISIS

1. Seymour Harris, *The Market for College Graduates* (Cambridge, Mass.: Harvard University Press, 1949), 107, table 22.

2. Robert A. McCaughey, *Stand Columbia: A History of Columbia University in the City of New York, 1754–2004* (New York: Columbia University Press, 2003), 258.

3. David O. Levine, *The American College and the Culture of Aspiration, 1915–1940* (Ithaca: Cornell University Press, 1986), 169.

4. Harry J. Carman, "Statement of Issues," in *Approaching Equality of Opportunity in Higher Education*, ed. Francis J. Brown (Washington, D.C.: American Council on Education, 1955), 89–92. Nor did colleges target needy students with their scholarships. Even in 1950 they were using scholarships to attract superior students from rival colleges, to the point where, in Carman's words, it had become "almost a 'racket.'" See Carman, "Statement of Issues," 92.

5. James B. Conant, "Education for a Classless Society: The Jeffersonian Tradition," *Atlantic Monthly* 165 (1940), 593–602.

6. Conant's father was a well-to-do real-estate developer. When Conant applied for a freshman scholarship at Harvard, he put his annual family income at $4500, a sum six or seven times greater than the average annual compensation in most industries; in 1948 he acknowledged that after reading *Who Shall Be Educated?* by W. Lloyd Warner, Robert J. Havighurst, and Martin Loeb, he had been appalled to learn that college attendance in the United States was so closely tied to parental income. Conant later related that during the 1930s a top official of the National Youth Administration, on hearing of his plans for scholarships at Harvard to establish a natural aristocracy, told him that all of the scholarships provided by private institutions could amount to no more than a drop in the bucket in view of the needs created by the Depression. Annoyed at the time, Conant later acknowledged that the official was "completely right." Conant, *Education in a Divided World* (Cambridge, Mass.: Harvard University Press, 1949), 43; James G. Hershberg, *James B. Conant: Harvard to Hiroshima and the Making of the Nuclear Age* (New York: Knopf, 1993), 18; Conant, *My Several Lives: Memoirs of a Social Inventor* (New York: Harper and Row, 1970), 138.

7. It was common knowledge during the interwar years that prep-school graduates neither needed nor valued high grades as much as did public-school graduates; see Arthur G. Powell, *Lessons from Privilege: The American Prep School Tradition* (Cambridge, Mass.: Harvard University Press, 1996), 277 n. 2. On the considerable gap between Conant's stated ideal of meritocracy and the reality of admissions on his watch, see Jerome K. Karabel, *The Chosen: The Hidden History of Admission and Exclusion at Harvard, Yale, and Princeton* (Boston: Houghton Mifflin, 2005), 166–99.

8. Hershberg, *Conant*, 16; Powell, *Lessons from Privilege*, 144.

9. Erwin O. Smigel, *The Wall Street Lawyer: Professional Organization Man* (Bloomington: Indiana University Press, 1964, 1969), 45–46. There was less objection in principle to Catholics than to Jews, but Catholics were even more severely underrepresented because they had not gone to the "right" schools. See also Kai Bird, *John J. McCloy: The Making of the American Establishment* (New York: Simon and Schuster, 1992), 57.

10. Clare Shipman and Katty Kay, *Womenomics: Write Your Own Rules for Success* (New York: Harper, 2009), 14–17.

11. Powell, *Lessons from Privilege*, 136.

12. In 1960 Harvard's admissions dean described his eight-year tenure as marking the greatest change in the student body in "our recorded history"; see Richard J. Herrnstein and Charles Murray, *The Bell Curve* (New York: Free Press, 1994), 30.

13. Powell, *Lessons from Privilege*, 141–42.

14. Benjamin DeMott, *Supergrow: Essays and Reports on Imagination in America* (New York: R. P. Dutton, 1969), 100–111.

15. Michael Young, *The Rise of the Meritocracy, 1870–2033*, new ed. (New Brunswick, N.J.: Transaction Publishers, 1994). For the publishing history of the first edition (1957), see Young's preface to the new edition, xi–xii.

16. John W. Gardner, *Excellence: Can We Be Equal and Excellent Too?* (New York: Harper and Bros., 1961), 115. Excellence was becoming a buzz word among policy planners around 1960; see *Recognition of Excellence: Working Papers of a Project of the Edgar Stern Family Fund* (Glencoe, Ill.: Free Press, 1960).

17. Gardner, *Excellence*, 67.

18. Ibid., 72–75; see also Norman Foerster, *The American State University* (Chapel Hill: University of North Carolina Press, 1937), 77.

19. George W. Pierson, *The Education of American Leaders: Comparative Contributions of American Colleges and Universities* (New York: Frederick A. Praeger, 1969), 72–74, 86–87, 96.

20. In 1960 sociologist Ralph Turner contrasted American "contest mobility" with English "sponsored mobility." The former kept laggards in the race for status as long as possible, assigned the public rather than an elite the role of judge, and admired those who advanced by common sense and enterprise more than by superior intelligence or academic brilliance; see Turner, "Sponsored and Contest Mobility and the School System," *American Sociological Review* 25 (1960), 855–67.

21. Suzanne Keller, *Beyond the Ruling Class: Strategic Elites in Modern Society* (New York: Random House, 1963), 265.

22. So many conflicting meanings have been attached to "modernity" and "modernization" that I am wary of using the terms, but neither can I avoid them. For recent insight into these concepts, see Dorothy Ross, "American Modernities, Past and Present," *American Historical Review* 116 (2011), 702–14.

23. For a portrait of Young's varied career, see Geoff Dench, Tony Flower, and Kate Gavron, eds., *Young at Eighty: The Prolific Public Life of Michael Young* (Manchester, U.K.: Carcanet Press, 1995). See especially the essays by Peter Willmott: "Resolving the Dilemmas of Bigness," 1–7; and "Directory of Main Organisations Linked to or Founded through the ICS," 235–41.

24. For an account of the forces working against academic achievement in schools, see James S. Coleman, "The Adolescent Subculture and Academic Achievement," *American Journal of Sociology* 55 (1960), 337–47.

25. John Stalnaker, "Recognizing and Encouraging Talent," in *The Discovery of Talent*, ed. Dael Wolfle (Cambridge, Mass.: Harvard University Press, 1969), 161–78.

26. Stalnaker, "Recognizing and Encouraging Talent," 168–69. For a critique of the National Merit Scholarships' underrepresentation of the disproportionately black children of day laborers and servants, see Horace Mann Bond, *The Search for Talent* (Cambridge, Mass.: Harvard University Press, 1959).

27. National Manpower Council, *A Policy for Scientific and Professional Manpower* (New York: Columbia University, 1953); *Proceedings of the Conference on the Utilization of Scientific and Professional Manpower* (New York: Columbia University Press, 1954). See also J. Frederick Dewhurst and Associates, *America's Needs and Resources* (New York: Twentieth Century Fund, 1947); Abram Jaffe and Charles Stewart, *Manpower Resources and Utilization* (New York: John Wiley and Sons, 1951); William Haber, Frederick Harbison, and Gladys Palmer, *Manpower in the United States: Problems and Policies* (New York: Harper and Row, 1954); National Science Foundation, *Scientific Personnel Resources* (Washington, D.C.: GPO, 1955).

28. Graduate School of Business, Columbia University, *A Report of the National Manpower Council* (New York: Columbia University, Graduate School of Business, 1954), 2; National Manpower Council, *Policy for Scientific and Professional Manpower,* 14–20. Dael Wolfle rationalized this preference for higher education on the principle that no one could be a specialist in a field that lacked a body of theory; see Wolfle, *America's Resources of Specialized Talent* (New York: Harper, 1954), 12–13.

29. President's Commission on Higher Education, *Higher Education for American Democracy,* 6 vols. (Washington, D.C.: GPO, 1948), 1:39. The Truman Commission did not assume that the veterans entering college under the G.I. Bill, who accounted for 1 million of the 2.4 million collegians in 1947, would have a long-term effect on enrollments or that the baby boom, already evident, would dictate a rise in enrollments. The rural South had the highest birth rate but the lowest rate of high-school graduation and college attendance.

30. Steven Brint and Jerome Karabel, *The Diverted Dream: Community Colleges and the Promise of Educational Opportunity in America, 1900–1985* (New York: Oxford University Press, 1989).

31. Seymour E. Harris, *The Market for College Graduates* (Cambridge, Mass.: Harvard University Press, 1949), 35.

32. Eli Ginzberg, *The Skeptical Economist* (Boulder, Colo.: Westview Press, 1987), 107, 115–16, 120–21.

33. Lee Kennett, *G.I.: The American Soldier in World War II* (New York: Charles Scribner's Sons, 1987), 10–11.

34. Christopher P. Loss, "'The Most Wonderful Thing Has Happened to Me in the Army': Psychology, Citizenship, and American Higher Education in World War II," *Journal of American History* 92 (2005), 864–91.

35. George Q. Flynn, *The Draft, 1943–1970* (Lawrence: University Press of Kansas, 1993), 140.

36. Daniel Bell, *The Coming of Post-industrial Society: A Venture in Social Forecasting* (New York: Basic Books, 1973), 409.

37. Ibid., 324.

38. Abraham Flexner, *Universities: American, English, German* (New York: Oxford University Press, 1930), 310–11.

39. Torsten Husén, *Talent, Equality, and Meritocracy: Availability and Utilization of Talent* (The Hague: Martinus Nijhoff, 1974), chaps. 2–4.

40. For example, England was a notable outlier of elementary education, which was not made compulsory until 1899, but it contained a remarkably diverse profusion of grammar schools that varied in prestige and bases of support. Germany and France were more explicitly credentialed societies than Britain. When Britain initiated examinations for its civil service, it did not require academic credentials as a prerequisite for sitting for the examinations; rather, it set minimum ages for taking examinations for different levels of the civil service, which in effect elevated the leaving ages of different grades of schools to the status of a credential. Within Britain, Scottish education was long thought, even by the English, to be more accessible and democratic than England's (see n. 89, below).

41. Fritz K. Ringer, *Education and Society in Modern Europe* (Bloomington: Indiana University Press, 1979), 25–29.

42. In 1972 two economists, Paul Taubman and Terence Wales, summarized the results of eight different studies that compared the rates of college attendance with performance on intelligence and/or achievement tests in 1925, 1929, 1934, 1946, 1950, 1957, 1960, and 1961. They concluded that the "mental ability" of graduates who in each of these years attended college was superior to that of the nonattendees, but that the difference, slight in the 1920s and 1930s, gradually rose with rising enrollments in colleges; Taubman and Wales, *Mental Ability and Higher Education Attainment in the Twentieth Century,* National Bureau of Economic Research, Occasional Paper 118 (Washington, D.C.: Carnegie Commission on Higher Education, 1972).

43. Conant, *Education in a Divided World,* 194. Conant also thought (63) that in Britain the "really brilliant boy—that is, brilliant in orthodox academic terms—has often had better scholarship opportunities than his opposite number in this country."

44. Michael Ackerman, "Mental Testing and the Expansion of Educational Opportunity," *History of Education Quarterly* 35 (1995), 279–300; Byron S. Hollinshead, "Who Should Go to College in America," *College Board Review* (No. 16, 1952), 249. Zook's ACE had its own equivalent of the SAT, called the ACE Psychological Examination. The Truman Commission established percentile equivalents between this examination and the AGCT data, probably to encourage wider use of the ACE examination. But two weeks after the publication of the Truman Commission report, the Educational Testing Service, the new home of the SAT, was chartered with Conant as board chair, and the ACE examination was immediately discontinued; see Nicholas Lemann, *The Big Test: The Secret History of the Meritocracy* (New York: Farrar, Straus and Giroux, 1999), 65.

45. Christopher Jencks and David Riesman, *The Academic Revolution* (Garden City, N.Y.: Doubleday, 1968), 64–74.

46. Eli Chinoy, "The Tradition of Opportunity and Aspiration of Automobile Workers," *American Journal of Sociology* 57 (1952), 453–59; Seymour M. Lipset and Reinhard Bendix, *Social Mobility in Industrial Society* (Berkeley: University of California Press, 1959, 1967), 103.

47. W. Lloyd Warner with Marcia Meeker and Kenneth Eells, *Social Class in America: A Manual of Procedure for the Measurement of Social Status* (1949; New York: Harper, 1960), 5. See also W. Lloyd Warner and Paul S. Lunt, *The Social Life of a Modern Community* (New Haven, Conn.: Yale University Press, 1941), 88. For a devastating attack on Warner's methodology, see C. Wright Mills's review of Warner and Lunt's *The Social Life of a Modern Community* in *American Sociological Review* 7 (1942), 263–71. Mills accused Warner of substituting class awareness for class.

48. Warner and Lunt, *Social Life of a Modern Community*, 5.

49. Kenneth Eells, Allison Davis, Robert J. Havighurst, Virgil E. Herrick, and Ralph W. Tyler, *Intelligence and Cultural Differences* (Chicago: University of Chicago Press, 1951).

50. Warner, Havighurst, and Loeb, *Who Shall Be Educated?* 49.

51. Ibid., 157–58. Robert K. Merton, another distinguished sociologist who moved in the same circles as Warner, warned that any society whose cultural values extolled success but whose structure of opportunity choked access to the symbols of success faced Durkheimian *anomie*; see Merton, "Social Structure and *Anomie*," *American Sociological Review* 3 (1938), 679–80.

52. William H. Whyte Jr., *The Organization Man* (Garden City, N.Y.: Doubleday, 1956, 1957), 45.

53. Kingsley Davis and Wilbert Moore, "Some Principles of Stratification," *American Sociological Review* 10 (April 1945), 242–49. I know of no significant rebuttal to this argument before 1953, when Melvin M. Tumin attacked it; see Tumin, "Some Principles of Stratification: A Critical Analysis," *American Sociological Review* 16 (1953), 387–94. Tumin contended that the Davis/Moore thesis was the sort of self-serving apology for its hegemony that the upper class had always devised. That it took so long, nearly a decade, for a response says something about the influence of the sort of functionalist analysis advanced by Davis, Moore, and Parsons; see Francesca Cancian, "Varieties of Functional Analysis," in *International Encyclopedia of the Social Sciences*, 17 vols., ed. David L. Sills (New York: Macmillan, 1972), 6:29. See also Talcott Parsons, *The Social System* (Glencoe, Ill.: Free Press, 1951), 184–85.

54. This is not to say that Warner got even the present right. Oscar Handlin pointed out that in 1930, when Warner and his research team started to study Newburyport, about 40 percent of the native-born population of the city had foreign-born parents and the city had been receiving large numbers of immigrants for the preceding nine decades; see Handlin's review of *The Social Life of a Modern Community* (the official title of the Newburyport study) in *New England Quarterly* 15 (1942), 554–57.

55. Margaret Mead, *And Keep Your Powder Dry: An Anthropologist Looks at America* (New York: William Morrow, 1942), 68.

56. W. Lloyd Warner and James C. Abegglen, *Occupational Mobility in American Business and Industry, 1928–1952* (Minneapolis: University of Minnesota Press, 1955); Warner and Abegglen, *Big Business Leaders in America* (New York: Harper and Row, 1955).

57. Uta Gerhardt, *Talcott Parsons: An Intellectual Biography* (Cambridge: Cambridge University Press, 2002), 48–49.

58. Mabel Newcomer, *The Big Business Executive: The Factors That Made Him, 1900–1950* (New York: Columbia University Press, 1955), 41. Warner examined three generations of company presidents and board chairmen: 284 men who reached their highest office between 1899 and 1903 (the 1900 group), 319 who made it to the top between 1923 and 1925 (the 1925 group), and 863 who became presidents or board chairmen between 1949 and 1953 (the 1950 group). The proportion of presidents and board chairmen in the 1950 group whose fathers headed their corporations was higher than for their 1900 counterparts (11.6 percent versus 7.8 percent); similarly, the proportion of higher-ups whose fathers were high corporate executives was higher in the 1950 group (7.3 percent) than in the 1900 group (2.6 percent).

59. Warner and Abegglen, *Big Business Leaders*, 209.

60. Ibid., 146; for the same view, see Warner and Abegglen, *Occupational Mobility*, 114. See also Lipset and Bendix, *Social Mobility in Industrial Society*, 103–10.

61. Lipset and Bendix, *Social Mobility in Industrial Society*, 143.

62. For a lively history of personality testing, see Annie Murphy Paul, *The Cult of Personality* (New York: Free Press, 2004).

63. C. Wright Mills, *The Power Elite* (New York: Oxford University Press, 1956), 142–43, 291, 295, 345. Both Whyte and Mills cited [Herrymon Maurer], "The Nine Hundred," *Fortune* 46 (1952), 132–35, 232–36. Maurer established that (1) the circulation of business executives was becoming increasingly sluggish (executives under 50 were much more likely than those 50 and over to have spent their careers with a single company) and (2) executive salaries were set more by custom than by the market.

64. For an overview of issues raised by the Coleman Report, see Donald M. Levine and Mary Jo Bane, "Introduction," and Godfrey Hodgson, "Do Schools Make a Difference?" in *The "Inequality" Controversy: Schooling and Distributive Justice*, ed. Levine and Bane (New York: Basic Books, 1975), 3–16, 22–44.

65. For an example of this debate, see Frederick Mosteller and Daniel P. Moynihan, eds., *On Equality of Educational Opportunity: Papers Deriving from the Harvard University Faculty Seminar on the Coleman Report* (New York: Random House, 1972).

66. Julie A. Rueben, "Merit, Mission, and Minority Students: The History of Debate over Special Admissions Programs," in *A Faithful Mirror: Reflections on the College and College Board in America*, ed. Michael C. Johanek (New York: College Board, 2001), 195–243; Christopher P. Loss, *Between Citizens and the State: The Politics of Higher Education in the 20th Century* (Princeton, N.J.: Princeton University Press, 2012).

67. 401 U.S. 424 (1971).

68. Ulrich Teichler, *Admission to Higher Education in the United States: A German Critique* (New York: International Council for Educational Development, 1978), 35.

69. 438 U.S. 265 (1978).

70. 78 F 3d. 932 (5th Cir. 1996).

71. 539 U.S. 306 (2003).

72. 539 U.S. 244 (2003).

73. John David Skrentny, *The Ironies of Affirmative Action: Politics, Culture, and Justice in America* (Chicago: University of Chicago Press, 1996), 37–50, 57–60.

74. Schultz had assisted the U.S. government in assessing the damage to German industry wrought by strategic bombing. Like many others, he had exaggerated the damage, and in his 1960 presidential address to the American Economic Association he traced his error to ignoring the human element. The remarkable revival of the German and Japanese economies after the war occurred because the Germans and Japanese possessed skills and bodies of knowledge that bombs could not obliterate. See Theodore Schultz, "Investment in Human Capital," *American Economic Review* 51 (March 1961), 1–17.

75. Gary S. Becker, *Human Capital: A Theoretical and Empirical Analysis with Special Reference to Education* (New York: National Bureau of Economic Research, 1964), 156.

76. Ibid., 64.

77. Gary S. Becker, *Human Capital*, rev. ed. (New York: National Bureau of Economic Research, 1975), 6.

78. For a summary of many of the New Left (or "neo-Marxist") criticisms of the functionalist descriptions of the relation between school and society that prevailed in the 1950s, see Randall Collins, "Some Comparative Principles of Educational Stratification," *Harvard Educational Review* 47 (1977), 1–25; see also Jerome Karabel, "Open Admissions: Toward Meritocracy or Democracy?" *Change* 4 (May 1972), 40–41.

79. Eli Ginzberg, *The Manpower Connection: Education and Work* (Cambridge, Mass.: Harvard University Press, 1975), 107–12.

80. Lester C. Thurow, "Education and Economic Equality," *Public Interest*, No. 28 (summer 1972), 66–81.

81. Barry Chiswick, "Schooling, Screening, and Income," in *Does College Matter?* ed. Lewis Solomon and Paul Taubman (New York: Academic Press, 1973), 150–58.

82. Christopher Jencks et al., *Inequality: A Reassessment of the Effect of Family and Schooling in America* (New York: Basic Books, 1972).

83. Donald M. Levine, "'Inequality' and the Analysis of Educational Policy," in Levine and Bane, *"Inequality" Controversy*, 305.

84. Jencks et al., *Inequality*, 226.

85. Christopher Jencks, "Higher Education and Social Stratification," *Harvard Educational Review* 38 (1968), 277–316.

86. Ibid., 314.

87. Ibid., 315–16.

88. Walter J. Blum and Harry Kalven Jr., *The Uneasy Case for Progressive Taxation* (Chicago: University of Chicago Press, 1953, 1978), 4, 84–85, 116.

89. Christopher Hurn, *The Limits and Possibilities of Schooling: An Introduction to the Sociology of Education* (Boston: Allyn and Bacon, 1978), 96. Studies from England, Holland, and France indicated a significant rise in the percentage of students from the industrial working class who were in selective schools or on selective tracks (the English data were from the interwar years, the Dutch and French data from the post-1945 period). Yet as Hurn notes, these data are consistent with data that, despite the increased presence of working-class children in selective European schools, middle- and upper-class children actually increased their representation in selective schools more than did the working class; the middle and upper classes were the first to take advantage of wider access to advanced education. See also Husén, *Talent, Equality, and Meritocracy*, 102–3; J. Gray, A. F. McPherson, and D. Raffe, *Reorganization of Secondary Education: Theory, Myth and Practice since the War* (London: Routledge and Kegan Paul, 1983), 213–26. Gray, McPherson, and Raffe interpreted the data as especially striking a blow against the folk wisdom that had long portrayed Scotland as different from England because of the greater historical attention paid by the Scots to identifying "the lad o' pairts," the brilliant working-class child who scored well on exams and earned a spot in a university. In reality, class differences in educational attainment were as great in Scotland as in England and other

Western societies. Remarkably, given the tenor of the American debate, Gray, McPherson, and Raffe concluded that class differences in educational attainment resulted from class differences in ability. Americans like Coleman, in contrast, assumed that ability was randomly distributed across classes and that class differences in educational attainment were best interpreted as evidence of a defective social and educational structure.

90. Raymond Boudon, *Education, Opportunity, and Social Inequality* (New York: Wiley, 1974), xiii, 29–30.

91. Pierre Bourdieu and Jean-Claude Passeron, *Reproduction in Education, Society, and Culture*, trans. Richard Nice (London: Sage Publications, 1977), 208.

92. Pierre Bourdieu, *Distinction: A Social Critique of the Judgement of Taste*, trans. Richard Nice (Cambridge, Mass.: Harvard University Press, 1984), 12.

93. For a revealing transatlantic dialogue on the nature of examinations, see International Examinations Inquiry, *Conference on Examinations, . . . 1938*, ed. Paul Munroe (New York: Bureau of Publications, Teachers College, Columbia University, 1939).

94. Quoted in Becker, *Human Capital*, 1975 ed., 123 n. 30. In the following footnote Becker cited Young's *Rise of the Meritocracy* for its portrayal of a society in which all social differences are based on differences in ability.

95. R. H. Tawney, *Equality* (1931; London: Allen and Unwin, 1964), 106–11.

96. James S. Coleman, "The Concept of Equality of Educational Opportunity," in Levine and Bane, *"Inequality" Controversy*, 207–9, 213.

97. John Rawls, *A Theory of Justice* (Cambridge, Mass.: Harvard University Press, 1971), 15.

98. For an illuminating review of Rawls, see Thomas Nagel, "Rawls on Justice," *Philosophical Review* 32 (1973), 220–34. The broader philosophical issues raised by the idea of "self-ownership" (each person enjoys full and exclusive rights to control and use his powers) are treated (from a Marxist perspective) by G. A. Cohen, *Self-Ownership, Freedom, and Equality* (Cambridge: Cambridge University Press, 1995).

99. Under the banner of "comparable worth," feminists after 1980 revived the idea of comparing the requirements of different jobs by such measures as physical effort, skill, mental effort, and responsibility in order to ensure equitable pay. See, e.g., Rita Mae Kelly and Jane Bayes, eds., *Comparable Worth, Pay Equity, and Public Policy* (New York: Greenwood Press, 1988); for a critical view, see Steven Rhoads, *Incomparable Worth: Pay Equity Meets the Market* (New York: Cambridge University Press, 1993). The "comparable worth" movement appears to have run out of gas since 2000, probably a victim of the success of feminists in shattering gender stereotyping in occupations.

100. Sidney Verba, *Elites and the Idea of Equality: A Comparison of Japan, Sweden, and the United States* (Cambridge, Mass.: Harvard University Press, 1987), chaps. 4 and 5.

101. Mary Jo Bane, "Economic Justice: Controversies and Policies," in Levine and Bane, *"Inequality" Controversy*, 293.

102. Franklin H. Knight, "The Ethics of Competition," in *The Ethics of Competition and Other Essays* (Chicago: University of Chicago Press, 1935), 48. Knight's essay originally appeared in *Quarterly Journal of Economics* 38 (1923), 579–624.

103. Ibid., 57.

104. Ibid.

105. Peter D. McClelland, *The American Search for Economic Justice* (Cambridge, Mass.: Basil Blackwell, 1990), 84–85.

106. Lester C. Thurow, *Generating Inequality: Mechanisms of Distribution in the U.S. Economy* (New York: Basic Books, 1975), ix–x.

107. McClelland, *American Search*, 70.

108. Joshua D. Angrist and Alan B. Krueger, "Does Compulsory Education Affect Schooling and Earnings?" *Quarterly Journal of Economics* 106 (1991), 979–1014; Thomas

L. Kane and Cecilia Rouse, "Labor Market Returns on Two- and Four-Year Colleges," *American Economic Review* 85 (1995), 600–614.

109. R. B. Freeman, *The Overeducated American* (New York: Academic Press, 1976).

110. Lewis C. Solomon and Cheryl L. Fagano, "Quality of Higher Education and Economic Growth in the United States," in *Higher Education and Economic Growth*, ed. William E. Becker and Darrell R. Lewis (Boston: Kluwer Academic, 1993), 155–57.

111. United States National Commission on Excellence in Education, *A Nation at Risk: The Imperative for Educational Reform* (Washington, D.C.: GPO, 1983), 5.

112. James E. Swiss, *Public Management Systems* (Englewood Cliffs, N.J.: Prentice-Hall, 1991), 157.

113. Yet in selling the CSRA to Congress, President Carter emphasized that it would strengthen political control over the federal bureaucracy even as he and other supporters of the SES spoke of increasing managerial discretion; see Christopher Pollitt, *Managerialism in the Public Service: The Anglo-American Experience* (Cambridge, Mass.: Basil Blackwell, 1990), 88.

114. Charles H. Levine and Rosslyn S. Kleeman, "The Quiet Crisis in the American Public Service," in *Agenda for Excellence: Public Service in America*, ed. Patricia Ingraham and Donald Kettl (Chatham, N.J.: Chatham House, 1992), 231.

115. James L. Perry, "Making Policy by Trial and Error: Merit Pay in the Federal Service," *Policy Studies Journal* 17 (1988–89), 390–91. "Comparability" with the private sector was established by the 1962 Federal Employees' Pay Comparability Act.

116. Perry, "Making Policy by Trial and Error," 392–404.

117. United States Performance Management and Recognition System Review Committee, *Advancing Managerial Excellence: A Report on Improving the Performance Management and Recognition System*, November 5, 1991 (Washington, D.C.: Performance Management and Recognition System Review Committee, 1992), 8–9, 13.

118. Ibid., 28–37. See also Derek C. Bok, *The Cost of Talent: How Executives and Professionals Are Paid and How It Affects America* (New York: Free Press, 1993), 243.

119. Carolyn Ban, "The National Performance Review as Implicit Evaluation of CSRA: Building on or Overturning the Legacy," in *The Future of Merit: Twenty Years after the Civil Service Reform Act*, ed. James P. Pfiffner and Douglas A. Brook (Washington, D.C.: Woodrow Wilson Center Press, 2000), 57–80. The law required each executive branch agency to initiate a program to eliminate the underrepresentation of minorities. The veterans' lobby succeeded in striking from the bill a proposal, strongly supported by feminists, to restrict bonus points for nondisabled veterans to ten years after their separation from the service. The law also authorized collective bargaining by unions of federal workers, a right they had enjoyed since 1962 under a succession of executive orders.

120. Patricia S. Wilson, "Politics, Power, and Other Reasons Why Senior Executives Leave the Federal Government," *Public Administration Review* 54 (1994), 12–19.

121. Hugh Heclo makes the point that a higher civil service must live or die on the basis of the perceived legitimacy of its constitutional calling. In the American republic, ruled by the ballot box, the idea of a higher civil service had little inherent legitimacy and needed the politics/administration distinction to gain a measure of legitimacy. In Heclo's view, performance appraisals can never substitute for the now decayed politics/administration distinction; see Heclo, "A Comment on the Future of the U.S. Civil Service," in *The Higher Civil Service in Europe and Canada*, ed. Bruce Smith (Washington, D.C.: Brookings Institution, 1984), 105–6.

122. David Osborne and Ted Gaebler, *Reinventing Government: How the Entrepreneurial Spirit Is Transforming the American Public Sector* (Reading, Mass.: Addison-Wesley, 1992).

123. National Performance Review, *Creating a Government That Works Better and Costs Less: Executive Summary* (Washington, D.C.: GPO, 1993). Managerialism also entered higher education through the portal labeled "value added." In my own university each department in arts and sciences was required to draw up a plan to evaluate how much value its courses added to the student. Regular course examinations to assess what students had learned did not count. See Pollitt, *Managerialism*, 179.

124. Donald F. Kettl, *The Global Public Management Revolution* (Washington, D.C.: Brookings Institution Press, 2001), 22–39.

125. Prepared Statement of Herbert N. Jaspers, "Performance Management, Benchmarks, and Reengineering within Government," Hearings before the Subcommittee on Government Management, Information and Technology, *House Docs.*, 104th Cong., 1st sess., June 20, 1995, 27.

126. On FSEE and the Urban League's suit, see David H. Rosenbloom, *Federal Equal Employment Opportunity: Politics and Public Personnel Administration* (New York: Praeger, 1977), 139–41.

127. Lee J. Cronbach, *Essentials of Psychological Testing*, 3rd ed. (New York: Harper and Row, 1970), 121–35; on the evolution of affirmative action from a system designed to make applicant pools more representative of racial diversity to a system of racial quotas, see Nathan Glazer, *Affirmative Discrimination: Ethnic Inequality and Public Policy* (New York: Basic Books, 1975), 58–59, 62–63, 225 n. 17.

128. The testing community was even more tone-deaf than the federal government to the implications of *Griggs*; it responded with proposals for "culture-fair" job tests without realizing that any test that resulted in a disparate impact had, by decree of the Court, become culture-unfair. See Nancy S. Peterson and Melvin Novick, "An Evaluation of Some Models for Culture-Fair Selection," *Journal of Educational Measurement* 13 (1976), 3–29; Lee J. Cronbach, "Equity in Selection—Where Psychometrics and Political Philosophy Meet," *Journal of Educational Measurement* 13 (spring 1976), 31–41.

129. U.S. Office of Personnel Management, *Biography of an Ideal: A History of the Federal Civil Service* (Washington, D.C.: GPO, 2003), 133–34. In collaboration with the testing community, the USCSC spent years developing PACE; for details, see Melvin H. Trattner, "Task Analysis in the Design of Three Concurrent Validity Studies of the Professional and Administrative Career Examination," *Personnel Psychology* 32 (1979), 109–19; James Q. Wilson, *Bureaucracy: What Government Agencies Do and Why They Do It* (New York: Basic Books, 1989), 139–40.

130. U.S. Merit Systems Protection Board, *In Search of Merit: Hiring Entry-Level Federal Employees* (Washington, D.C.: MSPB, 1987), 1–2.

131. Charles H. Levine and Rosslyn Kleeman, "The Quiet Crisis in the American Public Service," in Ingraham and Kettl, *Agenda for Excellence*, 228.

132. U.S. Office of Personnel Management, *Administrative Careers with America: Background Information and Sample Questions for the Examination for Careers in Law Enforcement and Investigation Occupations* (Washington, D.C., 1991), 8.

133. U.S. Office of Personnel Management, *Biography of an Ideal*, 164.

134. 129 S. Ct. 2658, 2671, 174 L.Ed. 2d., 490 (2009).

135. Nearly a dozen decisions interpreting Title VII came down from courts between *Griggs* and *Ricci*; more are likely. The majority opinion in *Ricci* invalidated the city council's actions on notably narrow grounds; see James Taranto, "There Is Such a Thing as Too Much Judicial Restraint," *Wall Street Journal*, July 6, 2009, 13.

136. Peter Novick, *That Noble Dream: The "Objectivity Question" and the American Historical Profession* (New York: Cambridge University Press, 1988).

137. Ibid., 628.

138. See, for example, Richard A. Watson and Rondal G. Downing, *The Politics of the Bench and the Bar: Judicial Selection under the Missouri Nonpartisan Court Plan* (New York: Wiley, 1969).

139. The reputation of merit has undoubtedly suffered since the economic crisis of 2008, when, along with several other investment banks, Goldman Sachs, a poster child for meritocracy, sold mortgage pools filled with assets it knew to be toxic to its customers; see Gretchen Morgenson and Joshua Roser, *Reckless Endangerment: How Outsized Ambition, Greed, and Corruption Led to Economic Armageddon* (New York: Times Books, 2011), 263–65, 294–95.

140. Adams to Jefferson, Nov. 15, 1813, in *The Adams-Jefferson Letters*, 2 vols., ed. Lester Cappon (Chapel Hill: University of North Carolina Press, 1959), 2:397–98.

141. Ibid., 398.

142. The emerging public relations and advertising industries combined with the mass media, mainly radio, in the 1920s to initiate the age of celebrities. See Charles J. Shindo, *1927 and the Rise of Modern America* (Lawrence: University Press of Kansas, 2010), chap. 3.

Index